THE CAMBRI
TO CICERO

MW00335455

Cicero is one of the most important and influential thinkers within the history of Western philosophy. For the last thirty years, his reputation as a philosopher has once again been on the rise after close to a century of very low esteem. This *Companion* introduces readers to "Cicero the philosopher" and to his philosophical writings. It provides a handy port of call for those interested in Cicero's original contributions to a wide variety of topics such as epistemology, the emotions, determinism and responsibility, cosmopolitanism, republicanism, philosophical translation, dialogue, aging, friendship, and more. The international, interdisciplinary team of scholars represented in this volume highlights the historical significance and contemporary relevance of Cicero's writings, and suggests pathways for future scholarship on Cicero's philosophy as we move through the twenty-first century.

JED W. ATKINS is the E. Blake Byrne Associate Professor of Classical Studies and Associate Professor of Political Science and Philosophy at Duke University. He is author of *Cicero on Politics and the Limits of Reason* (Cambridge, 2013) and *Roman Political Thought* (Cambridge, 2018).

THOMAS BÉNATOUÏL is Professor of Ancient Philosophy at the Université de Lille and a member of the CNRS research institute *Savoirs, Textes, Langage*. He is the author and editor of several books and articles in both French and English on ancient philosophy, in particular Stoicism and its contemporary reception, and is the co-editor of the journal *Philosophie antique*.

OTHER VOLUMES IN THE SERIES OF CAMBRIDGE
COMPANIONS

Continued at the back of the book

THE CAMBRIDGE COMPANION TO CICERO'S PHILOSOPHY

EDITED BY

JED W. ATKINS

Duke University, North Carolina

THOMAS BÉNATOUÏL

Université de Lille

CAMBRIDGE
UNIVERSITY PRESS

CAMBRIDGE
UNIVERSITY PRESS

University Printing House, Cambridge CB2 8BS, United Kingdom

One Liberty Plaza, 20th Floor, New York, NY 10006, USA

477 Williamstown Road, Port Melbourne, VIC 3207, Australia

314–321, 3rd Floor, Plot 3, Splendor Forum, Jasola District Centre, New Delhi – 110025, India

103 Penang Road, #05–06/07, Visioncrest Commercial, Singapore 238467

Cambridge University Press is part of the University of Cambridge.

It furthers the University's mission by disseminating knowledge in the pursuit of
education, learning, and research at the highest international levels of excellence.

www.cambridge.org
Information on this title: www.cambridge.org/9781108416665
DOI: 10.1017/9781108241649

© Cambridge University Press 2022

First published 2022

Printed in the United Kingdom by TJ Books Limited, Padstow Cornwall

A catalogue record for this publication is available from the British Library.

Library of Congress Cataloging-in-Publication Data

NAMES: Atkins, Jed W., editor. | Bénatouïl, Thomas, editor.
TITLE: The Cambridge companion to Cicero's philosophy / edited by Jed W. Atkins,
Thomas Bénatouïl.
DESCRIPTION: Cambridge ; New York, NY : Cambridge University Press, 2022.
| Includes bibliographical references and index.
IDENTIFIERS: LCCN 2021020778 (print) | LCCN 2021020779 (ebook) | ISBN 9781108416665
(hardback) | ISBN 9781108404037 (paperback) | ISBN 9781108241649 (epub)
SUBJECTS: LCSH: Cicero, Marcus Tullius. | Philosophy, Ancient.
CLASSIFICATION: LCC B553 .C36 2022 (print) | LCC B553 (ebook) | DDC 186/.2–dc23
LC record available at https://lccn.loc.gov/2021020778
LC ebook record available at https://lccn.loc.gov/2021020779

ISBN 978-1-108-41666-5 Hardback
ISBN 978-1-108-40403-7 Paperback

For Carlos and Malcolm

Contents

Contributors

JED W. ATKINS is the E. Blake Byrne Associate Professor of Classical Studies and Associate Professor of Political Science and Philosophy, Duke University. He is author of *Cicero on Politics and the Limits of Reason* (2013) and *Roman Political Thought* (2018).

SOPHIE AUBERT-BAILLOT is Professor in Latin, University of Lille (France). She is author of *Le grec et la philosophie dans la correspondance de Cicéron* (2021) and editor (with Charles Guérin) of *Le Brutus de Cicéron* (2014).

CLARA AUVRAY-ASSAYAS is Professor in Latin, University of Rouen Normandie (France). She is the author of *Cicéron* (2006) and *Cicéron: la nature des dieux* (2002). She has co-edited (with Daniel Delattre) *Cicéron et Philodème* (2001).

ELISABETH BEGEMANN is a research fellow at the Max Weber Centre for Advanced Cultural and Social Studies, University of Erfurt (Germany). She is the author of *Schicksal als Argument: Ciceros Rede vom fatum in der späten Republik* (2012).

THOMAS BÉNATOUÏL is Professor in Ancient Philosophy, University of Lille (France). His books include *Faire usage: la pratique du stoïcisme* (2006) and *La science des hommes libres: la digression du Théétète de Platon* (2020). He is the editor (with Katerina Ierodiakonou) of *Dialectic after Plato and Aristotle* (2018).

ANNE ISABELLE BOUTON-TOUBOULIC is Professor in Latin, University of Lille (France). She is the author of *L'ordre caché. La notion d'ordre chez saint Augustin* (2004) and has edited or co-edited many volumes, including (with Carlos Lévy) *Scepticisme et religion* (2016) and *Magna voce. Effets et pouvoirs de la voix dans la philosophie et la littérature antiques* (2021).

CHARLES BRITTAIN is a professor of Classics and the Susan Linn Sage Professor of Philosophy and Humane Letters at Cornell University. His publications include *Philo of Larissa: The Last of the Academic Skeptics* (2001) and *Cicero: On Academic Scepticism* (2006).

DANIEL J. KAPUST is Professor of Political Science, University of Wisconsin-Madison. He is the author of *Republicanism, Rhetoric, and Roman Political Thought* (2011) and *Flattery in the History of Political Thought* (2018).

CARLOS LÉVY is Emeritus Professor in Latin, Sorbonne University. Along with many articles on Cicero, Philo of Alexandria, and Hellenistic and Roman philosophy, he is the author of *Cicero Academicus* (1992). He has co-edited several volumes, including (with Jean-Baptiste Guillaumin) *Plato latinus* (2018).

SEAN MCCONNELL is Senior Lecturer in Classics, University of Otago (New Zealand). He is the author of *Philosophical Life in Cicero's Letters* (2014) and the editor of the forthcoming *Power and Persuasion in Cicero's Philosophy* (with Margaret Graver and Nathan Gilbert).

CLAUDIA MOATTI is Professor of Roman History at Paris 8 University and Adjunct Professor of Classics and Law at the University of Southern California. She is author of *La Raison de Rome: naissance de l'esprit critique à la fin de la République* (1997; published in English as *The Birth of Critical Thinking in Republican Rome*, 2015) and *Res publica. Histoire romaine de la chose publique* (2018).

WALTER NICGORSKI is Emeritus Professor, Program of Liberal Studies, University of Notre Dame. He is author of *Cicero's Skepticism and His Recovery of Political Philosophy* (2016) and editor of *Cicero's Practical Philosophy* (2012).

MARTHA C. NUSSBAUM is the Ernst Freund Distinguished Service Professor of Law and Ethics at the University of Chicago. She has published many books, most recently *Anger and Forgiveness* (2016), *Aging Thoughtfully* (with Saul Levmore, 2017), *The Monarchy of Fear* (2018), and *The Cosmopolitan Tradition* (2019).

PETER OSORIO is a Loeb Classical Library Foundation Postdoctoral Fellow at the Department of Classics, University of Toronto. His articles on the New Academy, Cicero's philosophy, Justus Lipsius, and Protagoras have appeared in journals such as *Phronesis, Classical Philology*, and *Mnemosyne*.

TOBIAS REINHARDT is the Corpus Christi Professor of the Latin Language and Literature, University of Oxford. His publications include *Das Buch E. der Aristotelischen Topik Untersuchungen zur Echtheitsfrage* (2000), *Cicero's* Topica (2003), and *Quintilian:* Institutio Oratoria *Book 2* (2006).

GARY REMER is Professor of Political Science, Tulane University, New Orleans. He is author of *Humanism and the Rhetoric of Toleration* (1996) and *Ethics and the Orator: The Ciceronian Tradition of Political Morality* (2017).

GRETCHEN REYDAMS-SCHILS is Professor in the Program of Liberal Studies, University of Notre Dame, and also holds concurrent appointments in Classics, Philosophy, and Theology. She is author of *Demiurge and Providence: Stoic and Platonist Readings of Plato's* Timaeus (1999), *The Roman Stoics: Self, Responsibility and Affection* (2005), and *Calcidius on Plato's* Timaeus: *Greek Philosophy, Latin Reception, and Christian Contexts* (2020).

MALCOLM SCHOFIELD is Emeritus Professor of Ancient Philosophy, University of Cambridge. His many publications within the field of Greek and Roman philosophy include *The Stoic Idea of the City* (1999), *Saving the City* (1999), *Plato: Political Philosophy* (2006), *The Cambridge History of Greek and Roman Political Thought* (ed. with Christopher Rowe, 2000), and *Cicero: Political Philosophy* (2021).

CATHERINE STEEL is Professor of Classics, University of Glasgow. She is the author of *Cicero, Rhetoric and Empire* (2002), *Reading Cicero* (2005), *Roman Oratory* (2006), *The End of the Republic, 146–44 B.C.* (2013), and editor of *The Cambridge Companion to Cicero* (2013).

RAPHAEL WOOLF is Professor of Philosophy, King's College, London. He is author of *Cicero: The Philosophy of a Roman Sceptic* (2015), translator of *Cicero:* On Moral Ends (ed. Julia Annas, 2001), editor and translator (with Brad Inwood) of *Aristotle:* Eudemian Ethics (2013), and editor (with Verity Harte) of *Rereading Ancient Philosophy* (2017).

Preface

Cicero's profound impact on Western intellectual history is undeniable. His esteem as a philosopher has fluctuated, ranging from the heights of the eighteenth century when he was widely regarded as the most important ancient philosopher, to the depths of the nineteenth and twentieth centuries, when his philosophy was largely ignored. In recent decades, Cicero's philosophical writings have once again received careful and sustained scholarly attention. This most recent scholarly renaissance, considered as a whole, is profoundly interdisciplinary. The field of course owes much to those working within different subfields of classical studies: ancient philosophy, Latin literature, Roman history, and Late Antiquity. But any picture of our present understanding of Cicero's philosophy that did not take into account the important work by philosophers, political scientists, and intellectual historians would be incomplete. Similarly, the most recent Ciceronian revival has been international in scope, with significant contributions coming from scholars working in North America, the UK, continental Europe, New Zealand, and beyond.

Our goal in this volume is to provide a guide to "Cicero the philosopher" as viewed through the lens of recent scholarship. We hope to provide an access point for readers who, interested either in the man himself or in one of the many philosophical topics explored by his writings, are approaching Cicero for the first time. But we also hope to invite those familiar with Cicero to view his philosophical writings afresh. We wish through this volume to encourage and shape the direction of future scholarship on Cicero's philosophy. In particular, we aim to bring into focus the different research questions that have grown up independently in the diverse and sometimes distant sectors of this field. The international, interdisciplinary team of scholars represented in this volume highlights the present diversity and richness of the field, and suggests future pathways for scholarship on Cicero as we move through the twenty-first century.

The first four chapters cover Cicero's creation of his philosophical oeuvre in its social and generic contexts. Chapters 5–7 have to do with Cicero's appropriation and transformation of Greek philosophy, especially as it relates to his self-identification as a Roman writing in Latin and as a Platonist. Chapters 8–15 have to do with Cicero's positions in and uses of philosophy within his Roman context. These chapters are arranged thematically: each typically focuses on one or two works that are especially important for the theme. Thus, readers will receive a helpful introduction to many of Cicero's most important philosophical works. Chapters 16–18 focus on a few case studies that highlight the way in which Cicero's writings have been useful for later philosophers to think with and against.

In completing this undertaking, we have incurred a number of debts over the years. I (Jed) would like to thank my research assistants, Alex Karsten (Duke) and Charlotte Champ (Princeton), who compiled the bibliographies of the individual chapters into a master bibliography and checked references. A trip to France in March 2018 gave Thomas and me an opportunity to work on the volume in person at an important stage of the project. I am grateful to Thomas for his hospitality in Lille and to Christelle Veillard, Juliette Dross, Jean-Baptiste Gourinat, and Charlotte Murgier for hosting me in Paris. Thomas also shouldered much of the burden of moving our project to completion during Fall 2020 as I began a term as departmental chair. The penultimate round of editing took place during my sabbatical for the 2019/2020 academic year. My sabbatical was made possible by the generous support of Duke University and, at Princeton University, the James Madison Program and the Politics department. I spent the Fall 2019 semester in Princeton. I am very grateful for the kind welcome offered by colleagues and staff in the departments of Politics and Classics, the University Center for Human Values, and the James Madison Program. Finally, I cannot imagine undertaking this or any other project without the love and support of Claire, William, and Caroline. When we were dating while I was in graduate school in Cambridge, Claire bought me Miller's Loeb edition of *De officiis* and Powell's OCT edition of *De republica*, *De legibus*, and other works, volumes now well-worn with use. She has patiently and lovingly encouraged me in both work and life in the fifteen years since.

I (Thomas) am very grateful to colleagues and friends who gave me opportunities to study Cicero as a philosopher in his own right, when I was mostly interested in his sources. Francis Wolff trusted me with an *agrégation* course on *De finibus* 3 in 1999–2000; I had various illuminating discussions about Cicero (often during sessions of the *Séminaire de*

Philosophie Hellénistique et Romaine in Créteil or Paris) with the late
Bernard Besnier, François Prost, José Kany-Turpin, Alain Gigandet,
Valéry Laurand, Mauro Bonazzi, Gretchen Reydams-Schils, and Margaret
Graver; the organizing committee of the *Symposium Hellenisticum* invited
me to give a paper for its 2010 Budapest meeting on *De finibus*. I also thank
all the participants in the monthly seminar on Cicero's *De republica*, which
I organized with Anne-Isabelle Bouton-Touboulic during the academic
years 2017/2018 and 2018/2019. A *délégation CNRS* allowed me to devote
all my time to research from January to July 2019; I was very fortunate to
spend this semester in Cambridge thanks to a French government fellowship at Churchill College. I very much appreciated the kind welcome offered
by colleagues and graduate students in the Classics Faculty, chiefly the
B Caucus, and in Churchill College. I thank James Warren, David Sedley,
and Ken Siddle for making me and my family feel very much at home in
Cambridge. Finally, I am very grateful to Jed Atkins for taking care of much
more than half of the editing work of this *Companion* when I was chair of my
department in 2018 and teaching in 2020.

We both would like to thank our editor at CUP, Michael Sharp.
Michael first suggested the possibility of a *Cambridge Companion to
Cicero's Philosophy*, and he patiently supported our project from conception to publication. We are also grateful to all of the contributors for the
diligence, care, and professionalism with which they worked to help bring
this volume to life. Above all, we are indebted to Malcolm Schofield and
Carlos Lévy. Malcolm first introduced us to one another, and both
Malcolm and Carlos read and gave us feedback on drafts of the original
proposal. However, our debts to both men go much deeper and will last far
longer. They directed our respective Ph.D. dissertations (Malcolm, Jed's
on Cicero's political philosophy; Carlos, Thomas' on the Stoic idea of
practice as use) and have generously offered their guidance and support
over the subsequent years. Given the immense debt that we, and indeed all
who work on Cicero's philosophy, owe to Malcolm and Carlos, we
dedicate this Companion to them.

Cicero's Philosophical Works

This table presents Cicero's major philosophical works and works dealing with philosophy, provides their date of composition (all dates BCE), and indicates the main chapter(s) where they are discussed in the *Cambridge Companion to Cicero's Philosophy* (*CCCP*). Many of these works are also discussed or alluded to in other chapters, especially the chapters devoted to historical context (Chapter 1), the dialogue form (Chapter 2), Latin translation (Chapter 5), Plato (Chapter 6), and reception (chapters 16-17). Please see the Index of Cicero's Texts for a complete documentation of treatments of Ciceronian works within the volume.

Work	Date	Chapter in *CCCP*
De inventione (*On Invention*)	91–80	13
Pro Murena (*On Behalf of Murena*)	63	4
In Pisonem (*Against Piso*)	55	4
De oratore (*On the Orator*)	55	6, 13
De republica (*On the Commonwealth*)	51	6, 14, 15
De legibus (*On the Laws*)	after 52	6, 15
Paradoxa Stoicorum (*The Paradoxes of the Stoics*)	47	1
Brutus (*Brutus*)	46	6
Orator (*Orator*)	46	6, 13
Consolatio (*Consolation*)	45	10
Hortensius (*Hortensius*)	45	16
Academica (*Academic Books*)	45	7
De finibus (*On Ends*)	45	11
Translation of Plato's *Protagoras*	45	5
Tusculanae disputationes (*Tusculan Disputations*)	45	10
De natura deorum (*On the Nature of the Gods*)	45	8
Translation of Plato's *Timaeus*	after 45	5, 8
De divinatione (*On Divination*)	44	9
De senectute (*On Old Age*)	44	18
De fato (*On Fate*)	44	9
De amicitia (*On Friendship*)	44	18

(*cont.*)

Work	Date	Chapter in *CCCP*
Topica (*Topics*)	44	4
De officiis (*On Duties*)	44	12, 15, 18
Epistulae ad Atticum (*Letters to Atticus*)	68–44	3, 6
Epistulae Familiares (*Letters to His Friends*)	62–43	3, 6
Epistulae ad Quintum (*Letters to Quintus*)	59–54	3

A Note on Abbreviations

The names of ancient authors and titles of ancient works are abbreviated according to the 4th edition of the *Oxford Classical Dictionary*.

References to modern works are not abbreviated, with the exception of the following:

> *SVF* = *Stoicorum Veterum Fragmenta*, I,. ed. Von Arnim
> *TLL* = *Thesaurus Linguae Latinae*
> SB = Shackleton Bailey

Note that "Powell" as a reference to the text of *De republica* = Powell 2006.

Introduction

Thomas Bénatouïl

For approximately the last thirty years, Cicero's reputation as a philosopher has been rising after close to a century of very low esteem.[1] The alleged reasons for this disrepute are numerous and varied. Cicero was Roman, and Romans were thought to be neither scientific nor philosophical. He wrote in Latin, when the genuine language of philosophy was and is Greek. No original thinker, he was not so much a philosopher as translator and compiler, pasting together various philosophical works from the second and first century BCE. This he did in his spare time, for Cicero was an amateur philosopher. His main pursuits were politics and judicial advocacy. When he turned to philosophy, he was content to adopt a form of eclecticism amenable to his own changing status in the troubled last decades of the Roman Republic. This short introduction won't be covering Cicero's philosophical works and their context (for which the reader should consult Chapter 1); it aims only to present the various and complementary ways in which this *Companion*, building on earlier studies, may answer these charges and allow us to gain a more accurate and richer picture of Cicero as a philosopher.

First, one must emphasize how crucial Cicero's philosophical writings were to the history of Western philosophy and culture. Cicero is one of our best sources of information about the doctrines and debates of the Hellenistic philosophers whose works have been almost entirely lost. About his teachers Philo of Larissa and Antiochus of Ascalon we would know next to nothing were it not for Cicero's dialogues. They are also our only sources about crucial physical or ethical tenets of the Stoics, the

---

[1] Among the seminal contributions to this now-booming trend: Boyancé 1970; Michel 1960; Burkert 1965; Douglas 1965; Grilli 1971; Görler 1974 and 1994; Wood 1988; MacKendrick 1989; Fortenbaugh and Steinmetz 1989; Lévy 1992a; Powell 1995a; Striker 1995; Inwood and Mansfeld 1997; Cambiano 2002; Auvray-Assayas 2006; Schofield 2008 and 2013b; Nicgorski 2012; Woolf 2015.

Epicureans, and the New Academy, and about many Hellenistic debates between these three schools.[2]

Cicero is also the creator of a considerable proportion of the Latin philosophical vocabulary, which had a major imprint on the history of Western philosophy lasting to our own day. In Chapter 5, Carlos Lévy analyzes Cicero's aims and methods in his translations from Greek into Latin. Cicero's contributions covered the fields of epistemology, ethics, and physics, and helped bequeath us terms such as the "individual" and "will."

Future generations from Seneca onwards regarded Cicero as an important philosopher whose philosophical works and positions were important in themselves. In Chapter 10, Anne-Isabelle Bouton-Touboulic focuses on Augustine's significant debts in style and substance to Cicero's philosophical writings. In Chapter 17, Daniel J. Kapust surveys the attitudes toward Cicero of a large number of eighteenth-century philosophers and political thinkers on a range of topics including ethics, rhetoric, civil religion, law, and the value of glory.[3] While authors in other periods have also turned to Cicero's philosophical writings with profit,[4] Cicero's thought most significantly contributed to the work of philosophers during Late Antiquity and the eighteenth-century Enlightenment.

But Cicero is not worthy of consideration merely because of reception history. Cicero's contribution to the topics just mentioned are important in their own right. First, his *De republica* (*On the Commonwealth*), *De legibus* (*On Laws*), and *De officiis* (*On Duties*) are major works in the history of political philosophy.[5] Chapters 12, 14, and 15 by Gretchen Reydams-Schils, Walter Nicgorski, and Jed W. Atkins, respectively, survey Cicero's views on human social relationships and community; his definition of *res publica* through liberty, his conception of equality and justice and of the best form of government; his discussions of imperialism, of justified and unjustified war, and of cosmopolitanism. While often

---

[2] Stoicism: the transition from self-appropriation to virtue (Cic. *Fin.* 3.16–23); Panetius' doctrine of virtues and duties (Cic. *Off.*). Epicureanism: the natural constitution of the gods (Cic. *Nat. D.* 1.42–52); the various definitions of friendship (Cic. *Fin.* 1.65–70). New Academy: Carneades' division of ethical positions (*Fin.* 5.16–23), his arguments against justice (Cic. *Rep.* 3) or theology (Cic. *Nat. D.* 3). Debates: the arguments about fate and human responsibility (Cic. *Fat.*).

[3] On Cicero in American republicanism, see also Nicgorski (Chapter 14) in this volume.

[4] See, for instance, the treatment of Cicero's legacy on the social and political thought of the late Middle Ages by Nederman 2020, and Schmitt 1972 on the influence of Cicero's *Academica* during the Renaissance. For other studies of Cicero's reception, see Steel 2013a: 233–350; Altman 2015.

[5] For two treatments of Cicero as an important political thinker, one seminal, the other very recent, see Wood 1988; Schofield 2021.

drawing on Stoicism for these topics, Cicero offers his own views, which were informed by his study of philosophy and, perhaps above all, his experience as a Roman statesman. Moreover, as Martha C. Nussbaum shows in Chapter 18, Cicero's discussions of cosmopolitanism, the duties of justice, and the conduct of warfare have vital relevance to current debates.

Nussbaum also devotes attention to practical ethics, where Cicero made original, albeit often overlooked, contributions on friendship and old age, which are still applicable to contemporary concerns. While practical ethics is often reduced to a personal search for peace of mind, Cicero's approach stands out for its focus on the social and political roots and implications of emotions or duties (as emphasized in Chapters 10, 12, and 18). In the *Tusculan Disputations*, Cicero deals with fear (especially of death) and grief, and, as Sean McConnell shows in Chapter 10, he adopts a pragmatic approach, which can be seen as a distinctive aspect of his philosophical practice.[6]

In fact, political philosophy and practical ethics are not so much discrete topics for Cicero as perspectives central to all his works. Cicero does not practice philosophy in a social void. In Chapter 1, Claudia Moatti puts his whole philosophical oeuvre into the context of the late Roman Republic and emphasizes his project of rationalizing Roman culture and politics. Cicero is not interested in theoretical elaboration in itself, let alone innovation, but concerned "with how the activity of philosophy might fit in with broader Roman social and cultural norms,"[7] and also claims to create a new style of doing philosophy.[8] This is why Cicero insists on judging philosophical doctrines not only on the basis of their consistency or adequacy to the facts, but also through the manner of discourse their proponents adopt and the efficiency of their arguments both inside and outside philosophical schools.[9] Consequently, Cicero's letters and speeches are also relevant for understanding Cicero as a philosopher, as shown in chapters 3 and 4, by Sophie Aubert-Baillot and Catherine Steel. The letters offer insights into the elaboration of Cicero's positions and testify to the experimental dimension of most philosophical doctrines in this corpus. The speeches use philosophy against Cicero's opponents but also as an implicit source of insights about political values and threats. This use of philosophy is theorized by Cicero in his dialogue *De oratore* (*On the*

---

[6] See also Luciani 2010: 49–130 on Cicero's original approach to time in the *Tusculans*.
[7] Woolf 2015: 4–6.   [8] Smith 1995; Wynne 2019: 15–16.
[9] Michel 1960; Aubert-Baillot 2008.

Orator) written in 55, as shown by Gary Remer in Chapter 13. Challenging both philosophical censures of rhetoric *and* widespread beliefs about philosophy's uselessness, Cicero conceives of rhetoric, politics, and philosophy as so interconnected that they are, or at least should be, a unity under the rubric "eloquence."

Cicero's later philosophical dialogues, written in the 40s under Caesar's dictatorship, are obviously not public speeches, but he conceived them as a continuation of eloquence and politics (from which he was forced to retire after Caesar's victory over Pompey) by other means.[10] It is crucial to take this agenda into account if we are to read Cicero's dialogues on their own terms. In Chapters 8 and 9, Clara Auvray-Assayas and Elisabeth Begemann show how preserving human responsibility both at the individual and the political level is a crucial issue in Cicero's approach to cosmology and theology. In *De natura deorum* (*On the Nature of the Gods*), Cicero emphasizes the historical, anthropological, and psychological aspects of Greek theology and uses skeptical arguments to define precise limits for political thinking on religion, while *De divinatione* (*On Divination*) and *De fato* (*On Fate*) can be read as seeking to combine Greek thought and Roman practice and as exhortations to act in the service of the *res publica* after the death of Caesar.

In response to all of these arguments for treating Cicero as an important philosopher, one might counter that he was content with an eclectic philosophy suited to the practical concerns of his Roman readers and that this is a long way from offering a systematic doctrine addressing philosophy's core issues in ontology and epistemology. Recent scholarship has shown, on the contrary, not only that Cicero's approach to philosophy as described so far is consistent throughout his late dialogues, and perhaps even his whole oeuvre,[11] but also that it is all of a piece with his affiliation to the New Academy. Cicero, like many other ancient and modern thinkers, has suffered greatly from the widespread disrepute of skepticism as a philosophy. But shunning new doctrines in favor of a critical survey of available ones, putting them into their cultural context, or assessing their practical implications are not the marginal approaches of an outsider but part and parcel of Cicero's skeptical practice of *philosophy*.

---

[10] Gildenhard 2007; Fox 2007; Baraz 2012; Begemann (Chapter 9) in this volume.

[11] Rheinardt (Chapter 7), Auvray-Assayas (Chapter 8), and Reydams-Schils (Chapter 12) in this volume trace crucial positions of Cicero's late dialogues to his earliest works. Discussions of possible shifts in Cicero's stance (between Antiochus and the New Academy) are found in Glücker 1988 and 1992; Lévy 1992a: 96–126; Görler 1994; and in Brittain and Osorio (Chapter 2), Schofield (Chapter 6), and Rheinardt (Chapter 7) in this volume.

Cicero often praises the New Academy for preserving the freedom (*libertas*) of judgment of its followers, unlike other schools that submit them to an authority: such a conception of philosophy is both epistemological and pedagogical, but also has political implications since *libertas* was an important republican value.[12] Yet there is still much debate about which type of skepticism should be attributed to Cicero. This problem is addressed by Tobias Reinhardt in Chapter 7, which shows that Cicero's stance in his *Academica* (*Academic Books*) shares certain features with mitigated skepticism but is formally a radical skepticism, and that his dialogues are unique sources about the enactment or the living practice of an Academic skeptical stance.[13]

Did Cicero really invent this Academic stance or did he borrow it from his Academic teachers? Was his epistemological contribution essentially literary (translating, selecting characters and a setting for each dialogue, adducing prefaces and Roman examples)[14] or really philosophical? A very promising line followed by recent scholarship has consisted in showing that this opposition misses the point. Cicero wrote *dialogues* for *philosophical* reasons. In Chapter 2, Charles Brittain and Peter Osorio present a few examples from the late and early dialogues to argue that Cicero's texts systematically enact, as well as represent, an Academic pedagogical methodology. While the dialogues mostly present doctrines which are not Cicero's own, they stage or frame original and searching philosophical debates between these doctrines.

Cicero's dialogues on ethics are a very good example, as shown by Raphael Woolf in Chapter 11: in *De finibus* (*On Ends*), Cicero writes as a skeptic, using the arguments to encourage his readers to consider the importance of accounting for a plurality of ethical goods and whether, once we do that, we can still usefully adhere to a "full-fledged" ethical theory. Thus, Cicero's philosophical stance can be captured only from a careful reading of each dialogue as a whole.[15] Cicero's dialogues must be read in the same manner as Plato's dialogues have been read during the last thirty years or so, that is to say *as philosophical dialogues*, in which no

[12] Auvray-Assayas 2006: 20–21; Atkins 2018a: 37–62. On the political implications of Cicero's skepticism, see Zarecki 2014; Nicgorski 2016; Cappello 2019.

[13] See also Bouton-Touboulic (Chapter 16) in this volume on Augustine's assessment of Cicero's skepticism.

[14] This is the main hypothesis of *Quellenforschung* (source criticism), originated by Madvig 1839 and Hirzel 1877, 1882, 1883, which was long dominant and criticized in Boyancé 1970: 199–221 (originally published in 1936); Douglas 1965: 138–142; Lévy 1996.

[15] As argued and practiced by Görler 1997; Schofield 2008; Atkins 2013a; Gildenhard 2013b; Zarecki 2014; Schultz 2014; Woolf 2015; Annas and Betegh 2016; Wynne 2019.

character (even a character bearing his name)[16] can be assumed to be a straightforward mouthpiece of the author and each argument must be read in its dramatic context. As a matter of fact, as shown by Malcolm Schofield in Chapter 6, Cicero himself identified with Plato in all his richness and abundance as a writer, thinker, and model for the politically engaged intellectual, but the imprint of Plato on Cicero's works evolved and is still much debated.

This introduction has tried to present the various ways in which Cicero has been read anew as a genuine philosopher during the last three decades or so, and how these approaches are represented in the eighteen chapters of this *Companion*. Our goal is to offer an overview and assessment of recent research on Cicero's philosophy and to encourage new research in this area. These lines of inquiry have been and are being pursued by many scholars all over the world and will surely not converge into one single picture of Cicero's philosophy. Some scholars focus only on Cicero's "strictly" philosophical dialogues, many take into account some or all of his other writings, while others study their various uses through different periods and cultures. Some scrutinize Cicero's arguments against the background of his Greek sources, others reconstruct his cultural and political agendas in the context of the late Roman Republic, and others emphasize their relevance to contemporary philosophical debates. Some view Cicero's Academic stance as radically skeptical, while others insist on the imprint of Stoicism or of Plato on many of his positions. Some emphasize Cicero's continuity across his entire body of philosophical writing, whereas others point out the various changes in style or substance between these works. Despite this diversity, all these approaches share the fundamental conviction that Cicero's philosophy will not be recovered against or at the expense of his other achievements and identities as a writer, advocate, politician, and Roman man of the first century BCE, but only in coordination with these other dimensions of his life. There is no one single way of reading Cicero as a philosopher; it clearly requires us to widen and diversify our practice and notion of philosophy. Renewed attention to Cicero can thus benefit the discipline of philosophy today, just as it did in the eighteenth century. Let us hope our century too will be Ciceronian.

---

[16] On the different "Ciceros" (author, narrator, character) in the dialogues, see Brittain and Osorio (Chapter 2) and Reinhardt (Chapter 7, p. 103–104) in this volume.

CHAPTER I

Cicero's Philosophical Writing in Its Intellectual Context

Claudia Moatti

For Cicero, intellectual inquiry was intimately related to historical analysis. When he took an interest in a specific discipline, dealt with a particular issue, or justified his interest in philosophy, Cicero situated the life of the mind in the long-term history of eloquence (*Brut.* 20), of Rome (*Tusc.* 1.1–6), or of humanity (*Div.* 1.1–3) – the forms of intellectual inquiry have a history. Cicero's association of intellectual inquiry and history is especially evident in the passages (letters or prefaces) in which he looks back on his work, as in the beginning of the second book of *De divinatione*, which allows him to explain what he understands by "philosophy": rhetoric, morality, theology, political theory, science itself, and of course logic, the art of demonstration (*Att.* 13.19.5).

The scholars of his time also sought to situate themselves within a broad historical horizon. They prepared chronologies or looked back on the past in order to define a word, an institution, or the sources of law. Antiquarians, grammarians, and jurists all broadened the horizon of the city by searching for origins, but also through comparatism or through the exercise of reason.[1] Cicero was therefore a true witness of his age. This is why it is important to put him into his context, provided we keep in mind that he himself contributed to create this context, which was influenced by his work, his thinking, and his erudition. Cicero was a historian and a witness, but he was also, among other things, an actor within an intellectual revolution.

Cicero the Historian

The Social Time of Disciplines

In a letter he wrote to Atticus in June 44, Cicero revealed that he had written a small volume of prefaces, a *volumen*

---

[1] On this intellectual context, see Rawson 1985, esp. ch. 16; Moatti 2015, ch. 3.

prohoemiorum.[2] These prefaces attempted in different ways to justify philosophical activity in Latin: this proves that such an activity still did not come naturally at the time. In one of these prefaces, he wonders: "why should accomplished Grecians read Latin poets and not Latin philosophers? Is it because they get pleasure from Ennius, Pacuvius, Accius, and many others who have reproduced not the words but the genius of the Greek poets?" (*Acad.* 1.10; trans. Rackham, modified). In another preface, at the beginning of the first book of the *Tusculan Disputations*, in which he engages in a sort of comparative anthropology of Greece and Rome, he laments again that philosophy was imported into the city very recently compared to rhetoric and even poetry (1.2–3). The sole exception, Cicero notes, was Epicureanism, which had been successfully promoted in Latin from the end of the second century (4.6–7).[3]

Cicero explains the reasons for this resistance to philosophy in detail in *De finibus*, which he wrote in June 45 and dedicated to Brutus (*Fin.* 1.1):

> Certain persons, and those not without some pretension to letters, disapprove of the study of philosophy altogether. Others do not so greatly object to it provided it be followed in dilettante fashion; but they do not think it ought to engage so large an amount of one's interest and attention. A third class, learned in Greek literature and contemptuous of Latin, will say that they prefer to spend their time in reading Greek. Lastly, I suspect there will be some who will wish to divert me to other fields of authorship, asserting that this kind of composition, though a graceful recreation, is beneath the dignity of my character and position.[4]

According to Cicero, two major obstacles prevented the development of philosophy: firstly, the status of culture (the status of Greek culture for the Roman elite in particular) – why would one waste time philosophizing when one should be at the service of the *res publica*?; and secondly, the translation of the treatises into Latin – why should they be translated if one could read Greek? In both cases, the relation between knowledge and power was at the heart of the problem: in a society in which only the skills necessary to the exercise of power were recognized by the elite (knowledge of law, the art of warfare, eloquence itself), what importance should be

---

[2] *Att.* 16.6.4: "I keep a volume of prefaces. From it I am accustomed to select one when I have begun some treatise." Here, Cicero confesses that he had already used the same preface in *De gloria* and in the *Academica*. He realized this on a boat journey. According to Yelena Baraz, this volume shows that the prefaces formed a whole and served as a kind of *captatio benevolentiae* (2012: 6–8).

[3] On the development of Epicureanism in Latin, see Sedley 2009: 39–40; Benferhat 2005: 58–73.

[4] See also *Acad.* 2.5: "There are many people who have no love for Greek literature at all and many more who have none for philosophy; while the rest, even if they do not disapprove of these studies nevertheless think that the discussion of such topics is not especially becoming for great statesmen."

given to philosophy, which was not only considered a difficult and studious hobby (*otium*) that was therefore likely to keep the ruling class out of politics, but also a discipline that could undermine the traditional modes of belief? This was an especially crucial concern in an age where senators were accused of having made the establishment of tyranny possible by deserting political life (Sall. *Cat.* 52; Caes. *BCiv.* 1.32.7; Cic. *Acad.* 2.4–7; App. *B Civ.* 2.82).

These issues did not first arise in the 40s. In the second century BCE, Ennius made his character Neoptolemus urge a moderate practice of philosophy: "I need to philosophize, but only a little (*philosophari mihi necesse, at paucis*)," he wrote (ap. Cic. *Tusc.* 2.1; *Rep.* 1.30). Likewise, Pacuvius, a contemporary dramatist, made a character from his *Antiope* an opponent of theory: "For my part, I hate men whose activity is idleness and whose thought (*sententia*) is philosophy (*philosophia*)" (Gell. *NA* 13.8.4). Also, in 92 BCE, the closure of the Latin school of rhetoric by the Roman censors, as part of their duty to enforce public morality, had revealed the ambivalent attitude of a certain part of the elite toward theory. Although learning Greek oratorical techniques was part of the education of young Romans, it aroused some hostility from Roman citizens. In *De oratore*, Cicero mentions a discussion on the subject that allegedly took place in 91 between the two great orators Crassus and Antonius: the former wondered why teaching law had always been a beautiful thing whereas rhetoric had a far more checkered history at Rome; the latter suggested that the successful orator must conceal the Greek science of rhetoric, thereby securing his popularity with his audience by giving the illusion of natural eloquence. Though *De oratore* was published in the mid-fifties BCE, Cicero could still hear the disparagers of philosophy using this very argument roughly a decade later (*Hortensius*, in August. *Contra Iulianum* 5.7.29). The point was that as long as the art of oratory remained a private, concealed choice, as long as it was learned in Greek and confined to a restricted social milieu, it did not question the social order. However, if it was taught in Latin, it became accessible to other social classes, it became visible, and even exhibited in the public space, which raised political issues. It is true that the edict of 92 had but a minor impact: several treatises in Latin were published during those years, such as *Rhetorica ad Herennium* or Cicero's *De inventione* (written between 87 and 81), and the schools of Latin rhetoric reopened in 81. However, social resistance to the spreading of this art lingered on, as is evinced by Cicero's caution in praising the culture of Lucullus in the 40s (*Acad.* 2.1–3).

The key issue of power and its relation to knowledge enables us to understand the reasons why poetry and theatre – even though they intimately depended on Greek literature – did not arouse the same hostility: these domains did not present themselves as new *sciences*; they gave people pleasures, emotions, and grace which could not divert them from politics, provided that they were considered as an intermittent entertainment. Lucretius' choice to write philosophy in the form of a didactic poem, like Varro's *Menippean Satires*, pertained to a strategy that fit Roman society: the poetic form, like theatre before it, enabled authors to spread doctrine among non-philosophers, and to overcome social resistance; these literary genres allowed these writers to turn philosophy into a literary pleasure while undercutting philosophy's status as "subversive knowledge." To a certain extent, Lucretius and Varro acted like Pompey, who had managed to defy the Senate's opposition to the building of a permanent theatre by passing his theatre off as an annex of the Temple of Venus Victrix.

The First Contacts with Philosophy

Although he reported on his contemporaries' resistance, Cicero nonetheless intended to demonstrate that philosophy already had a certain history in Rome and in Italy. For example, he argued that Pythagoreanism, a philosophy founded in the sixth century BCE by the Ionian philosopher Pythagoras, had already begun to influence Italian culture and Roman institutions by the fourth century BCE.[5] He dated the first contacts with Epicureanism to the third century, when Caius Fabricius was sent as ambassador to Pyrrhus in 279 BCE, while Epicurus was still alive (*Sen.* 43). This contact was followed by the important development of Epicureanism in Italy, as is suggested by Cicero in the *Tusculan Disputations* (*Tusc.* 4.6–7), and borne out by the expulsion of two Epicurean philosophers from Rome in 173 and 161 (Gell. *NA* 15.11). More importantly, Cicero dated the most significant influence of philosophy to the second half of the second century. He situated his important dialogue of political philosophy, *De republica*, in this period, and stressed the philosophical aptitude of its leading characters, including Scipio and Laelius, important Roman statesmen. In fact, Cicero places at the center of *De republica* an episode that he will also recall in his later *Tusculan Disputations*:

---

[5] Conversely, he rejected the belief in Pythagoras' influence on Numa (*Rep.* 2.28–29; *Tusc.* 4.3).

The study of wisdom . . . was of long standing among our countrymen, but nevertheless, I do not find any I can really call philosophers before the days of Laelius and Scipio. In their young days, I see that Diogenes the Stoic and Carneades of the Academy were sent as ambassadors to the Senate by the Athenians, and as these men had never taken any part in public life and one of them was a native of Cyrene and the other of Babylon, they would assuredly never have been called out of their lecture rooms or chosen for this office, unless the study of philosophy had been familiar to some of the leading Romans of that day. (4.5)

Here, Cicero mentions the famous ambassadorship of the three philosophers who came to Rome in 155 to defend the interests of Athens in its conflict against the city of Oropus: Carneades of Cyrene, Diogenes of Babylon, and Critolaus of Phaselis, a Peripatetic. Athens's very choice to send three (non-Athenian) philosophers as ambassadors suggests that the Roman elite's interest in philosophy was already well-known to the Greeks.[6] In any case, the event made an impression, particularly because of Carneades, a scholarch of the New Academy, who was bold enough to deliver two successive speeches: in the first, he spoke in defense of justice in public affairs; in the second, he pleaded the cause of injustice. This double argument, which Cicero reproduced almost entirely in the debate between Laelius and Philus in the third book of *De republica*,[7] resulted in Cato the Censor firmly enjoining the three philosophers to leave the city as quickly as possible. However, the effects of the ambassadorship were decisive: Laelius came around to Diogenes of Babylon's – and then Panaetius' – Stoicism (*Fin.* 2.24), as Scipio did. Even Cato took up Greek. In 45, Cicero wrote:

For my own part, as I have been told that Marcus Cato learned Greek literature in his old age, while history states that Publius Africanus [Scipio Aemilianus, who defeated Carthage in 146], on the famous embassy on which he went before his censorship, had Panaetius as absolutely the sole member of his staff, I need not look any further for someone to support the claims either of Greek literature or of philosophy. (*Acad.* 2.5)

In his account of this ambassadorship, in comparing Cato's ambiguous attitude with that of Scipio Aemilianus, Cicero shed light on both the contradictions of the second century, which was characterized by an

---

[6] A remark made by Cicero himself at *Tusc.* 4.5.

[7] See Ferrary 1974, 1977; on the political aspects and Roman reception of the embassy, Ferrary 1988: 351–363 and Vesperini 2012: 135–168; on Cicero's reconstruction of the event, see also Powell 2013b.

attraction to and a rejection of philosophy, and the imperial dimension of the first contacts with Greek culture.

Indeed, the turning point in the acceptance of Greek philosophy by elite Romans was forged from Rome's imperial conquests. From the slaves and the hostages brought to Rome after victories in battle to the artists who were summoned to celebrate Rome, including the ambassadors who came to plead the cases of conquered cities,[8] bonds were forged between Greek intellectuals and the Roman elite due to this mobility. Members of the Roman elite surrounded themselves with philosophers and rhetoricians: the Stoic philosopher Panaetius of Rhodes and his disciple Hecato lived with Scipio Aemilianus; another Stoic philosopher, Blossius of Cumae, and the rhetor Diophanes of Mytilene lived with the Gracchi (Plut. *Ti. Gracch.* 8.6; Cic. *Amic.* 36–37). Then, in the next century, Diodotus the Stoic stayed at Cicero's residence for a very long time; the Peripatetic Staseas of Naples stayed at Marcus Pupius Piso's (Cic. *Fin.* 5.8); and Philodemus of Gadara the Epicurean (110–40/35) settled in the villa of Calpurnius Piso Caesonius, Caesar's father-in-law, in Herculaneum. A former pupil of Zeno of Sidon (the scholarch of the Epicurean school of Athens from 100), Philodemus arrived in Rome after Zeno's death in 75. There, he created a sort of intellectual and moral community whose members were Roman citizens (among them, Quintus Varus, Quinctilius Varus, and Plotius Tucca) as well as Greeks (e.g. Siro the Epicurean, who lived on the other side of the Gulf of Naples, on the Posillipo hill, and who was Virgil's teacher): the papyri that were found in the ruins of this villa bear witness to his activity and his intellectual curiosity. These papyri include notes that come from Zeno's lectures (the Περὶ παρρησίας, "On Freedom of Speech," for instance [PHerc. 147]), his own treatises on such diverse subjects as theology, politics, ethics, poetry,[9] and books in Latin or in Greek, written by authors other than Philodemus.[10]

These philosophers who settled in Italy following sometimes dramatic escapes from their homelands (as was the case of Philo of Larissa, the last known head of Plato's Academy, and his pupil Antiochus of Ascalon, follower of Plato and Aristotle, who fled Athens in 86 as the city was being plundered by Sulla) often sought the protection of a Roman

---

[8] Such was the position of the Stoic grammarian Crates of Mallus, who was sent by King Attalus of Pergamon in 159 (Suet. *Gram. et rhet.* 2), and of Posidonius of Apamea the Stoic in 87 (Plut. *Mar.* 45).

[9] Asmis 1990.

[10] For an analysis of this aspect of the catalogue, see Houston 2013: 183 and passim.

"patron" over whom they would exercise great influence, as Antiochus did with Varro or Brutus (Plut. *Brut.* 2; Cic. *Att.* 13.25.3). But it was also in Greece that the Romans of the first century made their acquaintance, more specifically when they went there to further their education.

In his account of the two years he spent in the eastern Mediterranean between 79 and 77, Cicero mentioned his sojourn in Athens, where he and Atticus had the opportunity to attend the lectures of Antiochus of Ascalon and Demetrius Syrus the rhetorician (*Brut.* 313; *Acad.* 1.4), but also those of the Epicureans Zeno of Sidon and Phaedrus (*Fin.* 1.16; *Tusc.* 3.38). Cicero also mentioned his travels in Asia, in the course of which he followed the greatest rhetoricians, and his sojourn in Rhodes, where he attended the lectures of Posidonius, the head of the Stoic school, and Apollonius, Molon's son, who was also Caesar's teacher in rhetoric (Plut. *Caes.* 3.1). These ties also developed or were strengthened in the course of public or military missions: for instance, Cato the Younger, when he was a military tribune in Macedonia, took advantage of a two-month leave to go to Pergamon in order to meet Athenodoros, a famous Stoic and the keeper of the kingdom's great library, and talked him into following him to Rome (Plut. *Cat. Min.* 10.1–3). Likewise, as he passed through Rhodes after the campaign against the pirates in 67, Pompey attended the lectures of Posidonius (Strab. *Geog.* 11.1.6) and many sophists as well, according to Plutarch (*Pomp.* 42.5). Pilgrimage to the great places of Greece, such as the Academy or the Lyceum in Athens, was a powerful moral experience as well, but it could be undertaken purely out of intellectual curiosity, which was a truly new feeling at the time (*Fin.* 5.1–2).[11]

The conquests also made direct contacts with Greek manuscripts easier, as when the library of Perseus, King of Macedon, was brought to Rome in 167, or Apellicon's Aristotelian library was brought from Athens to Rome by Sulla in 84.[12] But books also circulated due to private initiatives. For instance, Philodemus brought a set of books with him when he settled in Italy, which may have been the private library he had inherited from his master Zeno;[13] and, above all, rich Romans took to buying and collecting books like works of art. In these villas where Ciceronian philosophical texts

---

[11] Moatti 2015: 152–153.
[12] According to Barnes 1997: 49 n. 200, after the death of Sulla, the library was bought by Lucullus, the tutor of Sulla's son Faustus. But there is little evidence for this. The library rather seems to have been transferred to Faustus' Campanian house at Cumae (*Att.* 4.10). For a discussion on this peculiar point, see Tutrone 2013: 164–166. About this library, see also Hatzimichali 2013, who is less skeptical.
[13] On Philodemus' library, see Cavallo 1983: 58–60, completed by Houston 2013.

were set (*De finibus, Hortensius, Tusculanae disputationes, De natura deorum, De divinatione*), a private library became the mark of a high social status (Vitr. *De arch.* 6.5.1–2). It was also there that people would have had direct access to ancient philosophy. In private libraries, men of culture would meet and talk far from the public space, as is evidenced by the *De finibus*: at the beginning of the third book, Cicero asserts (or claims) that he is relating a philosophical conversation he had had in 52 in the library of the young Lucullus, where, looking for Aristotelian commentaries to borrow, he had found Cato "sitting surrounded by many books of the Stoics" (*Fin.* 3.7).

Since they pursued the same studies and shared the same tastes, these educated Romans formed an intellectual community, a *societas studiorum*, as Cicero put it. They dedicated books to one another, debated via treatises, and exchanged books.[14] Therefore, more than a social milieu, the *societas studiorum* was an intellectual practice based on dialogue and the knowledge of Greek. Consequently, a question arose very naturally: what was the point of translating or writing philosophy in Latin if educated people knew Greek? Could the non-elite be interested in this discipline? Cicero was very clear on this point: to translate is first and foremost to know one's own language better, but it is also to spread the Latin language and literature, to make the geniuses of mankind accessible, and finally to complete the military conquest by transferring to Rome the Greek cultural patrimony.

Cicero the Witness

Undoubtedly, philosophy mostly interested the elite. It was also clear that its practice was a private choice and was restricted to this limited circle more often than not; but philosophy was not only an object of speculation for those who engaged in it: it offered above all methods to deal with the crisis the city was going through in the late Republic, to reflect better upon the past, knowledge, and politics. More than anything else, Cicero's work bears witness to an experience of philosophy serving the city.

A breach did open in the history of Rome at the end of the Republic. Initially, this breach was the result of Rome's imperial conquests and of a

---

[14] For instance, Caesar wrote his *De analogia* in response to Cicero's *latinitas* theory, which is mentioned in the *De oratore*. Cicero postulated that linguistic purity (*latinitas*) originated in *consuetudo* (the elite practice), while for Caesar, language could be regularized according to rational principles. On this debate, see Dugan 2005: 178–189; Garcea 2012: 13–18, 78–113.

part of the ruling class becoming tremendously richer. This process occurred due to the political violence that had developed since the age of the Gracchi, the incapacity of the elite to reform, the changes in the Roman political class that occurred after Sulla's proscriptions in 88 and in 82, and the extension of the civic body after the Social War (91–88). These changes raised important questions: How could a common civic memory, based on the contributions of a multitude of peoples and cultures, be constituted? How could this constant flow of goods and knowledge that had invaded the city since the second century be ordered? How could the conditions of certainty be established in a world where the source of authority was the subject of disputes, or the common utility defined when the city was torn apart by the struggles of factions, civil wars, and tyranny? How could one think when the *res publica* was on the verge of perishing? Greek philosophy offered fewer answers to these questions than tools to deal with the crisis.[15]

Crisis and Criticism: Reason in Rome

New ways of thinking and organizing did appear in this cultural and historical breach, as is evidenced by the appearance of a new language and the use of the same terms in every domain. Each of these terms became the *signifier* of an activity that claimed to be rational: *digerere* (to collect), *constituere* (to establish), *reddere rationem* (to account for), *in artem redigere* (to systematize), etc. These shared signifiers very precisely indicate what this spirit of rationality was: *an epistemological revolution* that manifested in three ways.[16]

The first aspect was *critical thinking*, that is, the search for the very foundations of human and divine affairs. In the first century, the entire domain of tradition and the forms of authority, which in the past had been merely a skill taught within the ruling class, became the subject of discourses and interpretations by scholars from various backgrounds who put them down in writing and created *corpora*. Making the past clearer, bringing out the coherence and the logic of knowledge, introducing distinctions between practices (for example, *religio*, or correct religious practice, and *superstitio*, practices that departed from the established civil religion), between modes of adherence (such as legend and history; or

---

[15] Moatti 2015, esp. ch. 5.
[16] On the influence of this epistemological revolution on Roman religion, see now Rüpke 2012, esp. 82–93, 144–151.

public worship and a purer, more natural practice of religion), or between disciplines (such as augural and pontifical law), or giving stable principles to contents – these were manifestations of the spirit of rationality in law, the administration, the domain of customs or that of cultural practices. Cicero's *De republica* and *De legibus* were both answers to this same concern. While referring to Plato, these works represented a continuation of the works of public law that appeared in the second century (e.g. T. Sempronius Tuditanus' *De magistratibus* and M. Junius Gracchanus' *De potestatibus*) and of the multitude of treatises that followed in the first century, of which only the titles remain in most cases (*De comitiis*, *De auspiciis*, etc.). Like Cicero's *De republica* and *De legibus*, these lost works were intended to establish discrete topics for inquiry – to select what was and what was not admissible historically and conceptually.

The search for precision was the second aspect of this revolution. Caesar's reform of the calendar, in which pontifical science was replaced by Hellenistic science, was clearly a victory of reason over tradition, of accuracy over instability and vagueness, as Macrobius saw it (*Sat.* 1.14.2). Grammatical research (Nigidius Figulus' *Commentarii grammatici*, or Varro's *De lingua latina*, and so many others), the attempts to clarify the state's archives, to build an authentic corpus of Plautus' works or to establish precise chronologies (e.g. Cornelius Nepos' *Chronica*, published before 63, the *Chronological Refutations* of Claudius [Quadrigarius?], or Atticus' *Liber annalis*) – all these activities were carried out in the same spirit. Alexandre Koyré wrote that the ancients lived in a world of approximations, but at the end of the Republic this was no longer the case – or, at the very least, the Roman elite sought to combat such a lack of certainty in order to get a grip on reality.[17]

The formalization of reality was the third manifestation of this new state of mind. In this age, there was an obsessive search for methods to put matter in order. It was necessary to systematize knowledge (i.e. to turn it into *artes*), but also to define new administrative entities that could subsume diversity under general categories: in this great movement of generalization and abstraction, everything had to be ordered and defined according to a logical order that transcended individual situations and historical singularities. Whether scholars classified various elements into types and species, according to a topical approach, or established principles from which all the rest followed, according to the deductive method of geometers, a process of intellectualization was at work to better grasp

[17] Koyré 1948 = 1971: 318.

matter and convey it more efficiently. Indeed, how could one learn if one got lost in the details of things? Systematization, which involved the reduction of contents and led people to privilege concision in everything, was supposed to be a pedagogical principle for all disciplines, including law: Cicero's idea to systematize civil law (*ius in artem redigere*, discussed in the *De oratore*) and to rationalize institutions (*De legibus*) was, no less than Pompey's and Caesar's projects of codification, intended to condense and simplify law, and consequently to make it more comprehensible. But the formalization of reality, especially when developed according to the geometrical method, also responded to a political need for "verticality." In the chaos of the previous century, while a part of the elite (the *populares*) defended the rights of the people and the validity of the laws voted by the assemblies, another part (some of the *optimates*) had searched for higher principles to serve as the source (*fons*) of human laws. Such, for Cicero, was the function of natural law, which he defined in the *De legibus*,[18] and to which he referred in the *Philippics* to justify the "illegal" but legitimate actions of Brutus and Cassius (11.28); such was, above all, the meaning of the qualification of the *res publica* as a transcendent norm, in the name of which it was possible to kill citizens, and of its institutionalization well documented by the developments of penal public laws (*leges de maiestate* [on treason] or *de vi* [on violence]), by emergency measures promoted for its defense, as well as by Cicero's efforts to conceptualize it.[19]

The unity of this intellectual revolution did not rest so much on the contents as on the methods of classification and division, on the search of unifying principles, as well as on the methods of demonstration and argumentation: in order to reason in the domain of probabilities, intellectuals turned to dialectic, like that which Aristotle applied in the *Topics*, or that of the Stoics, apparently used by some orators (*Brut.* 114, 205; *De or.* 3.78). Similarly, according to Cicero, Servius Sulpicius Rufus tried to apply dialectic to jurisprudential interpretation (*Brut.* 152). The influence of this art was strongly exerted in all the branches of science. As Cicero explained, "it defines the object, classifies genres, draws out consequences, formulates conclusions, separates the true from the false; it is the rational science of discourse" (*rem definit, genera dispertit, sequentia adjungit,*

---

[18] *Leg.* 1.19: it is from natural law that the origin of law must be brought out, because it is "the force of nature (*naturae vis*), the spirit and conscience of prudent man (*ea mens ratioque prudentis*), the norm of law and non-law (*iuris atque iniuriae regula*)."

[19] See Moatti 2015: 168–177, 2018, esp. chs. 3 and 5. Straumann, on the contrary, described this evolution as a step in the development of constitutionalism, the response to "what had effectively descended into a lawless state of nature: the late Republic with its civil wars" (2016: 150).

perfecta concludit, vera et falsa diudicat, disserendi ratio et scientia, Tusc.
5.72).[20] The most serious criticism he could address to certain thinkers was
a lack of rigor in their reasoning, especially in the link they made between
reasons. In short, he criticized them for not arguing according to the rules,
ratione et via (*Tusc.* 2.6), for not accounting for things.

The Benefits of Philosophy

Although the results of this process of rational examination seem inade-
quate to us, as they already were to Augustine, who mocked the inability of
those Romans to come to terms with their discovery of a natural religion
(*De civ. D.* 7.17); although the attempt to divide matters was sometimes a
vain effort, as in Varro's case; although the critical scrutiny applied to
tradition ended up praising it (such is the lesson of *De legibus*), this rational
activity was nonetheless a remarkable experience in human thought. The
elite proved itself able to subject its beliefs, its traditions, and even
irrationality to criticism; individually, the members of the elite proved
themselves capable of freeing themselves from their prejudices, supersti-
tions, and arbitrariness, and showed the ability to develop a sociability
based on universal values. Therefore, rather than undermining the established order, reason opened an inner space.[21] It opened a gap and created a
tension between critical thinking and tradition, a tension that Cicero
recreated using the dialogue form.[22] In the political conditions of the
end of the Republic, this intellectual experience even eventually became
a substitute for political action. This is what Cicero wrote to Varro in 46,
precisely when the *res publica* no longer required his services: let's "use
writing and books as the greatest scholars of the past did to serve the
Republic" (*Fam.* 9.2.5). He also developed this idea in one of the prefaces
of *De divinatione*, in which he remembers the years before Caesar's death:
"It was in my books that I made my senatorial speeches and my forensic
orations; for I thought that I had permanently exchanged politics for
philosophy" (*Div.* 2.7). During the crisis, freedom had to move from the
field of politics to the field of thought,[23] and philosophical commitment
had to take precedence over political commitment as long as the tyrant
occupied the city (*Div.* 2.7).

---

[20] Cf. *Part. or.* 40.139; *Orat.* 115 ff.   [21] Moatti 2015: 334.
[22] On this tension between reason and tradition, see Moatti 2015, esp. ch. 4; Atkins 2013a.
[23] See Moatti 2015: 168; Gildenhard 2007: 63–78.

Cicero: An Actor in the Intellectual Revolution

Born in 106 in Arpinum, a municipality in the Latium region that only acquired full Roman citizenship in 188 BCE, Cicero had never ceased to be interested in philosophy since his youth, as he confessed in *Brutus* (313). He applied his hand to philosophy in numerous ways: First through rhetoric, from *De inventione*, written between 87 and 81, in which he referred to the Socratic dialectic and to the Aristotelian tradition, to the *Topics*, which he wrote in July 44 and in which he used the techniques of the Old Academy and Aristotle; through the use of Hermagoras' theses and through the discussion of opposed positions (*in utramque partem disserere*), which he even applied in his letters, as in 49 when he had to choose between following Pompey to Epirus and staying in Rome with Caesar (*Att.* 8.3.1–4); through his translations of concepts, of excerpts, or of entire works (such as a work by Aratus, a Stoic of the third century, entitled *Phenomena*, which he translated between 89 and 77 BCE; or Plato's *Timaeus*, in the 40s);[24] and, finally, through dialogues and treatises written between 55 and 50 (*De republica, De oratore, De legibus*) and, more importantly, between 46 and 44.

Although Cicero constantly turned his attention to philosophy, he never produced a coherent system: as he often said, he took the liberty of "draw[ing] from the sources in such measure and in such manner as shall suit [his] purpose" (*Off.* 1.6). While he admired Plato,[25] he followed rather Philo of Larissa's New Academy, which was inspired by Carneades,[26] and sometimes Antiochus of Ascalon's more dogmatic principles.[27] Cicero's fundamental probabilism, that is, his commitment to following whatever position was most convincing in the moment, underpinned this attitude of openness and dialogue, which, it must be said, was also one of the features of Greek philosophy at the time.[28] It enabled him to reconcile the thought of different schools, which was unprecedented, or to recognize that two philosophical solutions stood in equal proximity to the truth (such as those of the Stoics and the Peripatetics regarding the issue of the highest good).[29] Finally, his probabilism enabled him to be as knowledgeable in Stoicism (as is evidenced by *De officiis*, written in 44 and dedicated to the ideas of Panaetius of Rhodes on moral good and usefulness) as in Epicureanism,

---

[24] See Lévy (Chapter 5) in this volume.   [25] See Schofield (Chapter 6) in this volume.
[26] See Reinhardt (Chapter 7) in this volume.   [27] Powell 1995b: 18–23.
[28] Gigante 2001: 41–44. This aspect clearly emerges from the two volumes edited by Sorabji and Sharples 2007.
[29] See Woolf (Chapter 11) in this volume.

the theses of which he knew well since he had met many Epicureans:[30] Atticus (*Leg.* 1.53); Memmius, to whom Lucretius dedicated his work (*Fam.* 13.1); Lucretius himself, whose work Cicero had read; Lucius Manlius Torquatus (who is presented in *De finibus* and who died in 46); Catius Insuber (*Fam.* 15.16), and maybe Philodemus, whom he quoted in *Against Piso* (Cic. *Pis.* 68; Asc. *Pis.* 68).

However, Cicero's philosophical choices evolved: references to Plato and Aristotle prevailed in *De oratore* (55 BCE), *De republica* (54 BCE), and *De legibus* (54–51 BCE), whereas Cicero mainly discussed Hellenistic philosophies in the rest of his treatises.[31] This comes from the fact that the times had changed between the two periods: between 55 and 51, the reform of the *res publica* still seemed possible, and Cicero very naturally turned to classical political philosophy in reflecting on the best political man (*De oratore*), in defining the best *res publica* (*De republica*), in describing the best laws and institutions, and their rational foundations (*De legibus*). In the 40s however, the *res publica* was under the power of one man, and social conditions had changed: Cicero therefore began to use Hellenistic philosophies and turned instead to probe into the soul, morality, emotions, and passions. At that time, Cicero proved to be as talented a conveyor of ideas as he was an author, and as talented a historian of philosophy as a philosopher. For two years, he wrote relentlessly: after the *Paradoxa Stoicorum* (*Stoic Paradoxes*) in 47, a work that developed seven philosophical themes inspired by Stoic philosophy but firmly rooted in the events of the time, and after *Hortensius*, written in the spring of 45, he wrote *De finibus* between May and July 45 (in which he compared systems of ethics) and the four books of the *Academica* (in which he discussed the foundations of knowledge); between July and August 45, he wrote the *Tusculan Disputations* (which focuses on ethics, death, passions, sadness, and virtues) and *De natura deorum* (the gods); then, between March and July 44, he wrote *De divinatione*, *De fato* (physics and theology), *Cato* (a tribute to Cato the Elder that explored old age), then *De amicitia*, a work on friendship, and the *Topica*; finally, between October and December 44, he wrote *De officiis*, a treatise on moral duties addressed to his son and composed at the time of his second *Philippics* against Mark Antony.

The *Hortensius* can be considered a sort of preface to these works. It was written in Cicero's villa of Astura, like the *Consolatio* he addressed to himself after the death of his daughter Tullia in February 45. This text,

---

[30] Maso 2015: 15.   [31] Powell 1995b: 23–25.

of which only fragments remain,[32] and which formed a trilogy with *Lucullus* and *Catulus* (also known as *Academica*), is an invitation to practice philosophy, a sort of protreptic:[33] Cicero portrays himself criticizing the false philosophers of the past (August. *Conf.* 3.4.7); he replies to the objections of the orator Hortensius, who rather praises eloquence (*Fin.* 1.1), or to those of Lucius Lucullus, who also wrote a history of the Social War and who supports the writing of history. Cicero also encourages the youth to learn philosophy, the only discipline that can lead them to happiness and help them reach the highest good (*Div.* 2.1–2).

Cicero's work thus not only exhorts readers to philosophize but, by resorting to the dialogue form, it depicts the *societas studiorum* mentioned earlier, that small nucleus of the Roman elite which was at that time considered both a substitute to the split political community and a way to transcend political differences. For example, Cicero dedicated his *De fato* to Hirtius, a partisan of Caesar, with whom he had a fraught relationship during this time. But was this *societas* of scholars a reality or a textual construction? Did Cicero's work reflect it faithfully? Members of the elite no doubt shared the language of philosophy, which can also be detected in Sallust's prefaces or Varro's works, but it is clear that their interest in culture did not correspond to Cicero's ideal vision.

Cicero himself was conscious of this issue. In a letter to Atticus, he explained why he was not satisfied with the first version of the *Academica*: he had chosen two characters to dialogue with himself, Lucullus and Catulus, but he quickly realized that the true Lucius Licinius Lucullus (consul in 74) and Lucius Lutatius Catulus (consul in 78) were far removed from the image of philosophers he gave of them in his book (*Att.* 13.16.1).[34] This is why he wrote a second version of the *Academica*, and replaced them with Cato the Stoic, who committed suicide in 46 in Utica in order to escape from Caesar, Brutus, the future tyrannicide to whom Cicero dedicated so many works, and Varro, the author of the *Antiquitates rerum humanarum et divinarum*: these three names were much more appropriate for the task.[35] But in the real world how many others of that kind were part of the *societas studiorum* he described or dreamt of? How many of these members of the elite wrote philosophical works in

---

[32] Straume-Zimmermann, Broemser, and Gigon 1990.   [33] Schofield 2013b: 76.
[34] On the history of the writing of the *Academica*, see Cappello 2019: 16–27.
[35] This second version was not completed, however, and was replaced by a third one, with Varro, Cicero, and Atticus as characters.

Latin at a time when written production was increasing in every other
domain of knowledge?

None of the Stoics of the time, who were quite few despite the influence
of Posidonius in the 80s, left a written record. Cato the Younger, who was
the main follower of Stoicism in Rome, owed his reputation to his life, not
to any book he wrote. The importance of Epicureanism is more certain.
Cicero quoted many Romans who belonged to this school, but this
philosophy does not seem to have necessarily influenced any personal
choice,[36] or to have gone beyond a certain milieu;[37] and how many of
them wrote anything besides Lucretius and Egnatius,[38] who both wrote a
De rerum natura? As far as the Old Academy is concerned, we could
mention Brutus and Varro, whom Cicero encouraged to write philosophical treatises; the former wrote *De virtute, De patientia, De officiis* (*Acad.*
1.12), while the latter wrote *De philosophia, De forma philosophiae, De
principiis numerorum*, and *Logistorici*, a series of moral meditations on
peace (*Pius de pace*), fortune (*Marius de fortuna*), the cult of the gods
(*Curio de cultu deorum*), etc.[39] As for Nigidius Figulus, considered by later
sources as a Neopythagorean, he wrote about everything (astronomy,
philology, morality, theology, natural history), and gathered around himself a group of learned friends.[40] Cicero was thus one of the few to leave
such a considerable body of philosophical work. He was the first and only
one to translate the philosophy of the New Academy and the fruits of the
probabilistic method into Latin, and the only one to produce a history of
philosophy in Latin and to expound so deeply on the debates and polemics
between all the schools.

Cicero and Varro

And yet, these educated men undoubtedly shared the common cause of
the search for truth. Does that mean that this search did not necessarily
require the practice of philosophy?

Varro's case enables us to qualify this assertion. His main subject
of study was the past, although his approach to this issue was reflexive:
what is called *antiquitates* was not the real past; it was the result of an
erudite approach of the *mores*, "traditions," of "human and divine things"

---

[36] Powell 1995b: 27 n. 69.
[37] On the Epicureans, see Benferhat 2005 (mainly the second part of the book); Sedley 2009.
[38] Hollis 2007: 43–43A.
[39] See for example Cardauns 2001: 69–76; Lehmann 1997; Moatti 2015: 94–164.
[40] On this group, see Musial 2001.

(*res humanae et divinae*), which concerned the city.[41] This erudition was double: surely it consisted in collecting details, but it was also a method to authenticate, criticize, select, systematize, organize, classify, and define. *Antiquitates* were to *mores* what erudition was to tradition. Turning the diversity of *mores* ("traditions") into *antiquitates*, so to speak, was turning the vagueness of the past and the *mos* ("tradition") into knowledge that was available to everyone and accessible through reason. The difference between Cicero and Varro is now clear: Cicero's philosophical project was to rationally account for institutions and knowledge (*De legibus*); Varro resorted to a rational and archaeological method to recover the diversity of *mores* in order to clarify and explain them, and to reveal their meaning.

However, a more profound, less visible movement was at work in Varro's project: indeed, Varro sought to understand the way things formed over time, and consequently tried to reach the origin beyond the Roman past, unity beyond historical diversity. Going back as far as possible in time, tracing the deepest roots of language, comparing societies, bringing philosophical systems closer and taking them back to an original philosophy (the Old Academy), describing an object from different angles – these were some ways of touching on something of this original unity, through a sort of reduction of differences. Undoubtedly, Varro always considered the origin an *adēlon*, an invisible thing that was fundamentally inaccessible: that is why he often confined himself to describing things, as when he discussed theology in its three dimensions (philosophical, civil, and mythological). But this attempt to get as close as possible to the origin of things was nonetheless constantly renewed.

It is why study of past institutions and antiquarian research were for Varro a sort of alternative to theoretical reflection. It was not mere patriotism, contrary to what Cicero suggested in the *Academica Posteriora*: he claimed to reach the knowledge of humanity and to search for the truth, but using other paths than the practice of philosophy.

Cicero and Varro therefore both aspired to understand the world beyond the walls of the city and both acknowledged that it was impossible to secure the truth. But the latter tried to get closer to the inaccessible truth through an archaeological method, tracing back the origin of every aspect of life; the former kept exploring the multiple paths of philosophy through the work of reason and the experience of thought.

---

[41] On this aspect, see also Leonardis 2019: 139–148; on antiquarianism, see Smith 2019; on the Varronian tradition and its reception under the Empire, see Arena and Piras 2016.

Further Reading

Useful introductions to the intellectual developments discussed in this chapter are provided in Rawson 1985 and Moatti 2015 (first published in 1997). On the earliest contacts of Rome with Greek philosophy, see Sedley 2009 (for Epicureanism) and Benferhat 2005 (who supplies a prosopography of the Epicureans); on the other schools, see Ferrary 1988 and more recently Powell 2013b. For a general approach to Cicero's philosophical work in the Roman context, Powell 1995b and Schofield 2013b are very useful and complementary. On Varro, see Moatti 2015: 94–149; Arena and Mac Góráin 2017. On the political implications of Cicero's philosophical interest, compare Gildenhard 2007 (who reads Cicero's project of creating a Latin philosophy as part of a program of civic instruction), Atkins 2013a (for whom Cicero tries to remedy the limits of reason in politics), Straumann 2016 (for whom Cicero is good evidence of the progress of constitutionalism in Rome), and Moatti 2018 (where I discuss the process of the formalization of the *res publica* at the end of the Republic).

CHAPTER 2

The Ciceronian Dialogue

Charles Brittain and Peter Osorio

Cicero's later dialogues, written in 45–44 BCE, tell us explicitly what their author wants: for the reader to become a good critic of philosophical disputes, practiced at weighing opposing arguments and forming their own judgment in response.[1] Cicero associates the shared protreptic goals of this group of late dialogues (specifically, *Hortensius, Academica, De finibus, Tusculan Disputations, De natura deorum, De divinatione,* and *De fato*) with the methods of the skeptical Academy, so we will call these his "Academic" dialogues. Contemporary critics of these dialogues have not taken great interest in Cicero's methodology or sought to determine the literary mechanisms he deploys to satisfy his pedagogic aim. Instead, two other questions tend to preoccupy philosophical study of these dialogues: scholars try to identify, first, Cicero's epistemology and, secondly, his own positions on the doctrinal problems raised by the dialogues.[2] In this chapter, we argue that pursuing Cicero's methodological practices frees readers from the need to answer these other two questions in order to understand these dialogues as compelling works of philosophy.

In the first part of this chapter, we review the central scholarly disagreement about the Academic dialogues, which derives from uncertainty about Cicero's epistemological stance. We suggest that this dispute should be put to rest in the light of the shared pedagogic aim of the later dialogues. Cicero may propose views of his own, but he does so in the service of effecting a change in the reader's powers of judgment, not in order to construct or advocate a philosophical system. We outline a number of textual devices by which the Academic dialogues seek to effect such a change in their readers, and use them to argue that Cicero's pedagogical aims constitute the core of his philosophical dialogues (rather than being merely a set of standard literary tropes).

---

[1] Powell 1995b: 30.   [2] On the first question, see Reinhardt (Chapter 7) in this volume.

Recognizing the sophistication of Cicero's methods for inscribing Academic practices into his later dialogues suggests that it may be rewarding also to look more carefully at his earlier dialogues, from the 50s BCE (sc. *De oratore, De republica,* and *De legibus*). We grant, of course, that these "Platonic" dialogues seem neither so skeptical nor so overtly Academic. But, we argue in the second part of this chapter, these dialogues already employ an array of pedagogical mechanisms that indicate the Academic aims of Cicero's literary work in this period.

The Academic Dialogues

A popular approach to the Academic dialogues is to read them as setting out, in combination with his Platonic dialogues and his non-dialogic works, Cicero's tentative philosophical system. For many, Cicero's skepticism affects only the degree of certainty with which he advocates Platonic, Antiochian, or Stoic doctrines.[3] That Cicero's skepticism is mitigated, and so not inclined toward the suspension of judgment reported in some accounts of Arcesilaus and Carneades, allows him to advocate certain views.[4] And that his dialogues present opposing arguments does not gainsay his desire to persuade others of his system: just as Cicero the orator argues in order to persuade his audience,[5] so Cicero the philosopher writes himself into his work so as to direct the reader to what he takes to be probable views.[6] On this system-building view of the Academic dialogues, the image of Cicero that emerges is of a philosopher not so very different from one who holds views with certainty.[7] Since Cicero does not reject holding philosophical views on the basis of arguments, critics often interpret the dialogues as committed to (insofar as they advocate or recommend) first-order views. The *Tusculans* is the dialogue most often interpreted in this way, perhaps unsurprisingly, given the one-sidedness of its disputes.[8] On this approach, then, Cicero uses the dialogue form in order to reproduce for readers the testing of opposing arguments that led

---

[3] Gawlick and Görler 1994: 1089; Gildenhard 2013b: 268–269 n. 116; Nicgorski 2016: 15–58.
[4] Gawlick and Görler 1994: 1097–1099; cf. Thorsrud 2012.
[5] See Leonhardt 1999: 28–29; Smith 1995.   [6] MacKendrick 1989: 25; Leonhardt 1999: 79.
[7] Leonhardt 1999: 78–81; Nicgorski 2012: 9; Hunt 1954: 189.
[8] Lefèvre 2008: 248–251; Gildenhard 2007; Koch 2006; Gorman 2005: 179–190; Schofield 2002; Görler 1996; Douglas 1995.

to his own determination of probable views, and his aim is for others to think likewise.[9]

Such *committed* interpretations of the Academic dialogues, however, face a number of serious obstacles, including: (i) Cicero's descriptions of his philosophical method that rejects affirming and advocating views (*Acad.* 2.7–9; *Tusc.* 2.4–9, 5.11; *Div.* 2.150) and (ii) explicit statements by Cicero that his aim in writing or speaking does not parallel that of a committed author or disputant who wants to persuade others of personally held views (*Fin.* 2.1–3, 5.76; *Tusc.* 5.33; *Nat. D.* 1.10–13; *Div.* 1.7, 2.8; *Fat.* 1); rather, Cicero wants his auditors and readers to be autonomous critics and does not mind if others leave unimpressed by his arguments (cf. *Fin.* 1.27, 1.29, 3.6). There are several ways to explain away these passages. They may form a kind a rhetorical technique that Cicero employs precisely where he lacks confidence as to the probable.[10] Or one may reinterpret passages like *Academica* 2.8, which stresses Cicero's independence of thought, as evidence of his commitment to a speculative system.[11] Others subordinate these passages, and the attitude toward method and authorship they support, to Cicero's more pressing rhetorical aim of persuasion.[12]

An opposing current in scholarship treats Cicero's Academic dialogues as genuinely dialogic or open-ended, and so *uncommitted*.[13] This view also tends to draw on a philosophical interpretation, but in this case one that denies that Cicero is a mitigated skeptic; rather, it is posited that Cicero writes as a radical skeptic who suspends judgment and reflects this in his writing.[14] This hypothesis is supported by noting that Cicero says he follows, albeit imperfectly, a Clitomachian interpretation of Carneades (*Acad.* 2.66, 78, 108), characterized by suspension of assent.

The radically skeptical reading of the Academic dialogues – which takes them to promote suspension of judgment in the light of opposing perspectives – is well-suited to explaining a range of features that support uncommitted interpretations: for instance, the presentation of arguments on either side, that characters do not change their opinions as the result of any single dispute, that a dialogue ends with the prospect of continued conversation, that characters are willing to be refuted, *vel sim*. But, while the committed approach seems incompatible with passages where Cicero

---

[9] See Nicgorski 2016: 77; cf. Douglas 1965: 50–51. Gildenhard 2013b offers a ream of further reasons to explain Cicero's choice of the dialogue form.

[10] Leonhardt 1999: 80–81.   [11] Görler 1997: 54.   [12] Nicgorski 2016: 59–96.

[13] Schofield 1986; Beard 1986; Fox 2007; Schofield 2008; Woolf 2015; Brittain 2016.

[14] This is most explicit in the case of Brittain 2016; see also Beard 1986: 35.

emphasizes the Academy's lack of conviction and his non-doctrinal aims in writing or speaking, the radically skeptical approach also faces difficulties. For (i) uncommitted interpretations in turn are compelled to minimize the import of passages where Cicero takes (or seems to take) an authorial position;[15] and, even when we recognize that he identifies himself as a Clitomachian follower of Carneadian skepticism, (ii) it is unclear why Cicero would be motivated to write in such a way that his dialogues somehow enact suspension of all judgment. Since Cicero understands radical skepticism in a way that still licenses judgments of probability, he has no reason not to express his own views while recognizing that they are likely only persuasive to him.

In order to resolve the problems that beset both committed and uncommitted interpretations of Cicero, it is useful to distinguish two (of many) reasons why a philosopher would be unwilling to advocate her ideas in writing. First, she may humbly think her preferred or attempted solutions to problems do not merit advertisement – and the radically skeptical approach takes Cicero to be a philosopher of this kind, whether rightly or wrongly. Secondly, though, a philosopher may write for any number of reasons *other than* the promotion of her own solutions to problems (e.g. to introduce philosophy into unfamiliar linguistic and cultural contexts); and some of these reasons may even positively exclude advocating solutions of her own. Our claim in this chapter is that there is excellent evidence that Cicero's principal motive for writing the dialogues was one such reason, viz. his *methodological* commitment to an Academic form of teaching. Hence, we advocate an uncommitted interpretation of Cicero's dialogues for this second reason, irrespective of our views about the first question, because it is Academic pedagogy, rather than skeptical epistemology, that is the proper ground for interpreting these dialogues.[16] Relying on Cicero's explicit claims about his motivations in this way has two clear benefits: (i) the interpreter needn't settle the debate about Cicero's epistemological position, since an Academic methodology that takes special care in how philosophy is received by an auditor or reader is compatible with both mitigated and radical forms of Academic skepticism and (ii) many more of the features of the dialogues can be explained without special pleading that Cicero is not expressing *real* views in this or that passage.

---

[15] Cf. Schofield 1986: 60; Brittain 2016: 34–40.
[16] This principle is implicitly followed in Schofield 1986 and Schofield 2008, where Cicero's epistemological views are not emphasized.

We can sketch Academic pedagogy and its motivations as follows: the Academic wants students to become reflective and thoughtful philosophers (perhaps even so much so that they also become skeptics, perhaps not). But, in order to achieve this, they must first become autonomous critics of arguments; and in order to become *that*, their judgments of arguments must not be prejudiced (e.g. by the rhetorical form of arguments or by the reputations of their proponents). In their live interactions, Academics tried to prevent preferential bias by a number of devices, including limiting their philosophical activity to Socratic refutations or to the dialectical method of argument on either side, such that their own views (if they had any) were not apparent.

To see how Cicero appropriated Academic pedagogy, we will examine a few techniques he uses to translate into literary form oral practices designed to limit prejudice. These techniques can be direct and brute or subtle and indirect, by working independently from, or relying on, the dialogue form. For the former, Cicero can describe his Academic aims in paratextual prefaces (cf. *Acad.* 2.7–9) or in dedicatory letters asking his dedicatees to read his dialogue with a critical but open mind (cf. *Fin.* 3.6).[17] As for the latter, the dialogue itself can dramatize models of dialectic. Thus, Cicero imitates Academic oral dialectic by representing himself as an impartial disputant arguing against another's arguments (e.g. in both editions of the *Academica*). But Cicero can dramatize not only his dialectical habits as a disputant but also his habits as a critical auditor of arguments by authoritative speakers, where the risk of prejudice is high. Finally, he can play off both non-dialogic and dialogic elements by creating intra-textual links between his prefaces and dramatic scenes.

Consider, for instance, the well-known interpretive problem at the end of *De natura deorum*, where Cicero reveals through his narratorial voice that "the argument of Balbus seemed to me to incline more to a likeness of the truth" (3.95). Disclosing this judgment seems inconsistent with his prefatory remark at *De natura deorum* 1.10 that "those who ask what my views are about every matter do so with more curiosity than necessary, for in disputation one ought to question the weight not of authority but of reason," and several interpretations have been put forward to make sense of the tension. There is a dilemma: one will think that *De natura deorum* 3.95 either (a) gives an authorial view – by this we mean either the view of the historical person, M. Tullius Cicero, or his authorial *persona* – or (b) it

---

[17] These direct, paratextual techniques would parallel brute admissions of pedagogic aims spoken by Academics (cf. *Acad.* 2.60).

does not. Readers who think that *De natura deorum* is a committed dialogue that advocates revised Stoic theological views favor (a),[18] while those who choose (b) suppose that Cicero isn't committed to advocating a particular theology.[19] Those who prefer (a) in order to build up a Ciceronian system do not satisfactorily ease the tension of the preface and *Nat. D.* 1.10. Those who choose (b), on the other hand, are hard pressed to explain how *Nat. D.* 3.95 does not provide an authorial view. (a) is certainly the natural reading, and, by taking into account the dialogue's didactic concerns as set out in the preface, we see that (b) is not at all necessary for an uncommitted interpretation.[20] Cicero can express his view as an example of an autonomous auditor weighing either side, in the manner he calls for in the preface. This is compatible with an uncommitted interpretation, especially because Cicero gives no grounds for his final evaluation and takes care to mark it as the view he had at the conclusion of *this* particular argument. A careful reader of the preface will see that it is in no sense a model for an authoritative view.

In the preface (*Nat. D.* 1.1–14) Cicero addresses three critical responses to his recent spate of philosophical works (sc. the four books of the *Academica* and five books of *De finibus*): curiosity both (i) as to the cause of his philosophical writing and (ii) what he thinks is certain (1.6: *quid ... certi haberemus*) on philosophical topics, and (iii) surprise at his adherence to the New Academy. We have already seen at *De natura deorum* 1.10 his reproach of the second response for needless curiosity, but he also rephrases their request in terms of his *views* (1.10: *quid ... sentiamus*), so that it is sensitive to his particular epistemological position that disclaims certainty.[21] While addressing the third group (*Nat. D.* 1.11), who are surprised that he follows the Academy given its present lack of representation, Cicero defends his choice on the grounds that views may remain live options even when no authorities currently represent them. Both the second and third class of Cicero's critics respond to his philosophical writing in a way that betrays an ignorance of Academic methodology. The second class, who ask Cicero for his certain beliefs, are unaware that he has only uncertain views *and* that he would have reason not to disclose even these, while the third class, who are shocked by his adherence to an outmoded form of philosophy, are unaware that choosing to follow the

---

[18] Görler 1974: 48; Gawlick and Görler 1994: 1044; Lévy 1992a: 588; DeFilippo 2000: 171–172.
[19] Pease 1955–1958: 1, 36; Levine 1957: 20–22.   [20] Taran 1987; Fott 2012; Wynne 2019.
[21] *Sentire*, as opposed to *adsentire*, is a blanket cognitive term in Cicero's *philosophica* that can be predicated of even radical skeptics like Arcesilaus (cf. Cic. *De or.* 3.67).

Academy in the face of a relative dearth of authoritative representation is, in fact, characteristic of the license of that method.

It is significant, then, that Cicero ends his preface with the wish that his readers join in making their own judgment, as a juror would, after listening to the ensuing dialogue:

> "Gods! Everyone! All young adults (*adulescentium*)!
> I cry for, demand, swear upon, pray for, beg, and implore your good conscience"
>   not concerning a most trivial matter, like that one who complains that
> ". . . capital offenses are happening in the state . . .."
>   "A woman for hire doesn't want to take pay from a loving lover!"
>   but so that you convene, discern, and consider what must be thought about religion, sanctity, rites, promises, oaths; what must be thought about temples, altars, and solemn sacrifices; what must be thought about the very auspices of which I am in charge. For all these matters must be referred to this inquiry about the immortal gods. (*Nat. D.* 1.14)

The quotation, from Caecilius Statius' translation of Menander's *Fellow Young Men* (*Synephebi*; cf. *Fin.* 1.4), features a call upon "young adults" to pay attention as though jurors of a case. The dialogue Cicero goes on to narrate takes place sometime between 77 (when Cicero returned from his studies in Athens) and 76 BCE (before Cotta becomes consul in 75). Cicero at this time would have been twenty-nine or thirty years old, at the end of the period of life called *adulescentia* and just old enough to become quaestor in 75 BCE.[22] Given this setting and his quotation of Caecilius, Cicero telegraphs a concern with how Romans of a similar age – both old enough to study philosophy and young enough that their professional lives have not yet fossilized their intellectual habits – would receive his work. The didactic aim of the dialogue, in other words, is to introduce nonspecialist readers to the practice of making philosophical judgments according to the method of argument on either side (cf. *Fat.* 1). It does not tell against an uncommitted interpretation, then, that Cicero discloses a past judgment of his in *De natura deorum* 3.95, because the dialogue sets out to show *how* a young Roman judged a dispute, without then defending or explaining it. The claim that what Cicero actually wants is to persuade others of his reformist theology seems to miss the point.

The *Tusculan Disputations* is a harder case, since the method employed here (sc. arguments against a thesis) is not the same as argument on either

---

[22] See *TLL* s.v. *adolescens* 795.49–52.

side. How can the dialogue have aims consistent with Academic pedagogy when it dramatizes a mode of inquiry that seems to privilege the protagonist? Proponents of an uncommitted interpretive approach have not applied it here:[23] Academic skepticism may even look irrelevant to the project of the *Tusculans*.[24]

However, there can be no doubt of the work's Academic credentials. The *Tusculans* has some of the clearest descriptions of Cicero's Academic aims in writing, despite also having some of the passages where Cicero comes closest to endorsing philosophical beliefs. But, while an interpretation that foregrounds Cicero's meta-philosophy can accommodate the apparent deployment of his own views, an interpretation that sees Cicero as writing just in order to advocate particular cognitive therapies cannot accommodate his meta-philosophical concerns. The dialogue is complicated, in other words, by having a dual aim. The first is a more or less standard *testing of a field of philosophy*, in this case, that of cognitive therapies for emotions. This is consistent with his general practice in the Academic dialogues, and Cicero justifies it in Academic terms (*Tusc.* 1.8, 5.11; *Fat.* 4). The second is a more complex testing of the *consistency of those therapies with a target reader's ethical views* (cf. *Tusc.* 5.21–34), which is a second-order, metaethical inquiry that requires or, at any rate, fits the distinctive method of Socrates and Arcesilaus, viz. argument against a thesis.

The second aim is introduced most clearly in the preface to the second disputation (*Tusc.* 2.1–9). Cicero here predicts critics of his dialogue, but distinguishes between two sorts. One sort is opposed to philosophy, whether as a whole or as practiced by Academics. Cicero won't concern himself with these readers further, but he still welcomes another sort of criticism:

> [I]t's so far from the case that we don't want to be opposed in writing that we actually want this most of all; for in Greece itself philosophy would never have been so valued had it not thrived by the contentions and disagreements of the most learned persons ... (*Tusc.* 2.4)

Cicero contrasts his willingness "to refute without doggedness and to be refuted without anger" with the partisanship of dogmatists (*Tusc.* 2.5), and

---

[23] Schofield 2002, for instance, interprets the dialogue in light of Philo's non-skeptical program of ethical instruction.

[24] So Gildenhard 2007: 226; cf. Gorman 2005: 69. Committed interpreters find further support in Cicero's catalogue of philosophical writings in the second preface of *De divinatione* (2.2), where he says that *Tusculans* "disclosed matters most necessary for living happily."

prior attempts at Latin philosophy by Epicurean authors such as Gaius Amafinius (cf. *Tusc.* 1.6, 4.6) are marked by the latter. He draws an important similarity between these Latin texts and their Greek counterparts by Epicurus and Metrodorus: they seek only to benefit committed Epicureans and so disregard precision and clarity (*Tusc.* 2.7–8). Epicurean texts are also contrasted with those of Plato and other Socratics: these authors of dialogue *are* methodical and elegant, and so are useful even to those who disagree with their philosophical commitments (Cic. *Tusc.* 2.8).

Cicero similarly aims to use his dialogues to engage a diverse range of educated readers (*Tusc.* 2.8), and he explains the steps he takes to achieve this:

> Therefore I always preferred the practice of the Peripatetics and Academics of arguing on either side about every matter, not only for the reason that what is truth-like in each thing could not otherwise be found, but also because that is the best exercise for speaking . . . (*Tusc.* 2.9)

Cicero does not explain his commitment to dialectic just by his desire to discover the truth-like; it also helps him speak (and write) in a way that, as with Plato and other Socratics, may "engage those who, liberally trained and supplied with a discernment of argument, philosophize rationally and methodically" (*Tusc.* 2.6). That is, Cicero wants to create a work that has philosophical value even for those with opposing doctrinal commitments. That "M.", the clearly Ciceronian protagonist, takes positions in the *Tusculans*, then, does not show that Cicero writes just in order to persuade others of largely Stoic therapies, since inciting reasoned disagreement from Roman readers is also the best means for philosophy to thrive in the Latin language.

But, one may well object, the *Tusculans* doesn't display meaningful disagreement. "A.", the anonymous interlocutor, becomes more combative by the end but, on the whole, does not oppose M.'s arguments against the proposed theses. What Cicero is *really* after, then, one may think, is to set out the ethical therapies he believes are most efficacious. This objection is disarmed, however, if we reflect about the effects of M.'s refutations of the theses on different readers. From the perspective of a philosophical novice like the interlocutor, M.'s arguments help to remove, at least temporarily, trenchant anxieties. For such a reader, the *Tusculans* serves to offer a variety of cures, and she may in fact find M.'s apparently authorial cures the most effective. But from the perspective of a philosophical adept – the sophisticated audience whom Cicero says in the preface of *Tusc.* 2 he has in mind to engage – M.'s preferred cures aren't new, and the adept already knows what therapies work for her. So what use, then, is the *Tusculans* for the adept? This reader, we propose, will see how M.'s favored positions throughout the five books are internally consistent and build upon themselves with an eye toward securing happiness. But the consistency of M.'s ethical progression should challenge a reader, and specifically, it seems, an Antiochian reader, who comes to the same practical conclusions as M., yet starts from different ethical bedrock.

This picture of the adept reader is, in fact, supported by the dialogue's only named audience, and its model reader: its dedicatee, Marcus Brutus. Cicero ends the *Tusculans* as follows:

> I think that I'll even write down [sc. our five disputations at Tusculum] . . . I will send this second set of five books to my Brutus, by whom I was not just driven but provoked to philosophical writings. (5.121)

The first five-book dialogue sent to Brutus was of course *De finibus*, in which Cicero asks Brutus to judge critically the represented disputes (3.6). We can see clearly in that work, even aside from Cicero's direct exhortations for Brutus to be a critic, that its structure serves to goad Brutus to a dialectical response. As the dialogue proceeds, Brutus faces progressively greater challenges to his own Antiochian position, culminating with Cicero's direct challenge to the Antiochian Piso in *De finibus* 5. We suggest that a similar dialectical structuring occurs in the *Tusculans*. Although Antiochus claimed to hold several of the same views as the Stoics in ethics (cf. *Acad.* 2.135), M. shows that their anthropologies, and therefore axiologies, differ significantly, so that the consistency of Antiochus' ethical doctrines, as well as their supposed closeness to the Stoics, is called into doubt.[25] The counter-theses M. argues for over the five days at Tusculum thus progressively reveal how Antiochus is *unlike* the Stoics in ethics, and the dialogue concludes by stressing that its intended critical reader is an Antiochian.[26] So Cicero's employment of argument against a thesis in the *Tusculans* both purges novices of dangerous certainties and tests the consistency of the systematic beliefs of philosophical adepts.

---

[25] See Brennan 2009 on the relation between Antiochus' ethics and those of the Stoics.

[26] M. holds the Stoic views (i) that the self is just the soul (*Tusc.* 1), (ii) that pain is not an evil (*Tusc.* 2), (iii) that emotions are beliefs (*Tusc.* 3 and 4), and (iv) that virtue is sufficient for happiness. Antiochus, on the other hand, (i) defines human nature as the conjunction of body and soul (*Fin.* 4.34–45; Aug. *De civ. D.* 19.3), and thus (ii) admits nonmoral evils, like pain (*Acad.* 1.19–23), (iii) accepts that emotions are natural and nonrational (*Acad.* 1.38; cf. *Fin.* 5.36–38); A. at last mentions Antiochus in *Tusc.* 5 as (iv) differing from Stoics by distinguishing happy and happiest lives. See McConnell (Chapter 10) in this volume for *Tusc.* 1 and 3.

The Platonic Dialogues

The Academic dialogues of 45–44 BCE present an explicit methodology in the paratextual prefaces and dedication letters, which is also represented and enacted in their narratives and dramatic scenes. But Cicero's earlier works in the genre from the 50s BCE are "Platonic," so-called for their rich allusions to scenes and conversational situations from Plato as well as their overt presentation as responses to particular Platonic dialogues.[27] And, like Plato's dialogues, these Ciceronian narratives do not come with paratextual instructions about how to interpret them.[28] As in the case of Plato, scholars have tended to pick up on one prominent feature of these dialogues – viz., that they focus on a single character who leads the discussion and defends definite positions (Crassus, Scipio, and Cicero, respectively) – as the key to their interpretation, and to interpret them accordingly as committed dialogues on topics dear to their author (sc. oratory, politics, and law).[29]

But this seems too easy a solution to the hermeneutic problem, given the complex dramatic structures of Cicero's Platonic dialogues and our knowledge of the sophistication of Cicero's later writing strategies. Cicero will say in a later preface, for instance, that he is projecting his view on a given topic onto characters to increase its persuasiveness (*Cato* 3), and in a letter that he is switching the protagonists to give the side he is arguing against the strongest case (*Att.* 13.19.5, on the second edition of the *Academica*). It is notable that, in the case of the Platonic dialogues, either there are prefaces but Cicero is not a character (*De oratore* and *De republica*), or Cicero is a character but there are no prefaces (*De legibus*) – which complicates any direct association between what characters, including the protagonists, say within a work and the views of its author.[30] So if the Platonic dialogues lack Academic prefaces, they are equally silent as to whether or how their conversations serve rhetorical ends. It seems, therefore, that we should look more closely at the philosophical drama as a whole and at the functions of its constituent features – characters, episodes, frames, etc. – to gain some direction. In the last part of this chapter,

---

[27] On Plato's influence on Cicero, see Schofield (Chapter 6) in this volume.

[28] For the relation between trends in scholarship on Plato and Cicero, see Fox 2007: 57–60.

[29] In the case of Plato, however, there has been much more resistance to monological interpretations; see, e.g., Frede 1992; Nails 1995; Frede 1996; Press 2000.

[30] *De legibus*, however, seeks to overcome its own dramatic form: Marcus identifies himself with the author of *De republica* (1.15) and *Aratea* (2.7), and Atticus and Marcus talk of their prospective conversation as an act of writing (*Leg.* 1.14–15).

we suggest that the Platonic dialogues are much more open-ended than they have standardly been read, because they function as representations and enactments of the same Academic modes of teaching as the "Academic" works of the mid-40s BCE. To this end we offer illustrations of three general – though less overt – mechanisms through which Cicero textualizes Academic pedagogy.[31]

The *first*, and most striking, case is the way in which the dialogues represent their interlocutors as readers of the dialogues of Plato.[32] Since Plato is Cicero's generic model, these episodes should be promising starting points for understanding Cicero's attitude toward the reception of *his* dialogues. Two prominent examples are scenes showing interlocutors' disagreements about the Socratic question (*Rep.* 1.15–16) and the apparent inconsistency between some of Plato's dialogues (*De or.* 1.47, 84–93).[33] In each case, Cicero represents his characters taking out of Plato's texts exactly what they read into them. The model of reading that emerges from these two episodes is one that fails to create interpretive consensus. It needn't follow from this that Cicero thinks "anything goes" when reading dialogue; but the model does show his awareness that interpretation is hard because it is easily shaped by antecedent commitments. This suggests that readers of Cicero's dialogues should be alert to the prejudices they bring to the act of interpretation and cautious in the way they use them to work out their own or the author's views.

The narrative in *De republica* starts with a brief argument between Tubero and Scipio over whether Socrates had any nonethical philosophical commitments, triggered by their appeals to the authority of Socrates in defense of their incompatible attitudes toward physics. Scipio takes a skeptical stance on the value of inquiries into nature, and bolsters it with the remark that Socrates was wiser because he thought they were "greater than human reason could follow," or, at any rate, "not at all relevant to human life" (*Rep.* 1.15). Although he doesn't mention it, Scipio's view of Socrates is the one found in the writings of most of the Socratics, including Xenophon (in his *Memoirs* 1.1.11–15) and Plato, at least in the *Apology*.[34]

---

[31] Cicero's letters give us some information about his choices of literary forms in the 50s and 40s, but it is an open question why he switched from "Platonic" to (mainly) "Academic" dialogues; see Further Reading below.

[32] *De or.* 1.47; *Rep.* 1.15–16; *Leg.* 1.15, 2.14.

[33] *De legibus* 1.15 and 2.14 is too complex to treat here, but see Powell 2001; Atkins 2013b.

[34] In the later *Varro* (1.15), the Antiochian Varro puts forward the same image of Socrates (cf. Cic. *Acad.* 2.123; *Brut.* 31; *Tusc.* 5.10), citing not only Plato but other Socratics (cf. Sext. Emp. *Math.* 7.8); for Xenophon's anti-physics Socrates in Cicero, see *Nat. D.* 1.31 (cf. Xen. *Mem.* 4.3.13–14) and *Div.* 1.122 (cf. Xen. *An.* 3.5–7).

Tubero, however, seems to take a more dogmatic line on physics; at any rate he responds to Scipio by citing Plato as the best source for Socrates, and noting that in Plato alone we find Socrates interested in scientific topics associated with Pythagoras (*Rep.* 1.16).[35] The conversation is cut short by the arrival of Philus, leaving unsettled whether Scipio or Tubero has the right interpretation of Plato's Socrates. Though brief, this interchange clearly models in miniature a serious set of interpretative problems both about historical questions – such as the scope of Socrates' inquiries – and about the reception and deployment of the history of philosophy as an argumentative trope in the late Hellenistic/late Republican period. The historical question was as controversial in the fourth and first centuries BCE as it is now. But it seems to be a question of which sources to trust;[36] and, since the Socratics had as much reason to shape the image of Socrates according to their own interests as Plato, the choice of which source to trust seems to be primarily a matter of one's philosophical views.

There is a close parallel for Tubero and Scipio's disagreement about the Socratic question in the similarly incompatible interpretations of Plato's Socrates by Lucullus and Cicero in the *Lucullus* (also known as *Academica* 2). Lucullus claims that Socrates' confessions of ignorance are ironic (*Acad.* 2.15), whereas Cicero defends their veracity (*Acad.* 2.74). It is no accident, of course, that Lucullus has the role of defending the dogmatic view that knowledge is possible and takes Socrates to endorse his view, while Cicero has the dialectical role of the Academic skeptic and takes Socrates to disavow knowledge. The main difference between the historical controversies in the Platonic *De republica* and the Academic *Lucullus* is that we cannot easily separate Cicero's dialectical role in the *Lucullus* from his personal views: he is both defending his preferred mode of philosophy and playing the Academic disputant. As a result, we cannot tell, by design, whether the authorial Cicero approves of his *persona*'s skeptical interpretation of Plato. In *De republica*, on the other hand, neither Scipio nor Tubero is characterized as playing a merely dialectical role, so we are in no

---

[35] As Büchner 1984, ad loc. notes, Tubero likely refers, among other passages, to the stretch of *Republic* 7 in which Socrates surveys the education of philosopher-kings and includes mathematics (522c5–526c7), three kinds of geometry (526c8–527c7, 528a6–e1, 528e3–530c1), and harmonics (530d4–531d4).

[36] Tubero ignores Xenophon's account, but the latter was already understood by some ancient readers to be a *parti pris* response to Plato (Gell. *NA* 14.3.6). Nor is Scipio's appeal to the biographical tradition decisive, since if Plato traveled to Italy after Socrates' death to study Pythagoreanism (cf. Cic. *Fin.* 5.87; *Tusc.* 1.38–39), he may have done so under Socrates' influence; cf. Numenius fr. 24 in Des Places 1973: "[Plato], following Pythagoras – he knew that Socrates said these same things and spoke of things he knew from no other source [sc. than Pythagoras] ...."

doubt about their positions on the Socratic question. But they are (effectively) fictional characters, and it is clear that their judgments about Plato's Socrates are represented as deriving from their own stated positions on inquiries in physics (i.e. from the positions they are designed to support). Because Plato writes dramatically, Scipio and Tubero can understand Plato's intentions in writing as they please. The problem seems recursive.

A second example of contested interpretations of Plato is from Cicero's first dialogue, *De oratore*. The agents here are the Academic philosopher, Charmadas, and his temporary student, the Roman protagonist of the dialogue, Crassus; and the interpretive challenge is how to make sense of Plato's seemingly inconsistent positions on rhetoric in the *Gorgias* and *Phaedrus*. In the dialogue, Charmadas is reported to have used a series of arguments from these Platonic dialogues that imply, indirectly, that they jointly support a specific view about rhetoric.[37] Thus he used positive material from the *Phaedrus* – Socrates' arguments that philosophical training will allow one to be persuasive – to support the view that philosophy is necessary for eloquence (*De or.* 1.84, 85–89, 93), while using destructive sentiments from the *Gorgias* – Socrates' arguments that rhetoricians do not practice an art – to support the view that eloquence is only a faculty, not an art (*De or.* 1.84, 90–92, 93). As a skeptic, Charmadas denied that anyone had succeeded in acquiring knowledge; and he also had a professional interest in denouncing rhetoricians offering a rival form of education. So Charmadas' procedure looks like an argument that harmonizes the apparently contradictory positions in Plato's two dialogues on rhetoric in order to support a view that happens to fit his own situation perfectly.

Crassus, on the other hand, holds not only that there is an art of eloquence but also that it requires a systematic understanding of all the arts, especially philosophy (*De or.* 1.46–57). His view of eloquence thus largely mirrors Socrates' in the *Phaedrus*, which endorses a similar view about what would make one a perfect orator (cf. Pl. *Phdr.* 269d2: *agonistēn teleon*).[38] Crassus later argues that Plato's Socrates had the joint knowledge of philosophy and rhetoric but said that the two are distinct because he disliked politics (*De or.* 3.59–61). The dialogue in which Socrates separates conventional rhetoric from philosophy, while professing an ignorance of political offices, is of course the *Gorgias* (cf. 473e6–474a1). But since

---

[37] Brittain 2001: 319–328.
[38] Socrates takes a comprehensive view of the fields of oratory (*Phdr.* 261a7–b2) and holds that philosophical knowledge is constitutive of a rhetorical art (*Phdr.* 261e6–262c3, 265c8–266c1, 269e1–271b5, 277b5–c6).

Crassus says, at *De oratore* 1.47, that he admires Socrates, and so Plato,[39] for their eloquence on the basis of their ridicule of Gorgias and the other interlocutors, we can infer that he interprets Socrates' separation of rhetoric and philosophy as *disingenuous*. Crassus thus holds an ironic reading of the *Gorgias*: Socrates' rhetorical prowess can only come from knowledge, so the *Gorgias* is only apparently inconsistent with the *Phaedrus*, since both in fact endorse the view Crassus happens to hold.

For Charmadas and Crassus, the kind of life they live – as a Greek philosopher-rhetorician or a Roman orator-statesman – determines their approach to Plato. Charmadas synthesizes from Plato's two dialogues a position that recommends both skeptical philosophy and rhetorical training. Crassus' position, on the other hand, leans heavily toward the *Phaedrus* and minimizes the doctrinal import of the *Gorgias*. Here again Plato is open to interpretive license, and how that license is taken is affected by the needs and views that each interpreter brings to the text. The Academics argued that our judgments tend to be affected by factors extraneous to the question at hand. In the Platonic dialogues Cicero does not express such Academic views, but he does enact them, by representing characters who show how problematic it is to cite philosophical literature, and especially dialogue, as certain support for one's views.

Our *second* case is an illustration of the way Cicero uses the prefatory frames to complicate the dramatic narratives of the Platonic dialogues and so prompt a critical reception from the reader. In our example, from *De oratore*, Cicero uses this formal device to both represent and undermine the deployment of authorities (just as he does in the Academic dialogues). In the preface of the first book (*De. or.* 1.5), Cicero constructs himself and his brother Quintus as authoritative figures on either side of the main question of the dialogue. Since the prefatorial Cicero holds here that eloquence follows from the knowledge contained in various arts such as philosophy, it is tempting to surmise that Crassus – who will develop just such a view over the course of the first and third books – is a mouthpiece for the author. In the second preface (*De. or.* 2.4), however, Cicero reveals that Crassus publicly disparaged the arts he is shown to favor within the dialogue. The prefatorial Cicero, seemingly influenced by his own view of eloquence, then proceeds to undermine the value of this explicit evidence for Crassus' beliefs. In so doing, Cicero represents himself as acting like

---

[39] Since it is *Socrates* who ridicules Gorgias and his interlocutors, Crassus must see Socrates as a Platonic mouthpiece, so that he simply says that *Plato* ridicules. We here differ from Lévy 1992a: 86; Altman 2016a: 30–32.

Scipio's Plato in presenting his own view through the authority of Socrates.[40]

It seems unlikely that Cicero's aim in this elaborate staging of the relation between his own and his protagonist's real and fictional views was to persuade readers or orators-in-training of the need of scientific knowledge by drawing on the authority of Crassus, since revealing this artifice undercuts the weight of authority. At best, the second preface may be construed as a strategic concession:[41] Cicero is compelled to acknowledge the fictional author-character relation, because readers wouldn't be fooled by it anyway. But even so, in doing this he draws the focus away from the weight of historical persons to the weight of their represented beliefs. It remains open, then, whether Cicero wants others simply to judge or also to accept the views he represents himself as giving to Crassus. In any case, the prefatory mechanism draws attention to authors' rhetorical habits of projecting commitments onto authorities; and it undermines any inclination to infer Cicero's actual view from his authorial statement of it in the first preface, by representing the same inference from Crassus' public statement of his views to his actual beliefs as erroneous in the second preface.

A *third* device by which Cicero renders the Platonic dialogues open for interpretation is his positioning of views within discursive contexts that set dialectical inquiry aside. So, notoriously, Marcus asks for silence from Epicureans and skeptical Academics in the first book of De legibus (1.39), as he sets out to support his view of natural law with a rationalist (Stoic) account that depends on virtue being a moral end (cf. 1.34, 37–38). The reasons that these philosophical groups in particular must be silenced are, it seems, first, that in Carneades' division of ethical ends they are the most prominent proponents of views according to which virtue is an instrumental good, not good per se;[42] and, secondly, that they are both skeptical, in different senses, of natural law. Of course, Marcus gives arguments when laying out his theory of law; still, while his theory recalls the complex architecture of the Stoic system, he does not allow debate to emerge concerning its physical (cf. *Leg.* 1.21) or ethical foundations.

---

[40] See Leeman, Pinkster, and Nelson 1985: II, 187 on Cicero's defense of his portrait of Crassus and Antonius as a literary game; representing his authorial behavior – as opposed to expressing it directly, as in *Cato* 3 – serves to mark it as an object for the reader's interpretive microscope.

[41] Gildenhard 2013b: 256.

[42] Along with the Peripatetic Hieronymous and the Cyrenaics, Epicurus and Carneades (not in *propria persona*) appear in the Carneadian *divisio* as the proponents of the set of views where virtue does not appear as a *summum bonum*: Cic. *Fin.* 2.35, 5.20; *Acad.* 2.131; *Tusc.* 5.84.

Rather, he lays out his account in a manner that corresponds to his rationalist commitments, gradually building it up with interdependent theses.

The Academic dialogues represent a similar phenomenon in Quintus' account of divination in the first book of *De divinatione*. There, the manner in which Quintus presents his view – cataloguing reported instances of divinatory successes – corresponds to his inductive acceptance of divination on the grounds of its attested results, not due to any rationalist understanding of its causes (*Div.* 2.10–11). Neither Marcus in *De legibus* nor Quintus in *De divinatione* is concerned with counterarguments. They are rather reproducing the kind of reasoning that leads them to hold their view. In *De divinatione*, however, and as one would expect in the Academic dialogues, Quintus' view eventually comes under Marcus' critique in the second book, while Marcus' exposition in *De legibus* is only contrasted with an implied refutation, represented by the silenced Epicureans and Academics.[43] While it is impossible to come to any certain conclusions about such a fragmentary work, it is hard not to infer that *De legibus* concedes the lack of a certain grounding for a theory of natural law. Marcus thus tells us what he thinks makes for the grandest philosophical support for law, without suggesting that his discourse can establish its truth. In this way, Cicero, at the very least, sets a limit on committed interpretations of *De legibus*: if, like Marcus, a reader finds its legislative policies persuasive, she also ought to ask whether it is only the result of her rationalist presuppositions.

Conclusion

Cicero employs a range of techniques besides the preface to fashion and promote his Academic philosophy. These techniques rely on the perspectival quality of dialogue and its dramatic aspect, and they are not limited to his overtly Academic dialogues. We hope to have shown by attending to just a few of these literary properties in the Ciceronian dialogues that there is scope for much further work in understanding Cicero's philosophical methodology.[44] We have also written with an eye to strengthening uncommitted interpretations of Cicero by placing focus squarely on his attitudes

---

[43] *Pace* Atkins 2013a: 179–185, we do not find that Marcus is engaged in a Carneadian method of witness corroboration.

[44] Further work of a different sort is required in the case of the *Brutus*, *De senectute*, *De amicitia*, and *Partitiones oratoriae*, which we have omitted here for reasons of space.

toward writing and reading philosophy. Accordingly, it may seem that we have argued against the fruitfulness of looking for Cicero's views in many of his dialogues, but this is not our intent: Cicero's views are there, but they aren't there to capture our belief.

Further Reading

Further valuable ways of investigating Cicero's dialogues include the detailed study of his literary models and methods of composition. Evidence for his deliberations regarding prefaces, settings, characters, and book divisions can be found in Cicero's letters. These topics are well treated in Anglophone scholarship on individual dialogues: Powell 1988; Zetzel 1995; Griffin 1997b; Fantham 2004: 44–79; Brittain 2006; Mankin 2011; Steel 2013b; Wynne 2019. Important earlier treatments include Hirzel 1895: 1, 457–552; Ruch 1958a; Zoll 1962. Comprehensive surveys of philosophical dialogue include Hirzel 1895 and Hösle 2013. The model for our own approach is Schofield 2008; Gildenhard 2013b is a useful counterpoint to our own essay.

CHAPTER 3

Philosophy in Cicero's Letters

Sophie Aubert-Baillot

While the renewal of scholarly interest in Cicero's philosophy over the last thirty years has extended to virtually all of his corpus,[1] his letters have received comparatively less attention. They are often quoted only as a source providing either chronological details for the composition of Cicero's major philosophical works or insights into his translation of Greek concepts in his dialogues. The letters are therefore a corpus still partly unexplored from a philosophical angle. Scholars who, after M. T. Griffin's groundbreaking works, have recently analyzed the philosophy in Cicero's letters, have concentrated their studies on a few texts which deal openly with Stoic, Epicurean, Aristotelian, or Academic theories,[2] but they have left aside discreet and fragmentary allusions to philosophy. In this chapter, I approach the topic of philosophy in Cicero's letters by examining such allusions, which are important because they highlight the experimental aspect of most philosophical doctrines in this corpus. From this point of view, the letters are a laboratory in which the origins and development of Cicero's thought appear more clearly than in his later works.

In this impressive, though incomplete, corpus of 954 letters, philosophy is everywhere, but in a fragmentary form. Both striking and allusive, serious and pleasant, its treatment is in keeping with the spirit of *sermo*, a "conversation between absent friends" (*amicorum colloquia absentium*), as Cicero himself defines the epistolary exchange (Cic. *Phil.* 2.7). Many philosophical topics are dealt with, ranging from logic and physics to ethical doctrines, which are predominant in Cicero. Behind these

---

[1] Lévy 1992a; Powell 1995a; Woolf 2015.

[2] Boes 1990; Baraz 2012; McConnell 2014; Gilbert 2015; Fletcher 2016; Cappello 2019: 13–81. See Griffin 1995; Griffin 1997a. See, above all, Cic. *Fam.* 9.22 on Stoic theory of language; for shorter philosophical arguments, see, e.g., *Fam.* 9.24–25 (letters to Paetus about Epicurean philosophy); *Fam.* 9.4 (letter to Varro about the Master argument of Diodorus Cronos); *Fam.* 15.16 and 15.19 (letters to Cassius after his conversion to Epicureanism).

apparently scattered and frequently allusive references to philosophy, some leitmotifs exist: the identification between happiness (*beatum*) and the good (*honestum*), between evil (*malum*) and the dishonorable (*turpe*),[3] the distinction between justice (*iustum*) and selfish interest (*utile*) as well as the equivalence between well-understood interest and *honestum*,[4] the opposition between selfishness and altruism as a criticism of Epicureanism,[5] the difficult reconciliation of freedom and fate (or chance),[6] the necessity to adjust to circumstances,[7] and finally the role of individual conscience.[8] From the earliest extant letters of the sixties BCE to those written at the end of Cicero's life, we find many allusions to philosophy. Even if their number increases as the political tension in Rome rises, these allusions are nonetheless abundant, rich, and varied as early as 63 BCE,[9] when Cicero, as a consul, had not yet written any of his major philosophical dialogues (which date to the years 45–44 BCE).

Considering the proliferation of philosophical references in the letters, I have chosen to focus on a small number of occurrences and to examine them from a precise angle: the use of Greek, the language of philosophy *par excellence*.[10] My purpose is neither to "highligh[t] the range of types of Greek within the letters"[11] nor to offer a sociolinguistic analysis of bilingualism in Cicero,[12] but to analyze the philosophical sources and uses of Greek words, phrases, and quotations in Cicero's letters,

Before Cicero undertook the ambitious project of translating Greek philosophy into Latin in his dialogues, he was trained in this discipline by Greek masters, both in Rome and in Greece. Whenever he alludes to philosophy in his letters, he quotes one or more Greek words: there is almost no exception to this rule.[13] Moreover, nearly one third of the total number of occurrences of Greek words or expressions in the letters (258 out of approximately 850) can plausibly be interpreted from a

---

[3] Cic. *Att.* 8.8.1, 10.4.4.   [4] Cic. *Att.* 7.3.2–3, 7.14.3, 8.2.4; *Fam.* 4.2.2, 5.19.1–2.

[5] Cic. *Fam.* 3.9.2, 3.10.9; *Att.* 7.2.4.

[6] Cic. *Fam.* 14.1.1, 5.21.5, 6.2.3, 12.23.4, 5.17.4; *Att.* 11.9.1.

[7] Cic. *Fam.* 1.9.21, 9.7.2, 4.8.2, 9.17.3, 4.9.1–2; *Att.* 10.7.1, 12.51.2.

[8] Cic. *Fam.* 9.16.6, 6.4.2; *Att.* 12.28.2, 14.11.1.

[9] The first letters we have preserved were written in 68 BCE and there are only eleven (excepting the *Commentariolum petitionis* by Quintus Cicero) predating Cicero's time as consul in 63 BCE.

[10] Greek and Latin bilingualism in Cicero's letters has aroused a keen interest among scholars since the late nineteenth century. See Clavel 1868; Font 1894; Steele 1900; Rose 1921; and more recently, Dubuisson 2005; Elder and Mullen 2019.

[11] Elder and Mullen 2019: 112. See Adams 2003: 308–346; Swain 2002.

[12] Elder and Mullen 2019: 111–174.

[13] For an exception, see, e.g., *Fam.* 1.9 (in the famous letter addressed to Lentulus) or *Brut.* 1.9. The solemnity of these letters may explain the absence of Greek words.

philosophical perspective. It must be noted that Cicero does not use philosophical Greek with all his correspondents, but mostly with Atticus, which can be explained by their intimate friendship, their shared admiration for Greek culture and language, and the tone of their letters, which is both allusive and lighthearted.

How is philosophical Greek used in Cicero's letters? Throughout his life, Cicero kept the habit of having discussions *in utramque partem*, both in Greek and Latin, which were strongly influenced by philosophy, though he called them "political theses" (θέσεις ... πολιτικαί) when they dealt with the civil war (*Att.* 9.4.1–3), mostly by Plato's thoughts on tyranny[14] or by Stoic precepts on moral goodness. His letters include many sketches of such discussions. They also display many Greek words that are related either to philosophical sources or to philosophical concepts.

In the former case, the use of Greek reveals a source which would be hard to detect without a hint, as when Cicero plans to leave Italy with Pompey, in March 49 BCE, though he knows this decision could cost him his life (Cic. *Att.* 7.20.2). The expression he uses, καὶ συναποθανεῖν ("even to die with him"), alludes to Plato's *Phaedo* (88d), where it is used to describe the alleged indissociability between body and soul. When human beings die, Socrates should assume that their souls perish with them (συναποθανεῖν), unless he succeeds in persuading Echecrates that this is not the case and that the soul will survive the body. In the context of the letter addressed to Atticus, Cicero, as a philosopher, considers himself the soul and Pompey, the man of action, the body. Together, they form an indestructible pair that cannot be separated by civil war.

In the latter case, and unlike in his dialogues, where he systematically translates into Latin every Greek philosophical concept, Cicero leaves many Greek philosophical terms untranslated in his letters, whether they refer to well-established concepts, such as καλόν ("good"), εὔλογον ("reasonable"), καθῆκον ("appropriate action"); neologisms, such as Stoic εὐθυρρημοσύνη ("direct and frank speech");[15] words without any exact equivalent in Latin, such as φιλοστοργία ("tenderness," "love between members of the same family"); or finally Greek quotes.

In this chapter, I shall study three different uses of philosophical Greek in Cicero's letters: (1) Greek language betraying the influence of a philosophical model on the letters (e.g. the influence of protreptic, long before the *Hortensius* was written in 45 BCE); (2) Greek language in implicit

---

[14] Gildenhard 2006.
[15] Cic. *Fam.* 9.22.5: ὁ σοφὸς εὐθυρρημονήσει. See Aubert-Baillot 2015; Aubert-Baillot 2021.

quotations,[16] whether they serve a purely philosophical purpose or inter-weave philosophy and literature, in contrast with the more rigorous reasoning of the major philosophical dialogues from 45–44 BCE; (3) Greek language revealing the progressive elaboration of a philosophical work contemporary with the letters (e.g. *De finibus* and its analysis of the Stoic theory of οἰκείωσις in book 3).

Philosophizing by Letter: The Protreptic Model

Scholars have frequently drawn a parallel between Cicero's letters and Plato's,[17] almost all of which are thought to be spurious today but were all considered authentic in antiquity. As for Cicero, he never suggests the opposite when he refers to letters 5, 7, and 9 in his works.[18]

However, Cicero's letters depend on other philosophical models than just Plato's letters. Among them is the protreptic genre, whose parallel with the epistolary genre is justified by several reasons. They both have a "dialogical" character and aim at changing the behavior of their addressees in a pragmatic way. As a matter of fact, the letter is conceived as a substitute for action, while the protreptic seeks to convert others to philosophy by diverting them from another way of life – an exclusive commitment to politics, for example. Here is a letter that Cicero sent to Atticus in 61 BCE about an upcoming consular election that was tainted with corruption:

> Therefore I suppose *one ought to philosophize* (φιλοσοφητέον), as you do, and not care a button (*non flocci facteon*) for these wretched consulships (*istos consulatus*).[19] (Cic. *Att.* 1.16.13; trans. Loeb)

This exhortation to philosophize, which aims at overcoming a tempo-rary disappointment, is tinged with irony. This is evident from the demonstrative adjective *istos*, with its derogatory connotations, which is applied (*istos consulatus*) both to the glorious consulate of 63 BCE that

---

[16] By "implicit quotations," I mean quotations that Cicero does not mention as such and whose author is not named.

[17] See Boyancé 1969 for a famous letter addressed to Lentulus (*Fam.* 1.9); see also Guillaumont 2008 and McConnell 2014: 62–114.

[18] See Guillaumont 2008 for all the references.

[19] Italics are mine whenever a Greek word is translated into English. See also *Att.* 2.13.2., written in 59 BCE, when Cicero, powerless against the ambitions of Caesar, addresses an exhortation to himself and to Atticus: "So take my advice and *let us philosophize* (φιλοσοφῶμεν). I can give you my oath (*iuratus*) that nothing is so rewarding" (after Loeb trans.). This Greek subjunctive, combined with the mention of the oath, already appears in Pl. *Ep.* 6.323d.

Cicero was so proud of and to the consulate of 60 BCE, which a man as mediocre as Afranius might hold. The irony is further enhanced by the neologism *facteon*, a hapax in Latin literature. The impression of technicality that emerges from this forged and seemingly Greek gerundive, based on the Latin verb *facio* in order to rhyme with the Greek form φιλοσοφητέον, is contradicted by the colloquial expression *flocci non facere* ("to care not a straw for," "to make no account of"), frequent in Plautus (*Cas.* 332; *Curc.* 713; *Epid.* 348; *Men.* 423, 994). However, this exhortation by Cicero can be interpreted as a real longing for Epicurean *ataraxia* and detachment from politics, two attitudes which would appeal to his addressee Atticus, given his sympathy for the Garden. Moreover, the gerundive φιλοσοφητέον is worthy of interest on a philosophical level. It was already mentioned in Plato's *Euthydemus* (282d, 288d) in a protreptic context and also in Epicurus' *Letter to Menoeceus*, an epistolary text endowed – once again – with a protreptic function. As stated in the prologue, "for no age is too early or too late for the health of the soul ... both old and young *ought to philosophize* (φιλοσοφητέον)" (Diog. Laert. 10.122; after Loeb trans.). Above all, the Greek word appears in Aristotle's lost *Protreptic*, as we can tell by the remaining fragments of this work[20] and also by Iamblichus' *Exhortation to the Study of Philosophy*, where this gerundive is repeated as a leitmotif in Chapters 5–12. These are chapters that I. Bywater deems to be authentic remains from Aristotle's own *Protreptic*,[21] which was written, according to some scholars, in an epistolary form.[22] Therefore, long before Cicero's publication of his *Hortensius* in 45 BCE,[23] his now-fragmentary protreptic to philosophy that asserted the urgent necessity to philosophize (*philosophandum*), long before the famous prologues of the philosophical dialogues written in 45–44 BCE, Cicero had already hesitated in his letters between his commitment to politics and his exclusive devotion to philosophy.[24]

With his letter of 61 BCE, he also tests upon himself the effectiveness of such an exhortation, which *prima facie* could have seemed rather abstract and vague. He proceeds in the same way as in the *Consolatio* he wrote to himself in 45 BCE, applying to his own case every philosophical method in

---

[20] Arist. *Prot.* frs. 5.3, 8.5, 9.7, 41.7, 92.2, 96.1, 110.2 Düring. See Van der Meeren 2011: 95–99.

[21] Bywater 1869.

[22] On the epistolary form of the *Protreptic*, see Hirzel 1895: 283 n. 2, 304; Jaeger 1923: 55–56. Van der Meeren 2011 leaves the discussion open.

[23] On Cicero's *Hortensius*, see Bouton-Touboulic (Chapter 16) in this volume.

[24] See also, as early as 59 BCE, *Att.* 2.5.2 and 2.12.4. On the debate between philosophical life and political life in Cicero, see Lévy 2012; McConnell 2014: 115–160.

order both to overcome his grief after Tullia's death and to prove that philosophy could have a powerful impact on human life in practice. Cicero's letters do not aim at promoting the views of the New Academy against other philosophical schools; nor do they aim at educating Romans by popularizing a Greek discipline like philosophy and bringing it into Roman culture and language. Most of them represent an effort to anchor philosophy in practice.

Philosophy and Allusions: Hidden Quotes

Let us now turn to quotations from Greek philosophy, whose number and importance seem to have been underestimated by J. N. Adams.[25] Focusing on Greek language allows us to detect them more easily. Since enumerating them all would exceed by far the limited scope of this chapter, I shall study only a few examples from Plato, Epicurus, and the Stoics. I shall start with a letter to Atticus from November 44 BCE:

> As for your admonitions, even if you were criticizing me (*si reprehenderes*) I should not mind, in fact I should be pleased, since criticism would be done with perspicacity and *kindness* (*quippe cum in reprehensione sit prudentia cum* εὐμενείᾳ). (Cic. *Att.* 16.11.2; after Loeb trans.)

The admonitions that Cicero feared so much concerned the *Second Philippic*. Atticus had just received the text and, as an editor, he did not correct it with "these famous little marks of red wax" (*cerulas ... miniatulas illas*), much to Cicero's relief (*Att.* 16.11.1). This is the reason why I have modified the translation by D. R. Shackleton Bailey and replaced the words "to find fault with" and "fault-finding" with "criticize" and "criticism," in order to emphasize the literary context of this passage. This change is also based on a Greek text that Cicero surely had in mind when he wrote these words. It comes from Plato's seventh letter, upon which Cicero draws openly in other letters,[26] and it brings together the noun φρόνησις (or "wisdom," rendered by *prudentia* in Cicero's letter, meaning rather "perspicacity," "clear-sightedness" here) and the adjective εὐμενής ("kind," "benevolent," transposed by Cicero as a noun, εὐμενεία):

> and it is by means of the examination (ἐλεγχόμενα) of each of these objects, comparing one with another – names and definitions, visions, and sense-perceptions – proving them by kindly proofs (ἐν εὐμενέσιν ἐλέγχοις) and

---

[25] Adams 2003: 323–342 analyzes seven categories of code-switching in Cicero's letters: critical terms, coding or exclusion, distancing or euphemism, proverbial or fixed expressions, *mot juste*, medical terminology, and evocativeness of a Greek word.

[26] See McConnell 2014: 62–114.

employing questionings and answerings that are void of envy – it is by such means, and hardly so, that there bursts out the light of wisdom (φρόνησις) and intelligence regarding each object in the mind of him who uses every effort of which mankind is capable. (Pl. *Ep.* 7.344b; trans. Loeb)

Although the elements of what is called the "philosophical digression" of Plato's seventh letter (342a–345c) are reorganized by Cicero in his passage, it is probable that Atticus' *reprehensio* echoes the Platonic *elenchus* through which wisdom and intellection can be attained. In this dialectic between the similarity of words and the difference of contexts (in one case, literary criticism of a political text; in the other, the method required for a complete theoretical knowledge of things), we can also notice Cicero's humor and his intellectual affinities with Atticus, who, as an editor of Plato's dialogues, knew them very well.

Epicurean quotes seldom appear in the letters,[27] and they are often mixed with reminiscences from other schools, including Stoicism and the New Academy. Thus, at the end of his proconsulate in Cilicia, Cicero is preparing to return to Rome. In October 50 BCE, he arrives in Athens, from where he sends Atticus a letter, written in a light and also anxious tone – the civil war is about to break out in Rome. It contains several philosophical allusions, some of which are due to Atticus, others to Cicero himself. Here is what he writes about a small sum of money bequeathed to him by Precius, which his freedman Philotimus is seeking to steal, even though Cicero needs money for triumph expenses:

> In that matter you shall find me, according to your precept (*ut praecipis*), neither *vainly anxious* in demanding (*nec me* κενὸν *in expetendo cognosces*) nor *thoughtless* in declining (*nec* ἄτυφον *in abiciendo*). (Cic. *Att.* 6.9.2; trans. Loeb)

Given Atticus' sympathy for the Garden, one would expect the thought and the terminology here to be entirely Epicurean, but this is not the case. Cicero certainly uses a Greek adjective employed by Epicurus at *Men.* 127 to describe groundless desires (κεναὶ <ἐπιθυμίαι>) that are neither natural nor necessary, such as, for example, the desire for wealth, as in this letter, or honors. He also adds the Latin verb *expetere*, which he will use five years later in his analysis of the ethical doxography of the Garden,[28] in order to describe the quest for pleasure inasmuch as it is the supreme good for the Epicureans.

---

[27] On the ambivalent attitude of Cicero toward Epicurus and his followers, see Lévy 2001; Maso 2008; Gilbert 2015; Warren 2016; Morel 2016.

[28] See, e.g., Cic. *Fin.* 1.11, 1.30–31.

On the other hand, the adjective ἄτυφος has a long and rich philosophical history, but not an Epicurean one. It is a key term among the Cynics[29] and Pyrrhonian philosophers,[30] and refers to the absence of vanity. It also appears in the self-portrait of Socrates in Plato's *Phaedrus* 229e–230a, which was certainly a source of inspiration for the Stoics when they drew up their own description of the wise man,[31] whom they considered to be "free from vanity (ἄτυφο[ς]), for he is indifferent to good or evil report" (Diog. Laert. 7.117 [= *SVF* 3.646]; after Loeb trans.). However, with the double negative *nec … nec*, Cicero rejects in his letter two attitudes he regards as equally reprehensible (*nec … κενὸν … nec ἄτυφον*). The word ἄτυφος cannot have a positive meaning here. Cicero would contradict himself if he said both that he will banish vanity (*nec … κενὸν*) in demanding his money and that he will not banish puffed-up pride (*nec ἄτυφον*) in declining it. Since the diseases of the mind include, among other things, "extravagant and groundless desires for … fame" (*cupiditates immensae et inanes … gloriae*, where *cupiditates … inanes* represents a Latin translation of the Greek κεναὶ <ἐπιθυμίαι>; Cic. *Fin.* 1.59; after Loeb trans.), according to Epicurean doxography as Torquatus presents it in *De finibus* book 1, the desire for vain glory (τῦφος) is neither natural nor necessary. The adjectives κενός and ἄτυφος are antonyms in this context.

The Stoics are the only philosophers to underline the ambivalence of the adjective ἄτυφος since, according to them, it modifies either the wise man or, on the contrary, the bad man (φαῦλος), "he who is ranked among the rash (εἰκαῖο[ς])" and acts in a thoughtless, random way (Diog. Laert. 7.117 [= *SVF* 3.646]; after Loeb trans.).[32] Although the first, laudatory meaning of ἄτυφος ("free from vanity") is much more common than the second ("thoughtless," "careless"), I suggest that Cicero attributes here a specifically Stoic meaning to this Greek word.[33] He thus makes Atticus defend a balanced wisdom, one that conforms partly to Epicureanism, partly to Stoic terminology and doctrine, and that does not sink into indifference and thoughtlessness as he denies that he is ἄτυφος.

---

[29] Brouwer 2014: 156–158.   [30] See Timo *apud* Eus. *PE* 14.18.19.

[31] See Brouwer 2014: 149–163.

[32] See, by contrast, Diog. Laert. 7.46 (= *SVF* 2.130) on the wariness (ἀνεικαιότης) of the wise man, which is "a strong presumption against what at the moment seems probable, so as not to be taken in by it" (Loeb trans.).

[33] See Shackleton Bailey 1965–1970: III, 276, who, without any allusion to Stoicism or philosophy in general in his commentary ad loc., translates ἄτυφον as "phlegmatic," "blasé," which comes close to my own hypothesis ("thoughtless," "careless").

Perhaps this proximity to Stoic doctrine explains why the next paragraph of the letter deals with the "suspension of assent" (ἐποχή): with a touch of humor, Cicero represents Atticus as an Academic who is prey to doubt, whereas he himself, in a very dogmatic way, no longer has any doubt at all. In this passage written in a cheerful tone, the philosophical roles seem to be reversed. Atticus had first joked with Cicero while applying the neo-Academic concept of ἐποχή to a context that was less philosophical than political, since he had written that he was experiencing "doubt" (ἐπ<ἐχ>ειν), a word that Cicero then translates as *dubitatio* in paragraph 3 when he imagines that Quintus Cicero, a tactless and irascible governor, will succeed his brother at the head of the province of Cicilia. This persistent hesitation (ἐπιχρονία ἐποχή, 3) on the part of Atticus, which Cicero interpreted less as a suspension of judgment than as a real negative judgment (in other words, a rejection, ἀθέτησις, 3), paradoxically helps Cicero to rid himself of his own ἐποχή (*me ... dubitatione liberavit*, 3).

Such a humorous use of a neo-Academic concept whose treatment here is quite unorthodox is all the more interesting if we compare this passage to a famous letter from August 45 BCE, a serious text this time, which is almost entirely devoted to the problem of the Latin translation of ἐποχή – a central concept in the dialogue Cicero was writing at that very moment, the *Academica*.[34] The chosen translation is no longer *dubitatio*, because it is too vague. Neither is it *inhibere*, which Atticus had suggested as a semantic calque, but the verb *sustinere*, because of its meaning ("to hold back" [one's horses and carriage], or "to rest on" [one's oars]) and its presence in a satire written by Lucilius, with the image of a driver holding back his team. This same image had already been used by Carneades in order to illustrate the suspension of assent.[35] Even though the reader does not face long, theoretical, coherent, rigorous philosophical developments in these letters, he cannot help noticing that philosophy is fundamentally a language which is used to discuss even nonphilosophical matters. By applying abstract concepts to practical cases from everyday life, even while distorting their original meaning or field of application, Cicero reveals his interest in major philosophical subjects about which he will write dialogues or treatises a few years later: exhortation to philosophy (*Hortensius*), suspension of assent (*Academica*), and fame (*De gloria*). Writing letters is

---

[34] Cic. *Att.* 13.21.3 (August 27 or 28, 45 BCE). See Lévy 1992b: 97–98.
[35] About Cicero's translation of assent in Latin, see also Lévy (Chapter 5) in this volume.

one of the ways in which Cicero practices philosophy, without reducing it to a mere intellectual discipline.

Interweaving Philosophy and Literature

Though present everywhere in the letters, philosophy is often kept at a distance by several devices like allusivity, humor, or the interweaving of philosophy and literature. An example of this conflation of a philosophical source and a literary allusion can be found in a letter written in July 59 BCE. Concerned about his enemy Clodius, who has just been adopted by a plebeian and will be elected tribune for the year 58, Cicero thinks he can either avoid without embarrassment the anticipated political struggles or face them with all honor (*cum dignitate*). Nevertheless, he reveals his uncertainties through a fictitious dialogue with Atticus, which he brings to a desperate conclusion:

> Perhaps you will say that we have had enough of honor – *le siècle du gland est passé* (*dignitatis* ἅλις *tamquam* δρυός) – and implore me to think of security. Oh dear, why are you not here? Nothing, I am sure, would escape you, whereas *I* perhaps *am blind* (τυφλώττω) and *have been* too much *affected by beauty* (*nimium* τῷ καλῷ προσπέπονθα). (Cic. *Att.* 2.19.1; trans. Loeb)

The Greek proverb quoted by Atticus, ἅλις δρυός ("enough acorns," i.e. "enough with these vain words from the past"), is all the more interesting since before Cicero's time, it is mentioned only by two Greek authors: Theophrastus and Dicaearchus.[36] These two Peripatetic philosophers disagreed on whether the contemplative or the active life was to be preferred, and Cicero mentions this disagreement in a letter to Atticus written two months before this one.[37] Although partly ironically, Cicero sides with Theophrastus and his "theoretical life" (θεωρητικὸς βίος), while Atticus prefers the views of Dicaearchus and the "practical life" (πρακτικὸς βίος).[38] Though the context in which this proverb appears in the fragments of the two philosophers – the frugality of the first men on earth – is very different from the political preoccupations of Cicero in his letter, its use reminds us of the famous debate between the two Peripatetic philosophers. Facing (*subire, Att.* 2.19.1) political storms or avoiding them (*declinare*), from Cicero's point of view, amounts to choosing between the two different

---

[36] See Porph. *Abst.* 2.5.36 (Theophrastus), 4.2.43 (Dicaearchus).
[37] Cic. *Att.* 2.16.3 (around May 1, 59 BCE).
[38] See Lévy 2012; Fortenbaugh 2013; McConnell 2014: 115–160.

kinds of lives described above. But between these two letters, written in May and July 59 BCE, Cicero has decided to stand more firmly against Caesar's political actions and not to stand aside, as Atticus recommended. The friends have swapped roles, or rather gone back to their initial schools, as if Atticus had finally yielded to his penchant for Epicureanism and advocated political disengagement, and Cicero, to his deep attraction to Platonic thought, which compelled him to fight against the immorality of Roman political leaders (*Att.* 2.19.3). The doctrine of Plato appears in the letter under the theme of blindness (τυφλώττω), since this is the fate that threatens those men who have left the cave, in the myth of the *Republic*, and have chosen to go back down there to transmit to others the knowledge of what they have contemplated, especially the idea of the good. No doubt this is the way to understand the Ciceronian expression, "*I have been too much affected by beauty*" (nimium τῷ καλῷ προσπέπονθα).

However, Cicero seems to employ a *contaminatio* between the Platonic text and a passage from Isocrates' *Encomium of Helen* when he uses the Greek verb προσπέπονθα ("to be affected in addition"), a rare word in the Classical era, especially as it is used in the perfect tense.[39] In this passage, Isocrates justifies the Trojan war by emphasizing the superiority of beauty (τὸ κάλλος) over all other goods and by drawing a parallel between aesthetics and ethics, so that virtue is especially admired because it is the most beautiful of all lifestyles (*El. Hel.* 54). From physical beauty (τὸ κάλλος), one moves toward moral beauty (τὸ καλόν):

> For in regard to the other things which we need, we only wish to possess them and we have not been affected in our soul in any way (οὐδὲν τῇ ψυχῇ προσπεπόνθαμεν); for beautiful things, however, we have an inborn passion (τῶν δὲ καλῶν ἔρως) whose strength of desire corresponds to the superiority of the thing sought. (Isoc. *El. Hel.* 55; after Loeb trans.)

Cicero's formula nicely sums up the second part of Isocrates' sentence. The interweaving between philosophy and literature highlights here the irresistible dimension, perceived in the Latin adverb *nimium*, of the attraction exercised by beauty – an aesthetic beauty above all in the case of Isocrates, and a moral beauty in the case of Plato and Cicero.[40] It also betrays the confusion that results from this attraction for Cicero, who is torn.

---

[39] The only two occurrences prior to Cicero are Pl. *Phd.* 74a (προσπάσχειν. Context: the theory of recollection) and Isoc. *El. Hel.* 55 (προσπεπόνθαμεν). Plato uses the verb προσπάσχειν in a transitive construction ("to experience in addition") and Isocrates in an intransitive construction ("to be further affected"), as Cicero will do in his letter.

[40] On the interweaving of emotional, even erotic, and philosophical considerations in Cicero, see also *Att.* 9.10.2.

Prudence would require him to agree with Atticus and decline political struggles, but his love for moral good prevents him from doing so. This example shows us the pervasiveness of philosophy in Cicero's letters, even when a Greek quotation seems insignificant from a philosophical point of view.

A Testimony on the Progressive Elaboration of a Philosophical Dialogue

I shall now turn to a last aspect of philosophy in Cicero's letters. Sometimes a seemingly insignificant Greek word may allude to a complex doctrine which Cicero is developing at the very same time in a treatise, and it helps us to define his philosophical position more precisely than we may by studying a dialectical debate between, for example, a Stoic such as Cato and Cicero in the role of an Academic philosopher in *De finibus* books 3–4. This is why I shall discuss here a key term in Stoic ethics, φιλοστοργία. Built on a double root, it joins the meanings of the verbs φιλεῖν ("to regard with affection" – a beloved person, a friend) and στέργειν ("to love tenderly, to cherish" – a verb that applies in particular to the love that parents feel for their children).[41] Above all, it designates the tenderness between members of the same family.[42] In his letters (which is significant, since the epistolary genre, with its intimate tone, is especially well adapted to the expression of affection and feelings in general), Cicero uses the word φιλοστοργία four times without translating it. Sometimes he uses it in the adverbial form φιλοστόργως or the comparative adjectival φιλοστοργότερον, in a sense that is slightly different from its traditional meaning. Apart from one text where the author is pleased that his son, the young Quintus Cicero, has sent him a letter written in an "affectionate" (φιλοστόργως) tone[43] (although here, it is the son and not the father who demonstrates φιλοστοργία, contrary to the standard classical meaning of this word), the Greek word does not apply to family relations in the strict sense. Even if Cicero could have a quasi-paternal connection with his young son-in-law Dolabella,[44] it is not natural to expect that one could describe by this model his relationship with Sestius the Elder[45] or with his host Sicca.[46]

---

[41] See Aubert 2011 for a more exhaustive analysis.
[42] See Theoc. *Id.* 18.13; Arr. *Epict. diss.* 1.11; Plut. *Mor.* 494d (*De amore prolis*).
[43] Cic. *Att.* 15.17.2 (June 14, 44 BCE). [44] Cic. *Att.* 13.9.1 (mid-June 45 BCE).
[45] Cic. *Att.* 15.27.1 (July 3, 44 BCE). [46] Cic. *Att.* 15.17.1 (June 14, 44 BCE).

Apart from the first text on his son Quintus, Cicero does not seem to assign to this Greek (and rare) term its classical meaning. In order to define it more precisely, we must examine the semantic proximity between two comparative adjectives, ἐκτενέστερον ("more friendly," "more forthcoming") and φιλοστοργότερον ("more affectionate"), both of which define, in an asyndeton, the conversation between Dolabella and Cicero (*Att.* 13.9.1). Cicero is the only Latin author to quote the Greek adjective ἐκτενέστερον (here in the comparative form) or the noun ἐκτένεια ("zeal," "assiduousness," a word applied to the speaker Hortensius, Cicero's friend and former rival, in a letter to Atticus).[47] The only previous mention of this Greek noun, according to the *Thesaurus Linguae Graecae*, appears in a Stoic testimony of Chrysippus transmitted by Clement of Alexandria. It also mentions φιλοστοργία and most probably influenced Cicero's conception of such a notion:

> Now love (ἀγάπη) turns out to be consent in what pertains to reason, life, and manners, or in brief, fellowship in life, or it is the intensity of friendship and of affection (ἐκτένεια φιλίας καὶ φιλοστοργίας), with right reason, in the enjoyment of associates ... And akin to love is hospitality (φιλοξενία), being a congenial art (φιλοτεχνία) devoted to the treatment of strangers ... Philanthropy (ἥ τε φιλανθρωπία), through which natural affection also exists (δι' ἣν καὶ ἡ φιλοστοργία), being a loving treatment of men, and natural affection, which is a congenial art exercised in the love of friends or domestics (ἥ τε φιλοστοργία φιλοτεχνία τις οὖσα περὶ στέρξιν φίλων ἢ οἰκείων), follow in the train of love. (Chrysippus[= *SVF* 3.292], *apud* Clem. Al. *Strom.* 2.9.41.2 – 6; trans. P. Schaff)

This text offers a philosophical re-elaboration of φιλοστοργία. The concept sees its original meaning broadened, through a play on its definition not as φιλοτεκνία (or "love for one's children," which corresponds to the traditional meaning of φιλοστοργία), but as φιλοτεχνία, in other words as a "congenial art," a "skill." This is how a parallel can be drawn between φιλοστοργία and the practice of hospitality (φιλοξενία), which is also called a φιλοτεχνία. On this basis, φιλοστοργία no longer applies to the sole relationship between parents and children: it extends to close relatives and friends, and more broadly to the entire human race, as φιλανθρωπία, just as in Cicero's letters. This analysis of φιλοστοργία is based on the Stoic theory of οἰκείωσις ("appropriation," "familiarization with oneself"), according to which every living creature, whether an animal or a human being, tries first instinctively, then rationally, to persist in its own

---

[47] Cic. *Att.* 10.17.1 (May 16, 49 BCE).

existence. It flees what is harmful to its nature and seeks, on the contrary, what is good for it – these primary things in accordance with (its) nature (*prima naturae*), among which are health or strength. But through their love for their children, parents both love themselves (if we consider that their offspring are part of their own being) and other people: therefore, the Stoics developed this argument in order to explain how οἰκείωσις contained in itself the origin of the social bond that unites all human beings to each other, because all human beings share in reason and virtue. The Stoics debated forcefully with the other philosophical schools, especially with the Garden, in order to show that parental affection toward children (φιλοστοργία) was rooted in nature (Diog. Laert. 7.120 [= *SVF* 3.731]). They wanted to prove that the ability of human beings to live in society, which stemmed from this original parental affection, was also inscribed in nature, as Cato highlights in *De finibus* book 3, where he tries, along with Cicero, to find Latin equivalents to the Greek technical words the Stoics used to express their ethical doctrines (3.62–63 [= *SVF* 3.340]).[48]

Behind the "parental affection for children" mentioned by Cato at the beginning of this passage (*Fin.* 3.62) lies the Greek word φιλοστοργία, the Latin equivalent of which here is not only the verb *amare*, used once in the passive voice ("nature creates in parents an affection [*amentur*] for their children"), once in the active voice ("it is clear that we derive from nature herself the impulse to love [*amemus*] those to whom we have given birth"), but also the verb *diligere*: "Yet it could not be consistent that nature should at once intend offspring to be born and make no provision for that offspring when born to be loved and cherished [*diligi*]" (Cic. *Fin.* 3.62 [= *SVF* 3.340]; after Loeb trans.). This suggests that Cicero struggles to find an exact Latin equivalent for the Greek φιλοστοργία. In any case, a verb seems to him preferable to the use of a noun (*amor* designates above all passionate love, while the verb *amare* has a wider range of meanings, from the love between lovers or friends to the affection between family members; as for the term *diligentia*, it does not mean "affection" or "love" in the first century BCE, but "attentiveness, diligence, industry, assiduity, care"). Moreover, if Cicero uses the verbs *amare* and *diligere* alternately, it is undoubtedly because the text deals at the same time with the love of parents for their children and the love of animals for their offspring. The word *diligere*, which designates a weaker affection, can apply to every living being (Cic. *Fin.* 2.33). As for the verb *amare*, it can only refer to human beings, which restricts the scope of the Stoic demonstration that nature itself teaches us, from the observation of

---

[48] On social ethics in Cicero, see Reydams-Schils (Chapter 12) in this volume.

humans and animals, that every living being is animated by an innate instinct of sociability. Moreover, as the Stoic φιλοστοργία is the source of the interest that each person feels for other human beings (φιλανθρωπία), it progressively designates, by extension, the affection mingled with tenderness that one feels for one's friends as well as for one's relatives, according to Stoic doctrine as preserved in Clement of Alexandria. Φιλοστοργία is thus akin to affection in a broad sense, φιλία, and it is precisely in the spring of 45 BCE, when he began to write his *De finibus*, that Cicero quoted for the first time in his letters a word close to φιλοστοργία, namely the comparative adjective φιλοστοργότερον, which he uses together with another comparative, the seemingly Stoic adjective ἐκτενέστερον (*Att.* 13.9.1).

Such a coincidence cannot be fortuitous: Cicero uses this word in his letters precisely when he is immersing himself in the study of Stoic ethics. Moreover, he gives it a much broader meaning than a mere "tenderness between members of the same family." By applying it not only to his son Quintus and his son-in-law Dolabella, but to his friend Sicca or to a political ally such as Sestius the Elder, Cicero suggests that he agrees with the Stoics when they say that οἰκείωσις contains in itself the origin of the social bond that unites all human beings to each other. Even in *De finibus* book 4, when he attacks Stoic ethics, he never calls this fundamental principle into question; instead, he tries to establish Aristotle as the inventor of οἰκείωσις (*Fin.* 4.15, 4.17). And when he launches a polemic against the Epicureans in *De finibus* book 2, he uses a Stoic argument and accuses them of ruining the moral good (*honestum*) by concentrating on their own interest, instead of considering humanity as a whole, whose members are united by a bond rooted in nature (2.45, 2.48). Though he quotes Plato's ninth letter here, saying that men are not born for themselves alone, but for their country and their relatives (Cic. *Fin.* 2.45; Pl. *Ep.* 9.358a), he returns to this point a year later, when he supplements Plato with Stoic οἰκείωσις in his description of justice in *De officiis* 1.22. Φιλοστοργία is a key term in this philosophical context: not only is it inseparable from the Stoic οἰκείωσις, it plays an important role in Cicero's conception of *humanitas*[49] as it illustrates both the natural origin of the social bond between all human beings and the feeling of deep affection between these same human beings.[50]

[49] See Prost 2006.

[50] This concept becomes so important that two centuries later, Fronto, a great admirer of Cicero's letters, insists on the absence of a Latin translation for what he calls a virtue (*virtuti*) because in reality (*reapse*), according to him, no one in Rome feels any warm affection: see Fro. *Ver.* 1.6.7 and Aubert 2011.

To conclude, philosophy in Cicero's letters does not typically take the form of long, coherent, and rigorous arguments such as those we find in the dialogues. It is necessarily less abstract and theoretical, as it is applied to the vicissitudes of Cicero's life, from exile and political struggles to grief at his daughter Tullia's death. It is also enhanced by many literary devices – fictional dialogues, images, proverbs, literary quotes – and illustrated by a more concrete, less technical vocabulary, and by a terminology which was not yet definitively established in the Latin language when the letters were written, hence the abundance of a Greek philosophical vocabulary in these texts.

Further Reading

Philosophy in Cicero's letters has mostly been studied by Lévy 1992b; Griffin 1995 and 1997a; Baraz 2012; and McConnell 2014. For good editions of Cicero's letters with translation and commentary (although not so rich when it comes to philosophical matters), see Shackleton Bailey 1965–1970, 1977, and 1980. On Cicero's appropriation of Greek literature and philosophy in the letters, see recently Bishop 2019, ch. 5; Aubert-Baillot 2021.

CHAPTER 4

Philosophy in Cicero's Speeches

Catherine Steel

Philosophy plays much less prominent and conspicuous a role in Cicero's speeches in comparison with the other genres of writing that he used. Indeed, there are just two discussions of philosophy of any scale in Cicero's surviving speeches, and in each case philosophy, in the guise of adherence to a specific philosophical sect, is introduced as the basis for an invective against an opponent. Thus a brief consideration of the topic might conclude that Cicero's speeches do not offer a helpful line of inquiry for his philosophy, being only marginally interested in the topic and only from a hostile perspective. The purpose of this chapter is to suggest that the picture is perhaps more complicated. A closer look at *Pro Murena* and *In Pisonem*, the two speeches which deal explicitly with – respectively – Stoicism and Epicureanism shows that neither suggests that philosophy, philosophical study, or even philosophical adherence are, in themselves, problematic or dangerous phenomena. Cato and Piso, the objects of Ciceronian criticism (albeit of rather different levels of hostility) are at fault not because they are interested in philosophy but because each, in his own way, has misunderstood how to be a philosopher. Even within the confines of oratory with its immediate ends, Cicero's approach to philosophy does not fundamentally clash with that which he adopts elsewhere. It is also possible to suggest that Cicero's philosophical studies can be linked to aspects of his political theory as expressed in his speeches. In particular, the development in *Pro Milone* and the second *Philippic* of an argument around the justification for murder can be connected to the argument around tyrannicide and human society that is articulated in the third book of *De officiis*. The aim of this chapter is to show that the speeches should not be ignored in an assessment of Cicero as a philosophical writer.

I am grateful to the editors for their invitation to contribute to this volume and their suggestions on an earlier draft; and to Walter Englert for his generosity in sharing his work on these speeches prior to its publication and for his comments on this chapter.

The forensic speech *Pro Murena* was delivered late in 63 in defense of
L. Licinius Murena, one of the consuls-elect for the following year, on
charges that he had used bribery in his campaign to be elected consul.
Cicero uses the adherence to Stoicism of one of his client's prosecutors, the
younger Cato, to build an argument against the credibility of the prosecution as a whole.[1] Cato was one of four speakers involved in the prosecution
of Murena but, unlike the other three, he did not have a direct personal
motive for his involvement.[2] Instead, the prosecution played to Cato's
hostility toward corruption in public life, a stance which would come to
be dominant in his public persona, and which had already become evident
in his tenure of the quaestorship the previous year.[3] Despite his junior
position at the time of the trial (he was tribune-elect), Cato's personal
probity gave authority to the prosecution: the only reasonable explanation
for his involvement must be his belief that Murena was guilty. Cicero's
response to the problem which that moral authority created for the defense
can be seen to underpin his presentation of Cato. He argues that Cato's
morality is unrealistically rigid, and he does so on the basis of Cato's known
adherence to Stoicism. If he could convince the jury not to see any
implication of guilt in Cato's presence as a prosecutor, it would go some
way to counter the feeling against Murena that arose from the circumstances
under which the charges had been brought and to reassure the jurors that
their own (hoped-for) leniency in reaching a judgment on Murena's behavior was not an indication of any moral failing on their own part.

The section of the speech (Cic. *Mur.* 60–66) in which Cicero sets out
this argument has been extensively studied.[4] It is distinctive in Cicero's
oratorical corpus for its wit and lightness of touch, and an anecdote that
Plutarch (*Cat. Min.* 21.5) records points to its effectiveness at the time:

> Cicero was consul when the case was heard and one of Murena's advocates.
> By criticizing and making a great deal of fun of Stoic philosophers and the
> so-called Paradoxes, because of Cato, he made the jurors laugh. They say
> that Cato smiled at what was going on and said, "Gentlemen, what an
> amusing consul we have."

---

[1] On *Pro Murena*, see Leeman 1982; Adamietz 1989; Stem 2006; Fantham 2013.

[2] Ser. Sulpicius (cos. 51 BCE), the other main prosecutor, was one of the unsuccessful candidates in
these elections and, if Murena were convicted and thus disqualified, he would have the opportunity
to stand again. The two *subscriptores* were closely associated with Sulpicius: see Alexander 2002:
121–127.

[3] See Morrell 2017: 160–162; Drogula 2019. Cato had announced in the Senate that he would
prosecute the successful candidates, given the prevalence of bribery, though he excepted his brother-
in-law Silanus (who was in fact elected): Cic. *Mur.* 62; Plut. *Cat. Min.* 21.2–3.

[4] Craig 1986; Riggsby 1999: 21–49; Fantham 2013: 166–173

Cicero wanted, and apparently had, his audience in gales of laughter at this point in the speech. Cato's recorded response to Cicero's witticism arguably draws on this authority as well, since the phrase ὕπατος γελοῖος, surely a translation of *consul ridiculus*, is no compliment: *ridiculus* can describe something which is the object of laughter as well as its cause.[5]

It is important to note that the jurors' laughter was directed very carefully at a specific kind of philosophical engagement. Cicero does *not* argue that Cato is a bad guide to conduct because he is influenced by his philosophical studies. Indeed, he demonstrates through a series of *exempla* that philosophical studies are eminently suited to the Roman elite.[6] But the men whom he identifies were, he claims, directed by their philosophical studies, even those conducted with Stoics, towards greater moderation and mercy, not less. The younger Cato has, it emerges, made a fundamental error in his philosophical practice. He has attached himself too firmly to one school, that of Zeno (when there were alternatives more suited to the reality of Roman life, in which mercy and moderation are valuable qualities), and he has misunderstood *how* to do philosophy. It should not be a matter of rigid adherence to a particular code of conduct but a process of investigation, in which one *sententia* can overcome another (Cic. *Mur.* 65) and minds can be changed.[7] If Cato would only use the Roman *exempla* that Cicero has brought forward (*Mur.* 66), he would understand what to do; the attitude which has led to his mistakenly over-zealous adherence is, after all, one that even Cicero as a young man shared: "I admit, Cato, that I too as a young man distrusted my own judgment and sought the assistance of rules" (*Mur.* 63). Cicero thus sets up philosophical study, if done properly, as a valuable part of Roman elite practice with a considerable history. It is entirely acceptable to spend time with philosophers, engage in discussion with them, and even, if you are young and inexperienced, to rely on *doctrina* – provided you have the sense, as Cicero did and Cato did not, to turn to Plato and Aristotle, whose tenets suit Roman practice in a way that those of Zeno do not.[8]

Throughout this section, form complements content as Cicero switches from oratorical address to the jury to setting up a philosophical dialogue with Cato himself. He marks the shift early on: "Since my speech is not

---

[5] See, e.g., Cic. *Rosc. Am.* 50; *Phil.* 11.13.
[6] He cites Scipio Aemilianus, Gaius Laelius, L. Furius Philus, C. Sulpicius Galus, and the elder Cato, all of whom would subsequently be used as characters by Cicero in his philosophical dialogues.
[7] On the practice of arguing *in utramque partam*, see further Brittain-Osorio (Chapter 2) and Remer (Chapter 13) in this volume.
[8] Cf. Cic. *De or.* 3.63–68.

delivered to an ignorant crowd or in a gathering of rustics, I shall discuss
the civilized studies which are well-known and dear to you as well as to me
with rather considerable freedom" (Cic. *Mur.* 61).[9] He then initially
expounds Stoic doctrine and describes Cato's adherence to it, but then
turns to direct address to Cato, and then (Cic. *Mur.* 65) apparently shifts
to prosopopoeia of Cato's voice, in which "Cato" states his position and
Cicero demolishes it. Cicero thus demonstrates to the jury the appropriate
use of philosophy by a Roman: it is not dogmatic but uses debate in order
to identify the best course of action. It is a matter of method, not content.
As a result, the jury is to understand, the problem with Cato is not that he
is a philosopher, but that he is a bad philosopher.

In Pisonem is one of the many speeches that Cicero gave after his return
from exile which endeavor to reestablish his authority within the Senate
and political community. One of the regular targets of his invective in
these speeches is L. Calpurnius Piso, consul in 58 who, on Cicero's view,
had betrayed him by failing to take steps to prevent the attacks of Clodius
which drove him into exile. At the time of Cicero's return in 57, Piso was
absent in his provincial command in Macedonia; when he returned to
Rome in 55, he and Cicero clashed in the Senate, and Cicero disseminated
In Pisonem as a record of their encounter.[10] Piso's adherence to
Epicureanism is presented as a major element in his moral worthlessness,
which is at the heart of Cicero's invective; he, unlike most of Piso's
audience, can see through the sham character of moral probity which
Piso presents to the world.[11] Similarly to *Pro Murena*, *In Pisonem* presents
an individual's erroneous adherence to a particular school of philosophy as
a fault which undermines authority within the public sphere. But there are
pronounced differences between the two speeches.[12] Piso's adherence is to
Epicureanism rather than Stoicism, and Epicureanism is presented as a
much less plausible philosophical position, even if Cicero holds back in
this speech from outright condemnation. Moreover, Piso's misunderstand-
ing of what it is to do philosophy feeds a fierce invective, in contrast to the
patronizing benevolence directed at Cato. Piso is drawn to Epicureanism

---

[9] In fact, Cicero's exposition of the Stoic doctrines that he attacks is so full that prior knowledge is not
required to follow his argument.

[10] Piso also produced a written version of his speeches; Cic. *QFr.* 3.1.11.

[11] On *In Pisonem*, see Nisbet 1961; Corbeill 1996: 169–173; Dugan 2005: 55–74.

[12] One important difference, as Walter Englert has shown, is in language. In his lecture "Philosophy in
Cicero's Speeches, 70s–55 BCE," delivered at the University of Glasgow on October 3, 2018,
Englert argued that Cicero does not use the term *philosophus* or *philosophia* in *Pro Murena*, whereas
there are eight occurrences in *In Pisonem* (56, 58, 65, 68, 69, 70, 71 [twice], 72). On the word
philosophus in Cicero's speeches, see Hine 2015: 14–17.

because of his vicious nature, and because it is Epicureanism to which he feels allegiance, philosophical study cannot amend his faults.

Piso's Epicurean adherence is treated as a given throughout the speech.[13] Systematic discussion of philosophy is concentrated at 63–72, where Cicero develops a series of arguments whose purpose is to discredit Piso both as a practitioner of Epicureanism and because of his Epicurean adherence. He is unable to live by Epicurean precepts, since he is affected by the fact that he is unpopular, though Epicureanism regards "reputation, shame, disgrace, and degradation as trifling words" (Cic. *Pis.* 65). He interprets Epicureanism in accordance with his own degraded standards, placing physical pleasure ahead of intellectual and aesthetic pleasure, and failing to understand the nature of true luxury; his study of Epicureanism lacks any rigor, as he was attracted to it because of his own voluptuous tendencies (Cic. *Pis.* 68–69). Finally, his practice is so debased that it has corrupted (the unnamed) Philodemus, his teacher, of whom Cicero says, "If he had had better luck in getting a pupil he could perhaps have been a more serious and respected figure" (*Pis.* 71). Cicero formally eschews judgment on the validity of Epicurus' arguments ("whether or not he is right is not our business, or if it is our business now is not the time," *Pis.* 86); the problem is thus not so much that Piso is an Epicurean, but that he is a bad Epicurean.[14]

In both these speeches Cicero uses defective philosophical adherence as a means to discredit his opponent.[15] His invective does not lack philosophical content, but there is no requirement for the audience to possess

---

[13] Cic. *Pis.* 20, *barbarus Epicurus* ("a barbarian Epicurean"); 37, *Epicure noster ex hara producte non ex schola* ("you, our Epicurean drawn not from the schools but a pigsty"); 92. The only explicit mention of Epicurus in the speeches besides the *In Pisonem* is at *Red. sen.* 14, where Cicero includes in his description of Piso the following observation: "When indeed he began to engage in literary study, and this prodigious monster began to philosophize with his little Greeks, he then was an Epicurean, not because he was deeply committed to that school (whatever it may be) but captured by this one word: pleasure." In brief compass, Cicero sketches the approach he takes at greater length in *In Pisonem*: a general caution around Epicureanism alongside Piso's incompetence as a student because of his moral depravity.

[14] How far Cicero's framing of Epicureanism here is affected by the Epicurean allegiances of some of his friends is difficult to ascertain.

[15] Other places in the speeches where Cicero explicitly refers to a specific philosophical school are at the start of *Scaur.* (3–6) and at *Rab. Post.* 23. In *Pro Scauro*, Cicero appears (the text is fragmentary) to invoke Plato's account of Socrates' death as part of an argument suggesting that the prosecution is ridiculous to claim that a Sardinian woman committed suicide because Scaurus was threatening sexual assault. The tone is distancing (*ut video … ut opinor*) and contemptuous (*Graeculi … multa fingunt*). At *Rab. Post.* 23, Plato's relationship with Dionysius is one of three examples of an intellectual whose life was jeopardized or even lost by his association with a tyrant, thus justifying Postumus' mistake in trusting Ptolemy XII; here Plato is presented as an acceptable guide to conduct. On Cicero and Plato, see Schofield (Chapter 6) in this volume.

any detailed knowledge of the philosophical ideas to which he refers, though Cicero implies that he and the jurors share a civilized understanding of philosophy and its proper use. It also appears that there is a basic level of fact underpinning his presentation. The philosophical allegiances of Cato and Piso were publicly known.[16] Moreover, the differences in the handling of Stoicism and Epicureanism correspond to what is known of Cicero's attitude towards each school.[17] It would seem that effective use of philosophical allegiance as a character trait in oratory required some correspondence with reality.

One function of philosophy in Cicero's oratory is, then, as a source for invective against opponents whose moral authority would otherwise prejudice Cicero's success, political or forensic. Another important area where Cicero's oratory engaged with philosophy is via his theoretical works on speaking.[18] These two disciplines were intertwined as intellectual pursuits at Rome from the foundational visit of the leaders of the three Athenian philosophical schools to address the Senate in 155 BCE, and the lectures they gave during their stay.[19] Even in Cicero's earliest work on rhetoric, *De inventione*, he seeks to transcend its handbook format with opening reflections on rhetoric and the origins of society which draw on Isocrates. The productive dialogue which should exist between oratory and philosophy and be embedded in rhetorical tuition underpins *De oratore*, in both its explicit demands that an orator have philosophical competence and its allusions to Platonic dialogue in the details of its framing.[20] The methodological implications, in terms of argumentation, of this relationship between oratory and philosophy were developed in the *Topica*: there, he set out the Aristotelian theory of τόποι in order to provide a method of generating arguments about general topics and thus escape the limiting specificity of standard status theory to specific questions.[21] In the safe generic context of a treatise in which Roman aristocrats can acknowledge their intellectual interests, Cicero introduces his treatment with a description of how his dedicatee, C. Trebatius, came across Aristotle's *Topica* in Cicero's library and asked him to expound the work.

---

[16] On Piso, see Griffin 2001; on Cato, see Craig 1986.

[17] In contrast to Piso and Cato, however, it is less clear that Cicero was widely known to have particular philosophical allegiances, though the presence of Diodotus in his household was presumably no secret. In *Pro Murena* 63 he claims to be guided by Plato and Aristotle, which establishes a middle ground in contrast to Cato's more rigid adherence to Stoicism. On the potential dissonance between our knowledge of Cicero and that of his oratorical audiences, see Morstein-Marx 2004: 207–230.

[18] See further Remer (Chapter 13) in this volume.   [19] See Erskine 1990: 188–192; Glucker 2001.

[20] See Wisse 1989; Zetzel 2003; Fantham 2004: 161–185.   [21] See Reinhardt 2004: 3–17.

Cicero initially refused, suggesting that Trebatius should do the reading himself and ask for help, should he need it, from "a most learned teacher of rhetoric"; but when Aristotle was too much for Trebatius, and his teacher confessed ignorance, Cicero felt himself obliged to step in (*Top.* 1–5).[22] The resulting work seeks to integrate the technique of using τόποι with existing rhetorical instruction, to expand but not radically recast the methods available to the well-educated orator.

Before considering other ways in which Cicero uses philosophy in his oratory, however, it is important to distinguish broader and narrower usages of the term "philosophy." Thus far, this chapter has only looked at those points in the speeches where Cicero explicitly refers to philosophy as an intellectual pursuit. These references depend on identifiable schools of philosophy and their associated philosophical positions. It is possible, however, to adopt a broader meaning of "systematic thinking," and so doing can reveal further potentially relevant aspects of the speeches. Gildenhard offers an example of such an approach, setting out a comprehensive analysis of Cicero's oratory in terms of its understanding of human psychology, society, and relationship with the divine.[23] He argues convincingly that the world that Cicero creates in his oratory across more than three decades offers a coherent picture of the nature of man and the consequences of this understanding of human nature for an orderly society, particularly in its dealings with internal threats. The cluster of modern academic disciplines which Gildenhard uses to structure his enquiry extend very widely; they intersect with the lines of enquiry pursued by ancient philosophy only at certain points. But at those points of intersection, it is worth exploring whether Cicero may be relying on his philosophical studies in articulating or implying a political theory underpinning the cases and advice he presents in his speeches. The fact that he may do so without explicit invocation of any philosophical authorities is not in itself evidence that there was no connection; caution over overt intellectualism, particularly in relation to Greek material, is a recurrent feature of his oratory.

---

[22] Cicero's initial reluctance to accede to Trebatius' request (whether or not it happened) can perhaps be explained as a reluctance to crystallize a disparity between him and Trebatius by assuming too openly the role of teacher. In Cicero's most openly didactic treatises (*Tusc., Part. or.*) his interlocutor is either anonymous or his own son, with whom an unequal relationship is appropriate. On the issues raised by the interlocutor in the *Tusculans*, see Gildenhard 2007: 70–76.

[23] Gildenhard 2011.

The intersection of Cicero's philosophical standpoint and his oratory in political theory can perhaps most productively be explored in the relationship he establishes in various speeches between the security of the *res publica* and the rights of the individual. This tension faced Cicero in 63 when, as consul, he responded to Catiline's uprising; in his fight with Clodius in the 50s; and at the end of his life in his opposition to Marcus Antonius. In each case Cicero used the priority of the *res publica* as the basis of his campaign to destroy his opponent, and in so doing he connected existing Roman legal frameworks and political practice with a theoretical framework developed from Stoicism and Academic skepticism. The result was a justification of how internal threats could trigger states of emergency and for the unilateral expulsion from the *res publica* of certain individuals.[24] The Roman Senate had developed a state of internal emergency through a form of decree which instructed the consuls "to see that the state suffered no harm"; first used in 121 BCE, it had been institutionalized by its repetition in subsequent crises in 100 and 77. Although its legality had never been established on a general basis, and was therefore subject to legal challenge on a case-by-case basis, practice indicated that it removed a citizen's individual protection from arbitrary capital punishment by magistrates in a civilian context.[25] In a parallel development, the irrevocability of citizen status was tested through the Senate's declaration that certain Roman citizens were *hostes*; this too was a preliminary to violent death. Sulla's creation of the process of proscription extended that process in terms of numbers and by breaking a link to a single moment of crisis.[26] Cicero was, therefore, operating within a political environment in which the Senate had intermittently claimed the capacity to protect the *res publica* by eliminating internal threats without the authorization of the people as a whole. He took the possibility of a set of enabling conditions for the suspension of individual rights and combined it with a Stoic-inflected theory of society to identify aspiration towards tyrannical power as the key to identifying those whose actions removed them from the *res publica*.

---

[24] See Harries 2006: 204–229; Hall 2013; Straumann 2016: 149–190.

[25] For an overview, see Straumann 2016: 63–117.

[26] Sulla had also attempted to remove the citizen status of entire communities. In some speeches earlier in his career (*Pro Caecina, Pro muliere Arretina*) Cicero had argued that citizenship could not be lost without the holder's agreement. Cicero's inconsistency can be explained by the specific forensic contexts of these speeches, but it was also an area in which the legal framework was developing fast.

The underpinning philosophical theory has its fullest articulation in *De officiis*, whose discussion of tyrant killing is clearly influenced by Caesar's death. In this work, written as Cicero began his campaign against Antonius in the autumn of 44 BCE, he provides the theoretical basis for rejecting tyranny. Killing a tyrant is the example he sets out to open up the topic of the work's third book (*Off.* 3.19) on the (apparent) conflict between doing what is right and doing what is useful:

> Often, as a result of circumstances, what is generally considered to be dishonorable is found not to be dishonorable. As an example, consider a case with wider ramifications. What can be a greater crime than killing someone who is not only a human but also a friend? Yet surely someone who kills a tyrant, however much a friend, has not embroiled himself in criminal activity?

As a result, the judgment concerning tyrants is "very straightforward" (*perfacile*, *Off.* 3.32): "We have no bond with tyrants; indeed, there is a total disjunction, and it is not against nature to rob him, if you can, whom it is honorable to kill, and this whole destructive impious group must be driven out from the society of men." Cicero's argument upholds the conclusion that tyrannicide is not dishonorable by asserting the bonds which link all humans, whether or not they belong to the same political community. Actions which threaten those bonds are invariably dishonorable. By threatening the basis of human society, tyrants put themselves outside that society, and as a result must be eliminated.[27]

It is possible to trace this theoretical position in the way that Cicero handles the death of Clodius in his defense of Milo some years previously in 52 BCE.[28] Milo was accused under the *lex de vi* for his role in Clodius' death; the *Pro Milone* is notable, among other features, for its dual structure, in which Cicero's demonstration of Milo's innocence of the offense of *vis* (because his killing of Clodius was in self-defense), which forms the first and largest part of the speech, is followed by a further demonstration that even if Milo had set out to kill Clodius, his actions would have been justified because of the threat that Clodius posed to the *res publica*.[29] The speech, at least in the form which Cicero circulated it, thus offers in sequence two incompatible arguments.[30] The second,

---

[27] See further Atkins (Chapter 15) in this volume.   [28] Clark and Ruebel 1985.

[29] The structure of the speech can be summarized thus: 1–71, defense of Milo on the charge of *vis* (the death of Clodius was self-defense); 72–91, hypothetical defense of Milo for deliberate killing of Clodius; 92–105, peroration (heroism and resignation of Milo). On the structure of the *Pro Milone*, see Fotheringham 2013.

[30] On the *Pro Milone*, see Stroh 1975: 31–54; Stone 1980.

so-called *extra causam*, section can be seen as the culmination of Cicero's arguments over the previous four and a half years since his return from exile that Clodius had expelled himself from the *res publica* through his behavior and actions.[31] In it Cicero summarizes Clodius' past actions in order to construct the praetorship for which he was campaigning at the time of his death as a threat to the entire community:

> If he had obtained that *imperium* – I pass over our allies, foreign nations, kings, and tetrarchs – you would be praying that he launched himself against them rather than against your property, your houses, your money – do I say money? He would never have kept his uncontrollable appetites away from your children, god is my witness, and your wives. (*Mil.* 76)

The argument moves towards Cicero's invocation of tyranny as the frame in which Clodius can best be understood:

> If he were this man's killer, would he, in acknowledging it, expect punishment from those he had freed? Greek people ascribe divine honors to those men who have killed tyrants – which I saw in Athens and in other Greek cities! What religious ceremonies, hymns, and songs are dedicated to such men!" (79–80)

Clodius is a *hostis* (78), and not only humans but also the gods have taken an interest in his obliteration.[32] The overt framework for Clodius' death is one informed by tyrannicide in Athenian political history and the divinity which adhered to those who committed it. Nonetheless, it is at the very least evident that, by creating an opportunity to explore Clodius' death as an event planned by Milo, Cicero sets out a vision of tyrannicide as a justifiable community response to individual power, and that this vision can be related to the subsequent analysis of the philosophical justification for tyrannicide in *De officiis*.

The argument in the *Pro Milone* depends on an emotional response to Clodius, compounded of disgust and horror in the face of sacrilege, violence, and assault on property rights. Cicero deploys a similar approach to Antonius in the *Philippics*, combining specific personal details, such as Antonius' relationship with Curio, with a more generalized threat to the integrity of the *res publica*. In Antonius' case, this threat emerges most clearly after Caesar's death, though its potential is present in the activity that Cicero describes at length prior to that moment. Cicero claims his

---

[31] On this "standard version," see Kaster 2006: 1–14.
[32] *Mil.* 85–86, building on the location of Clodius' death near a shrine to the Bona Dea.

immediate reaction to Antonius' behavior after Caesar's death was apprehension: "the *res publica* seemed securely established to others, but not remotely to me, who feared shipwreck with you as our helmsman" (*Phil.* 2.92). Antonius' return to Rome in early summer 44 throws Rome into confusion and provokes recollection of the rising triad of Cinna ("too powerful"), Sulla ("as master"), and Caesar ("as ruler," Cic. *Phil.* 2.108). These fears are not groundless: Antonius has confirmed them by summoning the Senate to a closed session under armed guard. "Surely it is better to die a thousand times than to be unable to live in one's own community without an armed guard? But that is no protection, believe me; you need to be protected by the affection and benevolence of the citizens, not by arms" (Cic. *Phil.* 2.112). By invoking the trope of being under armed guard, Antonius' behavior aligns him even more clearly with tyranny than that of Clodius. By suggesting that the only effective protection against assassination is his reputation among his fellow citizens, Cicero pushes his readers to reflect on the extent to which Antonius has indeed behaved in such a way as to create this protection for himself. The inescapable conclusion, brought out over the following two chapters, is that he has not; rather, he is responsible for a state of slavery. His actions show him to be a tyrant, and as such subject to the judgment of tyrants articulated in *De officiis*.

Within Cicero's oratory, philosophy plays a limited though significant role. His speeches were always directed towards a specific persuasive end, and philosophy plays a part only if it can contribute to that end. The breadth of the audiences of his speeches on the occasion of their delivery made technical or esoteric discussion inappropriate; even when speaking to senatorial jurors, Cicero was careful to distance himself from excessive or alienating learning.[33] Philosophy as a branch of intellectual activity fell clearly under this heading and was thus to be invoked with great caution. Nonetheless, it fulfills two functions. It is evident in Cicero's oratory of crisis insofar as it provides the theoretical basis for his construction of the *res publica* and the relationship between the *res publica* and his (and, on Cicero's telling, its) enemies. In this context, however, it is striking that the articulation of this theory is not framed in overtly philosophical terms. Greek philosophy combined with Roman jurisprudence to provide tools

---

[33] See *Verr.* 2.4; cf. *Arch.* 3 (this to an audience of senators and equestrians). Written speeches involved much smaller audiences than their spoken counterparts but verisimilitude of tone and approach, if not verbatim accuracy, was of central importance in the transition from speech to writing; for a useful survey of the issue, see Powell and Paterson 2004: 52–57.

but did not, it appears, contribute any authority which would make it worthwhile to invoke this aspect of the idea's history.[34] Indeed, Cicero's explicit invocation of philosophy is concentrated, within his oratory, in invective contexts. Although philosophical adherence itself is not presented as a weakness (a position which could easily have backfired for Cicero himself), he constructs his opponents' engagement with philosophical doctrine as flawed in a variety of ways, shaped by what seem to have been the public profiles of Cato and of Piso and by the level and nature of the attack which Cicero wished to launch. His approach is also adjusted to his audience, who are not required to deploy any specialized understanding in order to grasp what he says: all that is required is, at most, a broad familiarity with the terms "Stoic" and "Epicurean" and a willingness to identify Cato and Piso with those respective positions.

Cicero's use of philosophy in his speeches thus matches the prescription which Crassus offers in *De oratore*.[35] Philosophy is one of a number of bodies of knowledge which the orator should possess as a source of effective arguments. It also, in Cicero's case, underpins the beneficent relationship between the orator and the *res publica*: Cicero's philosophical knowledge and understanding enabled him to identify the ways in which he could serve the *res publica* and support his oratorical skill in explaining to a range of audiences what was required from everyone in its protection.

Further Reading

There is a translation of the *Pro Murena* in Berry 2000 and the *In Pisonem* can be found in Watts's Loeb (1931). Griffin 2001 offers a persuasive rehabilitation of Piso's Epicureanism; the significance of Stoicism in Cato's political practice is discussed in detail in Morrell 2017. On individual rights in Cicero's thinking, see Atkins 2013a and Straumann 2016. For consideration of philosophical material more broadly defined in the speeches, see Gildenhard 2011.

---

[34] Cf. *Fin.* 4.74, where Cicero contrasts his approach in the *Pro Murena* with the serious philosophical discussion with which he is currently engaged.
[35] Cic. *De or.* 1.52–57; cf. Remer (Chapter 13) in this volume.

CHAPTER 5

Cicero and the Creation of a Latin Philosophical Vocabulary

Carlos Lévy

It is both right and erroneous to say that Cicero was the creator of Roman philosophical vocabulary. Before him, at the outset of the Hellenization of Roman culture, poets like Ennius (c. 240–170 BCE) and Lucilius (180?/ 148?–102?/101? BCE) began to give Latin equivalents of Greek concepts.[1] This task was brilliantly pursued by Lucretius, after the rather disastrous attempts, at least according to Cicero (*Acad.* 1. 5–6; *Tusc.* 4.6), of Amafinius and Rabirius to propagate the Epicurean doctrine.[2] Lucretius was not only a great poet but also a prodigious demiurge of the language, trying to remedy the poverty of Latin, *patrii sermonis egestas.*[3] He succeeded in expressing a lot of Epicurean technical terms in Latin, though the Latin vocabulary of his literary predecessors did not seem at this time suited to accommodate an atomistic theory. By comparison, Cicero's originality lay in giving precise translations of many Platonic, Academic, Stoic, and Peripatetic concepts, in translating many Greek philosophical texts, and above all in strongly asserting the right of Latin to become a philosophical language. All those who pretend that Cicero dramatically lacked originality in the field of philosophy ought to imagine what a challenge it was to claim that there was no structural reason preventing Latin from becoming a philosophical language. While twentieth-century philosophers such as Heidegger still denied this fundamental Ciceronian intuition, many other philosophers throughout the history of philosophy acknowledged Cicero's achievement, especially those philosophers who wrote in Latin. Seneca, Augustine, Thomas Aquinas, Descartes, Leibniz, among so many others, testify that this Roman orator, so prudent in defining himself as a *philosophus*, made a most valuable contribution to philosophy.

---

[1] On Roman philosophy before Cicero, see Garbarino 1973.
[2] See Eckerman 2013; Maso 2015; Moatti (Chapter 1) in this volume.
[3] Fögen 2000; Benferhat 2014.

General Remarks

Consider the following statement: "Your individual qualities received strong assent." Almost all the terms in this sentence were coined by Cicero. This was not an overnight achievement, but the result of quite a long process.

Chronology is an element too often overlooked in studies of Ciceronian philosophy. It is crucially important, however, for understanding terminological creation. In Cicero's first rhetorical treatise, the *De inventione*, which he later explicitly dismissed as an underdeveloped work of his youth (*De or.* 2.5), there are no theoretical remarks about language. It is in the last book of his more mature *De oratore*, written in 55 BCE, that for the first time he proclaimed a kind of manifesto about the philosophical abilities of the Latin language (*De or.* 3.95).[4] Here he was affirmative without being dogmatic. He did not assert that Latin was already a philosophical language but that it could become such. Generally speaking, in the field of philosophy as well as in that of politics, he scorned any fatalism that denied human agency. Nature and history provide abilities which are put to work only if there is someone to make the decision. In light of this, the following sentence is particularly interesting: "The importation of the time-honored and outstanding wisdom of the Greeks for our habitual employment (*ad nostrum usum moremque*) is permitted by our language and by the nature of things (*natura rerum*); but it needs persons of advanced learning" (*De or.* 3.95).

Unlike the material world, language is not for Cicero an indeterminate material (*Acad.* 1.27).[5] It has natural characteristics, which he does not precisely define, since, unlike his contemporary Varro, Cicero seems to have had no special interest in linguistics and grammar. More subtly, the reference to *natura rerum* means that translation was possible because there was a kind of harmony, or at least of compatibility, between Greek wisdom and Roman national tradition, *mos maiorum*. Does this imply that a translation would be impossible if these conditions were not fulfilled? Cicero's expression is here too vague to allow this conclusion, but his "linguistic nationalism" is undeniable. In *Tusculans* 2.35, written ten years after *De oratore*, he dared to criticize Greeks because they were proud of the wealth of their language. Turning on its head Lucretius' pronouncement of the poverty of the Latin language in matters of philosophy, Cicero stressed that in reality the Greek language could sometimes be the poor

---

[4] Unless indicated otherwise, translations follow those of the Loeb Classical Library.
[5] On the structure of the target language, see White 2015: 7.

one. Some months before, in *De finibus*,[6] he had written that Latin was richer than Greek. All this shows that in a short period Cicero developed a much stronger view of the possibilities of the Roman language versus the generally admitted supremacy of Greek.

Translations of Platonic Dialogues

Cicero's activity as a translator of classical Greek philosophical texts seems to have been intense, though we unfortunately lack precise information about the date and length of these translations. He did not translate only Platonic dialogues. At *De officiis* 2.87, he makes a brief allusion to his translation of Xenophon's *Oeconomicus*. He says that he translated it at the same age as his son is now (i.e. at about twenty years old). We know still less about his translation of Plato's *Protagoras*. In *De finibus* 1.7, he seems to place on his schedule for the near future the translation of some Platonic and Aristotelian works, so let us suppose that he translated the *Protagoras* soon after he wrote *De finibus* in 45.

Georgina Frances White has given an impressive list of all the texts – Platonic, but also Peripatetic, Stoic, and Epicurean – that Cicero translated.[7] The most puzzling case is that of Plato's *Timaeus*. Textual tradition has preserved for us a fragmentary translation of this dialogue and a prologue.[8] Many questions arise about this pair of the texts' remains. The most important include the following:

(1) At what date did Cicero translate the *Timaeus*? The question is still debated. The prologue however speaks of Nigidius Figulus, the Neo-Pythagorean Roman philosopher, as someone who was dead.[9] We know that he died in 45 BCE, which gives us a *terminus post quem*.

(2) What could be the purpose of this translation? Two hypotheses can be considered: either it was for Cicero a pleasant and interesting linguistic exercise in which he could display both his bilingualism and his knowledge of Plato's dialectical proceedings, or it had a precise function in the Ciceronian program of exposition of philosophy, which he undertook in the 40s BCE. In the latter case, the translation of the *Timaeus* would testify to Cicero's return to a more dogmatic Plato than that of the New Academy. Similarly, in the

---

[6] *Fin.* 1.10, where he says that this theme is often stressed by him.   [7] White 2015: 147–230.

[8] This fragmentary condition can be explained by a problem in the transmission of the text or by the fact that Cicero himself left it unfinished.

[9] On Nigidius Figulus, see Ducos 2005.

Tusculans, Cicero's ethical Platonism is different from the skeptical approach to ethics he presented in the *Academica*.

(3)   How should we assess Cicero's translation? The debate can be summed up by the opposite opinions of Poncelet and Lambardi.[10] For the former, Cicero unintentionally demonstrated the inability of the Roman language to express abstract ideas. Taking a contrary position, Lambardi, following Alain Michel's intuitions, saw in this translation an implicit effort to define translation as a literary art.

One of the most interesting aspects of this translation is that Cicero translates Plato with the language and the concepts of someone deeply influenced by the dominant doctrine of his time (i.e. Stoicism).[11] Thus, he left, albeit almost certainly involuntarily, a precious testimony about certain aspects of the paradoxical symbiosis between Platonism and Stoicism, even before the rise of Middle Platonism, which had spread in the second half of the first century BCE, since Philo of Alexandria (first half of the first century CE) is often considered the first representative of this kind of philosophy. Actually, Middle Platonism can be defined as the return of a dogmatic Platonism after the skeptical interlude of the New Academy, but with the absorption of some Peripatetic and Stoic elements.[12]

The Circumstances of a Crucial Decision

In the *prooemium* of the second version of the *Academica* (1.9–14), Cicero describes the context of his decision to express philosophical ideas in Latin. Most probably this is an abstract of the many discussions that he had held with his friends on this topic. Three positions are clearly defined. The first belongs to Varro, a distinguished expert in linguistic problems, who expressed an opportunistic point of view: why work hard to provide Latin equivalents of Greek concepts if the unlearned will never be interested in these philosophical texts and the learned will read them in Greek? The second position, which belongs to Cicero's friend Atticus, can be

---

[10] On the Ciceronian *Timaeus*, see Poncelet 1957; Michel 1973; Lambardi 1982; Lévy 2003; Sedley 2013.

[11] See Lévy 2003. For example, at 37a, "the best of the intelligibles that always are," is translated by "the most excellent father," an expression that is close to that used by the Stoic Balbus in *De natura deorum* 2.45 about the immanent Stoic God: "there is nothing more excellent than him."

[12] On the elements of continuity between the New Academy and Middle Platonism, see Opsomer 1998.

defined as a prudential stance. In the *Academica*, Atticus says that he is waiting to see if Antiochus' philosophical ideas could be conveniently expressed in Latin, but in the slightly later *De finibus* he says that he is more pessimistic about this issue.

The third position belongs to Cicero himself. For Cicero, who recognizes with much praise that Brutus preceded him (*Acad.* 1.12.), philosophical translation is far from being a merely technical process. He stresses its historical roots, since Latin literature itself had its origin in the translation and adaptation of Greek models. Why would what was possible for literature not be possible for philosophy? But there is also a more political aspect. Like the satirist Lucilius before him, Cicero scorns those who despise their own language. The context of his decision is clear. Greece had lost its military power. In the field of culture, Roman literature and eloquence were constantly improving, not to mention Roman law. That is why to Cicero philosophy could appear as the last cultural province that still escaped Roman hegemony.[13] To win a cultural victory was a way to maintain his place in the public sphere. To make a useful work for all his compatriots remained his permanent goal in both the fields of philosophy and politics.

Problems of Method

Despite the generally negative image given by the *Quellenforschung* (source criticism) that dominated the study of Cicero's philosophical works at the end of the nineteenth century, Cicero was not an *amateur* trying to translate material he only superficially understood. He was instead completely bilingual, a view confirmed by the frequency and variety of Greek words in his letters.[14] His linguistic evaluation of Greek philosophical texts differentiated clearly between the various Greek schools of philosophy. Plato was for him the absolute master of style as well as of thought. Aristotle appeared to him the brilliant runner-up. In contrast to Plato and Aristotle, Cicero was harsh with Epicureans, whom he reproached both for erroneous doctrine and their lack of accuracy in the

---

[13] To describe Cicero's attitude towards the Greek texts, White 2015 rightly observes that Cicero uses the verb "to domesticate" many times. But for a Roman magistrate, "to domesticate" was not only a pedagogical and cultural process, it implied also the political project to make Rome the first, that is to put forward its *imperium*, its supremacy in all areas, even in that which was traditionally Greek: philosophy.

[14] See Horsfall 1979; Adams 2003. The thesis of Cicero's bilingualism has been criticized by Swain 2002.

use of language. With respect to the Stoics he was somewhat more nuanced. He accused them of having created new and superfluous terms, but at the same time, he recognized that they had achieved new ideas in the philosophy of knowledge (*Acad.* 1.40).

If, as I have suggested, Cicero is a creative and careful translator, by what principles did he achieve his verbal creation? As a translator he sought for himself a status in accord with the dignity of someone who twenty years before was a consul. To be just an *interpres*, a professional translator, was obviously not an identity of which he could be proud.[15] Cicero rather claims to "watch over" or "care for" (*tueri*) these Greek philosophical texts (*Fin.* 1.6). This formulation of his preferred status is quite interesting. The verb *tueri* means "to protect," but for a reader of Cicero's works it also had a strong political meaning and recalled the function of *tutor*, which is used in Cicero's famous definition of the *princeps* ("chief statesman") in the *De republica*. He was said to be a good and wise man who ought to be the *tutor et procurator* ("protector and governor") of the state (*Rep.* 2.51). With regard to translation, *tutor* indicates much more than a professional role. It is the expression of the authority of a person at the highest political level, who, once the *res publica* disappeared, transferred his sense of responsibility from politics to texts. The term implies respect toward them but also power over them. That is why Cicero says he will add to translating both his own *iudicium* and his stylistic abilities.[16]

Other aspects of his method of translation are more technical. He frowns upon giving new Latin equivalents of Greek terms with a well-established presence in the Latin language, such as *philosophia, rhetorica, dialectica, geometria,* or *musica*. He will accept the creation of neologisms if and only if it is impossible to do otherwise (*Fin.* 3.15). In expressing his reticence about using neologisms, Cicero was following his belief that the Latin language was full of semantic possibilities; however, he was also following a Platonic tradition since Plato himself was quite reluctant to create words.

But Cicero's method was driven by more than theoretical considerations. In some cases, Cicero observed the world that surrounded him in order to give the best translation. The best example of this attitude is to be found in a letter to Atticus (*Att.* 13.21),[17] about the translation of *epochē*, the suspension of assent. Though there are eleven occurrences of the verb

---

[15] In *Tusc.* 3.41 he says that he will assume the function of a translator momentarily, which proves that he does not identify with it.
[16] *Fin.* 1.6, where he denies that he is only a translator.   [17] Lévy 1992b.

dubitare ("to doubt") in Lucretius' poem *De rerum natura, epochē* implied much more (i.e. a specific conception of the functions of the mind). Cicero first accepted Atticus' suggestion that *inhibere* ("to prevent") was the most appropriate verb. But he was informed by sailors that *inhibere* did not mean to block the oars but to row in another way. This information prompted him to go back to his first choice, the verb *sustinere* ("to hold back"). He found a justification for this decision in the early Roman satirist Lucilius, who, acquainted both with the Stoic Panaetius and the Academic Clitomachus, served for Cicero as a kind of model (*Att.* 13.21, 23). But Cicero did not hesitate to use variations.

To Know and to Doubt

For Cicero the main difficulty in creating a Latin vocabulary for knowledge was to find terms adequate for expressing both the Stoic doctrine of a natural certitude, proceeding from mere sensation to the perfect knowledge of the sage, and the Academic assertion that no knowledge at all was possible.

First, consider Cicero's rendering of "sensation" and "assent" within Stoic epistemology.[18] In *Lucullus* 39, Lucullus, who in this dialogue (also known as *Academica* 2) defends an epistemology quite close to Stoicism and claims it was defended by the Stoicizing Platonist Antiochus of Ascalon, argues that a skeptical stance which allows for neither sensation nor assent makes action impossible in life. Unlike the radical skeptic Pyrrho, neither Antiochus nor the skeptical philosophers of the New Academy thought that it was possible to live without sensation. But Antiochus and his Academic adversaries disagreed on the value of assent: it was absolutely necessary in his opinion, and the main source of error in theirs.

Cicero's rendering of the term "sensation" provides one of the most striking examples of his ability to attribute new meanings to Latin words. Consider the following passage at *Academica* 1.41, where, in his description of the Stoic Zeno's innovations in the field of epistemology, Cicero writes the following strange-sounding sentence: "But what had been grasped by sensation (*sensu*), he called itself a sensation (*sensum*)."

Sensus was at the time of the redaction of the *Academica* a rather common word in Latin. It had been used by many writers, and by Cicero himself in his speeches, to mean both the organs of sensation and

---

[18] See Frede 1999.

the sensations they provided. The term had already received a first philosophical treatment in Lucretius. The following verse, which attacks the
theory of Heraclitus (Lucr. 1.693), is an especially interesting example
since, like in our Ciceronian passage, *sensus* is repeated: "For he himself on
the basis of senses fights against the senses." In this Lucretian verse,
repetition does not change the meaning of the word. However, in
Cicero's sentence there is a complex combination of permanence and
change. The first occurrence of *sensus* means that a sense takes possession
of the object, the second one expresses the result of this process – not only
a sensation but a sensation that has received the mind's assent. We know
the Greek equivalent of this sentence,[19] but it is not difficult to imagine
how hard it could be for a Roman, even one well trained in philosophy, to
understand it. At the same time, the efficiency of the Ciceronian method is
remarkable. He economically suggested that sensation was not a simple
mechanism but a complicated issue in which there was an implicit intervention of assent.

It was a great Stoic innovation to affirm that Nature had created a
fundamental rational harmony between humanity and the world. As a
consequence, error had no ontological basis in Stoicism, other than the
liberty given to the subject of giving or denying his or her assent. Still the
Stoics did not deny the existence of errors at all the levels of knowledge.
Explaining this fallibility was a real intellectual challenge that also needed a
profound terminological development in Greek; to translate these terms
into Latin thus required a serious effort.

One of the best examples of this effort comes from the term *sunkatathesis*, assent. This word was used in relation to the metaphor of "voting."
Stoicism transformed each human being in a permanent "voter" who,
faced with the representations that Nature offered to him/her, had to
choose to accept, to refuse, or, in some rare cases, to abstain from giving
assent. On the contrary, the philosophers of the New Academy said that
the only wise attitude was to abstain from assenting, since in their opinion
Nature was unable to give clear and evident representations. The process of
a free secret vote was not an essential element of Cicero's political culture.
In his ideal law code in *De legibus* (3.39), he recommends letting the
people vote with ballots, with the provision that these ballots be shown for
inspection to an eminent citizen. In Cicero's work, the concept of *sunkatathesis* occurs for the first time in the *Lucullus*, where he indicates that he

---

[19] Aetius Plac. 4.8.12 = *SVF* 2.72: Οἱ Στωικοὶ πᾶσαν αἴσθησιν εἶναι συγκατάθεσιν καὶ κατάληψιν.
Though Aetius, unlike Cicero, does not repeat αἴσθησιν, the meaning is exactly the same.

will translate it by *adsensio atque adprobatio*: *Acad.* 2.37: "Let us say a few words on the subject of 'assent *and* approval' [termed in Greek *sunkatathesis*]."

These two translations introduce an interesting shift in perspective.[20] Double translations were for Cicero a means not only to capture the greatest number of aspects of a Greek concept but also to express his perception of it. *Adsensio* did not mean the approbation that the voter gave to a proposition but that which the orator receives from his audience. *Adprobatio* also does not lack ambiguity. In Cicero's first rhetorical treatise, the *De inventione*, it means both "to approve" and "to demonstrate." But the most puzzling element is certainly the presence of *atque* ("and"), where one would have expected a *vel* ("or") giving the choice between alternative translations. The explanation of this doublet is in my opinion that *adsensio* expresses the idea of an approval, while *adprobatio* introduces something that is more than a nuance (i.e. the capacity, at least virtual, to give a demonstration of this agreement). A few paragraphs later, however, at 39, Cicero uses a new term, the neologism *adsensus*. The use of this word served not merely as a sign of Cicero's search for stylistic variation. As he progressed in the redaction of the *Lucullus*, he probably better realized that in fact *sunkatathesis* could have two meanings: the assent given to a particular proposition or the faculty of assenting itself. By using both *adsensus* and *adsensio*, he thus introduced a verbal distinction that in Greek was only expressed by the difference between the singular and the plural of the same name, *sunkatathesis*. At the same time, however, he did not always differentiate between *adsensio* and *adsensus*, as if he wanted to suggest the continuity between the faculty and its manifestations.

Now consider probability, a topic of special interest due to its scientific use nowadays. It was not a term coined by Cicero. It was used before him by the dramatist Afranius (c. 200 BCE) who spoke of a *probabilis voluntas*, "approvable will," which he seemed to praise. But this occurrence is the only one we know before Cicero's *De inventione*, where the word has a heavy presence. The rhetorical use of this notion is the background of its conversion into a philosophical concept. Its main features are defined at *De inventione* 1.46, where the *probabile* is said to have three aspects:

(1)   it can be based on frequency, as it appears in the example given by Cicero himself: "if she is his mother, she loves him";

---

[20] Glucker 1995: 118 evokes two "alternatives," but here they are rather complementary translations.

(2) it relies on ordinary beliefs, like the punishment of bad people in hell, or the atheism of philosophers;

(3) it can be defined by its phenomenological status, since it sometimes only appears to meet the two previous criteria.

The *probabile*, like the Aristotelian *endoxon*, could seem to be true without necessarily being so. In the *De inventione*, Cicero was mostly interested in the practical use of the *probabile*, but two other elements must be stressed. First he says that probability increases itself "both by its own dynamics and by reasoning" (*Inv. rhet.* 1.57). This assertion for the first time raises the problem of the articulation of and distinction between reason and another motivating autonomous faculty, which will recur later when Cicero develops the concept of will in his philosophical treatises. Secondly, in this first treatise of his youth, Cicero clearly stresses the link between probability and *disputatio in utramque partem* (i.e. antilogy, *Inv. rhet.* 2.48). He says that at least some of the *loci communes* (common topics) can be deduced from an antilogy.

Ten years after the *De inventione*, in the *De oratore* (1.63), he wrote: "In fact, that favorite assertion of Socrates, that every man was eloquent enough upon a subject that he knew, has in it some plausibility (*probabilius*) but no truth (*neque tamen verum*)." Actually, the Socratic idea that real eloquence was linked to knowledge had been taken up by the Stoics. Cicero does not reject it, but he deems it only probable, which means he was already interested in the difference between truth and probability within both his own rhetorical and philosophical traditions. In another rhetorical treatise, the *Partitiones oratoriae* (probably 46 BCE) where he clearly stressed his affiliation with the Academy, Cicero elaborated a sophisticated theory of the conditions of rhetorical probability, which confirms his permanent interest in the meaning of this concept (*Part. or.* 19).

When he decided to use *probabile* as a philosophical concept, in order to translate the *pithanon* ("persuasive") and *eulogon* ("reasonable") of both the Stoics and the Academics, he faced many difficulties, which are reflected in the way he introduces the term:[21]

> I take everything I decided to call "persuasive" (*probabilia*) or "truth-like" (*veri similia*) to be like this. But if you want to give them another name, I don't object in the slightest. It's enough for me that you understand properly what I'm saying, that you understand which things I am giving this name to: a wise person should be an investigator of nature, not a creator of terms . . . (trans. Brittain 2006)

---

[21] Augustine, *Contra academicos* 2.11.26, ascribed by Plasberg to *Academica*.

Here are the main problems created by the use of this term: First, inside the New Academy there was a difference between the concepts used by the two main masters of this school, the *eulogon* of Arcesilaus and the *pithanon* of Carneades. Both were concepts used by Stoics to suggest an imperfect rationality or a persuasive impression without a guarantee of truth. In a dialectical process, Arcesilaus and Carneades, each in his way, tried to demonstrate that they were the ultimate boundaries of human capacities.[22]

Second, neither *eulogon* nor *pithanon* suggested a statistical frequency. For the philosophers of the New Academy, they referred to logical deduction (*eulogon*) or to an impression of truth (*pithanon*). This was a notion that Cicero implicitly imported from his own rhetorical use of *probabile*. Though he never refers to a statistical meaning in the *Academica*, he makes the confusion possible by the use of this term.[23]

Third, Carneades had tried to create a hierarchy between persuasive representations, by defining degrees: "apparently true" representations, "persuasive and irreversible impressions" (i.e. those inserted in a chain of persuasive representations), and "persuasive, irreversible, and tested" (Sext. Emp. *Math.* 7.176). We find in Cicero some elements of this division, probably because he had been a disciple of the Academic philosopher Philo of Larissa, whom, strangely, he criticizes in the *Academica*. Moreover, due to his personal reading of Plato, he could not use the Neo-Academic terminology devoid of any ontological reference to truth. That may be one reason why he introduced the concept of *veri simile*[24] ("likeness to the truth"), for which we find no equivalent in our surviving Academic testimonies in Greek. It served as a bridge between Academic aporetism and a more dogmatic Platonism, but it also created a new problem which some centuries after would be stressed by Augustine in his *Contra academicos*: how to affirm a resemblance to something you claim not to know?[25]

It would be excessive to say that Cicero was the real inventor of probabilism, since he was trying to do his best to translate an Academic doctrine in which neither *eulogon* nor *pithanon* corresponded with the Latin *probabile*. In this case, however, because he did not create neologisms but used in his translation all of his experience as orator and theorist of eloquence, he introduced a new concept that was different from both the Academic ones and his own use of this term in other contexts.

---

[22] See Couissin 1983, and for a non-dialectical interpretation, Ioppolo 1986.

[23] This aspect was stressed for the first time by Burnyeat (unpublished).

[24] For Glucker 1995: 131, *probabile* translates *pithanon* and *veri simile* translates *eikos*, but Cicero's own creativity in translation must not be omitted.

[25] See Bouton-Touboulic (Chapter 16) in this volume.

Ethics: Romanization of Greek Words and Values

Especially in ethics, translation was also a way for Cicero to express a Roman vision of the world while introducing Greek concepts to his fellow Romans. While it is difficult to determine the extent to which this was a conscious process, in many cases it generated a translation conveying a multivalent meaning. Here we consider some examples of it: "the honorable" (*honestum*), love, and will.

The best-known example is perhaps Cicero's use of *honestum* to translate the Greek *kalon*, the word used especially in Hellenistic philosophy for expressing ethical perfection. In the Greek perspective, beauty was the external face of a virtuous interiority. Cicero was not actually the first to use *honestum* to render this idea, that is to say, he was not the first to remain inside social ethics rather than resorting to the linguistic expression of aesthetics. Once again, the poet Lucilius had preceded him. In his famous fragment about virtue, he expresses a conception quite close to Stoicism when he says, "For a human being, virtue means to know what is right, what is useful and honorable."[26]

Here *honestum* represents both social honor, at this time an essential value of the Roman society, and the implicit suggestion of a central dogma of Stoic ethics: nothing can be really useful if it is not ethically correct. No allusion to any kind of beauty occurs in this fragment. In contrast, *honestum* as an expression of ethical perfection is almost absent from Lucretius' poem. We find only the adjective in the context of the criticism of love, a passage in which everything suggests deception and fallacy (*De rerum natura* 4.1181). When the tearful lover is denied entry, he spends a lot of time crying at the door of the beloved. But if she at last admitted him, he would soon seek some honest pretext (*causas honestas*) to leave again. It is clear that Lucretius carefully avoided *honestum*, which certainly was for him a symbol of an erroneous ethics, based on the ignorance of pleasure, the only real principle of a right attitude. Cicero had been defining *honestas* as a key ethical word since his first philosophical work. In *De inventione* 1.43, in a professional context, he opposes it to *utilitas*, personal interest. But later, especially in *De officiis*, while presenting the Stoic doctrine, he insisted many times on the impossibility of disconnecting *utile* from *honestum*, as we can see in this passage: "Human beings

---

[26] In Lactant. *Div. inst.* 6.5.2 = fr. H 23 in Charpin 1991. On *honor* and *honestum*, see Jacotot 2013: 645–651 and passim.

pervert the elements of Nature (*fundamenta naturae*) when they separate interest (*utilitatem*) from ethics (*ab honestate*)" (*Off.* 3.101).

The link between *honestum* and *utile* was not only a Stoic tenet. It had deep roots in Cicero's own culture and beliefs. The great and wise man who, in the prologue of *De inventione* 1, brought humanity from a savage state to civilization is said to have taught them "everything that was useful and honorable." Further, the pairing "honorable-useful" occurs quite frequently in Cicero's political and judicial discourses before becoming a central concept in his presentation of Stoic ethics.

Translation was also a means to give a post-mortem life to ancient practices. Perhaps the most striking example is the translation of one of the main concepts of Stoic ethics, *oikeiōsis*. It is generally accepted that it was a Stoic innovation, though a minority of scholars still assert that it existed in Peripatetic doctrine.[27] In any case, at the time of Cicero the concept served as a general frame for the discussion between philosophical schools, as we can see in *De finibus*, where even the Epicurean Torquatus uses it. The concept of *oikeiōsis* was the exact opposite of the Platonic *fugē*, "flight." It meant that human beings had to look for the highest good, not by escaping the world, but by inserting themselves into the program scheduled for them by Nature. *Oikeiōsis*, from the Greek *oikos*, "house," means that at birth all living beings enter their specific nature as one enters his or her own house. At the beginning, like animals, human beings strive to remain alive. But after seven years, they adapt to the rational nature that is specific to gods and humankind. To translate this notion, Cicero could have used a neologism like *domesticatio*, which would have been a calque of *oikeiōsis*.[28] He preferred *conciliatio*, "conciliation," and *commendatio*, "recommendation," two words that belonged to the vocabulary of social and political relations of the world that he had known. For him, philosophical adaptation to nature was at a higher level, the kind of process he had experienced in his previous career.[29]

Another interesting shift appears in the expression of the dogma of *oikeiōsis*. Diogenes Laertius says that the first impulse of a living creature is *tērein* (i.e. to take care of itself), while Cicero adds a rather different concept, *diligit*, which expresses ideas of choice and of love.[30] Probably this latter idea was suggested to Cicero by Antiochus, who certainly

---

[27] Magnaldi 1991.

[28] On the concept of calque in the translation from Greek to Latin, see Nicolas 1996.

[29] See further Reydams-Schils (Chapter 12) in this volume.   [30] Diog. Laert. 7.85; Cic. *Fin.* 3.16.

preferred the concept of *philia* to the one coined by the Stoics (namely *oikeiōsis*). Actually Piso, who in *De finibus* 5.24 presents the ethical theories of Antiochus and of the Peripatetic Staseas of Naples, says that the first impulse of each living creature is to love itself. Thus, the idea of love for oneself as a creature's first impulse entered philosophy through a Roman gate. One century after Cicero, Aulus Gellius is even more insistent on this idea: he says that our natural principles are love and tenderness toward ourselves (*NA* 12.5.7).

It is rather common to read that Seneca or even Augustine were the inventors of our modern concept of the will. Actually, a great part of the job had already been done by Cicero. Here again his experience of human motivations from his work as a lawyer and a politician was very useful to him. In his day, *voluntas* was a very common word, one which had been often used by Plautus and Terence in their comedies. Especially in the *De invention*, Cicero mentioned will as an essential concept for describing human actions. But it was not easy to transform it into a philosophical term. In the Greek language there were plenty of words to express the autonomy of a human being. Cicero's solution was both elegant and efficient, since he decided to use only one word where he could have created many. Consider the following examples:

(1) *Acad.* 1.40: "the assent of our minds, which he wanted to depend on us and to be voluntary (*in nobis positam et voluntariam*)." In evoking the innovations introduced by Zeno, creator of the Stoic doctrine, Cicero uses the adjective "voluntary" to express the Stoic idea that our assent depends on us.

(2) In *Tusc.* 4.12, he uses *voluntas* to translate the Stoic *boulēsis*, a good passion (*eupatheia*), which could be found only in the sage. In this case, *voluntas* is an aspect of perfect reason.

(3) In *Fat.* 23, *voluntas* appears as the alternative solution to Epicurean atomism and to Stoic determinism. Coming from Cicero the Academic, the idea that *voluntas* is its own cause can be interpreted as an implicit reference to the Platonic idea of the self-motion of soul (*Phdr.* 245c–246a). This absolute autonomy of will, isolated both from the atomic swerves and from the universal network of causes, was a decisive contribution to our conception of will.[31]

---

[31] For Cicero's contribution to the development of the will, see Paulson forthcoming.

Physics of Individuality

We now turn to consider a philosophical term with an impact on the subsequent history of philosophy greater than any we have yet encountered: *individuus*.[32] Few people know that Cicero was the first to use the term *individuus*, of which we find no occurrence in any Latin text before him.[33] Actually Cicero began to use it in the *Lucullus*, late in his life. The term appears for the first time in *Lucullus* 55, which addresses the indivisible particles of Democritean physics. In this first use, Cicero gives no explanation of the meaning of the term: he says only that these particles are innumerable. This lack of explanation was certainly due to the fact that the etymology of the word *individuus* made it perfectly clear. *Atomus* appears at the end of the dialogue, also without any explanation, perhaps because it had been explained in his now-lost work the *Catullus*.[34] In any case, the adjective *individuus* is used, associated with *corpora*, in order to explain the Greek term *atomus* in *De finibus* 1.17. It is said that Democritus chose to call these little particles "atoms" – in Greek, the meaning is "impossible to cut" – because they are impossible to divide (*individua*). From this time, there was a kind of competition between *atomus* and *individuus* – one of the variations of which Cicero was fond. To give the precise statistics, *atomus* appears thirty-five times in his philosophical treatises, while the adjective, sometimes as a substantive, *individuus* appears only twenty-one times. *Individuus* is made still more evocative by the addition of other adjectives: "solid" (*Fin.* 1.18; *Nat. D.* 2.93) and "light and round" (*Tusc.* 1.42). One could have concluded that, after having hesitated, Cicero finally decided that he preferred *atomus*, without rejecting *individuus*. But if we except the *Timaeus*, he always used *individuus* in an Epicurean context, that is to say, when it was related to a precise physical context, without ever attempting a metaphorical use of it. In the *Timaeus*, however, things are quite different. *Individuus* is used to describe the indivisible matter from which divisible items are created (*Timaeus* 21, 25, 27). We are admittedly still far from our modern concept of the individual, but at least we see that the word had a kind of plasticity that allowed it to be detached from atomic theory.

---

[32] See Bourbon 2019. Another important word introduced by Cicero in Latin is *qualitas*, "quality." See Lévy 2008.

[33] Lucretius never used *atomus*. He preferred, obviously for poetical reasons, to use purely Latin terms (*corpora prima, corpuscula, primordia, semina rerum*, etc.).

[34] *Acad.* 2.125; cf. *Acad.* 1.6: *de corpusculorum* (*ita enim appellat atomos*) *concursione fortuita loqui*.

How did this word end up signifying an element of a set or a person in its singularity? It was a long process, in which the adjective first described certain qualities of a person. In the *Declamationes* of the Pseudo-Quintilian 5.3, we find the expression *individua pietas*, meaning a characteristic that could not be divided. More interesting perhaps, in *Troades* 401, Seneca says that death is individual, since it kills the body and does not spare the soul. He also gives another proof of the plasticity of the concept, by using it in a Stoic context when he speaks about things that are linked in the network of fate (*Dial.* 1.5.9). In *Ep.* 67.10, he uses *individuus* to suggest the solidarity of virtues, an idea of Socratic origin, which could evoke someone adorned with all the canonic qualities but without explicitly referring to his/her individuality. It is eventually in Roman legal language that *individuus* came to suggest more concretely a person. It was Cicero who started this process by using the two concepts, but he failed to establish an explicit relation between personality and individuality. For him, while *individuus* represented the ability of Nature to create indivisible elements, *persona* meant the plurality of aspects of a subject.[35] In his mind, the distance between the two concepts was huge, but he had the great merit of setting up the two poles whose association would later represent an essential moment in the constitution of the idea of subjectivity.

Conclusion

Cicero did much more than coin philosophical words in Latin. By rejecting categorically an opinion held by almost everybody at his time (i.e. that philosophy was the privilege of only one language, Greek), he opened the path that led to the Western conception of philosophy. His variations themselves, often a consequence of his search for greater precision, allowed his successors to feel freer in the use of Latin words and notions and in the creation of neologisms. It does not seem excessive to say that his decision to create a Latin philosophical language was also both a nationalistic endeavor and a matter of liberty and generosity.

Further Reading

Brittain 2001 is an essential book for the biography of Cicero as an Academic. A work by arguably the best specialist of bilingualism in Rome, Dubuisson 1992, embeds Cicero's philosophy within the larger

---

[35] See Lévy 2008.

context of a cultural and linguistic problem. MacKendrick 1989 provides an accurate presentation of Ciceronian philosophical works. Moreschini 1979 offers some interesting views on Cicero's translations by one of the best specialists of the history of Platonism. See also White 2015 on Cicero's methods as a translator. Reydams-Schils 1999 is essential for understanding how there was a partial mix of Platonic and Stoic themes in Hellenistic and Roman philosophy. For the issue of the translation of Greek into Latin by one of Cicero's contemporaries, Sedley 1998 is an important though controversial book that offers an exhaustive presentation of Lucretius' relation to Epicurus' *Peri phuseōs* and to the Presocratics.

CHAPTER 6

Cicero and Plato

Malcolm Schofield

Cicero was not a "Platonist."[1] He hardly ever described himself as a philosopher at all.[2] But Plato, the writer and thinker himself, was a presence of the greatest importance in Cicero's own writing and thinking. "No other individual philosopher," as A. A. Long has written, "is cited by Cicero as fully and frequently."[3] This chapter will not attempt to describe or assess Cicero's treatment of "Platonism" as a system. He inherited from his philosophical teachers – Philo and Antiochus – differing views of the overall stance from which Plato philosophized;[4] even in Antiochus' version of Academic history it was only subsequently that a "system" was articulated (*descriptio disciplinae*: *Acad.* 1.17) invoking his authority. Instead it will explore just what Plato himself meant to Cicero:[5] first in some of his letters of the period 54–49 BCE, then in the dialogues of 55–51, and finally in the theoretical writings of 46–44.

Letters

Cicero's engagement with Plato and his philosophizing is first evidenced not in his formal contributions to the literature of philosophy, but in his surviving letters. In letters he writes in 54 BCE, and then again in 49, as he reflects on his own political difficulties, he thinks of Plato deliberating in *his* letters (evidently assumed to be authentically Platonic) on how he ought to act. Thus in a long self-justificatory reply of December 54 to

---

Much of the material presented in this chapter was first published in Schofield 2017b.

[1] A contrary view has lately been revived by Altman 2016a.

[2] See Hine 2015: 14–19. Plutarch, however, says that he would often tell his friends that they should call him a philosopher, not an orator, oratory merely being his instrument (Plu. *Cic.* 32.5).

[3] Long 1995a: 44.

[4] Described by Lévy and Guillaumin 2018: 17, in a penetrating succinct overview, as "visions parfois contradictoires que Cicéron donne de Platon."

[5] The treatment of this topic by Boyancé 1970: 222–247 (first published in 1953) remains a rewarding read.

remonstration from his political ally Lentulus, he twice cites Plato (*nostrum Platonem*, "my Plato": *Fam.* 1.9.12; cf. 1.19.18). In the second passage he recalls Plato addressing in his fifth and seventh letters (*Ep.* 5.322a–b, 7.331b–d) the question of how one should act to try to put a society straight if it has gone off the rails. Cicero clearly thinks conventional Roman political wisdom incapable of addressing the state's current condition, but equally he considers it an issue that is now unavoidable.[6]

Hence the recourse to Plato: "I accept his authority in no uncertain terms." Plato had argued against the use of force, and for persuasion as the only alternative, but then, concluding that the Athenians were beyond persuasion, he simply opted out of public life altogether. Cicero does not take so low a view of the Romans, he says, and he is too much implicated in public affairs for abandonment of politics to be an option for him. So his own assessment of the wise course has to consist in seeing where the power lies (with Caesar, now the subject of warm tributes from Cicero, and with the whole "gang of three," constituted of Pompey, Caesar, and Crassus),[7] and not trying to fight it; in recognizing that they – not the Senate – are the leaders whose influence, like it or not, will and indeed ought to prevail; and in accepting that politics has to be a matter of adjusting to the times when things change and the sympathies of decent people with them.

If we fast-forward to the early months of 49 BCE, as Caesar and Pompey square up for civil war, we find Cicero commenting bitterly to Atticus in February of that year on how far short Pompey falls of the job description that the *De republica* had prescribed for the *moderator rei publicae*, or "calibrator of the commonwealth" (*Att.* 8.11.1–2; cf. *Rep.* 5.8) as we might say: a *princeps civitatis* (*Rep.* 1.25) at the helm of the state, equipped with the wisdom to understand the nature of the political change that is taking place and to guide the *res publica* through the perils ahead (*Rep.* 2.45). Back in December 54 and in the Lentulus letter, it sounded as though he might have entertained the hope that the "gang," with Caesar the chief driving force, would take adequate control of public affairs – and so (as the *De republica* puts it) do the work of calibrating. If so, the hope did not long survive. In early 49 Cicero thought that he himself might at least be able to act as peacemaker between the protagonists. He wanted to remain on good terms with both of them, and above all he wanted peace: "Even an unjust

---

[6] For discussion see Boyancé 1970: 248–255; McConnell 2014: 35–44.

[7] "More commonly now known by the spuriously formal title 'The First Triumvirate'": Beard 2015: 548 (cf. 218–219, 278–279).

peace," he writes near the end of January, "is more advantageous (*utilis*) than the most just wars with one's fellow citizens" (*Att.* 7.14.3; echoed in a letter to an old friend after the conflict: *Fam.* 6.6.5). (Here and elsewhere in his agonizings at this time, he articulates the choices before him in the terms of the Stoic ethics he will subsequently deploy in *De officiis*.)

But the prospect of any kind of rapprochement between the two warlords ebbs away, and Cicero is left with a decision, as he and Atticus see it, between staying put (at least until it becomes clearer how events may play out) or joining Pompey's entourage. This then mutates into a choice between staying in Italy, without necessarily committing to Caesar, or crossing the Adriatic to join the Pompeian forces. On February 17 he is still for remaining (*Att.* 8.2.4): leaving Italy he thinks advantageous neither for him nor for the *res publica* nor for his son and nephew, and moreover neither right nor honorable (*honestum*). He reminds himself that Socrates "never put a foot outside the gates" of Athens during the regime of the thirty tyrants.

A particularly low point is reached when in early March he receives a letter from Caesar, couched in friendly terms, which attempts to enlist his support just as Pompey is abandoning Italy. Cicero feels trapped. Books, letters, philosophical teaching, he tells Atticus in a letter of March 18, avail him nothing. However, Plato is clearly still very much with him – not Plato philosophizing, but Plato held effectively as a prisoner at the court of Dionysius II in Syracuse. He echoes Plato's words in the seventh letter, "gazing over the sea like the bird [i.e. the caged bird to which Cicero likens himself], longing to fly away" (*Att.* 9.10.2). In a further letter written five days later he refers again to Caesar's request, and quotes verbatim Plato's remark in the seventh letter, again with reference to Dionysius: "the requests of tyrants are mingled with compulsion, you know" (*Att.* 9.13.4). This is Cicero as *homo Platonicus* (as he was once described: *Coment. pet.* 46) in the direst and also most existential sense.[8]

Platonic Dialogues

In the five or six years before the outbreak of the actual hostilities of the Civil War in summer 49, Plato seems seldom to have been far from Cicero's thoughts, at any rate when such leisure (*otium*) as he could

---

[8] For fuller treatment of this and related material in Cicero's letters to Atticus of 49 BCE, see McConnell 2014: 62–114; cf. Schofield 2021: 197–206 and Aubert-Baillot (Chapter 3) in this volume.

contrive came his way, whether reflecting on his situation (as evidenced in the letters just reviewed) or devoting himself to the "gentler Muses" (as he refers to them in the Lentulus letter: *Fam.* 1.9.23) in the writing of dialogues. These first mature ventures into philosophical writing were conceived and constructed on a grand scale, indicating huge literary and philosophical ambition. The very idea of philosophy as a matter of dialogue, conversation, to which Cicero was evidently firmly wedded, is above all a Platonic inheritance. So also is the decision to stage these Ciceronian dialogues in carefully described locations, with no less carefully chosen casts of characters, assembled – certainly for the *De oratore* and *De republica* – at highly significant junctures in Roman history, comparable in this respect to Plato's choice (for example) of the indictment or trial of Socrates or the final days and hours of his life as similarly significant. Plato was clearly the main inspiration: *Platonis aemulus*, as Quintilian said of Cicero – "competing with Plato" (*Inst.* 10.1.120). This is obvious enough in the cases of the *De republica* (54–52) and *De legibus* (52–50), which explicitly advertise Plato's *Republic* and *Laws* as the precedent being followed (*Leg.* 1.15, 2.14). Something similar is true, if not immediately obviously so, of the *De oratore* (55 BCE).[9]

The key issues the *De oratore* debates – whether oratory needs broader knowledge than simply techniques of persuasion, how far it is a matter of experience and native talent and how far it is a sphere of expertise with rules that can be formalized – were subjects of theorizing that certainly have their seeds in Plato, although they were developed further in subsequent controversies, along with much of the detailed material associated with them that Cicero deploys. It is true that if we think of the *Gorgias* as Plato's primary contribution to the study of oratory, a Platonic precedent looks as though it might have been the last thing Cicero would have wanted to follow in composing his own dialogue on the subject. In fact he decided to take the *Phaedrus* as something of a model, a dialogue evidently one of his favorites in the Platonic corpus, and altogether friendlier to rhetoric and to its relationship with philosophy than the *Gorgias* (which is mentioned only rarely in the *De oratore*, and principally to represent its argument as self-refuting: if Plato's Socrates undermines

---

[9] In his letter to Lentulus, Cicero describes the *De oratore* as written in the "Aristotelian mode" (*Fam.* 1.9.23). Quite what he means by that in this context is a subject of scholarly debate, not helped by the loss of all Aristotle's exercises in the dialogue genre. I suppose that Cicero means to allude to his assigning the interlocutors lengthy sustained speeches presenting their opposing views (*De or.* 3.80), not the question-and-answer dialectic characteristic of the Platonic dialogue.

rhetoric, he does it precisely by employing superior rhetoric [*De or.* 1.47, 3.129]).

The report of the conversation occupying the three books of the dialogue is programmatically bookended by an emphatically explicit reminiscence of the physical setting of the *Phaedrus* (*De or.* 1.28–29), which inspires the Romans gathered to seat themselves for the discussion under a plane tree, and by the closing prediction of the young Hortensius' future eminence as an orator (*De or.* 3.230), echoing the similar prediction about Isocrates at the end of the *Phaedrus*. There are in *De oratore* many other allusions or possible allusions to passages in that and other Platonic dialogues. The suggestion that Antonius' anti-philosophical speech in book 1 does not represent his true opinion (*De or.* 1.263), which is explicitly confirmed by him subsequently after he has sketched a much more ambitiously drawn picture of the perfect orator (*De or.* 2.40), reminds commentators of Socrates' palinode in the *Phaedrus*. Cicero himself, in a letter already mentioned from around the beginning of July 54, explains the early exit from the dialogue of the augur and jurist Quintus Mucius Scaevola as modeled on the similarly early departure of Cephalus after the first few pages of the *Republic* (*Att.* 4.16.3).

When Cicero turned again to philosophical and theoretical writing in 46 BCE, just as in the late 50s so the first subject he addressed was oratory, initially in the dialogue *Brutus* (early that year), and subsequently after a number of shorter works in the *Orator* (later in that same year), composed in the form of an extended letter to Brutus. The *Brutus* is set in the garden of one of Cicero's houses. But more specifically, and of course highly symbolically, the participants discuss their topic – the nature and history of "true eloquence" – seated by a statue of Plato (*Brut.* 24). The *Orator* begins with a remarkable passage modeled on the ascent to Beauty in Diotima's speech in the *Symposium*, where Cicero develops the notion of a Platonic Form of the orator (*Orat.* 7–10). He continues by saying that he knows his recourse here to philosophy – ancient and rather obscure philosophy at that – will leave people astonished even if they do not object to it (*Orat.* 11). But then follows an avowal that he owes all he is as an orator to the Academy, and to philosophy: from Plato and other philosophers oratory draws "all its richness and what might be called its raw material (*silva*)" (*Orat.* 12).[10] Quintilian agreed that that was certainly true of Cicero: his hallmark was imitation of the Greeks – Demosthenes' power, Isocrates'

---

[10] Cf. *Acad.* 1.17; *Tusc.* 1.7. "Richness" (*ubertas*) is the quality Cicero had identified in Plato in the *Brutus* too (*Brut.* 120).

easiness on the ear, and Plato's abundance (*copia*: *Inst.* 10.1.108). If Plato had attempted oratory, Cicero himself will say in *De officiis* 1.4, the abundance and the weight (*gravitas*) he could have invested in it would have escaped all comparison. This is Plato as the paradigm for the grand style: rich and resourceful in its intellectual and linguistic resources, deeply impressive in its effect.

In contrast with his assessment of Plato as orator, Cicero's valuation of his standing as political philosopher, in the *Republic*, at any rate, is distinctly qualified. A celebrated remark in a letter to Atticus of June 60 about his contemporary the Stoic Cato conveys a key element. Commenting that for all his good intentions and integrity Cato sometimes does the *res publica* harm, Cicero complains that he gives his views in the Senate "as though he were in Plato's *Republic*, not Romulus' cesspool" (*Att.* 2.1.8). The idiosyncratic unworldliness of the political thinking of the *Republic*, contrasted with what Cicero represents as his own more realistic and historically based approach to the question of "the best constitution" for a *res publica* or a *civitas*, is a theme reiterated in *De republica*. It is adumbrated at the beginning of book 2 (*Rep.* 2.3), subsequently developed (*Rep.* 2.21–22), and appears again later in the same book in a discussion of the origins of tyranny (*Rep.* 2.51; conceivably in parts of book 2 now lost there were similar remarks). Nonetheless Cicero later states that in taking the Roman *res publica* as model, he will be applying the same principles as Plato to explain what separates public good and ill: what makes for a just and an unjust polity (*Rep.* 2.52). In other words, Plato was not wrong to suppose that using a model is the right way to do political philosophy.[11] In the *De officiis*, ten years or so later, he will urge the importance for those at the helm of the *res publica* to hold fast to two of Plato's principles (he has the *Republic* in mind): the insistence that they so focus on the good of the citizens as to forget their own interests, and secondly that they make sure that they look after "the whole body of the *res publica*," not sectional advantage to the detriment of everyone else (*Off.* 1.85; a reference to the quarreling crew of the *Republic*'s ship of state soon follows: *Off.* 1.87).

In the *De republica* we find Cicero exploiting material from Plato's *Republic* virtually from first word to last. Right at the beginning of the entire philosophical conversation of the dialogue Cicero has the participants recall with approval that in dealing with human affairs, the *res publica* included, Plato's Socrates couples such study with that of the mathematical sciences in Pythagorean style (*Rep.* 1.16). He is happy to

---

[11] See for discussion Powell 2013a: 51–57; Atkins 2013a: 56–61.

demonstrate that, difficult though it may be to do so, he can put into Latin a passage of Plato's richest prose. Near the end of book 1 he gives his translation of the account in book 8 of the *Republic* (which he clearly applauds) of the origins of radical democracy – sometimes a close rendering, sometimes freer – before switching finally to his own paraphrase of the subsequent Platonic treatment of the origins of tyranny (*Rep.* 1.65–68), which, however, he goes on to criticize in book 2. Later, as material for Philus' speech in book 3 against justice, he turns to Glaucon's account in the *Republic* of justice as a contract for mutual advantage (*Rep.* 3.23; the story of Gyges' ring in the same *Republic* passage would in due course be exploited in *De officiis* 3.38–39). The grand set piece with which *De republica* ends – the dream of Scipio – was apparently presented as a more credible literary device for conveying "the conjectures of wise people" than the play of Platonic fiction represented by the myth of Er that concludes the *Republic* (6.3). Here Cicero imitates, confident that he is also improving on the original. That said, homage to Plato resurfaces at the very end of the dream, where Cicero translates (without acknowledgment) one of his favorite passages in all the dialogues, the *Phaedrus*'s proof of the immortality of the soul (*Rep.* 6.27–28).

Of the *De legibus*, written as the sequel to the *De republica*, never put into circulation by Cicero himself, and indeed very likely never finished, James Zetzel rightly comments that it is in many respects his "most successful attempt at imitating the manner of a Platonic dialogue" – "a far more vivid and realistic conversation than those of *On the Orator* and *On the Commonwealth*."[12] In a letter to Quintus written in the autumn of 54 (*QFr.* 3.5.1–2), Cicero reports that a friend of his named Sallustius, following a reading of two books of the *De republica* (at that stage in draft), commented that if he himself were to be the main speaker on the subject (instead of a figure from the past he had never known – or rather a purely fictional Scipio), the treatment would be much more authoritative, particularly given Cicero's experience and high standing in Roman public life. Cicero writes there as though he will now redraft those two books of the *De republica* (presumably books 1 and 2) in line with the suggestion. Evidently he never did. But when it came to the sequel dialogue, *De legibus*, he did take the advice, and wrote himself into the conversation with the leading role, and took care to have the other characters – Quintus and Atticus – expatiate on his qualifications for philosophizing about law.

---

[12] Zetzel 1999: xxi.

Cicero is quite explicit in making the *Laws* his literary model for *De legibus*. Just as Plato (he apparently has no hesitation in identifying the Athenian Visitor as Plato, for whom, according to Atticus, Cicero has a special love, rating him above all others), discussed "the institutions of commonwealths and the best laws" (cf. Pl. *Leg.* 1.625a: "on both polity and laws," περί τε πολιτείας ... καὶ νόμων) with Cleinias and the Spartan Megillus among the cypress groves and forest paths of Cnossos, so Cicero with Atticus and Quintus will enquire into the same subjects among the poplars by the river running through his ancestral estate at Arpinum (Cic. *Leg.* 1.15; although here as in the preface to book 2, the studied echoes of the opening of the *Phaedrus*, describing Socrates' stroll with Phaedrus into the Attic countryside by the banks of the Ilissus are even stronger). Just as the *Laws* is throughout direct or scripted dialogue, not reported, so this is Cicero's unique exercise exclusively in this same form – without the authorial preface that introduces the *De oratore* and *De republica* (and indeed their several books), and would similarly introduce all the dialogues of the later sequence of 46–44; and with no authorial interventions introducing the participants.

Plato is his model, too, in writing first about the *res publica*, and then about its laws (*Leg.* 2.14). Whether that means he wrongly interprets the *Laws* of Plato as designing laws for the political system outlined in the *Republic* (as some interpreters suppose)[13] seems to me unclear but unlikely. When a bit later in book 2 (*Leg.* 2.23, recapitulating 1.20) he proposes for his part provision of laws which will be in harmony with the best form of *res publica* as expounded by Scipio in the *De republica* – that is, the constitution of republican Rome as it originally evolved – we need not suppose he thinks he will in that way be producing a close analogue of what Plato was attempting in the *Laws* relative to the *Republic*. What he takes the parallel with Plato to indicate in the first instance is in fact something else. The point he extracts from it is the advisability of following the Platonic precedent of a "double" presentation of laws, with what Plato called preludes or preambles prefacing the prescription constituted by the actual law itself. The intent – as with Plato – is to include in any piece of legislative activity an element of persuasion, conveyed by the preamble, not trying to do everything through the compulsion of force and the threat of force inherent in the law proper (*Leg.* 2.14). And in the immediate sequel Cicero will go on to write just such an introduction to the whole body of law on religious observance shortly to be presented

[13] So, for example, Zetzel 1999: 110 n. 18.

(*Leg.* 2.19–22), on which he will offer commentary and explanation throughout the rest of book 2. Expressly following Plato again, he calls this introduction a *prooemium* to law (*Leg.* 2.16).

It is not immediately apparent whether Cicero takes the Platonic agenda of "doubleness" in the business of legislation to be the natural consequence of associating a legislative project with a treatment of πολίτεια or *res publica*. A passage a little earlier in book 2 is suggestive in this regard, however. There Cicero says (*Leg.* 2.11):

> It is agreed, of course, that laws were invented for the safety of citizens, the security of states, and a life of calm and happiness for human beings: that those who first sanctioned statutes of this kind demonstrated to their peoples that they would write and propose rules which, once adopted and implemented, would enable them to live honorable and happy lives; and that the rules they composed and sanctioned on this basis were obviously the measures they called "laws."

Any prescriptions that inflict harm and injustice upon the relevant populations cannot accordingly be properly termed "laws," since those who devise them are actually doing the opposite of what they promised and undertook to do. That should make it clear that "in the understanding of the actual word *lex* there inheres the force and intent of choosing (*legendi*) what is just and true" (cf. *Leg.* 1.19).

Cicero's train of reasoning here makes clear three things in particular. The first is that he takes the whole point of legislation and a legal system to be promotion of the well-being of a political community and its members. If so, no wonder that Plato should decide to follow the *Republic* with the *Laws*, or that Cicero should take that example as his own model. The second thing to emerge is that law is only to count as true law if it is designed to achieve its ends by securing justice for the relevant community (i.e. provisions that will treat all constituencies within such a community fairly and equitably). Finally (and most closely pertinent to the rationale for prefacing laws with preludes or preambles), the legislator is seen not as an authority who simply promulgates a set of prescriptions, but as a political agent who is construed in his legislating to be promising the people that any laws enacted will promote the well-being of the community and its citizens, above all justice, and to be demonstrating to them that they can be relied upon to do exactly that. Persuasive preludes to particular legislative enterprises should therefore presumably be considered *inter alia* as one way in which a lawgiver can and should perform his duty to demonstrate to the population that the laws being enacted are properly conceived. The *De republica* had defined *res publica* as the *res* – the affairs, the business, the property – of the *populus* (*Rep.* 1.39). So if the *De legibus* continues in its own register the project of the *De republica*, the provision it makes for legislative preludes can be seen as a way in which lawgivers give practical recognition to the fundamental rights and interests of the *populus* in the *res publica* itself.

So far I have focused on Cicero's most general explicit statements of the way the *De legibus* will be modeled on Plato's *Laws*. But it is clear from various specific references to particular passages of the *Laws* in his own dialogue that Cicero had read relevant parts of the work pretty closely in preparing himself for its authorship. In book 2 he translates a passage on dedications of offerings to the gods from book 12 of the *Laws* in support of the law he proposes forbidding the consecration of land (*Leg.* 2.45), probably to enhance the authority of a provision that flew in the face of Roman tradition. Subsequently he gives a close paraphrase of another passage on tombs from a bit later in book 12 (*Leg.* 2.67–68). On his prohibition of gifts to the gods by the impious and wicked, he refers (*Leg.* 2.41) to a passage in book 4 of the *Laws* much quoted in later antiquity (Pl. *Leg.* 4.716c–717a).

Other echoes of the *Laws* may be suspected. When in book 1 Cicero announces that he is going to take as a first principle the doctrine he associates with the Old Academy, the Aristotelians, and the Stoics that nothing is to count as good – or at least as a major good – except what is to be valued in its own right, he rules out of court the Epicureans' rival view about pleasure "even if they speak the truth" (*Leg.* 1.37–39). We may be reminded of the version of the Noble Lie in book 2 of the *Laws*, where after taking the line that it is the life of justice that is most pleasurable, the Athenian Stranger suggests that even if that were not true, the legislator would find it a beneficial and effective fiction in persuading people to act justly (Pl. *Leg.* 2.663c–e). More generally, Julia Annas has argued recently that in the proposal in book 2 that the object of legislation is agreed to be the promotion of the virtue and happiness of the citizens, and in the development of the argument in book 1 to make that idea its eventual focus, Cicero certainly makes the same basic claim about the laws of the best state as Plato develops in the *Laws*.[14]

Neither the *De republica* nor the *De legibus* lacks a significant Stoic dimension. Early on in book 1 of the *De republica*, for example, we get the following exchange between Laelius (who has little patience with

[14] See Annas 2013, 2017, ch. 7.

theoretical enquiry) and Philus, another of those gathered for the discussion (*Rep.* 1.19):

> LAELIUS: So we have got to the bottom of questions that concern our homes and the republic, if the enquiry is to be about how affairs are in the heaven?
>   PHILUS: Don't you think it relevant to our homes to know how affairs are at home and what is happening there? Our home is not the one bounded by our house walls, but this entire universe, which the gods have given us as a home and a country to be shared with them.

Philus' response reflects the Stoic doctrine of the cosmic city. In his exposition of Stoic theology in the *De natura deorum*, Cicero's Stoic speaker, Balbus, explains what it is above all that the Stoics take gods and men to share: "They alone live according to justice (*ius*) and law (*lex*) by the use of reason."

In book 1 of the *De legibus* (see also Laelius' speech in *Rep.* 3.33 = 3.27 Powell), Cicero appropriates these ideas on his own account to specify what he takes to be "the source of justice itself." He sets out some Stoic-style syllogistic reasoning for the inference that to share in rationality in such a way is to form a citizen community (*Leg.* 1.23):

> Since nothing is better than reason, and this exists in both man and god, man's primary association with god is in reason. But those who have reason in common also have right reason in common. Since that is law, we humans must also be reckoned to be associated with the gods in law. But further, those who have law in common have justice in common. But those who have these things in common must be held to belong to the same citizen body (*civitas*).

And as Cicero then goes on to state, in exercising right reason, humans are obedient to the mind that is responsible for the celestial order of the universe. So the universe itself is the city that houses this community. It is the only true political community (i.e. the worldwide community of the properly rational). This was what the great Greek Stoic Chrysippus had maintained.[15]

It has often been thought that Cicero was just muddled in thinking that he could marry the Stoic idea of law with a political philosophy focused not on the cosmic city, but on the kind of *res publica* he envisages in both the *De republica* and *De legibus*.[16] He betrays no sign of any discomfort on

---

[15] See further Schofield 1999: 64–74.
[16] See, for example, Zetzel 1999: xxiii; Powell 2001: 34; Dyck 2004: 114–115, 410–411. Against that view, see Annas 2013: 219–222, to which the interpretation proposed here is much indebted.

this account. The Stoic theory of law may well have looked to him (and indeed to the Stoics themselves) like a more developed version of the notion of law in Plato's own *Laws*. And in effect he exploits only those elements of the theory that will prove useful to his purposes. The key elements for him are the idea that true law is in essence "the reason and mind of a wise being, as applied to prescription and prohibition" (*Leg.* 2.8; cf. 2.11), and the claim that the existence and force of such reason is rooted in the nature of things in a divinely ordered universe. Someone who thinks of natural law in this way is conceptualizing it as the rationality and ethical soundness inherent in any specific prescription or prohibition that a person whose mind is properly guided by reason will articulate – notably in the context of legislative or judicial activity within a particular political community.[17]

Plato in the Later Theoretical Writings

Cicero the Academic skeptic has so far made no appearance in this chapter.[18] There has been some debate in recent decades over whether or not he would actually have so identified himself at the period of his life with which we have so far been preoccupied – that is, the latter years of the 50s BCE, immediately prior to the outbreak of the Civil War. To my mind, an intervention Cicero as author has Atticus make in the conversation of book 1, immediately before what I have earlier called the Noble Lie passage, can scarcely be interpreted otherwise than as implying that Cicero ordinarily professes – and has probably long professed – allegiance to Academic skepticism. Cicero has indicated that the next section of the discussion will be included to meet the norms of scholastic Stoic methodology. Atticus exclaims (*Leg.* 1.36):

> I take it your own freedom (*libertas*) as to how to discuss things has gone missing – or else you are the sort of person not to follow your own judgment (*iudicium*) in a debate, but to submit to the authority (*auctoritas*) of others.

This is precisely the vocabulary Cicero will resort to when characterizing Academic skepticism in the philosophical writings of the later sequence of 46–44, when his own Academic stance is not in doubt.[19]

---

[17] See Atkins 2013a for fuller discussion of the presence of Plato in the *De republica* and *De legibus*.
[18] On the character of Cicero's skepticism, see Reinhardt (Chapter 7) in this volume.
[19] See Görler 1995: 103. For more on the continuity of Cicero's Academic skepticism, see Reinhardt (Chapter 7) in this volume.

Cicero's reply to Atticus stresses the requirements of a project in practical political philosophy. Here, he implies, a method and a stance need to be adopted to suit the purpose in hand, without thereby entailing surrender of a basic Academic allegiance. And Academics (as he will stress in the later sequence of philosophical writings) are not debarred from entertaining opinions by their inability to find conclusive proof of any proposition or its contradictory, provided that any such opinion is not asserted as though it were certain truth. In the later cycle of dialogues, however, the Academic strain is dominant, as it certainly is not in the earlier group. Now the very form of the dialogue shifts into the formal Academic mode of systematic presentation of opposed positions (*argumentum in utramque partem*).[20] There has, I think, been little discussion of a consequential question, which is surely suggested by our review of the prominence of Plato and devotion to Plato in the letters and dialogues of the 50s: what has now become of Cicero's deep preoccupation with Plato as master literary craftsman, as thinker on oratory and politics, even as exemplar with whom he is tempted to identify personally in times of political and personal crisis?

Cicero continues to refer to Plato as the supreme philosopher (e.g. *Fin.* 5.7; *Tusc.* 1.22). Throughout the later philosophical writings – from epistemology (e.g. *Acad.* 2.142) to ethics (e.g. *Tusc.* 5.34) and politics (e.g. *Off.* 1.85) – he is liable to recall with approval some key passage or other of Plato, whether in passing or of more crucial importance for his argument.[21] In some works, Plato's views become a main focus (as in book 1 of the *Tusculan Disputations*, where the fate of the soul after death is a key issue), or are very much grist to Cicero's mill (as in book 1 of the *De officiis*). He made translations in this period of the *Protagoras* (now lost) and of a substantial section of the *Timaeus* (which does survive, and whose purpose has recently been discussed and enticingly conjectured by David Sedley).[22] But Plato and his writings have disappeared almost completely from the letters of this period. And the arguments in the *pro* and *contra* style Cicero constructs in the dialogues he writes now for the most part present the reader with more recent systems of thought: Stoic, Epicurean, or Aristotelian in one version or another, whether representing the views of

[20] See Schofield 2008.
[21] See Long 1995a: 43–46, with further comments in Bénatouïl 2016: 217–220, and especially his remark at 218 n. 59 suggesting that "there is a common, albeit very discreet, Platonic thread in Cicero's three interventions as a character in the *De finibus*, namely book 2, book 4, and the end of book 5."
[22] Sedley 2013; see also Lévy (Chapter 5) in this volume.

Antiochus or of some other Peripatetic source or tradition. The intensity of the engagement with Plato, his philosophizing, his literary enterprise, his personal dilemmas, so characteristic of the earlier sequence, is apparently a thing of the past.[23] We recall his half apologetic reference in the *Orator*, near the beginning of this later sequence of theoretical writings, to Platonism as an "ancient and rather obscure" philosophy (11).

The 40s constituted a very different environment for philosophical composition. In the 50s, when Cicero wrote philosophy, his focus was on oratory and politics: on the public sphere, in which he still felt himself fully involved, and as his letters and prefaces at the time constantly emphasize, able to snatch few spare moments for his literary efforts. The richness in all its dimensions of the Platonic dialogue was the model to which he gravitated in the *De oratore* and *De republica*; and Plato's idealism offered a way of thinking about the issues confronting the conduct of public life that he wanted to address in those dialogues (and those he was forced in life to address), which he could use to help define his own approach. Imitating the *Laws* gave him something else: a broad framework for pursuing his own ideas for a legislative program in which he could debate *inter alia* salient contemporary issues such as the basis for the divinatory practices central to Rome's conduct of public business (*Leg.* 2.30–33) or the proper role of the tribunate (*Leg.* 3.19–26). But in the mid-40s any significant role for Cicero in public life appeared to have become impossible, as he would regret in his prefaces from time to time (e.g. *Brut.* 7–9; *Nat. D.* 1.7) and frequently in his correspondence. In philosophy he turned mostly to other topics, and to a new encyclopedic agenda needing presentation in a different style.

The most striking exceptions to the turn away from oratory and politics were the *Brutus* and the *Orator*, at the beginning of the new series, and the lost *De gloria* and the *De officiis*, which make a sort of final coda to it, composed when public life was once more a sphere with which Cicero felt he could engage, first in thought and then in action, following liberation from what he saw as Caesar's tyranny. In the *Brutus* and the *Orator*, Plato remains a significant presence, with Platonic metaphysical idealism more wholeheartedly embraced in the *Orator*'s delineation of the "best orator" (7–10) than it ever was in the writings of the 50s, as Ingo Gildenhard has brought out well.[24] However, the preface to the historical survey of oratory

---

[23] So Boyancé 1970: 233.

[24] Gildenhard 2013a, where he also discusses a similar strain in the opening pages of the *De officiis* (1.13–15).

in the *Brutus* closes with what is in effect an elaborate epitaph on the death of significant political oratory (6–9); and the *Orator*, to quote another recent discussion, "largely abandons the grand political and cultural ambitions for the orator" of the *De oratore*, and "takes a distinct turn towards the more technical issues of literary aesthetics."[25] Platonic idealism, in short, has here become a more attractive if distant vision – more attractive because there is now little scope for viable practical alternatives.

Further Reading

Useful introductions to the main works of Cicero discussed in this chapter are provided in Mankin 2011 (for the *De oratore*) and in Zetzel 1999 (2nd ed. 2017; for the *De republica* and *De legibus*; see also Zetzel 1995). The general study of Plato's place in Cicero's thinking and writing by Boyancé 1970: 222–247 (first published in 1953) retains its value; Long 1995a supplies a more recent treatment. On the letters of 54–49 BCE, see McConnell 2014: 33–114. For discussion of reflections of Plato's *Republic* in the *De republica*, see Powell 2013a, and of his *Laws* in the *De legibus*, Annas 2013. Atkins 2013a is a stimulating more general study of such echoes in both these Ciceronian dialogues. Altman 2016a offers a highly speculative general treatment of "Platonism" in the compositions of 46–44 BCE; remarks on Platonic moments in them are made in a more qualified register by Gildenhard 2013a; Bénatouil 2016; Lévy and Guillaumin 2018.

---

[25] Dugan 2013: 38.

CHAPTER 7

Cicero's Academic Skepticism

Tobias Reinhardt

Whose Academic skepticism? There is Cicero the man (consul 63 BCE), whose beliefs and attitudes we can try to reconstruct and infer, while acknowledging that they are ultimately as irretrievable as the beliefs and attitudes of any "real" individual, alive or dead (this is Cicero[1]). Cicero[1] gave the character Piso a long Antiochian speech in *De finibus* 5, but did not juxtapose it with the kind of detailed reply the Epicurean view receives in *De finibus* 2 or the Stoic view in *De finibus* 4. Then there is, one level up, Cicero[2], the author whose overall attitude we may want to describe (e.g. when we look at dialogues like the *De finibus* or *Academica* and ask what stance of the author emerges from the work as a whole). Cicero[2] may well be different from Cicero[1]; consider, for example, that the latter may have *wanted* to be an Academic skeptic but failed, whereas the former may emerge through the dialogues as a successful or consistent Academic skeptic. Or else Cicero[2] may have been deliberately designed to make the reader think that Cicero[1] may have held certain views which he did not want to map on those which can be hypothesized for Cicero[2]. The next level up is the speaker who features in the introductory frames of Cicero's dialogues and who is presented as explaining and justifying what he is doing and why in writing philosophy in Latin, or in pursuing philosophy at all when "men like him" are not supposed to indulge in meaningless introspection; we shall call him Cicero[3]. Finally, there is the character called Cicero (Cicero[4]), who features as an interlocutor in some dialogues, for instance the two editions of the *Academica* of which we have parts (*Lucullus* and *Academica posteriora*). Cicero[3] and Cicero[4] cannot simply be equated: for instance, in the *Lucullus* Cicero[3] speaks at the time the dialogue was written, whereas Cicero[4] speaks at the time the conversation is assumed to have taken place, about sixteen years earlier. Cicero[3] presents himself as an author of philosophical works, while Cicero[4] is warned by other interlocutors over the peril he is in for dealing with Catiline as consul in 63 BCE.[1]

It is desirable to keep these four Ciceros distinct, for reasons which will hopefully become apparent as we go along, for their versions of Academic skepticism should not just be assumed to be equivalent. Moreover, there is at least one further version of Academic skepticism to be found, that of the character Lucullus in the *Lucullus*. He delivers a speech against the Academic position, and in the process of attacking it, arguably fashions an additional position, not because he can clearly be shown to distort the Academic position to make his refutation more easily achievable, but because he delivers a speech intended to refute the cases made by two different Academic speakers of slightly different persuasion in the lost first book of the first edition of the *Academica*, the *Catulus*. These two speakers were Catulus the younger and Cicero (an instance of Cicero[4], that is, who also delivers the response to Lucullus in *Acad.* 2.64–147). Finally, in the *De natura deorum* we encounter another skeptical character, Cotta, who also features in the *De oratore*, although there he is not identified as an Academic and is given nothing to do that would reveal him as one. Cotta is a creation of Cicero[1] and in that sense further evidence for Cicero's Academic skepticism.

With these qualifications in mind, we can then ask what the nature of Cicero's Academic skepticism is. Is it to be characterized as radical or mitigated skepticism (a subject which has received considerable attention)? More specifically, is it to be characterized as something *we* would call mitigated skepticism, or is to be so characterized given distinctions between different types of skepticism which are drawn in the Ciceronian texts themselves? Is there a development over time, or an adaptation to particular contexts like the expository or dramatic needs of particular works? In order to address the last question, we shall discuss the evidence in roughly chronological order.

It will also be worthwhile to investigate to what extent skeptical positions that we find in Cicero's works are distinct from those of others, for example, his philosophical teacher Philo of Larissa, either because Cicero failed to follow the latter in adopting the position he held when Cicero sat at his feet, or because his skepticism ended up being different from any position Philo ever took, due, for instance, to Cicero's being Roman or writing in Latin, to name but two reasons that have been entertained.

---

[1] The concerns of Brittain and Osorio (Chapter 2) in this volume overlap with the present chapter.

Apart from Philo, who was head of the Academy until his death in 84/3 BCE, a number of other figures will feature in this chapter, and it may be useful to introduce them briefly. Zeno of Citium was head of the Stoa in the first half of the third century BCE and devised an empiricist theory of knowledge which was attacked by Arcesilaus, then head of the Academy. Under Arcesilaus, who appears to have invoked Socrates as a model, the Academy had turned skeptical and had shifted from formulating positive doctrines to scrutinizing the doctrines of other, dogmatic schools, notably the Stoa's. The debate about the Stoic theory of knowledge continued until the early first century BCE (as evidenced by Cicero) and reached its high point under another skeptical head of the Academy, Carneades, around the middle of the second century BCE. Carneades did not write any books, and his arguments gave rise to different interpretations, the two most prominent of which are usually referred to as "radical skepticism," associated with Carneades' pupil Clitomachus, and "mitigated skepticism."[2] While Philo was head, one of his pupils, Antiochus of Ascalon, broke with skepticism and developed a form of dogmatism that was informed by the prevailing dogmatic views of the time, notably Stoic epistemology, but tried to claim these doctrines for a broader Academic tradition. Antiochus became Cicero[1]'s second philosophical teacher a few years after Philo.

The Evidence from the *De Inventione*

The earliest text in the Ciceronian corpus in which the subject of skepticism features is the preface of the second book of the *De inventione*. This treatise is likely to be Cicero's first extant work, dating from the mid-80s BCE,[3] and unlike later compositions, including on the subject of rhetorical theory, it is comparatively unoriginal (which makes it invaluable in its own way, as evidence for Hellenistic rhetorical theory). The only sections in it which have the appearance of independent compositions (albeit informed by a number of sources) are the prefaces of books 1 and 2. The sense of enthusiasm projected by these prefaces, when set against the sobriety and derivativeness of the material in the body of both books of the *De inventione*, is apt to move the reader to believe that in the former Cicero[1] (or at least Cicero[2]) speaks to us through Cicero[3] about some of his most profound personal commitments at the time, but this may be the effect of a rhetorical ploy. The proem of *De inventione* 2 begins with a

---

[2] See Achard 1994: 5–10; Schwameis 2014: 169–181.   [3] See n. 2 above.

famous story about the artist Zeuxis, who selected several beautiful women as partial models in order to create a representation of the perfect woman, the mythical Helen. This sets up the idea in paragraph 4 that Cicero selected, by exercising judgment, the best elements from earlier treatises, while rejecting an approach which would have had him follow a single treatise. One cannot but think of remarks in the *Academica* which pit the judgment that Academics exercise (and foster in their pupils) against the blind following of a randomly selected authority practiced by the dogmatists (*Acad.* 2.8–9). In paragraphs 6–8, Cicero then characterizes the tradition on which he draws, which has Aristotle and Isocrates as its fountainheads. In paragraph 9 he states that he hopes to have chosen individual precepts well, but if he has made a mistake (perhaps omitting something important, or selecting the wrong thing), he will gladly change his mind. Then he states (2.9–10):

> For not understanding too little, but persisting stupidly and continuously in what is inadequately understood is disgraceful, because the first is attributed to the weakness common to all humanity, while the latter is attributed to everyone's very own fault. Therefore we shall, without any affirmation (*sine ulla affirmatione*), continuously enquire and make each statement with a degree of hesitation, in order to avoid the following outcome: while we achieve the small point of having written a reasonably useful book, we miss the most important one, not to give assent blindly and arrogantly to anything (*ut ne cui rei temere atque arroganter assenserimus*). This principle we shall pursue now and in our whole life diligently, as far as we are able to.

Cicero's stance is here characterized by universal suspension of judgment, not by a rejection of rash assent (which would leave scope for assent that was not rash); on these grounds, one would call him a radical skeptic, not a mitigated skeptic.[4] And yet Cicero feels able to put forward rhetorical precepts, not as injunctions he regards as unqualifiedly true, but as ones which he endorses with a proviso. This suggests that he thinks there is a mode (or modes) of endorsement available to him which falls short of assent (i.e. of regarding something as true). Moreover, the context here

---

[4] By "radical skeptic" I mean someone who suspends judgment universally and who aspires to not assent to (i.e. accept as true) any view or impression, including in situations where he follows a view or impression without thereby expressing an "opinion" of his own. A "mitigated skeptic" is someone who is ready to give qualified assent, which means assent given with the proviso that one might be wrong. The "mitigated skeptic" is sometimes called a "dogmatic skeptic" in the secondary literature (e.g. Frede 1987), because he will accept as true (sc. under proviso), for instance, the claim that nothing can be known. I believe that in Cicero the difference between these two versions of Academic skepticism is confined to the attitude regarding assent; no particular argumentative practices or epistemic attitudes accrete around either radical or mitigated skepticism.

does not suggest that Cicero is speaking *ad hominem* and setting out an alternative which an opponent should find as compelling as his own avowedly held one, given his own assumptions. Rather, Cicero sets out his stance on his own terms and is speaking non-dialectically. Note also that Cicero claims to conduct his whole life, and not only, say, the composition of rhetorical treatises, along the lines he has set out.

Thus we derive from the *De inventione* a starting point against which we can judge later pronouncements in other works – that Cicero[1] chose to cast Cicero[3] as a radical skeptic in the 80s BCE.

From the 80s BCE to the 50s

From the 80s BCE down to the mid-50s, Cicero pursued his career as an advocate and politician. Only letters and speeches are extant for this period. While the letters do make frequent reference to philosophical subjects, they do not contain any clear statements on Cicero's philosophical stance comparable to *De inventione* 2.9.[5] We do find numerous instances of Cicero rehearsing, by speaking on either side (*in utramque partem*), a difficult political problem on which he must take a view, clearly in the hope that this will help him opt for the right course of action.[6] In a letter to his friend Atticus (2.3.3), written in late 60 BCE, Cicero calls arguing *in utramque partem* on Caesar's first agrarian reform bill "speaking on either side in the Socratic manner" (in Greek, not by coincidence), and says that he will state his preferred position at the end, "as those men used to do" (*ut illi solebant*) – "those men" surely being Academics, on the most plausible reading.[7]

The speeches rarely mention philosophy positively, since a Roman jury and larger audience would have resisted an orator who cast himself as an intellectual.[8] The dialogues written in the mid-50s – *De oratore*, *De republica*, and *De legibus* (the latter not published at the time) – are indebted to Platonic models in terms of their format.[9] This is interpreted by some as evidence that Cicero was during that phase of his life a follower

---

[5] The letters and speeches were of course written by Cicero[1]. On our classification, the speaker of the letters is Cicero[3], who allows us to reconstruct the intentions of Cicero[2]. (Some readers would no doubt be inclined to equate the intentions of Cicero[1] and Cicero[2].) We are hesitant to read the speeches in terms of the fourfold scheme.

[6] See Aubert-Baillot 2014, 2018, and in this volume (Chapter 3).

[7] See McConnell 2014: passim, but esp. 8 n. 19, 51–52 on *Letters to Atticus* 2.3.3, and ch. 4.

[8] See Steel (Chapter 4) in this volume.   [9] See Schofield (Chapter 6) in this volume.

of Antiochus of Ascalon,[10] his second major philosophical teacher, whom
he encountered after Philo around 79 BCE, but programmatic passages that
might seem to support this reading have been shown to offer no actual
support (*Acad.* 1.13; *Nat. D.* 1.6).[11] Additionally, the three works
contain enough gestures to a skeptical stance as well as suitable formal
features to make it preferable to view them as exploring vaguely Platonic
themes in a Platonizing format from a skeptical standpoint. In *De oratore*
3.145 Cotta says in reply to Crassus' final contribution to the conversation
that he was now won over by the Academy; nothing Crassus said would
associate him with Antiochus' Old Academy in particular, and Cotta
features as a proponent of skepticism ten years later in the *De natura
deorum.* In *De republica* 3.8 (= 3.7 Powell), Philus assumes that enquiry on
either side is a format familiar to interlocutors and audience alike, and uses
it to enquire into justice.[12] In *De legibus* 1.36, Atticus alludes to Cicero's
freedom to form his own view guided by reason and his avowed lack of
dependence on authority (a theme we first encountered in the preface to
De inventione 2).[13]

The Works of the 40s BCE

In the 40s, after Caesar's victory over Pompey the Great in the Roman civil
war and during Caesar's dictatorship that followed it, Cicero returned to
philosophical writing and produced a substantial number of works in
quick succession. The first of these was the dialogue *Hortensius*, conceived
and probably begun in the second half of 46. It has the same ensemble of
speakers and (roughly) dramatic date as the first edition of the *Academica*,
which consisted of the *Catulus* (lost) and the *Lucullus* (extant). The three
dialogues thus formed a triptych, whether or not they were first so
conceived; they were in any event written in succession. What is relevant
to our purposes is that in the *Hortensius*, in which the eponymous
character is converted to philosophy after other areas of expertise to which
he might equally devote his spare time are found to have a weaker claim
(art, poetry, history), the character Cicero (= Cicero[4]; no Cicero[3]

---

[10] On Antiochus see Glucker 1978 and the articles collected in Sedley 2012.
[11] See Görler 1995, refuting Hirzel 1883: 488–491; Glucker 1988; Steinmetz 1989.
[12] On the fact that the *De republica* does not relinquish Philus' or the Academic perspective after
Philus' speech, see also Lévy 1992a: 506; Atkins 2013a: 37–43.
[13] The *De legibus* has no frame, and the Cicero character in it should be seen as a conflation of Cicero[3]
and Cicero[4].

statements are preserved among the fragments of *Hort.*)[14] wins the protreptic competition for philosophy generally and makes statements that dovetail with *De Inventione* 2.9, as well as (we can anticipate) with Cicero[3] and Cicero[4] statements in the *Academica*. Thus Augustine has himself say in *Contra academicos* 3.14.31:

> Cicero loudly declares that, while he himself may be a great holder of opinions (*magnus opinator*), he is enquiring about the sage [cf. *Acad.* 2.66]. If you young people do not know this work yet, you have certainly read in the *Hortensius*: "If there is nothing certain and holding opinions is not what the sage does, the sage will never approve anything."[15]

Note the manner in which a programmatic statement made by Cicero[4] in his speech in *Academica posteriora* 4 (reproducing *Acad.* 2.66) is linked to a statement of the character Cicero in the *Hortensius*. The latter was committed to universal suspension of judgment.[16]

The *Academica* is cited in later dialogues as a foundational work, as the place where Cicero explains his philosophical position. The first edition (i.e. *Lucullus* and *Catulus*), has a frame (on the evidence of the former), offering Cicero[3] statements on the subject, as well as Cicero[4] statements; in addition, it features another Academic speaker, Catulus the younger, who adopts a different position from Cicero. In the final edition of the *Academica* in four books, of which we have perhaps half of the first book (*Acad. post.*), in all likelihood drawing on the first part of the *Catulus*, there is no frame, and the Cicero character (Cicero[4]) assumes features confined to Cicero[3] in the *Lucullus*, notably the property of being an author who reflects on the practice of writing philosophy in Latin. Moreover, the material presented by Catulus in the *Catulus* was introduced by Cicero[4], which must mean that he introduced a position which was somewhat different from his own in one part of the text (i.e. the lost part of *Acad. post.*) and promoted the one his character adopts in the *Lucullus* (and elsewhere, or so we believe).

In the preface of the *Lucullus* there are comments by Cicero[3] on the nature of his stance, which we can examine for consistency with those found in earlier works. Having dismissed criticism on account of his portrayal of distinguished Romans as engaging in philosophy or as having more expertise in it than they could conceivably have had in real life,

---

[14] One would assume the *Hortensius* to have had a preface like the *Lucullus*.
[15] See Bouton-Touboulic (Chapter 16) in this volume.
[16] Cf. also *C. acad.* 1.3.7, lines 15–27 (in the edition of Green 1970), with Schlapbach 2003: 95–97 for the probable ascription to *Hort.*

Cicero responds to those who criticize him for adopting an Academic stance in particular (*Acad.* 2.7–8). In doing so, he characterizes it, in a manner that is most plausibly read as non-dialectical, even though it involves a contrast with the dogmatist view; what is more, while Cicero appears to speak generally, the preface of the *Lucullus* presupposes the *Catulus*, from which it must have emerged that, while Academics are ready to scrutinize anyone's knowledge claims as well as the theory underpinning them, it is the Stoic epistemological theory as promoted by Antiochus that is identified in *Academica* as the main target of the Academic speakers. Cicero contrasts those *qui se scire arbitrantur*, which should be taken to mean "those who think they have knowledge of certain things" (rather than "those who have the exalted disposition of knowledge," namely that with which one would credit a sage), with himself or people like him, "who are in possession of many plausible impressions, which we can follow easily, but which we cannot affirm" (*nos probabilia multa habemus, quae sequi facile, affirmare vix possumus*). Just before this (*Acad.* 2.7) he has stated that in his discussions – deliberately ambiguous between real-life discussions as depicted in the dialogues and the discussions in the dialogues *qua* artistic creations – he has but one goal, to extract, by presenting arguments on either side and by listening to them, what is either true or comes as close as possible to it.

As in *De inventione* 2.9, Cicero's position is characterized by a commitment to suspension of judgment. He is looking for the truth about philosophical questions, as the context makes clear, and he deploys the technique of argument on either side to reach truth or, failing that, to get close to it. While he hopes to find the truth with this method, he is prepared to settle for what comes as close as possible to it. He does not believe he has knowledge, in general and – or so the context suggests – as the Stoics understand it, and this view is quite likely to stem from his qualified endorsement of the so-called core argument.[17] To be sure, some endorsement of the argument is required, or else it would not leave Cicero with a view in a non-dialectical context. But the endorsement does not translate into a belief as conceived by the Stoic framework, since a belief so

---

[17] The "core argument," a term coined by Brittain 2001, argues toward the conclusion that there are no cataleptic (= self-warranting) impressions, and looks like this (cf. *Acad.* 2.40): (i) of appearances (= impressions), some are true and some are false; (ii) what is false cannot be apprehended; (iii) but any true appearance is of such a kind that something false which is exactly alike could appear in the same way; (iv) with respect to appearances without a difference between them, it cannot happen that some of them can be apprehended, and others cannot; (v) therefore there is no appearance that can be apprehended.

conceived requires assent, and assent is explicitly rejected, as we have seen. Instead, Cicero claims for himself a lesser form of belief, which has two components: the content of his beliefs has the status of a *probabile* rather than of a truth, and the endorsement he is entitled to is characterized as *sequi*, "to follow," in *Lucullus* 8. All of this is consistent with *De inventione* 2.9. Issues that would seem to require further explanation include what conception of a *probabile* is employed here and what kind of endorsement is envisaged in the quasi-beliefs that Cicero grants to the Academic by allowing for "following."

As mentioned above, another speaker in the first edition of the *Academica*, Catulus the younger, is also an Academic, but he adopts a slightly different position from Cicero ("mitigated skepticism"; I will return to problems of terminology in the conclusion of this chapter). From *Lucullus* 148 there emerges one respect in which this position is different from Cicero's (i.e. Cicero³'s and Cicero⁴'s). While Cicero is committed to universal suspension of judgment, tries to avoid assenting universally (although as a matter of fact he does not always succeed; see below), and regards the form of endorsement of impressions to which he is entitled as a form of non-assent, Catulus is ready to assent and therefore to have beliefs or opinions as the Stoics define "opinion" (i.e. assent to a non-cataleptic impression), but his assent is qualified by an awareness that the impressions which he takes to be true in assenting to them may in fact be false. We shall return to the issue of whether Catulus' and Cicero's positions differ only on the narrow issue of endorsement.

The nature of "following" emerges from a passage (*Acad.* 2.104) in which Cicero, in contravention of his usual practice, directly translates from a Greek work, in this instance one by Carneades' loyal pupil Clitomachus. In it Clitomachus draws a distinction, ascribed to Carneades, between two modes of non-assent (= suspension of judgment),[18] unqualified non-assent and non-assent that involves approval or disapproval, so that one neither affirms nor denies. The second, somewhat baffling, mode of non-assent is then characterized further: it amounts to (i) following *probabilitas*, (ii) applies to actions as well as problems discussed on either side (i.e. philosophical problems; see below), and (iii) is like saying "yes" when one approves a position in an interrogation on either side.

---

[18] I use the term "mode" to signal that the two varieties of non-assent are, on my construal, not mutually exclusive: the scheme envisages that one can embrace both simultaneously.

(iii), a point which I cannot defend here in detail, suggests question-and-answer *logoi* as dramatized in Plato's early dialogues, codified in Aristotle's *Topics*, and retained as an occasional reference point in argumentation theory in the Hellenistic period and beyond. In particular, we need to think of a particular kind of scenario in which the questioner confronts an answerer with a problem – "Is the cosmos eternal or not?" – and the respondent then selects one option, making it incumbent on the questioner to introduce premises from which the contradictory of the respondent's position follows. The important point to appreciate here is that, usually, this would not be an exchange in which the respondent's beliefs are at issue: he may not feel strongly about the cosmos either way, may never have given it much thought, and may only have opted for one view because it seemed true or at least more plausible than the second option available.[19] In this situation, one criterion which premises offered by the questioner would need to fulfill in order for the respondent to accept them is that they appear true on rational grounds, which means that they cohere with other propositions which appear true to us, possibly imply them or are implied by them, possibly make them more intelligible, and so on. What distinguishes them from the content of his beliefs is the dialectician's attitude of detachment: he brings his rational faculties to bear on them, and on their relationship with other propositions, but without thereby making them, or revealing them to be, "his" beliefs.

"Approval" or "following" – on our construal of Clitomachus' interpretation of Carneades' distinction as translated by Cicero – is like this: an acceptance on the grounds of appearing true, which does not issue in or reveal a belief (as defined in the context of this debate, this equals assent to a non-cataleptic impression). Whether or not the two modes of non-assent featured in Clitomachus' work in a dialectical context (i.e. as an alternative to the Stoic model of what is involved in action and acceptance of philosophical claims which ought to carry weight with the Stoics), Cicero claims approval or "following" in non-dialectical passages for himself, as we have seen.

In *Lucullus* 104 (*Acad.* 2.104), the second mode of non-assent is characterized as "following *probabilitas*." This brings us back to the related question of what the *probabile* is in itself, for Cicero. The etymology of the term helps us little, given that it only suggests that the *probabile* is something one can "approve" of. The *Academica* offers no official

---

[19] Alternatively, the respondent might choose one pole because it seemed easier to defend; yet, arguably, what seems easier to defend would usually appear true to a higher degree.

statement on the matter, since the parts of both editions where we would expect this information – Catulus' speech in the *Catulus* and the later part of Cicero's speech in the *Academica posteriora* – are lost. Lucullus' speech in the *Lucullus* offers in paragraphs 32–36 (*Acad.* 2.32–36) what I take to be a backward reference and short summary of the relevant part of Catulus' speech in the *Catulus*; I will return to it later. One way of getting closer to the *probabile* is to start from the Greek term it translates – *pithanon*, "persuasive" – as conceived by Carneades. The most detailed passage on the *pithanon* is in Sextus Empiricus, *Adversus mathematicos* 7.159–89.[20] One can use it to determine what the *pithanon* is and to see if the conception which emerges from Sextus' evidence would work for Cicero. According to the account in Sextus, an impression which is *pithanon* is not an island but comes with its own peculiar "syndrome" of impressions. The notion of a syndrome is, on one level, a way of thinking about the phenomenal content of an impression in an articulated way. Thus, the syndrome which is associated with the *pithanon* that "this is Socrates" would include impressions whose content may be characterized as "this is a man," "this is an ugly person," "this is a person who is typically to be found on the agora," etc. (*Math.* 7.178). What accounts for the initial persuasiveness is the internal consistency of the syndrome (i.e. the fact that none of the component impressions appears to be false). A perceiving subject's confidence in a given *pithanon* increases, moreover, if an impression is also clear, if one has enough time to take a careful look, and so on. Sextus speaks of two different types of scrutiny which one can apply to a *pithanon* in order to test for the two kinds of quality which account for its persuasiveness.

The evidence from Cicero is consistent with what we learn from Sextus. Lucullus mentions two different types of test to which *probabilia* are to be subjected, clearly rehearsing material introduced by one of the Academic speakers in the *Catulus* (most likely Catulus). And later in *Lucullus* 146 (*Acad.* 2.146), in a context where it is clear that reliance on *probabilia* is at issue as opposed to reliance on cataleptic impressions as envisaged for the Stoics, Cicero points out that a reluctance to make unequivocal knowledge claims and the corresponding epistemic attitude had a long-standing tradition in Rome, evidenced, for instance, in the somewhat hedging way in which Roman judges traditionally issued their verdict. Although the passage does not explicitly make the point, it seems safe to assume that

---

[20] Sextus Empiricus (approx. 160–210 CE) is the main representative of the second major skeptical school that existed in antiquity, Pyrrhonism.

the comparison of pieces of evidence for consistency is one of the crucial mental operations which a judge has to perform in order to arrive at a verdict.[21]

We noted above that in the *Academica* there are two different Academic positions being promoted by Cicero (= Cicero[4], in line with Cicero[3] on this point) and Catulus, respectively (in the first edition; in the final edition the material given to Catulus is introduced by Cicero, too). A clear difference between them is that Cicero's position envisages complete suspension of judgment (while allowing for approval), while Catulus' allows for self-aware assent. In a passage early in his speech in the *Lucullus*, Cicero[4] relates his stance on the question of endorsement of impressions to one which envisages assent. He says that, as a matter of fact and because he is not a wise man, he will often assent to impressions (*Acad.* 2.66, whose counterpart in the final edition of the *Academica* is cited by Augustine in *Contra academicos* 3.14.31, quoted above). This, however, is not due to a hold which the alternative Academic view has on him as a theoretical position (i.e. it is not due to the rational appeal of said view), but because, due to human weakness, Cicero cannot help but assent on many occasions when he should suspend judgment (cf. *Acad.* 2.68, 2.108, 2.115).

It is a striking feature of Cicero's stance in the *Lucullus* that it is linked to Arcesilaus, who functions as a kind of figurehead. Arcesilaus was the first skeptical head of the Academy who started the long debate with the Stoics and Zeno in particular over the cataleptic impression. It was Arcesilaus who urged that, if there are no cataleptic impressions, one should suspend judgment universally (*Acad.* 2.66–67). By contrast, the position promoted by Catulus could not invoke Arcesilaus in the same way. The search for the truth as a motif is linked to Arcesilaus' and Carneades' argumentative practice alike (*Acad.* 2.76 and *Nat. D.* 1.4, respectively).

One can now ask whether Cicero[2], the implied author of the *Academica*, can either be aligned with Cicero[3]/Cicero[4] or characterized differently, bearing in mind that any answer will be a matter of the interpretation of the dialogue as a whole.[22] Relevant evidence would consist in the palpable promotion – for instance, by means of structural features – of Antiochianism over Academic skepticism (or vice versa), or in the palpable promotion of mitigated skepticism over Clitomacheanism (the latter being crucially characterized by an injunction and an aspiration to suspend judgment universally). A natural heuristic assumption would be that

---

[21] On the *pithanon*, see Reinhardt 2018.

[22] See Brittain 2016, who considers similar questions with respect to the *De finibus*.

Cicero[2] agrees with Cicero[3]/Cicero[4]. We can note that the *Lucullus* ends with Catulus saying (paragraph 148) that he sides with his father's view introduced in the discussion on the previous day (*Catulus*), so Cicero[1] – the historical individual who wrote the *Academica* – has built a character into the text who is not won over by Cicero[4]'s reply to Lucullus; this should make us hesitate to see Cicero[4] as being made to prevail because he speaks last (a formal feature sometimes cited). In one of the letters to Atticus which documents the conversion of the first edition of the *Academica* into the final version (*Att.* 13.25.3 = SB 333), Cicero[3] worries that Varro (cast as the Antiochian speaker in that edition, who replaced Hortensius and Lucullus) might feel that Cicero had given himself the upper hand in the exchange with the Varro character. Cicero[3] would regard this as unwarranted, but he also seems to think that Varro might take this view in any event, without there being any actual reason for it. Obviously a more detailed argument would be required, but on the evidence of the *Academica*, it is arguable that Cicero[2] should be taken to present both sides dispassionately and equally compellingly, leaving it – in line with the avowed intention of Academic characters in the dialogue – to the judgment (*iudicium*) of the reader to make up his mind. This may, however, be a deliberate ploy on the part of Cicero[2], who could "actually" and "secretly" be favoring the stance of Cicero[3]/Cicero[4].

It could be shown that the *De finibus* and *De natura deorum*, which are comparable in formal terms, as well as the *Tusculans* and the *De officiis*, which are formally different, feature statements by Cicero[3] that are consistent with the picture that emerges from the *Academica*. With respect to the *De finibus* and *De natura deorum*, this is largely uncontentious, and the preface of *De natura deorum* 1 (1–12), delivered by Cicero[3], is especially full of points of contact with the *Academica* and refers to the latter as the place where Cicero had explained why he is an Academic (11). *De natura deorum* 1.1, while technically not precluding that Cicero[3] allowed for self-aware assent, is more plausibly read as a commitment to universal suspension of judgment. The five books of the *Tusculans* are not dialogues like the *De finibus* and *De natura deorum*; instead, a pupil character formulates a thesis, and an unidentified speaker who may be taken to be Cicero argues against them. The format is identified as Socratic and designed to discover what is "most similar to the truth" (*veri simillimum*) in 1.8 (cf. 3.46, 4.7). In 2.5 the speaker declares: "We follow *probabilia* and cannot advance beyond what is *veri simile*." In the *De officiis*, a treatise rather than a dialogue, the speaker, Cicero[3], professes to follow the Stoics on a specific point "today" (*hoc quidem tempore*, 1.6), but explains later in the work that the Academy allows him to adopt as his view what strikes him as "similar to the truth" (*veri simile*) at a given time (3.20) and that being an Academic does not mean that his mind wanders around aimlessly or that he has nothing at all which he could follow (2.7).[23]

The Practice of Academic Skepticism

What makes the works of Cicero[1] unique as evidence for Academic skepticism is that they contain a number of second-order statements on what we might call the enactment or the living practice of an Academic skeptical stance.

In *Lucullus* 112 Cicero[4] presents his stance as a function of the position and attitude adopted by his opponent. When he is talking to Stoics or an Antiochian who embraces the Stoic conception of the cataleptic impression, he will play defensively and deny that there is knowledge, but when faced with a Peripatetic, who operates a more relaxed conception of knowledge, there is less reason to disagree. Similarly, in *Lucullus* 98 he proposes to leave behind the nitpicking mode of argument which the Stoics adopt in the field of logic, and instead proposes to show "who we are." He goes on to cite a Clitomachean division of impressions. Arguably, there are two separate points being made: when arguing *ad hominem*, the Academic's stance will be determined by the opponent's stance up to a point. An unrealistically stringent conception of knowledge will be met with a punctilious and unforgiving counterargument. The second point is that a non-dialectical exposition of the Academic's "views" will only be possible in an environment which is not hostile, as it were: the Academic will not lay out how he operates cognitively on his own terms when he feels he has to adopt a defensive posture.

The Academic is also happy to be refuted by rational means: he is not the obstructionist he is often painted as by his opponents, nor does he have the personal ambition of winning merely for the sake of it. This is so because he genuinely seeks the truth. An unsustainable counterargument against the dogmatist deserves to fail, or so he thinks. Thus in *Tusculans* 4.4 Cicero[3] says that he does not simply not mind when others oppose him in writing, he positively hopes for it, and in 2.5 he says that he follows what is *probabile* and cannot advance beyond the *veri simile*, which is why he is happy to be refuted, will not show misplaced persistence, and is prepared to be proven wrong without any danger of him getting irate. In

---

[23] Passages that speak to Cicero[4]'s stance in the *De divinatione* include 2.8 and 2.28.

3.51 he says that he will happily yield to those who tell the truth. More teasingly, Cotta (another Academic speaker) says to Balbus in *De natura deorum* 3.95 that he is happy to be refuted and that he knows Balbus will be able to do so easily.[24]

However, there are some passages where Cicero[3] (or the character Cotta) maintains his skeptical stance while expressing a hope or a wish that a particular view is true. In *Tusculans* 5.20 Cicero wishes to reward those who enable him to believe more firmly in the sufficiency of virtue for happiness. In *De natura deorum* 1.61 Cotta wishes to be firmly convinced of the existence of the gods (cf. 3.7). Such passages are indicative of background intuitions and convictions which the speakers in question entertain, but which do not come up to the firmness or quality of doctrinal beliefs, and are therefore compatible with a skeptical outlook. However, they do form part of the make-up of the particular speakers, and it is in every case worth asking where the particular intuition comes from. Cotta is a priest, and *De natura deorum* dramatizes (among many other things) the question of how one can be a priest as well as an Academic at the same time, given that a priest may be assumed to believe *ex officio* a great many things on which an Academic may prefer not to take a view. Conceivably some of these background intuitions may also be what makes the characters in question distinctively Roman.[25]

Conclusion

The characterization of Cicero's Academic skepticism that I have given will be contentious in some respects. It is at variance with the view that Cicero presented himself (i.e. Cicero[3] and Cicero[4]) at least in some works as a mitigated skeptic.[26] Rather, I would say that Cicero was a radical skeptic whose skepticism accommodated many of the features which others would associate with mitigated skepticism, like the use of argument *in utramque partem* in search of the truth and in the hope that a *veri simile* might emerge, or the holding of views (in a suitably qualified way, i.e. not as a result of assent or self-aware assent). This is so because, on the evidence of Cicero[1]'s texts, radical and mitigated skepticism differed mainly on the fairly narrow question of which conception of belief they allowed for,

---

[24] For Socrates' avowed happiness to be refuted if he is wrong, see, for instance, Plato, *Gorgias* 458a; it is natural for a Clitomachean to invoke Socrates because Arcesilaus invoked Socrates, and the Clitomachean position shares with Arcesilaus' stance the commitment to suspension of judgment.

[25] See Wynne 2014.   [26] See, for instance, Frede 1987: 218; Brittain 2001: 218; Thorsrud 2012.

specifically what mode of endorsement of persuasive impressions the skeptic is permitted ("approval" or qualified assent).

Further, it is sometimes said that the conception of the *pithanon/probabile* employed by radical skeptics is different from that of mitigated skeptics in that the former, in invoking persuasiveness, give psychological self-reports, or merely the grounds for their (qualified) acceptance of a *pithanon*, while mitigated skeptics regard persuasiveness of *pithana* as evidence for the truth of the propositional content of the impressions in question.[27] I recognize the conceptual distinction, but do not think it can be used to differentiate radical and mitigated skepticism as both stances present themselves in Cicero's works, because I think that a radical skeptic using and citing *pithana* outside of a dialectical context will already be treating them as (albeit ultimately inconclusive) evidence, given how persuasiveness was construed in the Carneadean scheme which he followed.

Finally, one might ask to what extent Cicero's works contain evidence of a skepticism that is peculiarly Ciceronian in a specific sense. According to an influential view,[28] Philo was a mitigated skeptic when Cicero[1] heard him in the early 80s BCE, someone who embraced self-aware assent rather than a lesser form of endorsement, that is, approval (cf. *Acad.* 2.104). Now it is possible that Philo promoted mitigated skepticism, while merely mentioning Clitomacheanism, and that Cicero[1] came away thinking that the Clitomachean position was superior, but it is not a natural assumption to make, unless evidence from elsewhere suggests so (we have largely confined ourselves to Cicero in the present chapter). It is also remarkable that, some forty years after he first identified himself (that is, Cicero[3]) as a radical skeptic in *De inventione* 2.9, Cicero[1] should create another character, Cotta in the *De natura deorum*, who heard Philo at one point between 91 and 89/8 BCE.[29] He, too, is a radical skeptic. This suggests the hypothesis, to be tested against evidence from non-Ciceronian sources, that in one important respect Cicero's Academic skepticism is not uniquely Cicero's, because Philo's stance at the time when Cicero[1] was

---

[27] See Brittain 2008: section 3.3.   [28] See Frede 1987; Brittain 2008: section 3.3.

[29] According to *De natura deorum* 1.17, Cotta and Cicero "learnt to know nothing from Philo" (in the character Velleius' words). Cotta was exiled under the *Lex Varia* in 91 BCE and did not return to Rome until after Sulla's victory in 82; cf. Cicero, *Brutus* 206 and Gruen 1965: 64. He heard Philo in Athens (*Nat. D.* 1.59).

his pupil is likely to have fallen on the radical side of the radical-mitigated skepticism divide, in virtue of its attitude to assent.[30]

Further Reading

Brittain 2006 provides an accessible introduction to Cicero's philosophical outlook as well as an annotated translation of the *Academica*. A wide-ranging collection of articles on the same work is Inwood and Mansfeld 1997. Two rather different but equally stimulating attempts to characterize Cicero's skepticism are Görler 1994 and Brittain 2016; other studies which offer or incorporate fundamental characterizations of Cicero's skepticism include Lévy 1992a, Leonhardt 1997, Thorsrud 2009, Woolf 2015, and Cappello 2019. Brittain 2001 is devoted to Philo of Larissa, but offers penetrating and insightful readings of many Ciceronian texts drawn from the *Academica* and elsewhere in the corpus.

---

[30] *Lucullus* 78, which links Philo with assent, will require careful explanation if it is to be reconciled with my reading.

CHAPTER 8

Cosmology, Theology, and Religion

Clara Auvray-Assayas

Cicero's writings on religion, *De natura deorum* (*On the Nature of the Gods*) and *De divinatione* (*On Divination*), are open to a large range of interpretations, as shown in the long history of their receptions from the early Christian writers down to the philosophers of the Age of the Enlightenment.[1] The two dialogues were composed in 45 and 44 BCE, ten years after a first group of works on politics, *De oratore*, *De republica*, and *De legibus*. In both *De natura deorum* and *De divinatione*, Cicero puts under examination the views expressed by philosophers on the subject of the gods, including their nature and their participation in the world and in human life, in order to understand and to give rational explanations for religious practices and human beings' representations of the gods. Thus, the discussion of theological questions is meant to be decisive for the city and, for that reason, a strong emphasis is given to the historical and anthropological aspects of the subject.

In considering Cicero's dialogues on religion within the context of the philosophical debates of the mid-first century BCE, two main issues need to be examined. First, on matters of religion and theology, the radical opposition between the Stoics and the Epicureans sets the agenda, and for that reason the books written by the Epicurean philosophers Lucretius and Philodemus, Cicero's contemporaries, should be considered as the intellectual background to Cicero's dialogues.[2] The second issue concerns the relationship of Cicero's works to the deep and complex heritage of the

---

[1] General sketch in MacCormack 2013; references in Pease 1955–1958: I, 59–61; Dyck 2003: 15–16; for nineteenth-century German scholarship on these works and its long-lasting influence, see Begemann 2015.

[2] Lucretius' poem was read by Cicero in 54 BCE (*QFr.* 2.9.4), and Philodemus' *On Piety*, dated by paleographical analysis to the mid-first century BCE (Obbink 1996: 74), reports the arguments used by the Epicurean Zeno of Sidon to defend Epicurus' conception of piety against the Stoics: Cicero knows the precise arguments used by both sides, from Zeno himself if not from Philodemus and from the Stoic Posidonius.

Platonic tradition and its conflicting interpretations.[3] The skeptic and the dogmatic readings of Plato's books, which are part and parcel of the history of the Academy itself,[4] are embodied by two leading figures in Cicero's times, Philo of Larissa and Antiochus of Ascalon.[5] The influence of both men on Cicero's thinking cannot be neglected.

In his *Academica*, Cicero puts in a wider perspective the debate between the dogmatic Antiochus and the skeptical Philo on the possibility of knowledge: the mere decision about who is the most legitimate heir of Plato's philosophy entails a discussion of whether or not Aristotle and the Stoics are Plato's true followers. Thus, on the interconnected subjects of cosmology and theology, the choice between Antiochus and Philo has crucial consequences: is Cicero ready to accept a cosmology based on a simplified and syncretic physics, combining the accounts of Plato, Aristotle, and the Stoics, such as the one Varro offers in the name of Antiochus?[6] Or does he stick to the main epistemological stance defended by Philo, who argued that the withholding of assent is justified by the limitations of the human mind?[7] As Cicero reminds his opponent Lucullus in the *Academica* (2.116–17), this cautious attitude is considered to be particularly necessary when the matters under investigation include difficult questions related to ancient "physics," mainly concerned with cosmology, theology, and the first causes. The complete disagreement on physics among learned men makes the choice between different doctrines impossible: "all these things are hidden, Lucullus, and shrouded in deep darkness: no gaze of the human intellect is strong enough to penetrate the heavens or enter into the earth" (*Acad.* 2.122–26; trans. Brittain).

It is impossible to conclude from Cicero's books that he has made a choice between Philo and Antiochus.[8] This chapter will argue that he goes beyond this alternative by developing his stance from the texts of Plato himself, where the use of mythical discourse is a clear indication that a firm knowledge of cosmology and theology is not the necessary condition for a rational discourse on religion. Cicero is a careful reader of Plato's *Republic*,

---

[3] See Schofield (Chapter 6) in this volume.   [4] Tarrant 1985; Brittain 2006: xxxv–xxxviii.
[5] On Philo, see Brittain 2001; on Antiochus, see Barnes 1997; Sedley 2012.
[6] See *Academica* 1.24–29 (with Brittain 2006: 96–99) on the Peripatetic interpretation of Plato's *Timaeus* and the conflicting Stoic elements in this compressed passage.
[7] The main testimonies, including large parts of Cicero's *Academica*, are in Long and Sedley 1987: 1, 438–449; Brittain 2001: 357–363.
[8] Two opposite views are presented by Görler 1995 and Glucker 1988.

Laws, *Phaedrus*, and *Timaeus*,[9] and he makes good use of the complex narrative strategies which allow Plato to give cosmological theory a specific status when discussing the city, its rulers, laws, and religion. If no solid and uncontroversial cosmology can lay the foundation for a political and ethical discourse, one can still resort to some form of "provisional" physics: a mythical discourse along the lines of the myth of Er in Plato's *Republic* (10.614b–621c), or a common view presented as the most convincing, such as that commended in the persuasive prelude to the religious laws of Plato's *Laws* (10.886a, 891c).[10]

Thus, the first extended cosmological description in Cicero's works is a vision appearing in Scipio's Dream in *De republica* 6: here the Platonic and Pythagorean background is completed with standard or sometimes over-simplified Hellenistic astronomy and with Aristotelian and Stoic physics.[11] This vision of the cosmos is not meant to be an up-to-date scientific explanation such as the one alluded to in *De republica* 1,[12] but a poetic description whose philosophical background implies a syncretic, Antiochean conception of the history of philosophy. While Cicero will put such a view under scrutiny in his later *Academica*,[13] in *De republica* it helps him build the cosmic frame he needs to provide a general back-ground for the ethical and political values he promotes.[14] In that respect, Scipio's Dream brings only partial answers to the questions raised in the preliminary discussion of *De republica* 1: what is the use of scientific knowledge in public affairs? Should political thinking be related to the macrocosm?[15] Was Socrates right to reject physics or should Plato be trusted when he represents Socrates discussing politics and physics together in a Pythagorean manner (*Rep.* 1.15–16, 19, 23–33)?

---

[9] Cicero seems to have read much more (including *Protagoras*, *Phaedo*, and *Apology*), but these four texts had a strong and explicit influence on his own writings: see Schofield (Chapter 6) in this volume.

[10] Cf. Laks 2000: 285–290. Following Plato, Cicero in his *De legibus* has his Epicurean friend Atticus agree to a "Platonic-Stoic" stance (1.21) for the sake of the discussion to follow; this stance is then used as a preamble to the presentation of the laws of the city (2.8–16).

[11] Zetzel 1995: 235–237 stresses the vagueness of the description and its analogical purpose; see pp. 223–253 for a precise identification of the various elements composing the cosmological description presented in *De republica* 6.17–19, 20–21, 24.

[12] The precise mechanisms of the sphere conceived and built by Archimedes are described in 1.22 in order to explain the meteorological phenomenon called "parhelion."

[13] Cicero's answer to Varro is lost but from his answer to Lucullus, in the first version of the *Academica*, it is clear that the main objection to Antiochus' syncretism as a whole is that it amounts to Stoicism in the guise of the Academy (2.69–70).

[14] On astronomy as a metaphorical political science in Cicero's *De republica*, see Gallagher 2001; Atkins 2011a, 2013a.

[15] See Reydams-Schils 2015 and her contribution, Chapter 12, in this volume.

A few years later, Cicero would tackle these unresolved questions again in another group of works which he seems to have conceived as an overall project: *De natura deorum*, *De divinatione*, *De fato*, and a dialogue commenting upon an important part of Plato's *Timaeus* translated into Latin.[16] Although the last two works on this list are uncompleted drafts and the first was meant to be revised by its author,[17] it is clear that Cicero intended to map out the connected issues of the representations of gods and their role in the organization of the world as well as in human life. Focusing on *De natura deorum*, this chapter will highlight the way Cicero selects and reworks different materials to raise original questions and to shape his own philosophical inquiry about nature.

The dialogue, set out in three books, is introduced by a general preface in which Cicero offers a detailed explanation of his philosophical method after a short presentation of the subject and of its main issues. Cicero the author then becomes the auditor of a dialogue set thirty years before between three members of the Roman political elite who act as qualified representatives of the main philosophical schools of their time. In book 1 Velleius, a member of the Senate, expounds Epicurean theology and is refuted by Cotta, a pontiff, who is a member of the Roman priesthood, speaking as a follower of Carneades' New Academy. Book 2 is dedicated to a presentation of Stoic theology by Balbus (also a member of the Senate) and book 3 to its critical examination by Cotta.

Since Mayor, Cicero's dialogue has been mostly analyzed according to a doxographical approach comparing the alternate presentation and refutation of each doctrine.[18] This approach is essential to the precise understanding of Cicero's rich dialogue but needs to be completed, as this chapter does, by an analysis of the questions which appear repeatedly throughout the dialogue in the confrontation between Epicureanism,

---

[16] In the preface of the second book of *De divinatione*, Cicero makes his plan explicit: "I finished three volumes *On the Nature of the Gods*, which contain a discussion of every question under that head. With a view of simplifying and extending the latter treatise I started to write the present volume *On Divination*, to which I plan to add a work on *Fate*" (trans. Falconer). No mention of his translation of Plato's *Timaeus* can be found in his works or his letters but one can guess from the use of some specific words which do not appear in Cicero's vocabulary before his *Academica* that it was a work being elaborated during the last two years of his life (45–43 BCE). See entries under *fabricator-molitio-opifex-aedificator mundi* in Merguet 1905 and the parallel between *Nat. D.* 2.47 and Plato's *Timaeus* 17 (see Sedley 2013).

[17] Mayor, Hirzel, and Plasberg have suspected that the *De natura deorum* was under revision, mainly on the basis of lacunae and discrepancies in the setting of the dialogue. A new analysis of the manuscript tradition and of the testimonia gives more arguments in support of this thesis: see Auvray-Assayas 2016 and, for further details, Auvray-Assayas 2019.

[18] See Mayor 1880–1885 and, more recently, Wynne 2019.

Stoicism, and the New Academy and which allow for a better understanding of Cicero's authorial strategies.

In his preface to the dialogue *De natura deorum*, Cicero begins by addressing two major problems. He explains that the inquiry that follows is vital for the regulation of religious observance and, therefore, for politics and religion (1.14) but that it should also rely on strong assertions about cosmological matters:

> There is particularly wide disagreement on the most important element in the case: are the gods inactive and idle, absenting themselves totally from the supervision and government of the universe, or is the opposite true, that they created and established all things from the beginning, and that they continue to control the world and keep it in motion eternally? (1.2; trans. Walsh)

The first opinion leads to political disturbance and chaos: "if reverence for the gods is removed, trust and the social bond between men and the uniquely pre-eminent virtue of justice will disappear" (1.4; trans. Walsh). But the opposite view is not presented symmetrically as the most efficient way to insure political order: although they are "of high and noble stature," the philosophers who hold that the intelligence of the gods is the governing principle of the universe will have to face the skeptic Carneades' many arguments (1.4).[19]

As the dialogue unfolds, Cicero's authorial strategies and the sharp objections addressed to one another by the different speakers gradually suggest that the preliminary question needs to be rephrased: if physics cannot help the discussion move forward, then a change of focus is needed. Thus, in order to give a philosophical justification for the almost universal acceptance of the existence of the gods, as asserted in 1.2 and 1.62, Cicero concentrates on the psychological and epistemological processes which account for human conceptions of the gods. In so doing, not only does he display a sound methodological accuracy,[20] but he emphasizes what the Epicureans and the Stoics have in common: the "natural" preconceptions as epistemological starting points.[21] As a consequence, the radical opposition between the two Hellenistic doctrines on the activities of the gods and their role in the cosmos and in human life, although often alluded to by

---

[19] On Carneades, see Thorsrud 2010.

[20] Sextus Empiricus in *Against the Physicists* follows a similar pattern, thus confirming the strong influence of New-Academic epistemology upon the structure of the Ciceronian dialogue: "But since, in regard to every inquiry, the conception of the subject of inquiry must come first, let us consider how exactly we acquired the notion of God" (9.12; trans. Bury).

[21] Texts and discussions in Long and Sedley 1987: 1 (chs. 17, 19, 32, 39, 40).

Velleius and Balbus,[22] is not the main issue in the discussion of this particular dialogue: Cicero chooses to address it more specifically in *De divinatione* and *De fato*.[23]

As regards the fundamental question of the rationality of the cosmos, Cicero makes a very significant decision: the Platonic heritage of the *Timaeus* is to be discussed in another dialogue, where a Neopythagorean, Nigidius Figulus, and a Peripatetic teacher, Cratippus, are to play the leading parts. The dialogue was left unfinished, but we can draw an idea of its general purpose from the few lines introducing Cicero's incomplete translation of Plato's *Timaeus*: "I have gathered many arguments in the *Academica* against the natural philosophers, arguments I often discussed in the Carneadean vein and manner with P. Nigidius."[24] The translation of Plato's text is limited to 27d–47b, that is, to the cosmogony and the creation of human beings as the main beneficiaries of divine benevolence: humans have been given eyes so as to be able to make inquiries about the cosmos and practice philosophy. If this selection is Cicero's choice, as is most plausible, and not a fragment resulting from a chaotic textual transmission,[25] it could help explain why, in *De natura deorum*, the discussion about the gods can do without a thorough examination of the rationality and the providence of the world, as we shall see below.

The shift of emphasis from a cosmological to an epistemological and anthropological point of view seems to be due, on first examination, to the non-cosmological theology developed by Epicurus. Velleius, the Epicurean speaker in the dialogue, recounts in a disparaging tone the opinions that twenty-six philosophers,[26] from Thales to Diogenes of Babylon, held about the gods (1.25–42):[27] none of the ancient philosophers, not even

---

[22] Epicurean criticism of Stoic doctrine: Cic. *Nat. D.* 1.18–24, 36–41, 54–55. Stoic criticism of Epicurean doctrine: *Nat. D.* 2.45, 93–94, 162.

[23] The Stoic speaker Balbus says he would prefer to postpone the big issues of the providence of the gods and of their special care for humankind (2.3 and 3.65) and asks Cotta to treat separately the questions of divination and fate (3.20). See Wynne 2019 on the issue of gods' care for mankind.

[24] Trans. after Reydams-Schils 1999: 121.

[25] Cicero's intense political activities and his sudden death could explain the state of this translation: it is a coherent piece prepared for a dialogue not yet written. Sedley 2013 considers the selection as Cicero's own choice but thinks that the dialogue it was meant for was interrupted when Cicero started to write *De natura deorum*.

[26] Velleius' *persona* is modeled after Lucretius' poetic *persona*, combining didacticism and dogmatism, as is obvious from many allusions (1.18, 43, 56, 58, 91).

[27] This piece of doxographical erudition has parallels in Philodemus' *On Piety* (see Obbink 2002: 183–221) but its purpose is quite different. Philodemus (after Zeno) criticizes the Stoics for claiming that ancient poets and philosophers hold the same views as them on the gods; see Obbink 1996: 84–85. For an analysis of its Aristotelian and Theophrastean origins, see Mansfeld 1995: 22–44.

Plato or Aristotle, much less the Stoics, were able to give a proper definition of the gods because they did not rely on human natural preconceptions. According to these *prolepses*,[28] gods are immortal beings who have a human shape and live the most pleasurable life far away from the world inhabited by human beings (1.43–54). Therefore, the gods cannot be thought of as an elemental principle or a pure mind or the world itself with the stars and the heaven: no cosmology is needed to explain the nature of the gods.

Such a radical conclusion is not discussed by Cotta: as a speaker for the New Academy, he sticks to the skeptical position[29] and reminds his interlocutors that "on almost all topics but especially on natural philosophy I more readily pronounce on what is not true than on what it is" (1.60; trans. Walsh). Therefore, in his refutation of the Epicurean doctrine, Cotta does not make use of the long list of philosophers, most of whom define gods as cosmic principles, in order to oppose Epicurean physics: he takes it as a mere indication of what most people are inclined to think (1.91–92). Thus the doxographical material on physics, which is used to reach a skeptical attitude in *Academica*, has quite a different function here and a positive one: although it does not offer an historical starting point for philosophical inquiry as in Aristotle's *Metaphysics* (1.983b), nor an argument in favor of a consensual cosmology, as Antiochus would have it,[30] it points to a widespread conception of the gods and of the cosmos, grounded in common reasoning:

> [Y]ou directed withering criticism at those who took account of the magnificent and pre-eminent works of creation, who contemplated the universe itself and its parts ... and accordingly conjectured that there was some outstanding, pre-eminent nature which had created them, and now impelled, governed and guided them. Even if such men are off-target, I can understand their line of thought. (1.100; trans. Walsh)

As such, the doxographical material on physics proves useful for opposing Epicurus' claim that he alone was able to set the *prolepsis* of the gods as an anthropological universal (1.43).

---

[28] On Epicurean *prolepsis* as a criterion of truth, see Diogenes Laertius 10.31, 33, 37–38 with Asmis 1984: 91–103. On *prolepses* of the gods, see Schofield 1980; Sedley 2011.

[29] This position is given a brief and polemical definition in the introductory setting of the dialogue (1.17): Philo of Larissa has taught Cotta and Cicero "to know nothing."

[30] Although it is a product of Aristotelian and Peripatetic science, the doxographical material can easily fit many different purposes (Mansfeld 1990): the links, exposed with a polemical intent by the Epicurean speaker, between the first natural philosophers, Plato, and the Stoics could also be taken as a sound confirmation of Antiochus' syncretism.

The presentation of Stoic doctrine by Balbus follows two different lines of argument.[31] The first is based on the notion of a cosmic god whose intelligence and benevolence toward men permeate the whole cosmos. He first offers this notion as the main proof for the existence of the gods (2.19, 23–44) before developing it in a description of the universe and of the ordered movements of the heavenly bodies (2.47–60). Platonic and Aristotelian elements are explicitly inserted as authoritative contributions to Stoic theology.[32] The second line consists in the development of two of the four reasons which, according to Cleanthes, cause human beings to conceive of the gods: the advantages human beings take from the fertility of land and other blessings, and the wonderful sight of the ordered movements of the stars in the heavens (2.13).

The first type of argumentation is methodically refuted by Cotta, following Carneades, on the basis of physical science: nature alone explains the regular movements of the stars and the planets and all the cohesive forces which maintain the world, so that there is no need for divine intervention (3.23–28). And if the gods are perceived as natural beings, in the same way as stars or the world itself, how could they escape mortality and destruction (3.29–37)?

As regards the second line of argument, no objection can be found in Cotta's refutation. The traditional hypothesis that some important development has been lost in the transmission of the text[33] does not take into

---

[31] These two different approaches are easy to delineate when one compares the two families of manuscripts transmitting the text: the first approach is the first version of the Stoic exposé written by Cicero, the second is a second version grafted onto the first in order to modify it. The graft (of the portion of the text from 2.86 to 2.156) is located at 2.15 in one family and 2.16 in the other. Cotta refutes the first version and plans to refute the second (see 3.17–18), but the latter was left unfinished at Cicero's death (Auvray-Assayas 2016).

[32] Plato's definition of "spontaneous movement" (*Phaedrus* 245c) is used to prove that the universe is alive (2.32); Aristotle's distinction between three types of movements (*Metaphysics* 12.1071b35) is used to prove that the stars have a voluntary movement (2.44). This kind of borrowing from philosophical authorities could have been intended by Cicero to suggest how dependent the Stoics are on Plato and Aristotle, unless it bears testimony to the Stoics' practice of integrating Platonic and Aristotelian physics into their own system.

[33] A long lacuna has been suspected in Cotta's refutation at 3.65 (Pease 1955–1958: II, 1142–1143; Walsh 1997: 207). There is obviously something missing, but its content needs to be assessed according to the testimony of the manuscript tradition. The first version of the Stoic presentation is mainly concerned with the proofs for the existence of the gods and with the description of their cosmic nature. The second version gives weight to the notion of admiration toward the universe, as is made clear by the vocabulary and by its location in the manuscripts: it is not, as has been thought since the correction made by Renaissance philologists, a proof for the providence of the gods. That should explain why there is no refutation of this part as such. The signs left on some Carolingian manuscripts may go back to the revision work itself; see Auvray-Assayas 2016.

account the following observation: this second line of reasoning develops at length the various and numerous causes explaining how humans came to conceive the gods. When the Stoic Balbus adopts this uncontroversial perspective, Carneadean arguments are useless because what is at stake is not a scientific definition of nature but a psychological experience. If Cotta has nothing to say against the long description of the beautiful and efficient organization of the world, nothing against the astonishing capacities of the human mind and body,[34] it is because the Stoic chose to arouse an aesthetical emotion and, for that purpose, resorted to the full power of ekphrasis, the rhetorical device using description as the best way to attract readers' eye. Thus the poets are best qualified to give a precise expression to this emotion:[35] Aratos' verses are quoted at length in the Latin translation made by Cicero,[36] even though they do not give an accurate astronomical description of the stars and the heavens.[37] Offered as a convincing explanation of how humans infer the existence of the gods from the admiration they have for the beauty of the world, Aratos' cosmological poem is an extensive development of what was already expressed by Aristotle in an otherwise unknown passage quoted by the Stoic Balbus:

> Imagine that there were people who had always dwelt below the earth ... through rumour and hearsay they had heard of the existence of some divine power wielded by gods. A moment came when the jaws of the earth parted ... They were confronted by the sudden sight of earth, sea, and sky ... they gazed on the sun, and became aware of its power and beauty ... When they observed all this, they would certainly believe that gods existed, and that these great manifestations were the works of gods. (2.95; trans. Walsh)

The Platonic imagery of the cave is here given a new signification, illustrating the way men discover the natural world after having spent their life below the earth, in a place abundantly furnished with works of art. Aristotle is thus quoted as an authority on the subject of how men

---

[34] As developed in 2.98–119, 133–53.

[35] The quotation from Accius' *Medea* at 2.89 emphasizes the astonishment of the shepherd when he sees the vessel of the Argonauts for the first time.

[36] On Aratos' *Phaenomena*, see Kidd 1997; on Cicero's translation, see Ewbank 1933. On Cicero's astronomy, see Gee 2001.

[37] In his *De republica* (1.22) Cicero has Philus say that Aratus described the ornamentation of the old globe (due to Thales) "drawn from Eudoxus, not using any astronomical knowledge but through his ability as a poet" (trans. Zetzel 1999).

come to think that gods exist,[38] not on the subject of providential design.[39]

How epistemological issues merge with anthropological ones can be understood from the argumentative strategies of the three speakers: Epicurean *prolepsis* is based on what human beings think and dream of (1.44) and the Stoics rely extensively on age-old beliefs (2.5). By contrast, Cotta's criticism resorts to the infinite variety of religious practices and representations of the gods to dispute the Epicurean and Stoic claims that the notion of the gods is universal:

> Velleius, will you maintain that risible stance of yours, if we find that it is wholly untrue that when we think of a god, the sole appearance that comes to mind is that of a human being? It perhaps works out as you say in the case of Romans like ourselves, for from childhood onward we identify Jupiter, Juno, Minerva, Neptune, Vulcan, Apollo, and the other deities with the features which painters and sculptors have decided to plant on them ... But Egyptians, Syrians, and virtually all the uncivilized world do not envisage gods in this way. (1.81; trans. Walsh)

In this manner, Cicero underlines the philosophical difficulties inherent to the definition and the use of common notions. Through the exchange of arguments, a distinction is being elaborated between what all human beings, with the exception of a few atheists,[40] have in common – the idea that the gods exist – and the extreme diversity of human conceptions of their shape or their activities.[41] This distinction proves useful for several reasons: it enables the very idea of the gods to be preserved from the criticisms usually directed at the Epicurean anthropomorphic and inactive gods or at the round and revolving Platonic and Stoic cosmic deities.[42]

Furthermore, Cicero's distinction helps to draw a clear line between two separate inquiries, one concerning what needs to be rationally grounded, the other concerning what is relevant to cultural history: contrary to the

---

[38] The meaning and the function given to this fragment by the Stoic Balbus in Cicero's work are corroborated by Sextus Empiricus (Aristotle, *De philosophia* F 12b in Ross 1958) and by Philo of Alexandria (F 13 Ross).

[39] As thought by Furley 1989: 214, who does not take into account the location of the whole development in the manuscripts.

[40] The names of Diagoras, Protagoras, and Theodorus appear in the preface (1.2) and again in Cotta's refutation of the Epicurean doctrine (1.63); a longer list including Critias, Prodicus, and Euhemerus is quoted by Sextus Empiricus (*Math.* 9.51–57). It is plausible that it comes from Carneades via Clitomachus.

[41] This distinction first appears in the preface (1.2) and shapes the presentations of the Epicurean doctrine (1.45) and the Stoic doctrine (2.12, 45) as well as the New-Academic refutation (1.61–62, 65; 3.7, 17, 20).

[42] Respectively 1.94–95, 102, 123 and 1.18, 52.

Stoics' claim, the accumulation of cults and statues, developing from the very beginnings of civilization and scattered throughout the vast Roman empire, as documented by mythographers, historians, and geographers,[43] cannot be subsumed as embryonic forms of a more developed notion of the gods. If that were the case, all forms of religious practice should be accepted without limitations and, as a consequence, the fundamental links established between the city and its cults by the legendary second king of Rome, Numa, would be destroyed. This point is well emphasized through Cotta's persona, both as a speaker for the New Academy and as a *priest in charge of religious regulation*, which allows for a rich and multilayered discourse on religion.[44] Cotta indeed resorts to a very efficient dialectical tool known as the *sorites* not only to deride the Stoics' weakness in logical reasoning but also to show that they are unable to draw valid distinctions, among religious practices as well as representations of the gods, between what is essential to Roman political life and what belongs to the various local communities.[45]

The political issue is all the more important because Rome at this time has expanded to such an extent that the old traditional religious practices, grounded in the religious reforms of Numa, are disappearing under the many layers of more recent accretions.[46] According to Cicero, political legislation on religion needs help from philosophers[47] but neither the Epicureans nor the Stoics offer relevant material for discussion. As Cotta remarks, Epicurus' doctrine allows a minimal observance of traditional cults and therefore escapes the frequent charges of impiety levelled at it: "his sole concern is not to presume to deny their existence, in case he

---

[43] The display of erudition in 3.42–61 is based on Alexandrian sources (used in Rome by a friend of Atticus Demetrios of Magnesia) and on the vast inquiry conducted by Varro (on his *Antiquitates rerum divinarum* and religion, see Jocelyn 1982).

[44] Cotta insists on his role as a *pontifex* at 1.61 and 3.5–6 (as Cicero draws attention upon his own office as augur at 1.14). The implications of having a philosopher and priest as a speaker (in the dialogue *De divinatione*) have been analyzed by Beard 1986 and Schofield 1986. See also Begemann (Chapter 9) in this volume.

[45] See for example 3.47: "A further point. If these figures which we have accepted and now worship are gods, what objection have you to including Serapis and Isis in the same category? And if we accept them, why should we reject the deities of the barbarians?" (trans. Walsh). On this use of the *sorites* against Stoic theology inspired by Carneades, see Burnyeat 1982.

[46] Beard, North, and Price 1998: I, 156–166.

[47] In his *De legibus*, Cicero gives a full legislation on religion which does not differ from that of Numa (2.19–23), but it comes after a philosophical analysis of the links between natural law and civil law, and it is commented upon with explicit reference to Plato. This is the background of the question Cotta asks Balbus after saying that the foundation of the Roman state had been laid by Romulus and Numa (3.6): "Since you are a philosopher, I must exact from you a rationale for religion, whereas I am to lend assent to our forebears even when no rationale is offered" (trans. Walsh).

incurs some odium or indictment" (3.3; trans. Walsh).[48] Epicurus' conception of anthropomorphic gods seems in accordance with the most common religious representations, but because he thinks the gods do not interfere with human life, he deprives all the prayers, vows, and sacrifices of their meaning and function.[49] The Stoics defend the opposite view, including the gods' benevolence toward men in the overall divine rationality of the cosmos: in so doing they seem to offer a theoretical justification for cults, but, as is made clear by Cotta's arguments, the assertion is not firmly grounded and leads to undiscriminating acceptance of any form of worship and communication with the gods (3.15).

These two aspects of the question are developed at length so that preeminence is given to the political issues raised by Stoic philosophy: the gods' benevolence cannot be proven by apparitions on a battlefield or signs sent through prophecies, premonitions, and predictions (3.11–13). These tales are part of the legendary stock from which the Roman people have written their own history: they are anthropological documents, not proofs. The Stoics should not exploit the history of Rome for their own purpose: no divine design can be grasped through the chaotic succession of generations of men (3.80–81). The misfortunes of good men and the successes of bad ones, as shown in numerous historical examples, suffice to prove that there is no such thing as divine justice (3.82–85). As a consequence, human freedom is only limited by human laws: ethics does not originate in divine teachings but in human reason, limited or dangerously powerful as it can be. The tragic figures of Medea and Atreus should remind the Stoics that reason has not been bestowed upon humans out of divine benevolence and that the free use of reason is the necessary condition for men's ethical choices (3.68–69, 87–88).

The clear-cut distinction between what is relevant to human decisions and actions and what should be left to theoretical speculation is the main line of Cotta's argument: playing a mute role in the dialogue, Cicero the author does not make any comment on the Neo-Academic speaker's position but has the Epicurean Velleius give his enthusiastic approval. Could it be that the Epicureans offer some arguments against the Stoic tenet that gods are omnipresent in the world and in human life, thereby preserving human freedom and ethical responsibility? This question will be

---

[48] Cotta takes the charge of impiety from the Stoics (as shown by the argumentation in Philodemus' *On Piety*) and quotes the Stoic Posidonius in his book *On the Nature of the Gods* (1.123).

[49] This point is the conclusion of Cotta's refutation (1.121–123).

explored further in *De fato*.[50] From the few words Cicero, the character in the audience, delivers about what the Stoic Balbus has just said, the reader can only guess that the Stoic presentation is, at best, "closer than the others to a semblance of the truth" (3.95: *ad veritatis similitudinem propensior*; trans. Walsh). This should not be understood, as Cicero's brother, Quintus, does in *De divinatione* and many readers after him, as "closer to the truth" (*Div.* 1.9: *ad veritatem propensior*). The "semblance of truth" (*verisimilitudo*) is as much as human beings can reach, because we live in a world made in a semblance of the true one and our discourse on the world we see cannot have a better ontological status, as is made clear by Timaeus in Plato's eponymous work (29b–c). Should we conclude that the Stoic presentation is the best available? That would be correct if Cicero had not opened a new path with his *Timaeus*: when he translates Plato's text at 29c he has the speaker say that, as a human being, he will be able to state only *probabilia*,[51] a term which refers to the ensuing cosmological discourse, but has nothing to do with the model/copy vocabulary previously used.[52] Unless Cicero is considered a careless writer, unaware of the precise meaning of words and semantic roots, it should prove useful to pause on the distinction he introduces here between the semblance of the truth (*veri similitudo*), that is, what human beings can hope to grasp when talking about images, and *probabile*, a word which has no link with the ontology of images and appearances mentioned in Plato's text, but only with proof, approbation, and testing (*probare*). Using this distinction, one can offer the hypothesis that the Stoic Balbus gave the best of what human beings can say when they talk about images (like the poet Aratos describing an artifact, the sphere), but that his vision of the world has not been put to the test. Platonic and not Stoic cosmology was to be the subject of the last discussion on physics, in the dialogue Cicero intended to write, and eventually gain a rational – if provisional – acceptance.[53]

Moreover, if the word "religion" means "cult of the gods," as Cicero puts it (*Nat. D.* 2.8), and refers more precisely to the forms of worship and rites which have been accepted and regulated in the course of the historical

---

[50] See Begemann (Chapter 9) in this volume.

[51] *Timaeus* 8. On this notion developed by Cicero to give ethics, politics, and physics an epistemological foundation that is not based on Platonic ontology, see *Acad.* 2.8; *Tusc.* 1.17, 4.7; *Nat. D.* 1.12; *Fat.* 1; *Off.* 2.8; and Auvray-Assayas 2006.

[52] The Platonic vocabulary is maintained only when Cicero translates the general rule at *Timaeus* 8: *cum de re stabili et immutabili disputat oratio talis fit qualis illa: neque redargui neque convinci potest; cum autem ingressa est imitata et efficta simulacra bene agi putat si similitudinem veri consequatur.*

[53] Though she takes *veri simile* and *probabile* as equivalent, Hoenig 2018 emphasizes the importance of Academic methodology in Cicero's translation.

development of Rome, then it cannot be a matter of theoretical discussion only: an historical point of view is the most legitimate and, as in *De republica*, Cicero makes it clear that no speculative theory can supersede a thorough analysis of historical facts. None of the philosophical doctrines put under examination offer a rationally grounded explanation of the nature of the gods and, therefore, of how we should honor them: at best they provide some understanding of the psychological conditions which account for the formation of human conceptions of the gods.

De natura deorum thus clears the way for further analysis by delineating distinct types of inquiries. In the course of the discussion, Cicero has developed a multilayered examination of the ways humans find happiness in the contemplation of superior beings, whatever they are. This is why the dialogue set between three conflicting positions on cosmological and theological matters leads to a possible common acceptance of what is the highest ethical accomplishment, a pure and elating contemplation: the pleasure and the reverence felt while considering the outstanding nature of the gods is described with a similar enthusiasm by the Epicurean and the Stoic as by Cicero himself in the dialogue *De divinatione*.[54] In a truly Socratic manner, Cicero reminds his readers that the main philosophical objective is to understand the human mind: hence, exploring the subject of the gods, difficult as it may be, is the noblest study leading to *cognitio animi*, knowledge of the human intellect (1.1).

Further Reading

Mayor (1880–1885) and Pease (1955–1958), monumental critical editions with abundant notes, are still very useful to trace the long history of the interpretations of the dialogue *De natura deorum* and offer access to the numerous parallels, *testimonia*, and summaries gathered by previous scholarship. Dyck 2003 provides the best recent study of the dialogue, to be complemented with Graver 2009, Fott 2012, Woolf 2015, and Wynne 2019.

---

[54] See *Nat. D.* 1.45, 49, 56, 96, 100; 2.4; and *Div.* 2.148 echoing *Acad.* 2.127 on the pure pleasure offered by contemplation.

CHAPTER 9

Determinism, Fate, and Responsibility

Elisabeth Begemann

Setting the Scene

In 44 BCE, Cicero was again on the brink of returning to the political arena. The dictator, Caesar, was dead; the conspirators had raised the hope of a return to republican forms of politicking; and Cicero, who had withdrawn into a philosophical exile in the absence of opportunity for independent political action (cf. *Att.* 12.21.5), was eager to return to the Forum and the Senate. Eager, but cautious. The way forward was unclear, the future uncertain. Cicero did not return to the *curia* right after Caesar died. He rather continued what he had started, the writing of philosophy (Cic. *Div.* 2.2).[1]

The two texts discussed here, *De divinatione* and *De fato*, belong to this period and span an interesting moment in Roman history. *De divinatione* was begun before the Ides of March 44 BCE and the first book was more or less completed while Caesar was still alive.[2] Book 2 is headed by a new introduction which points to the changed political situation following Caesar's assassination.

Cicero had announced the writing of the two treatises in his book *De natura deorum*, and *De divinatione* both points back to the earlier treatise and forward to *De fato* (*Nat. D.* 3.19; *Div.* 2.3). Circumstances being hopeful but uncertain, Cicero continued with his enterprise of making philosophy accessible in Latin so that Romans would no longer need to follow the Greeks but be able to develop their own wisdom. In these two works, he explicitly addresses the (elite) Roman youth to prepare them for the political offices they will one day hold (*Div.* 2.4). The introduction to book 2 of *De divinatione* summarizes all the relevant philosophical, political, and rhetorical works Cicero had written, as well as the order in which

---

[1] On Cicero's motivation to write philosophy, see Schofield 2013b; Baraz 2012.
[2] Some revisions were introduced later; cf. Wardle 2006.

he intended them to be read. The goal of this program of study was to develop the ideal, philosophically educated, Roman politician.[3]

However, what Cicero presents is not a handbook of Roman divinatory practices and their theoretical background. It is, rather, a discussion of forms of divination practiced in Rome, both those that were accepted and those that were socially deviant. His discussion includes, and to a certain degree focuses upon, those practices that do the most to undermine and ridicule Roman cultic practices, especially as they pertain to the divination that accompanied any political action.[4]

Scholars have often supposed that the period of the late Roman Republic in which Cicero wrote was a period of religious decline. While there is a superficial attraction in the idea of political and religious developments mirroring one another, this notion is contradicted by our evidence for the period.[5] In fact, a rich diversity of lived religious practices prospered at the time,[6] including active literary discussion of religion and religious practices, such as Appius Claudius Pulcher's *Liber auguralis*, Varro's *Antiquitates*, Lucretius' *De rerum natura*, and, of course, the writings of Cicero. Caesar's calendrical reform and Augustus' imaginative use of religious forms are products of this lively debate. It is true that Roman authors of the time speak *as if* they were living through a period of religious decline,[7] but it is far more accurate to understand the developments of the period in terms of *change*.

In his presentation of divination, an old Roman practice that was firmly established in both the political processes of the *res publica* and in Roman life in general, Cicero mirrors that change. He presents divination as no longer (broadly) being understood as communicating the gods' consent (or lack thereof) to the plans of human agents but, rather, as predicting future events (and, ideally, solutions for avoiding problematic outcomes). This change in the conceptualization of divination mirrors an increasing need in both everyday life and political life to seek special sanction by proclaiming closeness to a particular deity (as did Sulla, Caesar, Pompey, and Augustus, but also Cicero himself), and to seek preferential divine knowledge. (Marius was accompanied by a Syrian prophetess, Appius practiced necromancy.)[8] In brief, the Romans sought assurances and sanction through divination.

---

[3] See Altman 2008, 2016b.   [4] Wissowa 1912: 410.   [5] Momigliano 1984.
[6] Albrecht et al. 2018; Gasparini et al. 2020.
[7] Cic. *Div.* 1.25, 105; *Leg.* 2.33; *Nat. D.* 2.9. Varro in Aug. *De civ. D.* 6.2.
[8] Plut. *Mar.* 17; Val. Max. 1.13.4. Cf. Gilbert 1973: 106; Kragelund 2001: 89. Cf. Cic. *Div.* 1.132.

Cicero's *De divinatione* and *De fato* were written in opposition to these trends. Cicero stresses that any action undertaken is decided upon by a human agent, and that the responsibility for that action thus also always belongs to human beings. It is significant that Cicero writes *De fato*, a treatise on an obscure and, from a political perspective, seemingly irrelevant topic at a time when the political future of Rome was entirely undetermined. (His decision to include this discussion is all the more striking since he never presents a complete philosophical "canon" in his works: logic, for example, is one topic he never discusses.) That he chooses to do so should be read as a clear statement on contemporary politics: what will happen next is not determined but depends entirely on the actions (and is therefore the responsibility) of human beings. To stress his point, the treatise is dedicated to Aulus Hirtius, the designated consul for 43 BCE, a man hardly known for his philosophical inclinations. Understood in this way, *De fato* is an exhortation to act, or rather, a rebuttal of the *refusal* to act, just as *De divinatione* seeks to refute the more superstitious divinatory practices current in Rome. All of these divinatory forms were directed at the well-being of the individual rather than the political community to which Cicero had dedicated his life. As such, he sees them as a threat to the unity of Rome.

Much has been made of whether Cicero the augur argues against divination,[9] since he presents the skeptical case in this discussion and does not seem to underwrite the Roman practice in which the gods either warn of their displeasure or give their consent to proposed action. But although these practices are questioned, Cicero states repeatedly that they must be upheld for the sake of tradition and because of their utility to the *res publica* (*Div.* 2.28, 43, 70; see also 2.148). He argues against divination on rational grounds (*Div.* 2.8), but recognizes the antiquity of the practice and its value for the administration of the *res publica*, which lies in the contribution it makes toward the reaching of consensus on what might otherwise be divisive issues. In the rest of this chapter, I will show how Cicero argues his case, upholding those ancient Roman practices of divination focused on the *res publica* while refuting the Stoic theory of fate. His goal is to show that the impulse to action, the decisions one makes, and responsibility for the future are all firmly in the hands of human agents.

---

[9] Schofield 1986; Beard 1986; Rosenberger 1998: 78–90; Rasmussen 2003: 183–198; Momigliano 1984; Krostenko 2000.

To understand the thrust of both texts, it is necessary not only to see them as part of a triad with *De natura deorum*, but also to read *De divinatione* and *De fato* together, as the interpretation of each is aided by the other. In particular, many of the logical problems raised in *De divinatione* can be considered in the much more theoretical framework of *De fato*. Thus I draw extensively on the later work in order to interpret positions in the earlier. The analysis of divination is closely interwoven with the question of fate; in fact, it is the precondition for the discussion in *De divinatione*. Its subject matter is, however, determined by *De natura deorum*: Quintus points in *De divinatione* 1.9 to Cicero having omitted the question of divination in the earlier treatise because it calls for more extensive discussion in its own right, which will now be done – in private and between two brothers. As in *De natura deorum*, where the nature of the gods can neither be proven nor disproven (their existence is tacitly affirmed), so in *De divinatione* the discussion is open-ended: divination also cannot be said to exist (there being too many examples that prove its existence) or to not exist (it cannot be logically proven).[10]

In contrast to the earlier text, the discussion in the later treatises is set in the present. The two works mirror one another with regard to the political circumstances to which they refer: there is time for philosophical discussion because there is currently no opportunity to be involved in the *res publica* (*Div.* 1.11), or the *res publica* does not currently demand immediate attention (*Div.* 2.7; *Fat.* 2). The setting of *De divinatione* is one of tranquility and leisure: Marcus and Quintus take a walk to the Lyceum at Cicero's Tusculan villa, which they reach at the beginning of book 2, seating themselves in the library.[11] The circumstances have shifted in book 2: after the death of Caesar, philosophy may be undertaken only in the time remaining after one has fulfilled the service owed to the *res publica* (*Div.* 2.7).

This situation is repeated in *De fato*, which is set at another of Cicero's rural homes, at Puteoli. Only after he and Hirtius have exhaustively discussed the current political situation do they turn their attention to "lighter" matters.[12] Hirtius, himself hardly a philosopher, asks for a rhetorical exercise and that is what he gets: Cicero will take on the role of the teacher and will argue against a proposition set by Hirtius the student. An unfortunate lacuna means we cannot be entirely sure of the

---

[10] Cf. Volk 2017: 336.   [11] Mirroring the schools they represent: Schultz 2014: 67f.
[12] On the choice of Hirtius, see Levine 1958; Kerschensteiner 1986; Begemann 2012: 25ff.; Schofield 2013b: 82.

phrasing of the thesis advanced by Hirtius, but it was most likely formulated as "all things occur by fate," *omnia fato fiunt*.[13] That Cicero approaches this topic as an orator rather than as a philosopher gives the reader a clue as to what to expect: as orator, he need not address the topic fully and cover all its aspects. Rhetorical exercise is geared toward persuasion rather than discovery; the good orator will choose those arguments which are most likely to support his cause and will abbreviate, distort, and misrepresent others that might weaken it (Cic. *De or.* 2.312; *Orat.* 24).[14]

Writing Philosophy

In the Stoic curriculum, the treatment of theology, to which the discussion of divination and fate belongs, marks the culminating point of the systematic presentation of philosophy,[15] dealing with physics, but also touching on issues of logic and ethics (Cic. *Fat.* 1).[16] In a Stoic manner, Cicero had begun his theological triad with an inquiry into the nature of the gods, followed by the question of how they communicate with men (*De divinatione*) and under what conditions foreknowledge of the future is possible, even for the gods (*De fato*). Since the Epicurean school held that the gods do not involve themselves in human affairs, they play no part in *De divinatione*, although they do play a role in *De fato* as the major opponents of Stoic determinism.

In *De divinatione*, Cicero pairs himself (Marcus) with his brother Quintus as interlocutors.[17] Quintus speaks for the Stoic side in the discussion, arguing that divination and prediction of the future are both possible and common, while Marcus argues against these claims from a skeptical, Academic perspective.[18] Marcus is a natural spokesman for the Academic position, since he had claimed in earlier writings to be an adherent of the school. Quintus, however, is an uneasy fit for the Stoic

---

[13] Not extant, but lost in lacuna B. Cf. Sharples 1991: 18.   [14] Cf. Schofield 2013b: 82.

[15] Diog. Laert. 7.39–41 (*SVF* 1.45, 46, 482; 2.37, 41 43), and esp. Plut. *De Stoicorum repugnantiis* 9.1035A–B.

[16] The treatise *De fato* is only extant in fragmentary form, with the introduction and end missing; a (probably rather extensive) lacuna between what are now paragraphs 4 and 5, as well as a shorter lacuna between paragraphs 45 and 46, leave us with a tantalizingly incomplete text.

[17] On the choice of Quintus as spokesperson for the Stoa, see Görler 1974; Beard 1986; Schofield 1986; Begemann 2012; Santangelo 2015.

[18] It is common to distinguish between Cicero, the author of *De divinatione*, and "Marcus," the Academic spokesperson within the treatise: see Santangelo 2015: 11. See Brittain and Osorio (Chapter 2) and Reinhardt (Chapter 7, p. 103–104 in this volume).

role, as he inclined rather toward the Peripatetic school of thought. In *De natura deorum* 1.16 the Academic Cotta voices the claim that the Stoic and Peripatetic schools were similar in thought, and disagreed with each other only in words.[19] Quintus' admission halfway through Marcus' exposition that he holds some Stoic views to be *superstitiosus* and in fact agrees with his brother can be read as an expression of this viewpoint: the Stoics accepted too many, and implausible, ways to divine the future, whereas the Peripatetic school restricted themselves to accepting "natural" divination (dreams and oracles) as true divination only (*Div.* 2.100).

In *De natura deorum*, Cotta, the priest, is given the task of representing the skeptical, Academic viewpoint in arguing against the Epicurean and Stoic views of the nature, power, and benevolence of the gods (raising the question of theodicy, which remains unanswered).[20] Cicero mirrors this move in *De divinatione*, once again assigning the skeptical perspective to a man who, by virtue of his position, should defend the practice: Marcus, the augur. However, this reversal of expectations is not a blunt tool. The topic is carefully framed in a way that allows the augur to not, in fact, argue against divination *per se*, but rather to criticize a certain specific understanding of divination while simultaneously upholding the Roman practice.

This reading hinges on the definition of divination, which sets the stage for the discussion: Quintus defines divination in *De divinatione* 1.9 as *earum rerum quae fortuitae putantur praedictio atque praesensio* ("the prediction and presentiment of things which seem to happen by chance"). The definition is then slightly, but tellingly, altered by Marcus in book 2: *divinationem esse earum rerum praedictionem et praesensionem quae essent fortuitae* ("divination is to be taken as the prediction and presentiment of things that happen by chance," *Div.* 2.13). If these things happen by chance, how can they be predicted? And if they are predictable, how can they be said to happen by chance? (*Div.* 2.18).

Here lies one of the major differences between the two expositions: Quintus argues his case empirically, while Marcus bases his *oratio* on *ratio*;

[19] In *Nat. D.* 1.16, Cicero makes the definition of *bona* the central point of disagreement. While, for the Stoics, *virtue* is the only true *bonum* and apparent physical and social goods are merely "indifferents," the Peripatetics would regard all of these as *bona*, albeit varying in degree. All three, in their opinion, were to be sought after, unattainable wisdom as much as physical well-being (i.e. the absence of pain and need) and social recognition (*honores*, books 3 and 5 of *De finibus*). See further Woolf (Chapter 11) in this volume.

[20] See Auvray-Assayas (Chapter 8) in this volume.

Quintus the *how*, Marcus the *if*. Marcus presents the problem as a logical one, applying philosophical reasoning to a controversial topic. The basis for the discussion is not a kind of divination that is to be understood as mere communication between gods and humans in which the gods make their consent or displeasure known. The discussion is rather concerned with an understanding of divination that touches directly upon the possibility of human agents acting independently and of their own volition (*voluntas*).[21] The reason for this is that if divination is to be understood as the prediction of that which only *seems* to happen by chance but is actually the prediction of things that are already determined to happen (whether by divine will or a chain or network of causes: Cic. *Div.* 1.125),[22] then the value of divination is very limited and Marcus is right to be skeptical. What is the use of knowing what is to happen if whatever happens does so independently of one's actions? In *De divinatione*, Cicero criticizes both the idea of a deterministic, let alone fatalistic, background to divination and to specific divinatory practices (i.e. those that promise to do more than give "agree/disagree" answers and those that pertain to the individual rather than to the *res publica*).

The problem of fate and human agency is discussed in *De fato* as the "Lazy Argument": if whatever happens is already determined, independent of human action, then the opponents of the fate doctrine can conclude that it is rational to be lazy (*Fat.* 29). While Cicero also quotes Chrysippus' refutation, which distinguishes between different kinds of causes, he much prefers Carneades' conclusion, which insists on human agency ("There is something in our power" – *est autem aliquid in nostra potestate, Fat.* 31), a move that reflects his commitment to the republic. After all, if everyone were to wait for their fate to happen, how could a political community or any form of human society continue to exist? A healthy political community depends on active individual agents who choose to participate in it and make decisions for the common good. At this crucial juncture in Roman history, Cicero the self-made man cannot see inaction and dependence upon fate as viable options for the aspiring Roman politicians for whom he writes (*Fat.* 29).[23]

---

[21] For Cicero's time, we cannot yet speak of a discussion of "free will." Cicero speaks throughout of *voluntas*. The term *libertas* carries its own, rather different, connotations: cf. Bobzien 1998: 330ff.; Frede 2011. For Cicero's contribution to discussions of the will, see Lévy (Chapter 5, p. 84) in this volume and Paulson forthcoming.

[22] Cf. Bobzien 1998: 50.   [23] Cf. Schubert 2017. Cf. Bobzien 1998: 192, 221ff.

Reading *De divinatione*

The figure of Marcus in this dialogue (as well as in *De natura deorum*) has long been understood as a cipher for the author himself. This position was rightfully challenged in the late 1980s, and it is now commonly agreed that neither dialogue comes to a definite conclusion, the open-endedness rather being part of the charm of these particular treatises.[24] Cicero does not want to produce dogma in his writings but, as Brittain and Osorio argue in this volume (Chapter 2), "for the reader to become a good critic of philosophical disputes." Thus while in *De divinatione* Cicero draws attention to his person by participating in the debate or providing numerous examples of successful instances of divination, he warns against too much interest in his own opinion (*Nat. D.* 1.10): the reader is to be convinced by *ratio* rather than *auctoritas*, while the author, as follower of the skeptical Academy, will assent to that which seems most probable to him in any debate, without holding firm to just one conviction.

The question of fate is of course not the primary focus in the treatise on divination, which rather seeks to come to terms with an ancient Roman practice that had, in the late Republic and along with other religious practices, come under considerable stress. The major question is rather whether the gods communicate with mortals, care for them, and participate in their lives. But by focusing on the conditions of that communication, Cicero draws attention to the unity of the Theological Triad and the pitfalls of applying dogmatic Greek philosophy to Roman practice.

In reading *De divinatione*, it is important to bear in mind the different approaches taken by the two interlocutors. Quintus argues that the future can be known and predicted by a number of means, both typically Roman (augury, haruspicy, interpretation of the Sibylline books) and supposedly foreign ones (oracles, prophecies, astrology, dreams).[25] His understanding of divination is less rooted in the idea of the gods' will to communicate with men and more in the observability of signs and divinatory experience. Only rather late in his exposition does he first turn to fate-based divination, by which he means divination based on a notion of causal determinism,[26] and then to divination "from nature" (*a natura*, i.e. dreams and ecstatic forms of divination). The basic division between divinely willed communication and the observation of signs and causes is

---

[24] For *De divinatione*, see Beard 1986; Schofield 1986; Leonhardt 1999; Krostenko 2000; Altmann 2008; Volk 2017; Wynne 2019.
[25] On dreams, cf. Kragelund 2001; Harris 2003; ten Berge 2013.   [26] Cf. Bobzien 1998: 33.

introduced at the very beginning of the treatise, where Cicero the author claims that the Greek word for the phenomenon, μαντική ("divination"), derives from μανία, while the Latin word is rooted in the divine, *a divis*. He thus expresses a preference for artificial divination over natural forms. Quintus' brief discussion of divination *a natura* in book 1 is a consequence of this preference, as the observability and experience of artificial divination implies a rational endeavor, whereas the μανία, frenzy, connected to natural divination is unbecoming for a Roman statesman.

Marcus, on the other hand, takes his point of departure from the (intentionally) misunderstood definition given in the first book, but he lays much greater stress on personalized deities, ready to determine the future by their will in one instance, only to be swayed by gifts and ritual means in the next. His argument is a logical one: chance events cannot be predicted, since predictability bars them from happening by chance. By the same token, it is illogical (not to mention unbecoming) for the gods to communicate by means which can be ignored or are so obscure that they cannot be understood (Cic. *Div.* 2.131–135). He finds it irking that the Stoics, "philosophers ... not of the meaner sort but those of the keenest wit, competent to see what follows logically and what does not," have adopted and propounded positions that, in his eyes, contradict reason. Throughout *De divinatione* and *De fato*, Marcus/Cicero bases his arguments on *ratio* and seeks to disprove the position that fate determines all things and that future events can therefore be predicted.

Both interlocutors in *De divinatione* base their discussion and understanding of divination on the assumption that the future must already be present in "traces" (*semina* in *Div.* 1.128; *vestigia* in *Fat.* 33). Without these, even a god could not predict the future.[27] The prediction of future events is, then, strictly bound to some form of determinism. Marcus/Cicero denies this. He must consequently also deny that divination, understood as the prediction of future events, is possible.

In fact, Marcus finds neither value nor content in divination (2.9–12). In his eyes, it does not seem to be a topic with which a serious philosopher should concern himself, being mere speculation. Indeed, in book 1, Quintus repeatedly insists that the relevant question is not *why* divination works but *how* it works (*Div.* 1.86, 109). His presentation is cumulative and his subject often blurred. Does he speak of divination as the expression of divine will or as the foreknowledge of future events? He grapples with a

---

[27] Cf. Cic. *Fat.* 32f.

number of examples, both foreign and Roman,[28] mixes different kinds of divination, and draws on different genres – epic, poetry, and history – as much as on personal experience. He does not look for systematic reasoning, but uses an approach that has already been put forward (and rejected) in *De natura deorum*: that the *communis opinio* is proof of anything (*Nat. D.* 1.62, 3.10; *Div.* 2.81).[29]

Marcus' exposition is much clearer, and he bases his reasoning on *ratio* and proof rather than (invented) examples (although Quintus also insists that his exposition is rational; *Div.* 1.84). Marcus prefaces his discussion by taking a systematic approach to the topic before disproving the various examples Quintus has advanced.[30] Regarding divinatory practices, he also distinguishes between artificial and natural divination, and he holds that, in order to predict future events, traces of these must already be present now. However, he does not see this as an expression of determinism.

In fact, it is important to note that in neither treatise is determinism denied *per se*, for Cicero was committed to the view that nothing happens without a cause (*sine causa*, *Div.* 2.61; *Fat.* 47). Every event has preceding causes and causal determinism is, to a degree, accepted.[31] However, this determinism is not meant to be understood as fate: *voluntas*, for example, is also considered to be a cause (Cic. *Fat.* 23ff.). Cicero accepts causal determinism because it is rational, but he rejects the belief that fate predetermines human motion: Cato's coming to the Senate is not determined by immutable and eternal causes (*immutabilis easque aeternas*), but rather by his choice to go.

Reading *De fato*

Chrysippus, on whose teachings Cicero predominantly draws for the Stoic view of fate in *De fato*, also held that the soul (*animus*) was free of *necessitas*, that the subject's choice was free of fate. In trying to establish an ethical determinism that upheld the fate doctrine *and* the idea of human responsibility, Cicero has Chrysippus distinguish between different kinds of causes, *causae perfectae et principales* ("complete and principle causes") and *causae adiuvantes et proximae* ("aiding and proximate causes"), which can be understood as internal and external causes (Cic. *Fat.* 41).[32] Internal

---

[28] Schofield 1986: 50 calls his exposition "leisurely and expansive, reliant more on batteries of examples than on subtleties of philosophical argument."
[29] Cf. Begemann forthcoming.   [30] Cf. Krostenko 2000.
[31] Bobzien 1998: 18; Henry 1927: 34.   [32] Cf. Görler 1987.

causes correspond to the nature or character of a body (the soul also being a body), while external causes are those that act on a body from without, including *visa* ("impressions"). The distinction is important: if all causes are of the same kind, everything would indeed be determined by fate, including assent to external impressions and the resulting impulse to act. This Chrysippus tried to avoid. Only internal causes can really be counted as sufficient causes that necessarily bring about the implied effect.

To explicate his meaning, Chrysippus had introduced the image of the cylinder and spinning top. Both are by their nature round objects. If they are pushed, the ensuing motion occurs according to their nature (i.e. they spin a certain way). The same, he says, is true of human agents: the disposition of their soul determines if and how they react to impulses. *De fato* 40 is to be read in this light: To emphasize the moral side of the question of fate, Chrysippus held that the soul met with external impressions (*visa*), to which it could either assent or dissent. If assented to, the impression leads to an impulse, which leads to motion. While the impression has an external origin, assent is entirely internal and is determined by the nature of the agent. Assent thus remains within the power of the human agent and, by consequence, the agent remains responsible for his or her actions. However, circumstances are fated in Stoic doctrine, and these contribute, as prior experiences and knowledge, to forming the agent's soul. Therefore, just like the cylinder or the spinning top, the way in which human agents react to external impulses is determined by the constitution of their souls and their previous experiences. This diminished scope of human responsibility was clearly not enough for Cicero, and the question remains as to what is *really* in the agent's power, and what can thus be predicted (*Fat.* 28, 39).[33]

In *De fato*, which is much more philosophical than *De divinatione*, Cicero also discusses (or skates over) other problems related to the question of fate, such as the Law of the Excluded Middle and the Principle of Bivalence that Epicurus famously rejected in order to preserve the independence of human action. Instead, he introduced the so-called atomic swerve, which provided a means to avoid the deterministic necessity of future events in the context of Epicurean atomism (Cic. *Fat.* 22f., 47f.).[34]

---

[33] Cf. Bobzien 1998: 263; Schallenberg 2008: 252.

[34] Cf. Purinton 1999; Brunschwig and Sedley 2003: 163. Epicurus' teaching is further complicated by interpretative difficulties. It is unclear whether Epicurus held that the swerve brought about decisions, in which case these decisions would indeed be random; or whether he thought that decisions were the impulses that made atoms swerve. If the latter is correct, then *voluntas* would certainly be within human power, but one wonders why the introduction of the swerve would then

Epicurus had introduced his theory of the swerve to avoid the consequence that, if all atoms were moved only by gravity and impact, everything, including human decisions, would be predetermined by their prior motions. By introducing the notion that atoms randomly swerve spontaneously by a minimal amount, Epicurus sought to solve this problem by injecting an element of indeterminacy into what would otherwise be a fundamentally predictable physical system. However, by having atoms swerve randomly, Epicurus also runs the risk of making human decisions a matter of random chance, which does little to protect the notion that they are directed by the will of independent agents. Cicero points toward this conclusion when he writes: "we should have no freedom whatever [in this case], since the movement of the mind was controlled by the movement of the atom" (*nihil liberum nobis esset, cum ita moveretur animus, ut atomorum motu cogeretur, Fat.* 23).

Cicero relates Epicurus' introduction of the atomic swerve to his rejection of the Principle of Bivalence. This principle states that every proposition has exactly one truth value, true or false.[35] With regard to future events, the proposition "this stone will break" is thus either true or false. If it is true, it has always been true. If it is false, it has always been false. Was it, then, also always determined? Epicurus prefers to take the bold step of denying the validity of the Principle of Bivalence rather than accepting that human actions are necessarily predetermined. Admittedly, Epicurus is not known as one of the great logicians of antiquity. His solution is extreme, but understandable if considered in the context of future-tense statements. If the future is undetermined, it is *now* not possible to say whether X will happen or not; thus the proposition "this stone will break" is *now* neither true nor false. Cicero ridicules Epicurus for his lack of logic. While he recognizes the shared goal (i.e. refuting the doctrine of fate), he sees Epicurus' proposed solution as far-fetched (*Fat.* 47) and unnecessary. For Cicero, the insistence that something is in our power (*Fat.* 31) is enough to prove his point. The fact that society functions through its system of praise (*honores*) and punishment (*supplicia*) is taken to bear him out, as such inducements and deterrents would be meaningless if people have no choice over how they will act (*Fat.* 28).

---

have been necessary at all. Cicero does not much care for this solution: nothing, he says, seems to affirm the fate doctrine more than "solutions" as far-fetched as Epicurus' swerve (*Fat.* 48).

[35] Not identical with the Law of the Excluded Middle, which states that either a proposition or its negation is true, *tertium non datur* (cf. *Fat.* 20f.).

Conclusion: Predicting the Future

In both treatises, Cicero argues his case by drawing on Greek sources, while at the same time rewriting them for and integrating them into the Roman context. He argues logically: something can only be upheld if there is good cause to assume that it "has the semblance of approaching nearer to the truth" (Cic. *Nat. D.* 3.95.). Causal determinism can, thus, be accepted, for it is clear that nothing happens without a cause. Teleological determinism, on the other hand, must be rejected as it is not compatible with the administration of a political community. It follows that it is only possible to predict that of which there are causes *now* that will bring about the event in the future (such as "he will die" in reference to a mortally ill person: *Fat.* 17).

With regard to all predictions other than the strictly logical, Marcus/ Cicero's position is clear: "I deny that divination exists" (*esse divinationem nego*, *Div.* 2.15). If divination is based on fate, then whatever is predicted must come about necessarily (cf. Cic. *Fat.* 11).[36] But if this is the case, then the value of divination is thrown into doubt, for if fate is the basis for divination and fate cannot be altered, what is the use of divining the future in the first place? Cicero's understanding of fate is decidedly negative: "the very word 'fate' is full of superstition and old women's credulity" (*anile sane et plenum superstitionis fati nomen ipsum*, *Div.* 2.19). In consequence, the kind of divination that is based on "superstitious fate" cannot have any bearing on "public" divination, the kind of divination that was relevant to the Roman *res publica*.

In writing about divination in a philosophical framework, Cicero discusses both the kind of divination that was practiced in Rome at the time and his ideal version of what divination should be. Quintus and Marcus discuss a form of divination that involves the prediction of future events; Roman political practice rather asked for divine consent to planned actions or choices, especially in war and elections.[37] Divination was highly ritualized and referred in each case to a specific question, such as, "If we proceed with the planned action, can we expect that you will not disapprove?" This form of divination was a form of communication both with the gods and a human audience, since a positive public response sanctioned the proposed action and contributed to the creation of a consensus. Thus, divination

---

[36] Cf. Kreter 2006: 172.

[37] Although this does not rule out prediction, e.g. in the case of the Sibylline books, cf. Santangelo 2015: 85. Divination in the political decision-making process: Rüpke 2013: 14ff.

that pertained to political decision-making was meant to take place in public, as when it accompanied ritual offerings. This had the added bonus that the public could partake in the ritual feast to follow, and that even negative responses would be observable, adding to the credibility of the process. The Roman public could have confidence that the gods did not simply "nod through" whatever the Senate decided to do. They also communicated their displeasure by refusing to accept offerings or in spontaneous signs, *signa oblativa*, such as floods or earthquakes.[38] Thus, divination as it was practiced in Rome was never a question of ritual action not being able to alter predicted or indicated future events, since the gods could (on occasion) be appeased by renewed sacrifices or special holiday-making. Nor did it ever render human decisions unimportant, since it was humans who decided on what needed to be done, while the gods "merely" gave, or withheld, their consent to human decisions. Divination was, in the public realm, part of the decision-making process and thus a communicative strategy.[39] Why, then, does Cicero discuss a version of divination in his introduction to Roman philosophy (cf. *Div.* 2.4–5)[40] that does not coincide with Roman practice?

Cicero states at the outset of his theological triad that he is now dealing with a dark and most obscure subject: "There are a number of branches of philosophy that have not as yet been by any means adequately explored; but the inquiry into the nature of the gods, which is both highly interesting in relation to the theory of the soul, and fundamentally important for the regulation of religion, is one of special difficulty and obscurity" (*Nat. D.* 1.1). It cannot rationally be proven whether the gods exist or not, and, if they do, of what kind they are. The same holds true for divination: human beings may have had the experience of gods speaking to them (or at least, they may ascribe such an experience to the gods), but this does not prove that it is indeed the case. On this matter, we may consider the discussion between Quintus and Marcus, in which Quintus cites plenty of examples, and even Marcus himself, as proof, whereas Marcus, by contrast, asks for the *rationale* behind it all and finds none. However, even if no certainty can exist about a topic, there remains plenty of room for speculation and false beliefs (Cic. *Div.* 1.7), and these can be avoided through rational investigation.

---

[38] Cf. MacBain 1982. Cicero's speech *De haruspicum responso* is one famous case of negotiation of the interpretation of signs sent by the gods.
[39] Cf. Rüpke 2006: 226. See further Belayche et al. 2005.   [40] Baraz 2012.

De divinatione and *De fato* are texts that seek to come to terms with the intellectual challenge of combining Greek thought and Roman practice. They reflect messy everyday practices rather than the idealized practices invoked by the political elite. With the political elite in mind as his audience (*Div.* 2.4–5), Cicero seeks to (re)establish divination as a practice with relevance to the *res publica* rather than the individual (cf. *Leg.* 2.21), to seek consent between human and divine agents, and to dismiss the superstitious beliefs and practices of his contemporaries (*Div.* 1.132). In dismissing the notion that divination is the prediction of the future, and in rejecting the corresponding idea of (individual) fate along with it, he upholds the need for individuals to act and to bear responsibility for their actions. In doing so, he insists on the preconditions for a moral community, one in which "praise and blame, honor and punishment" are deserved, because the subject is responsible for having earned either one or the other (*Fat.* 1, 40).[41]

Cicero's commitment to the *res publica* above all explains why he carefully outlines in the preface of these texts the need to be involved in the everyday affairs of the republic: only once matters of the political community have been discussed in sufficient detail, or when one does not have the possibility of being involved in the administration of the state, is it becoming for the educated man to turn to lighter matters, such as the very speculative discussion of divination and the strictly rhetorical, though highly technical, discussion of fate. For Cicero, these matters must remain speculative, since there can be no proof, and they must remain merely rhetorical, since the question "what if there is something like fate?" is rendered meaningless by the decisions each one of us takes every day. Cicero agrees with the Academic Skeptic Carneades in underlining the necessity for human action by arguing that the mind moves of its own will (*Fat.* 23) and that something is within our power (*Fat.* 31). With the political future of Rome uncertain, he calls on his fellow Romans not to hide behind philosophical doctrine, but to do what is necessary to preserve the *res publica* as it once was, and as he wishes it to be once again.

Further Reading

The question of fate and its relation to Ciceronian theology is discussed in Begemann 2012. Seminal for the reading of *De divinatione* are Beard 1986

---

[41] Cf. Henry 1927.

and Schofield 1986. See also the recent study by Wynne 2019. For a commentary of book 1, see Wardle 2006 and Schultz 2014. On the practice of divination, see Rüpke 2006 and Rosenberger 1998. Schallenberg 2008 offers a philosophical commentary of *De fato*; for a reading within the framework of Stoic philosophy, see Bobzien 1998.

CHAPTER 10

Cicero on the Emotions and the Soul

Sean McConnell

By the time of the first century BCE, the Greek philosophical tradition contained a sophisticated and disparate set of views on the nature of the emotions and the soul. Cicero's engagement with this tradition can be seen across his speeches, his letters, and his rhetorical and philosophical works. His most detailed and systematic philosophical treatment of the emotions and the soul, however, appears in the *Tusculan Disputations*, a work composed in the second half of 45 BCE at a time of grief following the death of his daughter Tullia and of personal failure in the political realm following Caesar's success in the civil war.[1] The *Tusculans* comprises five books in dialogue form,[2] in which the interlocutors A. and M. (the latter is usually identified with Cicero himself) discuss a host of issues concerning death, pain, and suffering: the first book focuses on the soul and whether or not death is an evil; the second book, on the endurance of pain; the third book, on the alleviation of grief and suffering (*aegritudo*); the fourth book, on other emotional disorders of the soul; the fifth book, on whether virtue is sufficient for happiness. The first, third, and fourth books are the most pertinent with regard to Cicero's views on the emotions and the soul, and they form the focus of this chapter.[3]

The critical approach that Cicero employs in the *Tusculans* deserves some comment. In the preface to the first book, he tells his readers that he is adopting the manner of Socrates: he will argue against an opponent's propositions so as to reach conclusions that are closest to the truth (*veri simillimum*, 1.8). In later books he reaffirms his use of the Socratic adversarial method, but he also signals his use of the less combative

---

[1] For biographical and historical details for the period, see Rawson 1975: 203–247.

[2] On the literary form of the *Tusculans*, see further Douglas 1995.

[3] Note that in the context of rhetorical theory and practical oratory Cicero's treatment of the emotions differs substantially from what is to be found in the *Tusculans*. In short, he stresses that the emotions should be aroused in the process of persuasion (see in particular *De oratore* 2.188–214). For further discussion, see Hall 2007; Wisse 1989.

practice of weighing the arguments on both sides of the issue (*in utramque partem*) so as to reach conclusions that are closest to the truth or most persuasive (*probabile*), a method he associates with the Academic and Peripatetic philosophers (2.5, 9; 4.7, 47; 5.11).[4] All in all, these are highly rhetorical modes of philosophical discourse that Cicero adopts in many of his philosophical treatises and dialogues,[5] but in the *Tusculans* we can sense Cicero's deep personal investment in proceedings: his critical examination of the nature of the soul and the emotions is intimately connected to the therapy of his own emotional suffering (*aegritudo*), a process that also found expression in his *Consolatio*, his consolatory epistle to himself following the death of his daughter, a work that now survives only in a few fragments but is at times referred to or quoted in the *Tusculans*.[6]

This chapter, then, sets out to achieve two things: first, it traces some of the key features of Cicero's adversarial and *in utramque partem* argumentation, in which he appears to favor Plato on the soul but the Stoics on the emotions; second, it draws attention to the ways in which Cicero employs and evaluates these philosophical resources in the realm of therapeutic practice, as he reflects on his own experience of suffering and loss.

The Nature of the Soul

Cicero considers the nature of the soul in the first book of the *Tusculan Disputations*, in the framework of a discussion of the commonplace philosophical question of whether death is or is not an evil. The interlocutor A. offers the thesis that death is an evil, both for those who are dead and for those who are destined to die, and M. advocates the opposing view that death is not an evil at all but a good (1.7–17).[7] The dispute leads immediately to two questions: what does death actually involve and what is the nature of the soul? There are various competing views, as a brief survey of the Greek philosophical tradition makes clear (1.18–24), so which is correct? Do we still exist after death or not? Is the soul mortal or immortal, and are we sensate or subject to rewards and punishments after death? The answer to these questions will of course have major implications for the question of whether or not death is an evil.

---

[4] On the Latin terminology and its links to the epistemological position of the skeptical New Academy, see in particular Glucker 1995 and Lévy (Chapter 5) in this volume.

[5] See further Brittain and Osorio (Chapter 2) and Reinhardt (Chapter 7) in this volume; also Woolf 2015: 10–33; Brittain 2016 and 2006: viii–xliii; Gorman 2005.

[6] For the collected fragments and *testimonia*, see Vitelli 1979.

[7] See Warren 2013 for critical analysis of the arguments in this passage.

Four major competing positions on the soul are laid out and examined by Cicero over the course of the first book, only one of which posits the soul's immortality:

(1)   The soul is a thing that is separate from the body; it lasts forever and is immortal. This position is associated most of all with Plato, and in particular with the arguments put forward by Socrates in the *Phaedo* (1.24, 39–40, 53–77).

(2)   There is no soul at all, a radical claim attributed in particular to the Peripatetic philosopher Dicaearchus. This position also covers the more nuanced view that there is no soul separate from the body, present in various physicalist models whereby the soul is really the heart, the brain, blood, or breath, and in the harmony theory of soul (associated by Cicero with the Peripatetic philosopher Aristoxenus of Tarentum in particular) in which the soul is really a phenomenon of bodily attunement (1.19, 21, 24, 41, 51, 77).[8]

(3)   The soul is a material thing, separate from the body, but there is the dissolution of the soul at death and so it is mortal. This is a view ascribed to the atomist Democritus and the Epicureans (1.42, 77).[9]

(4)   The soul is a material thing, separate from the body; it lasts a long time and can survive death, but it is not immortal. This is a view that Cicero ascribes in particular to the Stoics (who hold that the soul is fire) and also, it would appear, to Aristotle (who holds that the soul is an unnamed fifth element). These philosophers also maintain that the soul has a natural home that fits its material nature: being composed of fire or the pure fifth element, it belongs in the rarefied heavenly realm alongside the stars, and progresses there quickly upon death, which frees the soul from the body and the constraints it

---

[8] Cicero had firsthand knowledge of Dicaearchus' works on the soul: in a letter to his friend Atticus from this period (13.32) he names *The Descent* (Καταβάσεως) and a two-book *On the Soul* (περὶ Ψυχῆς), and in the *Tusculans* itself he refers to a three-book discussion set at Corinth (1.21) as well as a three-book work entitled *Lesbiaci* (since the discussion takes place at Mytilene) that aims to prove the mortality of souls (1.77). The scattered evidence for Dicaearchus' views on the soul is collected in Mirhady 2001: frr. 13–32. For discussion of whether he actually denied the soul's existence or was instead a harmony theorist like Aristoxenus, see Caston 2001. As Cicero himself confirms (1.41–42), Aristoxenus was (and still is) best known for his work on harmonics and musical theory. Cicero's report suggests that his status as a harmony theorist was extrapolated from his musical theory more generally. On the harmony theory of soul, see further Gottschalk 1971.

[9] Evidence for Democritus' views on the soul is collected in Taylor 1999: frr. 106–12 (= frr. B242–8 in Diels-Kranz 1951–1952). The third book of Lucretius' *De rerum natura* presents the Epicurean position on the nature of death and the soul, and much further evidence is collated and discussed in Long and Sedley 1987: I, 65–72; see also Kerferd 1971.

imposes (1.19, 22, 40–47, 51, 77–81).[10] This all matches Plato's views on the fundamentally separate natures and capacities of soul and body, with the crucial differences concerning the questions of immortality and immateriality.

The interlocutor M. suggests to A. that they should assess the arguments for these competing positions in an open-minded fashion, seeking to identify that which is closest to the truth (1.23); A. agrees and then immediately signals that he inclines strongly toward assenting to the position that posits the soul's immortality (1.24):

> M.: The opinions of the rest bring the hope, if this by chance delights you, that souls are able, when they part from bodies, to find their way to the heavenly realm, as if to their own dwelling place.
>
> A.: It really does delight me, and in the first place I would like it to be so, and then, even if it is not, I would like to be persuaded of it nonetheless.
>
> M.: What need, therefore, do you have for our help? Surely we cannot surpass Plato in eloquence? Turn over with attention that book of his, which is about the soul, and you will long for nothing more.
>
> A.: I have done so by Hercules, and indeed quite often; but, why I do not know, while I am reading I agree; when I put the book down and I begin to think to myself about the immortality of souls, all that agreement slips away.

Of particular interest is A.'s rejoinder that reading Plato's book about the soul (the *Phaedo*) over and over again has not proven sufficient grounds for his assenting firmly to the soul's immortality, so further persuasion is needed above and beyond what Plato offers in that dialogue.[11] Cicero (as M.) thus begins with a series of arguments for the soul's immortality that appeal instead to the authority of popular cultural traditions.

Cicero first observes that the ancient Romans held that people remained sensate after death, hence the sacred burial rites, the pontifical law, and the ingrained beliefs about the afterlife – the esteemed go to the heavenly realm, the rest to a place under the ground (1.27). The Greeks, he notes, have similar pre-philosophical traditions (1.28–29). The continuing

---

[10] Evidence for Stoic views on the soul is collated and discussed in Long and Sedley 1987: 1, 313–23. Aristotle's views on the soul are notoriously complicated and controversial – the essays in Nussbaum and Rorty 1992 are a good starting point for further critical discussion. Unlike with the Stoics, it is not clear that Cicero had firsthand access to Aristotle's writings on the soul.

[11] For discussion of Cicero's literary and philosophical engagement with the *Phaedo* in the first book of the *Tusculans*, see Stull 2012.

ubiquitous presence of these ancient beliefs and practices apparently confirms that they do indeed capture the truth. An appeal to nature follows: all peoples believe in the gods and likewise in the existence of their loved ones after death, hence the universal human experience of grief and mourning for the dead (1.30); these universal human beliefs do not arise from any reasoning (*ratio*) or learned practice (*doctrina*), but purely from the prompting of nature (*natura*), which confirms their truth. Nature itself gives further grounds for believing in the immortality of the soul since people universally have all kinds of concerns about the future after their own death – for their fame and glory, for their children, for their wealth, and so forth (1.31–36). These natural impulses only make sense if there really is a self after death, which implies the immortality of the soul.

The harmonious accord of nature and traditional pre-philosophical culture promises to be an effective line of argument for persuading A. of the immortality of the soul. However, although it offers a clear indication that the soul is immortal, Cicero stresses that the nature of the soul's survival after death is not accounted for properly in popular tradition – the bodily afterlife is emphasized erroneously, because the ancients were unable to grasp the life of the soul separate from the body (1.36–38). This is where the philosophers come into their element: the Pythagoreans are identified as the first to distinguish the soul from the body, with Plato in particular then following their lead by supplying rigorous proofs (1.38–39).

The stage is now set for the presentation of Plato's arguments for the soul's essential nature, and in particular its immortality. But Cicero does not proceed so straightforwardly. He first offers a sympathetic account of the materialist positions of Aristotle and the Stoics (1.40–47). He then recounts the argument from Plato's *Phaedrus*, in which the soul is identified as a self-moving thing without origin or birth (1.53–55),[12] and also the recollection argument in Plato's *Meno* and *Phaedo*, in which learning is explained by the soul having acquired knowledge of the Forms in a prenatal mode of existence, before being entombed in a body here on earth (1.55–59).[13] At this point an important tension emerges, for the material nature of the soul sits uneasily with its immortality: in the *Phaedo* Plato posits the view that the immortal soul is distinguished from the mortal body, among other reasons, by virtue of its immaterial and divine nature. At this point Cicero appears to favor the Stoic or Aristotelian materialist position regarding the soul's

---

[12] See *Phaedrus* 245c–e. Here Cicero quotes directly from the Dream of Scipio that concludes his *De republica*, where he translates Plato's Greek into Latin (6.27–28).

[13] See *Meno* 81a–86c; *Phaedo* 72e–78b. On the recollection argument, see further Ackrill 1973.

constituent nature, coupled with a Platonic commitment to its immortality; but are the two positions compatible?

Cicero is thus obliged to consider the soul's material nature once more. He dismisses again the atomist and other physicalist views, but he is now strikingly ambivalent, declaring his ignorance and suspension of judgment (1.60):

> M.:   Whether it [the soul] is of breath or fire, I do not know, and
>   I am not ashamed, like those others were, to admit that I do
>   not know what I do not know: but one thing, if I am able to
>   affirm any other things about a dark matter, whether or not
>   the soul is breath or fire, I would swear that it is divine.

The question of the soul's material nature is left open, but we can see that, for Cicero, the absolutely key thing is that the soul has a divine nature on any account.[14] In the Greek tradition this is established by appealing to affinity arguments: either the soul is assimilated with the heavenly and divine in terms of shared material substance, in the manner of the Stoics and Aristotle (fire, the fifth element), or the soul's attributes and capacities are connected with things divine, an argument developed by Plato in the *Phaedo* and elsewhere.[15] Cicero argues that the soul is divine because it is pure and unblended with any of the base earthly elements, but it is the Platonic line that the soul is divine because it has the capacity for memory, and for thought and contemplation about divine things, that holds pride of place (1.60–65). Whatever the soul's material or constituent nature may be (and it may be separate from all perishable matter, 1.66), Cicero is adamant that it must be the same as god's – and that, like god, it must be a thinking and self-moving thing, eternal and divine (1.65–71).

Now, even if this point about the soul's divine nature is accepted, it is not clear that the soul is thereby immortal. Indeed, Cicero states at length that the Stoics accept the soul's divine nature, and that the soul exists for a long time and can survive death, while still denying the soul's immortality, since they have objections to the arguments given by Plato. In particular, Cicero says that Panaetius argued that souls have an origin and are born, as can be seen in the fact that children resemble their parents, and so souls

---

[14]   At 1.65 he reaffirms this point.

[15]   See *Phaedo* 78b–84b; *Republic* 476e–480a; *Timaeus* passim. On the affinity argument in the *Phaedo*, see further Apolloni 1996. Note that Cicero had a good working knowledge of the *Timaeus*: he completed a partial Latin translation, and there are some explicit allusions to the *Timaeus* in this sequence of the *Tusculans* (1.63–4). See further Sedley 2013 and Lévy and Schofield (Chapters 5–6) in this volume.

must perish (1.77–81). Cicero quickly rejects the Stoic resemblance argument as feeble (1.80–81), but only after he has offered a further argument from Plato's *Phaedo* to support the soul's immortality – the so-called final argument, which proves that the soul by its very nature must be deathless and indestructible (1.71).[16] Just as in the *Phaedo*, this argument seems to settle matters, as attention turns to the implications concerning the fear of death. More arguments are drawn straight from the *Phaedo*: the soul is subject to reward and punishment after death (1.72), and death is welcome to the good person (1.73–75).[17] Both A. and M. find that the Platonic arguments for the soul's immortality are persuasive (1.76–77). Just as importantly, it appears that they find the arguments against immortality unpersuasive (1.77–81). Thus, despite going on to argue for the conclusion that death is not an evil regardless of whether the soul is immortal or not (either premise, Cicero demonstrates, leads to the same conclusion; 1.82–116), Cicero himself appears to favor the Platonic position that the soul is immortal.[18]

In sum, although he begins by considering the nature and the authority of traditional cultural practices and beliefs, Cicero's critical assessment of the competing positions in the Greek philosophical tradition is distinguished foremost by the positive presentation of arguments for the immortality of the soul taken directly from Plato. The one area of real contention is the question of the soul's material nature. Although seriously entertaining the materialist views of the Stoics and Aristotle, Cicero suspends judgment on that particular detail, while stressing that on any model the soul has a godlike, eternal, and divine nature. Ultimately, Cicero's philosophical treatment of the soul is engaging and well-informed, but it does not lead to any dramatic or startlingly novel conclusions.[19]

---

[16] See *Phaedo* 102b–107b. For sympathetic critical discussion, see Frede 1978.

[17] See *Phaedo* 59c–69e, 84d–85d.

[18] The same Platonic view is expressed at *Rep.* 6.26–29 = 6.30–33 Powell, *Leg.* 2.27, and *Sen.* 66–85. However, given Cicero's skeptical persona and argumentative methods, there is no compulsion to see him as a dogmatic advocate of the Platonic position; on which, see further Setaioli 2013: 455–469. On this point, see also Görler 1974: 20–26, who argues that Cicero presents not only a strong (and preferable) position on the soul (that it is immortal), but also a weaker (but perhaps more realistic) position (that it is mortal), without determining definitely between them; in terms of the overarching argument regarding the question of whether or not death is an evil, Cicero shows that either position on the soul is bearable in so far as the implications are the same (although the weaker position is less noble than the first since it makes virtue less important).

[19] For an alternative view, see Lévy 2002b; Brittain 2012, who both maintain that Cicero offers an original argument for the soul's immortality based on its perceptions and knowledge of itself, which emerges with his engagement with Plato's *Phaedrus* at 1.50 f.

The Emotions

In the third book of the *Tusculan Disputations*, Cicero shifts his focus to the emotions. In the preface philosophy is praised as the medicine of the soul, which, like the body, can be in a state of sickness (3.1–6).[20] Cicero relates that the soul by nature is striving toward truth and virtue, its healthy state, but it can become corrupted and sick owing to various factors that foster false beliefs and lead the soul into error, causing it to suffer grief (*aegritudo*) and desire (*cupiditas*), emotions that are themselves indicative of the sickness of the soul. The soul can, however, heal itself through philosophy, which will engender correct beliefs and thus alleviate the emotions of grief and desire.

After this engaging preamble that lays out the central conceit of the third book in laudably clear terms, the interlocutor A. presents the thesis for debate: the wise man is susceptible to *aegritudo*; moreover, he is susceptible to the emotions of terror (*formido*), lust (*libido*), anger (*iracundia*) – indeed, all the emotions (Greek πάθη) that are "movements of the soul that are not obedient to reason" (*motus animi rationi non obtemperantes*, 3.7).[21] The discussion then revolves around the following issue: are all these emotions indicative of unsoundness of soul (*insanitas animi*), in which case the sage would not be susceptible to them since by definition he has soundness of soul (*sanitas animi*), or are there some emotional responses that are compatible with a sound soul, in which case the sage may be susceptible (3.8)? The interlocutor M. states his support for the view that the sage is not susceptible at all to emotions of this kind, since such disturbances are indicative of a sick and unsound soul. This view, he argues, is already clear from the testimony of the Romans of old, and it is also the view of the Stoics, who follow the model of Socrates and hold the view that all who are not wise have unsound souls; hence, only those who are not wise are susceptible to emotions such as *aegritudo* (3.8–11).[22]

---

[20] Schofield 2002 demonstrates that this therapeutic concern, which is so central to the *Tusculans* as a whole (see in particular Cicero's final concluding words at 5.121), rests on a Socratic attitude toward the practical purpose of philosophy (cf. 3.8, 4.24, 5.10), which can be traced to the Academic skeptic Philo of Larissa (145–79 BCE).

[21] Here Cicero also explains his translation of Greek πάθος as *perturbatio* ("disorder") rather than *morbus* ("disease"), so as to delineate clearly a flaw of the soul rather than of the body (cf. 4.23–32).

[22] The Stoic sage experiences none of the emotions that are disturbances of the soul, but he is not devoid of emotions altogether: he experiences "equable feelings" (*constantiae* or εὐπάθειαι), which are by definition not disturbances of the soul (4.12–15). The evidence for Stoic views on the emotions is collated in Graver 2002: 203–223; see also Long and Sedley 1987: I, 410–423. For sympathetic critical discussion of the Stoic model, see Frede 1986.

The discussion then proceeds to critically address the competing positions of the various Hellenistic schools, most of which share A.'s view that the wise man is in some way susceptible to emotions such as *aegritudo*, with a clear indication from the start that Cicero finds the Stoic position to be the most persuasive. The interlocutor M. informs A. that his view is shared by the Academic philosopher Crantor, who maintains that the soul is by nature sensitive and susceptible to *aegritudo*, and who explicitly rejects the position of the Stoics (3.12–13, 71). Cicero himself clearly had been sympathetic to Crantor's position: his own *Consolatio* drew on Crantor's work *On Consolation* (περὶ πένθους), as well as other sources (*Tusc.* 1.115; *Att.* 12.14.3, 12.18.1, 12.20.2, 12.22.2),[23] and the letters to Atticus suggest that in it Cicero promoted, among other things, the view that grief and suffering are valid to some extent – it is a natural response to the death of a daughter to feel grief, and grief is fitting so long as it is proportionate and does not persist too long (*Att.* 12.20.1, 12.28.2).[24] This also accords closely with the Peripatetic approach to the issue, in which the sage suffers proportionate states of disturbance in the soul, an appropriate emotional mean (*Tusc.* 3.22, 74; 4.39–47). In the *Tusculans*, however, Cicero advocates the more austere Stoic line that the emotion of grief (*aegritudo*) should be extirpated completely, presenting at length the Stoic proofs for the incompatibility of wisdom and virtue with such disturbances of the soul (3.13–21; cf. 4.8–38).[25] The Stoic argument is clear: any "proportionate" emotional response still involves some evil in the soul, since it involves some disturbance, and the proper aim is the health of the soul, no evil at all, so the Academic and Peripatetic positions, which may appear comfortingly moderate and reasonable, are in fact fundamentally misguided (3.22, 4.39).

At this point attention turns to the Stoic explanation for what causes the soul to suffer emotional disturbances – a diagnosis of the cause promises in turn a cure (3.22–23). If it is an external source, remove it and the soul should be undisturbed. If it is an internal source, something inherent to the soul itself, it can be targeted for removal by the soul itself – by doing philosophy, the internal activity of the soul. The Stoic model makes it plain that the sources of emotional suffering are in the soul itself: external factors – the vicissitudes of fortune – do not play the key causal role, and

---

[23] For discussion of Cicero's engagement with the tradition of consolatory literature, see further White 1995; Hutchinson 1998: 49–77; Graver 2002: 187–194.

[24] See in particular Baltussen 2013, an engaging reconstruction and analysis of the *Consolatio*. See also the consolatory letter of Servius Sulpicius to Cicero (*Fam.* 4.5), and Cicero's reply (*Fam.* 4.6).

[25] See further Nussbaum 1994: 359–401.

our emotions are under our own control. A fourfold schema is then presented to clarify the nature of emotional disturbances in the soul and how they relate to external things (3.24–25): (1) elation (*voluptas gestiens, id est, praeter modum elata laetitia*) arises when one judges oneself to have some perceived good in the present; (2) lust (*cupiditas* or *libido*) when one desires some perceived good in the future; (3) fear (*metus*) when one thinks one will suffer some threatening evil in the future; (4) grief (*aegritudo*) when one thinks that one is suffering some evil presently.[26] The Stoics have, then, a cognitivist model of the emotions whereby they are the result of (erroneous) judgments about the value of external things. These emotional disturbances can be extirpated by altering one's judgments so that they are correct, which ultimately relies on gaining proper beliefs about the true worth of external things (3.25–26; cf. 4.58–84).

After this fourfold division, *aegritudo* is presented as the worst emotion of all: it causes the soul to be in an anguished state of wretchedness, and it poses the greatest therapeutic challenges (3.26–27). The alleviation of *aegritudo* now forms the focus of the remainder of the third book of the *Tusculans*.[27] Before addressing the effectiveness of the Stoic therapeutic approach, however, Cicero diverts attention to the hedonist philosophical tradition as he confronts the question of whether it is natural, and hence unavoidable, to feel *aegritudo* in the presence of some perceived evil (3.28). Cicero sympathetically relates the Cyrenaic view that anticipating evils in the future is key to developing mental fortitude and strength in the face of sudden misfortunes (3.29–34, 52–59) – since one has anticipated suffering bad things, it does not seem so terrible when misfortune strikes, and this helps to alleviate *aegritudo*. This Cyrenaic observation about the therapeutic power of contemplative reflection bolsters the essential claim that evil lies "in belief" rather than "in nature" (3.31), contrary to what Epicurus maintains (3.32–35). Epicurus holds that emotional suffering is natural in the presence of an evil (which, for Epicurus, is experiencing a pain), but we are able to bear the unavoidable reality by the memory of past and the anticipation of future pleasures, and by reflecting on the fact that no pain

---

[26] There are subdivisions within each category: the names given to various forms of *aegritudo* are expounded at 3.83–84, and in the fourth book Cicero gives a list of definitions of distinct emotional terms, following the practice of the Stoics (4.9–22).

[27] Given the nature of the Stoic cognitivist model, Cicero's treatment of the other emotions in the fourth book, such as love (4.68–76) and anger (4.77–79), more or less mirrors that of *aegritudo*. This section thus focuses solely on the case of *aegritudo*, while noting parallel passages in the fourth book.

lasts long (3.32–33, 35).[28] The Cyrenaic position accords more with the Stoic view that the virtues are the good states of soul that cause us to be unmoved by the vicissitudes of fortune and to suffer no distress at all (3.36), the only real evil and source of suffering being vice, the bad internal state of one's soul (3.34). Cicero harangues the Epicureans since they are unable to account for the role played by the virtues in the alleviation of *aegritudo*, as they place our emotional responses at the mercy of fluctuating external factors outside of our control (3.37–51).[29] Cicero thus presents the Epicurean approach as deeply flawed: the truly wise and virtuous person would not be afflicted by either positive or negative emotional disturbance in the face of external things.

By this point in the *Tusculans*, the major competing accounts of the emotions in the Greek philosophical tradition have been presented and criticized from essentially a Stoic set of commitments. Many of the criticisms are compelling only if one accepts the cogency of the Stoic position from the outset, which leaves significant room for dissent. The interlocutor A. never intervenes assertively in support of his original proposition, but the Stoic model does come under critical scrutiny of a different sort: for the remainder of the third book, Cicero explores its utility and effectiveness when confronting the actual experience of emotional distress.

Emotional Therapy

Cicero observes that time is the key factor in the actual therapy of grief (3.54). This suggests that reason alone is not sufficient for the alleviation of *aegritudo*: even if one accepts the Stoic arguments and sees where reason points, healing is a process. This prompts further comment on the role played by reason in emotional therapy. It is certainly helpful to anticipate future evils (3.55–59), to consider the experiences of others and the ways in which they bore *aegritudo* (3.56–58), and to admit that pain and misfortune are unavoidable realities in human life, challenges that can

---

[28] Epicurus, *RS* 4 and *Sent. Vat.* 3–4. On past and future pleasures, see further Warren 2001; 2006.

[29] For the Epicureans, the emotions are responses that indicate whether something is an immediate source of pleasure or pain; see further Konstan 2008: 1–25. The evidence for Epicurean and Cyrenaic views on the emotions is collated in Graver 2002: 195–201. Cicero's account of the Epicurean position is inaccurate, since they do stress that the virtues allow us to maintain control and equanimity in the face of the vicissitudes of fortune; see further Long and Sedley 1987: 1, 112–125.

and must be borne with virtue and honor (3.59–61). In all these cases, contemplative reflection is the key process in identifying that one has false beliefs (3.58), the rectification of which will bring the soul into a state of health (3.61). Cicero will stress the themes of time and continuing reflection as the third book reaches its culmination.

At this point, however, Cicero diverts attention to a pressing moral issue: there is a very strong intuition that it is right and fitting to feel grief in certain instances, such as the deaths of relatives, which implies that the beliefs causing distress are, at least in some instances, not false but valid (3.61–71). Cicero once again stresses the Stoic view that grief is a matter of belief, not of nature (3.65, 71), and that it is not the perceived misfortune (the external thing) that is the cause of suffering but rather one's own beliefs (3.67). These common moral intuitions thus do not reflect anything substantial; rather they are the result of ingrained cultural practices and expectations, which may in fact be pernicious – for nothing good is gained by suffering as a result of false beliefs. The counterargument is attributed to the Academic Crantor: it is natural to feel grief since evidently when something bad happens *aegritudo* still affects a person who has the right beliefs; this indicates that the emotional response is independent of that cognitive state (3.71–72). Moreover, it is evident that words and arguments are frequently of no comfort to the one suffering when misfortune strikes, which again shows the limitations of reason and the Stoic model (3.73). Cicero's own experience with regard to his daughter Tullia affirms these observations: he was by his own account inconsolable, despite the reasoned advice and arguments – and the admonishments – offered by the canon of consolatory literature and by Atticus and his peers (*Att.* 12.14.3, 12.18.1, 12.20.1–2, 12.22.2, 12.28.2; *Fam.* 4.5–6). In these letters Cicero appears to accept the criticism of both the magnitude of his grief and its excessive duration, and he expresses to Atticus his hope that the *Consolatio*, as well as being an exercise in self-therapy, would present to others an image of his propriety in grieving, even if it were at odds with reality. Cicero is evidently aware that his intense and prolonged period of grieving is indecorous and reflects poorly on his standing as a composed, equable Roman statesman. It is time that has helped him to heal, as he makes clear in the reflections on his own experience in the *Tusculans*, written some months after the intensity of his grief had faded (3.76–77, 4.63).[30] Cicero thus appears to be drawn to both sides of the argument

---

[30] See further White 1995.

and, ultimately, he offers a nuanced conclusion that judiciously captures
the two most relevant factors – time and contemplation (3.74):

> M.:   But certainly this is the greatest proof [that *aegritudo* is due to
> ourselves and not to nature], since it is agreed that *aegritudo* is
> removed by a long duration of time (*vetustate*), this intense
> blow (*vis*) is not laid aside in a day, but in continual reflection
> (*in cogitatione diuturna*). For if the circumstances are the same
> and the person is the same, how is it possible for anything to be
> changed with regard to grief, if there is neither any change with
> regard to the thing on account of which one feels grief, nor any
> change with regard to the one who feels grief? Therefore,
> continual reflection (*cogitatio diuturna*) that there is nothing
> evil in the circumstances has a healing effect on grief, not the
> continuance of time itself (*ipsa diuturnitas*).

Cicero is well aware that the experience of emotional suffering is all too real
for those of us who are not Stoic sages; but he is also adamant that the
Stoics have the therapeutic model fundamentally right: alleviation of
emotional pain is all about thinking correctly, realizing that what seems
to be an evil is in fact nothing bad at all, a process that is under our control
but that takes time (3.74–76; cf. 4.58–84).[31]

As the third book reaches its conclusion, Cicero stresses first and
foremost that emotional disturbances such as *aegritudo* are strictly a matter
of belief and do not arise by nature (3.80–83), while also emphasizing that
the successful practical therapy of emotional suffering is vexed and complicated (3.76–84). How can others help us to think correctly and alleviate
our suffering? What makes for effective consolation? Cicero surveys a range
of views in the tradition: Cleanthes maintains that the consoler should
deny the existence of the evil; Epicurus, that he should shift the sufferer's
attention to thinking about pleasures; the Cyrenaics, that he should convey
that nothing unexpected has happened; the Peripatetics, that he should
show that the evil is not that serious; Chrysippus, that he should remove
the sufferer's erroneous belief (3.76). Cicero says that his own *Consolatio*
combines all of these approaches (3.76). Ultimately, however, it is the
particularities that really matter when attempting to show the suffering

---

[31] Cicero's emphasis on the importance of time anticipates its prominence in contemporary work on
grief and mourning, including "neo-Stoic" cognitive accounts such as Nussbaum 2001. Here Cicero
also anticipates key features of modern cognitive behavioral therapy (CBT), especially the device
called "reattribution," where one develops over time the ability to assign different values to
unpleasant experiences. On the avowed affinities between CBT and Stoic philosophy, see in
particular Robertson 2010. Seneca, Epictetus, and Marcus Aurelius figure most prominently, but
Cicero's richer and earlier discussions of emotional therapy also have much to offer.

person that they suffer only because of their own judgments and beliefs, which they can change: the character of the person who is suffering, the timing of intervention, the fittingness of certain consolatory arguments and examples, all such things must be taken into account (3.77–83). Cicero's pragmatic approach suggests that therapy has its own aims and rules and is not strictly dependent on the explanation of the emotions: while he clearly favors the Stoic explanation, he does not feel compelled to recommend only the therapy in agreement with that explanation.

Although every case will pose its own challenges, Cicero appears optimistic about the general practical utility of a flexible therapeutic model that focuses on the transformation of beliefs, presenting himself as a person who has benefitted from it, and he sums things up with admirable sensitivity and nuance (3.82–83):

> M.: But one must go back to the same fountainhead, that all *aegritudo* is far removed from the wise man, since it is empty (*inanis*), since it is undergone for no purpose, since it does not originate in nature but in judgment (*iudicio*), in belief (*opinione*), in a certain invitation to grief when we have decreed that we ought to feel this way. By the removal of this, which is wholly up to us (*totum voluntarium*), *aegritudo*, being in a state of grief, will be laid aside, but nevertheless a sting (*morsus*) and certain symptoms of the shrinking of the soul will remain. Let them say that this is quite natural (*sane naturalem*), provided that the offensive, hideous, sorrowful term of *aegritudo* is absent, since it is not able to be with wisdom and is, so to speak, in no way able to share its home.

The admission of a natural sting and diminishment of the soul is telling: the experience of loss is real, and it has real emotional effects on all of us, even the sage, as is natural and appropriate; but, as the sage illustrates, loss can and should be borne in an emotional state of equanimity and constancy, rather than in the disturbed and feverish emotional state of *aegritudo*.

In sum, in his philosophical treatment of the emotions, Cicero strongly advocates the supremacy of the Stoic cognitivist view that places our emotional responses completely under our own control. He affirms this time and again in the third and fourth books of the *Tusculan Disputations*. Cicero's preference pertains not only on a purely intellectual level: he showcases the therapeutic power of philosophy, and how such a model of the emotions can serve as a genuine aid in the therapy of *aegritudo* and other disturbances of the soul. He uses his own recent experience as an illustrative example: unlike what we see in the private correspondence to

Atticus, in the *Tusculans* Cicero presents an image of himself bearing up to loss in an exemplary fashion – time and continual contemplative reflection on what is truly bad have alleviated his grief and allowed him to retain the equanimity and control befitting a Roman statesman, and they may do so for others too.[32]

Conclusion

In the *Tusculan Disputations* Cicero demonstrates his familiarity with the major views on the emotions and the soul in the Greek philosophical tradition. He conveys a clear impression of his own intellectual preferences: Plato's views on the immortality of the soul and the Stoic position on the emotions. He does not present anything overly innovative in terms of philosophical theory, preferring to assess the persuasiveness of the competing views in the tradition. Most impact comes in the therapeutic realm: drawing on his own recent experiences, and against the backdrop of civil war and political crisis, Cicero conveys how thinking deeply about the nature of the emotions and the soul can help one to deal with grief and loss in the present, and to avoid anxiety about shocks and upheavals in the future. In the *Tusculans* Cicero thus showcases the practical utility of philosophy to his Roman audience, while presenting himself as an exemplar of the benefits that follow.

Further Reading

Setiaoli 2013 offers an engaging general assessment of Cicero's treatment of the soul, incorporating further relevant material from the dialogues *De republica* and *De senectute* in particular. For Cicero's engagement with Plato's treatment of the soul in the *Phaedo*, see Stull 2012 and Brittain 2012: 110–119. For Latin text and English translation of the *Tusculans*, see King 1971. On the treatment of the emotions in the third and fourth books of the *Tusculans*, the translation and commentary of Graver 2002 is indispensable. Accessible critical discussion can also be found in Woolf 2015: 201–247. Gildenhard 2007 makes the case for a pointedly political reading of the *Tusculans*, and he also has much to say on Cicero's

---

[32] This is pertinent to the wider intellectual project of the *Tusculans*, in particular the legitimizing of the beneficial roles philosophy might play in Roman political life, on which see Gildenhard 2007 in particular.

treatment of the emotions and the soul. White 1995 is excellent on the therapeutic theme in particular. Altman 2009 assesses Cicero's self-presentation in the *Tusculans* within the framework of Roman masculinity. Wisse 1989 offers detailed discussion of Cicero's treatment of the emotions in the context of rhetorical theory and oratorical practice.

CHAPTER 11

Ethical Theory and the Good Life

Raphael Woolf

In the *Tusculan Disputations*, Cicero praises Socrates for having been "the first to have called philosophy down from the heavens and placed it in cities and even brought it into homes, compelling it to ask about life and ways of living, and about things good and evil" (5.10). Cicero's formulation portrays Socrates as not simply enquiring about value but doing so in a worldly fashion – bringing philosophy into the city and the home. These two aspects – the need for philosophical ethics to engage with human life and to adopt a questioning rather than dogmatic approach – constitute a central focus of Cicero's main work on ethical theory, *De finibus*. It is on these aspects that I shall focus in this chapter. Given its short compass, I take a selective approach, highlighting features of Cicero's discussion that I hope readers may find of particular philosophical interest.

De finibus: Title and Structure

The title of the work refers to the ends or goals that one might pursue in one's life.[1] So *De finibus* invites us to reflect on what the chief human goods are, the attainment of which will give us the best possible life. Cicero considers in this regard three leading ethical theories of his day: Epicureanism, which proposes that the chief good is pleasure; Stoicism, which holds that the chief – in fact the only – good is virtue; and the theory of Antiochus' Old Academy, which, while including goods other than virtue within its conception of the supreme good, places virtue higher than the rest.

The basic structure of the work is as follows: for each theory, Cicero puts into the mouth of a proponent an exposition of that theory, followed

---

[1] It may literally be translated as *On Ends*, though the full Latin title of the work – *De finibus bonorum et malorum* (literally *On the Ends of Goods and Evils*) – raises puzzles of its own, on which see further Allen 2014.

by a critical response delivered by Cicero himself. Thus Epicureanism is propounded and criticized in, respectively, books 1 and 2; then Stoicism in books 3 and 4; and finally Antiochus' theory in book 5, which contains both the case in its favor and Cicero's response. This structure offers Cicero's readership the resources to compare and contrast the different theories and make up their own minds about which, if any, is more likely to be correct.

Ethics and Nature

The opening part of the exposition by Torquatus, Cicero's Epicurean spokesman, emphasizes two features that Cicero had announced as part of the common framework of his enquiry, though neither is an obviously indispensable feature of ethical theory. The first is the idea that there is indeed only one highest good. In his preface Cicero spoke of investigating "the goal, the final and ultimate thing, to which all deliberations about living well and acting rightly are to be referred" (1.11). Torquatus picks this up at 1.29 as "the final and ultimate good, the thing that all philosophers are agreed must be such that all things should be referred to it, while it is itself referred to no other thing."

The notion of an ultimate goal is normative: both Cicero and Torquatus speak of it as being that to which other things are to be, or should be, referred. Whether or not all agents actually do structure their aims in this way, they ought, rationally, to do so. The question then becomes: how should one determine what that ultimate goal actually is? Here the second key feature of Cicero's framework comes into play: nature. Cicero states that we need to investigate what nature pursues as the most desirable thing (1.11); and Torquatus will justify the choice of pleasure as the ultimate goal by calling it the "uncorrupted and sound judgment of nature" (1.30).

Torquatus' recommendation for following nature is that we observe that "every animal, as soon as it is born, seeks pleasure and rejoices in it as the greatest good, while shunning pain as the greatest evil" (1.30). He declares that in the behavior of animals, especially (at least in the human case) the very young, nature is uncorrupted, and this in turn he connects to the making of uncorrupted judgments (1.30, 71). Judgment is corruptible, by implication, when based on sources other than such behavior. Torquatus takes it as an empirical fact that creatures do instinctively seek pleasure and avoid pain. And he also takes it that instinctual behavior, insofar as it represents an uncorrupted state, guides us toward what is good and away from what is bad.

Nature and Reason

It is our senses that testify that pleasure is good and pain bad (1.30, 71) and it is from our senses that all our knowledge of the world is ultimately derived (1.30, 64). The senses are thus basic in two ways: they serve to guide us before our higher faculties have developed; and they supply the information on which the functioning of those faculties depends. For this reason, their evidence is to be regarded as truthful, on pain of rejecting the whole idea that knowledge is attainable (1.64). This indicates that, for Torquatus, while the reports of our senses are closely correlated with the reliability of instinctual behavior, our senses are not the sole guide to our good. Indeed he tells us that, according to some Epicureans, the intrinsic desirability of pleasure and undesirability of pain can be grasped by reason, such that we have an innate conception of these features in our minds; still others consider that precise argumentation is needed to establish the goodness of pleasure against the many philosophers who deny it (1.31).

That it is more than instinctual behavior that the Epicureans recommend is further confirmed when Torquatus reveals one of the most distinctive features of their position: the idea that the greatest pleasure is to feel no pain (1.39). This view is based on a particular piece of Epicurean reasoning: the denial that there is any middle state between pleasure and pain. It is not possible, they hold, for any sentient being to experience neither pleasure nor pain; if so, then it is reasonable to conclude that once one has removed all pain, pleasure has reached its maximum, and can vary in kind but not in amount (1.38).

Its emphasis on nature does not mean that Epicureanism neglects elements that we might regard as distinctively human. Torquatus has plenty to say also about Epicurean views on virtue and on friendship (1.42–54, 65–70). Nonetheless, its prescriptions about the highest good are evidently supposed to apply to humans without restriction. If animal nature is our basic guide to what is good, then social and cultural norms that seem to be inconsistent with that guidance will be dismissed as mistaken, evidence of a corrupted way of thinking that prevents us from fulfilling our true nature.

The Values of Rome

Cicero's main response to Torquatus, in book 2, is previewed in his initial, critical outline of Epicurean theory in book 1. At 1.23–24 he appeals to the behavior of two of Torquatus' ancestors, both stern military men who treated their sons harshly (execution for cowardice and banishment for taking bribes, respectively), treatments which in Cicero's view can only be explained by their having put the wider public interest ahead of their own pleasure, contrary to Epicurean prescription. Pointedly, Cicero describes the first Torquatus as acting against the "very nature" of a father's love for his son (1.23).

It is no coincidence that the main elements of Cicero's examples here are military and family, both central to ancient Roman values. Torquatus defends his ancestors' behavior in terms compatible with Epicurean theory (1.34–35). Focusing in particular on the first Torquatus, he argues that he acted to uphold his authority at a time of war, and therefore to enhance his own security and so, ultimately, pleasure. More striking than the details of Torquatus' explanation is that he feels the need to give it. Why could he not have said that his ancestors were misguided and that it took later generations to see the Epicurean light? Torquatus says explicitly that he has no reason to fear he cannot "accommodate" his ancestors to the Epicurean view (1.34). That he rises to Cicero's challenge in this way indicates that ancestral behavior has normative force for him: his ancestors must be read as acting from (what he considers) the correct motives.

Interestingly, it appears that Torquatus' own father was an Epicurean, whom Torquatus evidently admired. He reports with enthusiasm his father's rebuttal of a Stoic argument against hedonism (1.39); and, though this is not said explicitly, perhaps was influenced by his father in adopting Epicureanism himself. Cicero thus slyly reinforces the sense that ancestral piety is an ineliminable part of the value system that Torquatus shares.[2] He has induced Torquatus to agree that it would be a *problem* for the validity of Epicurean ethics if it did not sit comfortably with the norms of Roman culture. The reader is thus encouraged to reflect on whether, and if so how, the abstract and general features of an ethical theory are to fit with outlooks and practices which, at least in part, carry normative weight precisely because they represent adherence to a particular tradition.

This issue is picked up in Cicero's sustained critique of Epicurean ethics in book 2, where he sets out a vivid comparison of lives at 2.63–65. Cicero contrasts one Lucius Thorius, who was unrestrained in his appetites but had the taste and resources to satisfy them, feared neither death nor the gods, and was healthy and popular. Much less happy was he, declares Cicero, than the Roman general Marcus Regulus, who promised his

---

[2] On the place of such piety in the history and reception of the Torquatus family, see further Feeney 2010.

Carthaginian captors that, if his mission failed, he would return to captivity having been sent by them to Rome to negotiate a prisoner exchange. Urging the Senate upon his arrival never to agree to such an exchange, Regulus thence returned – in effect voluntarily – to be tortured and executed by the Carthaginians.

One of the striking things about this comparison is that Thorius is given some virtuous qualities. The proof that he had no fear of death is that he died in battle for his country (2.63); and Cicero tells us he would have endured pain robustly (2.64). But evidently his virtue pales into insignificance beside that of Regulus, and that is the dimension against which a happy life must be measured. Cicero tells us that the judgment about Regulus' happiness is made by "virtue herself," and he uncorks the memorable oxymoron that people are often happy even when sad, if they are steadfast and true (2.65).

These sorts of descriptions have two noteworthy features, one of method, the other of substance. In reverse order, they put pressure on Epicurean theory to explain why we admire Regulus' actions so much (assuming that we do); and they show the importance of concrete examples in testing the credibility of ethical theory. This is not of course to say that the Epicureans would have no response to such cases. For a start, there is the important question of who are the "we" that admire Regulus. Here and elsewhere in book 2 Cicero uses predominantly Roman examples to illustrate his favored (and, for that matter, disfavored) kinds of life. It is open to an Epicurean to respond that they have no obligation to simply accept Roman values as authoritative. Epicurean theory is professedly a radical one that sees most humans as having been corrupted by false values and blinded to what nature demands.

Yet the value we place on a particular way of life is, it might be argued, inevitably colored by the cultural assumptions we bring with us. Cicero evidently expects his readers to respond to a comparison such as that between Regulus and Thorius by seeing some force in the idea that, even if Regulus were not (as Cicero claims) the happier, his heroics in returning voluntarily to captivity at least show that in some significant sense his life was the worthier or more admirable. One can, however, imagine other ways of responding to the Regulus case: that it was an act of masochism, for example, that showed a rather twisted sense of what counted as virtuous behavior; that he would have been of far more use to Rome had he not handed himself back, and so on. Cicero in fact does imagine his Roman readers raising such objections to Regulus (which he goes on to rebut) in book 3 of *De officiis*.

Society and Integrity

So what should we, as non-Roman readers, make of Cicero's discussion? Even if we accepted that he demonstrates an incompatibility between Roman and Epicurean values, it is not clear that this should have any hold on us – or even that Cicero would have thought that it should (we are not ancient Romans). We are surely both able and entitled to assess the Epicurean case on its own merits. On the other hand, we are no less the inheritors of cultural assumptions and outlooks than the Romans, even if ours are different, and even if the "we" implied by that are a great and diverse plurality. Disentangling a thing's "own merits" from the values we bring preloaded, so to speak, to an encounter with it is neither a simple nor perhaps a viable task.

This is not of course to say that our perspectives cannot be changed by such encounters. Ethical theory, particularly of the professedly radical sort that many of the ancient theorists propounded, would hardly have a point if that were the case; and Cicero's project of communicating such theories would be equally unintelligible in that light. But coming to a theory from outside of any perspective *is* unintelligible. What Cicero's holding up of Epicurean ethics against the canvas of Roman tradition is supposed to convey is a point about how ethical theory in particular must conform, not so much to specific values and traditions, as to certain basic elements of what makes us human, without which it would be hard to discern how an ethical theory could have any purchase at all: above all, perhaps, our status as social creatures shaped by our relation to specific histories and traditions.[3]

Epicureanism, despite its advocacy of a quiet life largely free from political participation,[4] does not deny that humans are essentially social beings: the importance of friendship in its ethics bears witness to that. If so, then Cicero proceeds to raise a problem for a theory that lays emphasis on the social nature of humans: the difficulty of publicly proclaiming one's (in this case) Epicurean beliefs.[5] Torquatus, as a typically ambitious and well-connected young Roman, has not allowed his Epicurean sympathies to deter his pursuit of the higher reaches of public office, and Cicero asks him to consider what effect it would have if he publicly announced that his

---

[3] On the centrality of the social dimension in Cicero's ethical thought, see further Reydams-Schils (Chapter 12) in this volume.

[4] Cicero treats what he regards as Epicurean political quietism with scorn at *De republica* 1.9–11.

[5] See here Inwood 1990: 154–155.

aim was the maximization of his own pleasure, rather than serving the public interest (2.74). Cicero points out that Torquatus does *not* present himself in public in terms of the Epicurean rationale but speaks instead of duty and fidelity, of what is right and honorable, of risking all, even to the point of death, for his country (2.76).

The example is couched by Cicero in highly Roman terms. Could not an Epicurean reply that all the case shows is that Roman values are so corrupted that an enlightened Epicurean in Rome will have to dissimulate in order to find favor with fellow citizens? This response misses something important about the example: it does not turn on whether Roman values are right or wrong; rather, it asks us to acknowledge the undesirability of having to live a lie – of presenting oneself to others in a way that misrepresents one's true motives (2.76–77).

No doubt the idea that a conventionally ambitious Roman cannot be a consistent Epicurean presents a practical challenge for a would-be advocate of Epicurean doctrine. But Cicero is after more than the highlighting of a tension between Epicurean theory and Roman convention. It is not, after all, as if we read Cicero's critique and think: the problem of public proclamation is one peculiar to the culture of ancient Rome. In the political sphere, it is hard to imagine any politician in any age being able to assert (however truthfully) that they are acting to promote their own interest rather than the public good. It is equally hard, in many other vital areas of human association (friendship, for example), to imagine justifying one's participation to those with whom one is associating by reference to one's own pleasure rather than concern for those other participants (cf. 2.78–79).

Part of Cicero's point, then, is that an ethical theory goes wrong just insofar as its principles cannot be openly proclaimed. But he is unwilling to leave us with the thought that hypocrisy or lack of integrity might nonetheless be a requirement for social cooperation to work – a necessary (if regrettable) oiling of the wheels. On the contrary, his response to Torquatus implies a conception of openness and integrity as ethically paramount for a social being, and his targeting of their perceived lack in the Epicurean case indicates that he would expect any reflective Epicurean to be of the same view.[6]

---

[6] For a contemporary standpoint from which to compare and contrast Cicero's critique of ancient Epicureanism, see Williams 1973 on modern utilitarianism as failing (among other things) to account for values of openness and integrity. See also n. 9 below.

Virtue and Reason

We shall see below that Cicero mounts a similar critique in book 4 against Stoic ethics. But first, in book 3, the Stoic theory is laid out by its spokesman Cato the Younger, arch defender of the traditional values of the Roman Republic. Indeed, Stoicism, with its emphasis on the supremacy of virtue and the value of political participation, seems on the face of it to conform much more readily than Epicureanism to traditional Roman values.

As a preliminary, Cato gives a concise account of the motivation for the Stoic claim that virtue is the only good (3.10), namely that otherwise one cannot say that virtue suffices for happiness (3.11), or that the wise person – who it is assumed will be virtuous – will be happy (3.42). At 3.11 Cato explains that the value of virtue could not be accounted for if it turned out that virtuous people could have miserable lives. His point about value is brought out with particular emphasis in an argument that Cato later gives to the effect that the happy life is the honorable life. One cannot, the argument goes, take pride in one's life unless it is a happy one; so only a happy life is one that merits pride. But since the only life that merits pride is an honorable one, the honorable life and the happy life are the same (3.28).

The first premise of the argument might be questioned. That is, we might wonder whether it is true that a life that is not happy cannot be a matter of pride. But the Stoics are asking us to consider what it would mean if we could say of our lives that they were happy but not a matter of pride or miserable yet a matter of pride. That would perhaps mean regarding oneself as not the agent of one's own life, insofar as happiness or misery would be things that happened to one rather than resulting from what one does, the latter being the proper basis of pride. A happy life, then, must be one in which pride can properly be taken. But since the only such life is an honorable one, the happy and the honorable life must be the same.

Reflection on the relation between value and agency offers one way of understanding the Stoic insistence that to live happily is to live virtuously (3.29), and their rejection of any other good than virtue. It also explains why Cato is able to describe the Stoic wise person as the only one who is truly free and subject to the dominion of no other (3.75). The Peripatetics (the followers of Aristotle), by contrast, in admitting that there are goods other than virtue, namely goods of the body (such as health) and external goods (such as wealth), have to say that happiness will increase the more of

these goods one possesses (3.43), despite their value not being a matter of
the subject's own agency: they are things that might simply happen (or not
happen) to one.

If this is so, how does Cato meet the charge that virtue has no material
to work with? If it is the only good, how can one make sense of agency at
all, given that it would seem the agent has no basis for making the choices
by means of which virtue is exercised? If virtue is the only good, then it
would seem there is no discrimination to be made between other things in
a way that would explain rational choice and action. It is here that Cato
makes particular use of Stoic technical terminology, reflecting (as he would
argue) a position distinct both from the Peripatetic view – that there are
goods other than virtue – and the view that there are no value discrimi-
nations at all to be made between things other than virtue.

Between virtue as good and vice as bad, the Stoics identify a further class
of items which they term "indifferents." These are neither good nor bad,
but some have value, some have disvalue, and some are neutral (3.50).
Examples given by Cato of indifferents with value – also known as
"preferred indifferents" – are health, well-functioning senses, freedom
from pain, fame, and wealth; examples of indifferents with disvalue – also
known as "dispreferred indifferents" – are the opposites of these: pain,
illness, poverty, and so on (3.51). These items seem quite intuitive: other
things being equal, health is preferable to sickness, lack of pain is preferable
to pain, and so on. But a good theory should be able to tell us why such
things are in these categories. The Stoics, like the Epicureans, appeal to
nature as the ultimate source of value; but, as expounded in *De finibus*,
they have a different view about what is to be picked out as natural, and
hence as of value.

On the Stoic view, it is to its self-preservation, and the things that
conduce to that, that a creature is drawn from birth, while being averse to
its own destruction and whatever seems to threaten that (3.16). Cato
interestingly claims that for a creature to have these sorts of desires it must
have both self-awareness and self-love, these being the basis for our seeking
the things that we do at this stage, things that Cato dubs "the primary
objects of nature." With the exception of soundness of limb, Cato does not
spell out what these are, but one can readily see that if self-preservation is
the primary objective, there will be a range of things other than pleasure
that have value – Cato in fact reports that the Stoics do not even hold
pleasure to be amongst these objects (3.17).

This approach may offer, in outline, the basis of a rational theory of
choice. But Cato needs to show why it is virtue that turns out to be our

ultimate, indeed our only, good. He remarks that once a person becomes capable of understanding, they observe a kind of order and harmony in the things that one ought to do, and infer by the use of reason that this is the highest good and the only thing to be sought on its own account. Cato labels this harmony "consistency" and says that this is what acting honorably consists in (3.21). He also notes that the fact that honorable action was not included amongst the primary natural objects does not mean it is not in accordance with nature (3.22).

The naturalness of action that is honorable evidently derives, on this view, from its adoption being a product of the development of our reason. And indeed we might well think that order and harmony are only discernible by reason, and as such deserving of special value. Thus the Stoics are able to term their highest good as "living consistently with nature" (3.26, 31, 61). As we just saw, it is order and harmony in one's actions that has particular significance. For the Stoics it is in agency that the supreme human good must lie, and the test of whether our actions are of the right sort is that they exhibit order and harmony. But why should this be? What, in particular, is the connection between one's actions being honorable or morally right and their exhibiting order and harmony?

One way of approaching this is to take note of a further Stoic distinction that Cato discusses, that between an "appropriate action" and a "right action." An appropriate action is any action for which a reasonable justification can be given (3.58); a right action is a "complete appropriate action" (3.59). What does "complete" mean here? Cato gives an example of the relation between right and appropriate action as that between returning a deposit "justly" and (simply) returning a deposit – by "deposit" Cato likely means some valuable item lent for safekeeping. We can readily say that returning a deposit is an appropriate action, since there is reason to return it: the item was lent for safekeeping, not donated. But now let us adapt the famous example (which Cato may be alluding to) given by Socrates in book 1 of Plato's *Republic*: one borrows a knife from a neighbor who subsequently goes mad. Once this factor is taken into account, there is reason not to return it, and the return would no longer be justified.

Part of what I take Cato to mean by a "complete" appropriate action, then, is one that is performed on the basis of *all* relevant reasons. That is why Cato describes, in his developmental account of human nature, the key difference between the regular choosing of appropriate actions and the acquisition of virtue as consisting in one's choices being "in accordance to the ultimate degree" with nature (3.20). Hence, too, Cato speaks of right actions as containing "all the measures of virtue" (3.24):[7] each right action, when one is sufficiently developed to perform it, is a full expression of the agent's wisdom. Thus the wise person's actions will be unified by the wisdom they each fully exemplify; and the order and harmony in what one ought to do that Cato spoke of can be understood in that light.

It may seem, however, that a significant gap remains between the idea of a fully developed rational nature and the performance of right actions. Take, for example, a reason one might have for not returning the borrowed knife: that it is very useful for one to keep it. Perhaps the agent might see this as outweighing the fact of its having been borrowed. Can one say that the rationality of such an agent is defective? Cato continues his exposition by noting another aspect of the Stoic developmental account that is concerned with the bond we have with our fellow humans as such: starting from the basic natural desire to procreate, Cato observes that it would be inconsistent of nature to then not have us love our offspring (3.62). From that impulse arises our natural kinship with our fellow humans, based on "the very fact that they are human" (3.63).

In speaking here of the natural desire to procreate and to love one's offspring, Cato explicitly refers to nature as including all animals (3.62). Indeed his reference to nature not being inconsistent alludes to the Stoic doctrine of nature, as a whole, being a rationally organized providential system. But it is still evidently human nature that is his primary focus – he will go on to speak at 3.64 of the Stoic idea (their "cosmopolitanism") of the whole universe as a single community of gods and humans who, conversely, have no relationship of justice with other animals (3.67). Cato speaks of the bond between humans as "much closer" than that between other animals (3.63), and this perhaps implies that it is not just the fact of our common humanity that grounds our concern for our fellow humans but our rational capacity both to recognize that humanity and to see it as the source from which our obligations to our fellow humans flow.[8]

It would follow that the knife's being useful to me gives me no particular reason to prefer keeping it to returning it. A fully developed reason will see my own interests as carrying no special weight over those of a fellow human being. More pragmatically, Cato's account of the distinctively social character of humans, based on our rational nature, enables him to put in a bid for what one might call "the Roman vote." Given that we

---

[7] See also Cicero's attribution to the Stoics of complete appropriate action as involving "all the numbers" at *De officiis* 3.14.

[8] On Cicero's engagement with cosmopolitanism, see further Atkins (Chapter 15) in this volume.

are all members of a single human fellowship, we should place the common interest above our own, and this explains why dying for the republic is praiseworthy (3.64), why we make wills and appoint guardians for our children in the event of our death (3.65), and why it is in accordance with nature to take part in government as well as marry and have children (3.68).

Value and Virtue

It is no accident, in the context of a work written primarily for a Roman readership, that Cato picks out these Roman values of family and country as part of the upshot of Stoic theory, nor that Cicero's response in book 4 makes it clear that he sees difficulties with Stoic ethical theory in precisely this regard. It turns out, in fact, that the Stoics as Cato presented them, and not just the Epicureans, are vulnerable to the charge that their ethics cannot be publicly proclaimed. This is a consequence not just of their thesis that virtue is the only good and vice the only evil, but also of a certain Stoic view about the character of virtue itself, namely that it does not admit of degrees (3.48). Recall that every right action expresses "all the measures" of virtue (3.24). As I interpreted this, no action counts as right for the Stoics unless it is taken in the light of every reason relevant to a decision to perform it; and this explains why the Stoics take it to follow that unless one has this maximal wisdom, one is not wise at all and, correspondingly, virtue is not possessed: the single reason which one overlooks might be the difference between the action's being right or wrong.

Both the doctrine that virtue is the only good and the conception of virtue as not admitting of degrees are regarded by Cicero as linguistic distortions of positions already held by the Peripatetics and other ethical theorists (4.56–57, 60). But despite (as Cicero contends) not differing from the Peripatetics in substance, the Stoics have a theory which, in the terms they express it, cannot be proclaimed in those contexts that define the sphere of public life for a Roman: courts, assembly, Senate house, and battlefield. A lawyer, observes Cicero, could not credibly conclude the case for the defense by declaring that the punishments of exile and confiscation were not evils, but merely to be "rejected" (the Stoic technical term, counterpart of "chosen" or "selected," for aversion toward dispreferred indifferents); nor could an orator announce, with Hannibal at the gates, that captivity, enslavement, and death were no evils (4.22). Moreover, the Senate would not be able to speak of Scipio Africanus' triumph as won by his valor, since he did not meet the standards of perfection required, in Stoic terms, for virtue (4.22).

This sort of objection is perhaps even more potentially damaging for the Stoics, with their emphasis on agency and public participation, than for the Epicureans. While the Epicureans could not proclaim their hedonism in the public sphere without in effect disqualifying themselves from participation in that sphere, the Stoics cannot express their doctrines about virtue in such contexts without incurring ridicule or incomprehension (or both). What they are left with, according to Cicero, is hypocrisy: the use of ordinary language in public, their own language in their writings (4.22). This hypocrisy cannot even be justified as a "realist" defense of the need to deal with ordinary people's views, since if Cicero is right about Stoic ethics, it is much closer to such views than their technical terminology would suggest.

No doubt there is much that the Stoics, like the Epicureans, could say in response. Cicero's aim is to provoke debate, not close it down. Still, the notion that the central Stoic doctrines cannot be publicly proclaimed retains its unsettling effect as an objection, all the more for a theory that, unlike Epicureanism, strove in Cato's hands to present itself as friendly to political activity and to the values of Rome. In raising such problems for a theory that regards virtue as the only good, Cicero has paved the way for consideration, in book 5, of an ethics that is rather more generous in the goods that it recognizes.

The Power of Pluralism

In book 4 Cicero regularly contrasted the Stoics with the Peripatetics, if only to assert that their theories about what is good differ only in terminology, with Zeno the founder of Stoicism pictured in effect as wrapping in new clothes the doctrines of his teacher Polemo (Plato's third successor as head of the Academy), who seems to have been the first explicitly to formulate the good life as being one that accords with nature (4.3, 14, 45, 61). At the same time, although today we regard Platonic and Aristotelian ethics as quite distinct, Cicero here treats Plato, Aristotle, and the early leading lights of their respective schools as espousing in essence the same ethical theories (4.3–5). This approach is shared by Piso, the expositor of Antiochus' ethics in book 5, a system which is generally labeled that of the "Old Academy," since Antiochus took himself to be reviving what he saw as the authentic doctrines of the original Platonic Academy before it fell under the sway of the skeptical philosophy of the New Academy. Thus

Piso, who has studied under Antiochus, will expound the doctrines that he regards, and tells us that Antiochus regarded, as held in common by the early Academics and Peripatetics (5.7–8, 14, 21–22).

Let us look at some aspects of the theory that Piso expounds. He affirms that every creature loves itself and strives from birth for self-preservation, seeking what conduces to that, at first instinctually and later more reflectively as it becomes aware of what is suited to its nature (5.24). Piso specifies that while for all creatures the goal is the realization of their nature, so that the good life will be life in accordance with (that) nature, each kind of creature has its own nature. Therefore, the good will be different for different creatures (5.25). So in the human case the highest good is "to live in accordance with fully developed human nature that is in need of nothing" (5.26).

The reason why Piso is so explicit on the seemingly obvious point that it is human nature we are dealing with is connected with his sense of what human nature encompasses. The Stoics work on the basis that we are essentially rational creatures, a feature which for them we share with the gods, so that their theory can be read as concerned with rational nature as such. The Epicureans, on the other hand, emphasize what connects our nature to that of living creatures generally. Piso is presented by Cicero as occupying what one might call the middle ground. A human being consists of body and mind, although the faculties of the body are less important than those of the mind. The human mind in turn consists of both the senses and the intellect, the latter being the natural ruler of the human whole (5.34).

It follows from this that it is in accordance with nature for our bodies and our senses to be healthy and well-functioning (5.35–36). The intellect has two main types of virtues: Piso calls "non-volitional" those that are spontaneous, such as receptivity to learning and good memory; and "volitional" those that the agent is responsible for, adding that only the latter are virtues properly speaking. These include prudence, temperance, courage, justice, and so forth (5.36). There is thus a ranking of goods, those of the mind ranked higher than those of the body, and the volitional virtues ranked higher than the non-volitional. Piso explains that the (volitional) virtues rank highest because they spring from reason, the most divine element in a human being, virtue being the perfection of reason (5.38).

What, though, is the connection between reason and virtue? It is not clear that Piso successfully offers an account of how virtue represents reason's perfection. In fact, when he does consider how we develop virtue and come to value it in the right way, reason does not feature prominently in explanatory terms. He tells us that children exhibit semblances of virtue, in that they have a natural propensity to act and to show affection, generosity, and gratitude (5.43; cf. 5.61), which would certainly establish virtue as a natural good, but does not explain its connection to reason or (thereby) its ranking in the scheme of goods. Although Piso offers a similar account of our development as social beings to that given by Cato, culminating in a sense of devotion to the whole human race (5.65), Piso's version lacks the simple but crucial explanation that it is in virtue of our shared humanity that this arises, which in the Stoic case ties the account to the operation of reason.

This reflects a further distinctive feature of Piso's position, deriving ultimately from Aristotle's *Nicomachean Ethics*: there are in fact two types of true virtue, one already noted, embracing the regular virtues of justice, courage, and so on and their exercise in the practical arena, the other embracing scientific pursuits, in particular the study of the celestial universe (5.57–58). One might call these two types of virtue practical and contemplative, respectively.

Contemplative virtue can be regarded as natural by reference to the eagerness of children to find things out (5.48) and as virtue by reference to the admiration we have for high intellectual achievement (5.50); and it is evidently not hard to see how contemplative rather than practical virtue flows from our rational capacities. While stressing the primacy of the whole category of virtue, Piso ranks contemplation as the highest kind, followed in effect by a subdivision of practical virtue: the knowledge and practice of politics, and then the exercise of the practical virtues in general (5.58).

In fact Piso seeks to blur even the rankings that he offers: not to make a better match with some preexisting Roman scheme but, on the contrary, to emphasize the pluralism, even within the volitional realm, inherent in his theory's recognition of varieties of human excellence: "The types of [virtuous] activity are several," he affirms at 5.58, having noted at 5.54 that sometimes we go without sleep for the sake of some piece of "action or study" without indicating that one should be valued over the other. At 5.57 he declares that the best people do not find life worth living if they cannot take part in the management of affairs, suggesting if anything priority for the political conception, before speaking of how those of superior outlook either seek public office or – though it is unclear whether these are still supposed to be the superior ones – devote themselves to study.

Although this slackness about ranking will open up Piso to criticism, it is I think constructed by Cicero as an important feature of Piso's ethics: its pluralism is its point. What, after all, is an ethical theory for? Is its purpose to imply that there is a mechanical method, to be uncovered by the theory in question, of arranging our values? That seems to misrepresent the complex way that different values compete and cooperate both within and across individuals and societies. If a purported ethical theory ends up failing to capture this organic quality of lived human experience and decision-making, we must ask whether the notion of a theory, with its necessary generalizations and simplifications, is helpful or even applicable in the ethical realm. Piso's exposition is, to this extent, anti-theory, emphasizing plurality not just of values but of the relations between values; and, true to its Aristotelian spirit, setting more store by the way people actually think about value than by artificial abstraction.

Part of Cicero's task in the final portion of *De finibus* is to deliver some criticism of Piso's account, but it is noteworthy that Piso, unlike the Stoic and Epicurean spokesmen, gets a right of reply at the end. Piso holds that virtue is sufficient for happiness but that there are also bodily goods such as health and freedom from pain, the possession of which, when added to virtue, will render the subject not just happy (as virtue on its own does) but "happiest" (5.71). Cicero wonders whether treating such items as goods will not simply mean adopting the view of Aristotle's distinguished successor Theophrastus who, while providing a good deal of the resources for Piso's account (5.12), also acts as something of a Peripatetic outlier for having claimed that no life could be happy if caught up in pain or misfortune (5.77).

Cicero asks Piso to consider whether, even if one were to allow that a single misfortune might not affect the happiness of the virtuous, an accumulation of them would: could someone wracked by pain, disease, and other misfortunes plausibly be thought of as happy, let alone happiest? (5.84). Shrewdly turning against him the Aristotelian method of canvassing the views of both the many and the wise, to which Piso had appealed at 5.63 to support his view of the supremacy of virtue, Cicero declares that ordinary folk would deny, and experts be unsure, that someone being tortured could be happy (5.85). Piso responds by at last giving a more worked out "lexical" account of the relation between virtue and the other goods, so as to underpin his view that virtue suffices for a happy (even if not for the happiest) life: the smallest amount of intellectual excellence is ranked ahead of all bodily goods; and no foul-but-pleasant action is better than any honorable-but-painful one (5.93). Virtue can thus be equated with happiness, while happiness can be enhanced through the addition of other goods (5.95).

But does not this theoretical tightening come at a cost? The advantage of Piso's looser exposition is that it accorded with the views about goods and evils of those, as Cicero puts it, who have never come across a philosopher even in a painting (5.80). Piso is allowed to reiterate the criticism – indicating its importance for Cicero – that the Stoics adopt one set of terms in life and another in the lecture room (5.89). But when Piso asks disapprovingly whether philosophers should speak in a different way from human beings (5.89), it is hard to avoid the thought that in his case the terminology of the street now dresses a more radical and rigid substance. In becoming full-fledged theory, his discourse is in danger of losing what made it distinctive and attractive as an account of the good human life.

Conclusion

One of the most distinctive aspects of *De finibus* is the way in which, in properly skeptical fashion, it seeks to cast doubt on the viability of ethical theory itself. While insights and arguments within a theory may play an invaluable role in the enrichment of human life, as whole systems such theories have, for Cicero, an endemic flaw: if they posit a number of separate ends in an unstructured way, they provide no means of organizing one's choices and hence one's life. But if, like Stoicism and Epicureanism, they posit one (highest) end, be it pleasure or virtue, they fail to reflect the complexity of human values and, as we have seen, can thus turn out to be unlivable in practical contexts.[9]

If this leaves us uncertain about which ethical theory, if any, is to guide us, that is as Cicero would have wished it. He points out at the end of Piso's main exposition that a skeptic is entitled to accept any doctrine that he finds plausible, including the theory Piso has just expounded (5.76). But perhaps what matters is not which ethical stance Cicero himself may endorse, but that we his readers continue to explore, in open-minded and critical fashion, the basis of a good human life. Cicero's Socrates would, one feels, have approved.[10]

[9] For an influential contemporary critique of ethical theory, with which Cicero's discussion of ancient theories may usefully be compared, see Williams 1985.

[10] My thanks to the Editors for helpful comments on an earlier draft of this chapter.

Further Reading

The interpretation of *De finibus* laid out in this chapter draws in part on the fuller treatment in Woolf 2015. The work is edited and translated with introduction and notes in Annas and Woolf 2001. Annas and Betegh 2016 is an excellent recent collection of essays devoted to *De finibus*, with extensive bibliography. On aspects of Cicero's method and strategy in *De finibus*, see also Patzig 1979; Lévy 1984; Inwood 1990; Görler 2011; Long 2015. The literature on Stoic and Epicurean ethics is vast. For an overview of Stoic ethics, see Schofield 2003, and of Epicurean, see Erler and Schofield 1999. On the ethics of Antiochus, see Barnes 1989: 86–89; Bonazzi 2009; Sedley 2012, chs. 6–8

CHAPTER 12

Nature and Social Ethics

Gretchen Reydams-Schils

In one of his letters to his friend Atticus, Cicero congratulates him on the birth of his daughter with the following teasing reflection:

> I am glad your little daughter gives you pleasure and that you agree that affection for children is a part of nature. Indeed if this is not the case there can be no natural tie between one human being and another, and once you abolish that, you abolish all society. "And good luck!", says Carneades – an abominable thing to say, but not so naïve as the position of our friend Lucius and Patro [Epicureans]; when they make self-interest their only yardstick while refusing to believe in any altruistic act and maintain that we should do good only to avoid getting into trouble and not because goodness is naturally right, they fail to see that they are talking about an artful dodger, not a good man. (*Att.* 7.2.4; trans. Shackleton Bailey)

Atticus leans toward Epicureanism, yet feels genuine affection for his little daughter despite the fact that Epicureans are supposed to deny that parents' affection for their children is natural, to hold that our relations with others are governed by self-interest, and to enjoin human beings to do good merely in order to avoid getting into trouble (see also *Fin.* 2, esp. 78–85; the opening of *Rep.* and 3.26 ff.). That Cicero is alluding here to a philosophical debate about the value of human relations is also borne out by the fact that he uses a Greek phrase for parental affection: φυσικὴν esse τὴν <στοργὴν τὴν> πρὸς τὰ τέκνα ("affection for children is a part of nature"; lines 1–2 in the previous quotation).[1] It is noteworthy, too, that in this context Cicero parts ways even with the Academic Carneades, contrary to his self-avowed Academic leanings elsewhere. Cicero leaves

---

I would like to thank Jed Atkins, Thomas Bénatouïl, Carlos Lévy, Ermanno Malaspina, Fausto Pagnotta, and the reviewer of this volume for their comments on and assistance with earlier versions of this contribution. A portion of this chapter was previously published in Reydams-Schils 2015.
[1] On the role of the language of *philostorgia* in Cicero's correspondence, see also Aubert-Baillot (Chapter 3, p. 54–57) in this volume.

no doubt that if one abolishes the notion of natural parental affection, one does away with *all* human relations, indeed with society as a whole.

In this chapter we will take a closer look at the philosophical foundation in Cicero's *De officiis* and his other philosophical writings for the social virtues and sociability in general as he sees them, from his distinctive Roman perspective. Cicero, I will argue, consistently anchors his social ethics in the Stoic notion of the cosmopolis as the community of gods and human beings, who share reason. How Cicero attempts to combine this broader cosmopolitan perspective with his patriotism and his call for loyalty to the specifically Roman Republic and its laws is addressed in this volume by Jed Atkins (Chapter 15).

The philosophical debate he echoes in his letter to Atticus already indicates that for his social ethics Cicero is quite willing to borrow key tenets from the Stoics, who, as he tells us himself, endorse the view that the sage will marry and take part in politics (*Fin.* 3.68).[2] This view implies that in order to assess the role of sociability we need to treat together the more "private" sphere of personal relations with the public one of "active participation" in politics (to the extent that this distinction holds in the Roman Republic). Moreover, we need to look beyond the two topics pertaining to Cicero's attitude toward Stoicism that have received the most attention in the scholarly literature, namely the criterion of knowledge and the notion of the "good" as the goal of human life.[3]

Cicero's *De officiis* (*On Duties*) is his last philosophical work, written in October–November of 44 after the murder of Caesar on the Ides of March, while Mark Antony was on the ascendant and the latter's rivalry with Octavian was increasing. The political situation was unstable and the Republic had not been restored after Caesar's death, but Cicero still had some hope that all was not lost, and that he could reenter the political arena with renewed influence and vigor.[4]

Though the work, which focuses on the relation between the *honestum* (honorable) and the *utile* (beneficial), sometimes reads like an etiquette manual and is addressed to Cicero's son Marcus, then studying philosophy in Athens with the Peripatetic Cratippus, it clearly has a broader aim too. The weighty theme that underlies the entire exposition is how to provide a philosophical foundation for the social virtues and the common good as

---

[2] See also Diog. Laert. 7.121; on participation in politics, see the so-called Arius Didymus doxography, Stob. 2.7.11[b] and 2.7.11[m] Wachsmuth; Sen. *De otio*; Dio Chrys. *Or.* 47.2–3; Plut. *De Stoicorum repugnantiis* 1033B–1034B.

[3] On the issue of Cicero's Academic allegiance, see Reinhardt (Chapter 7) in this volume.

[4] Baraz 2012, ch. 6.

incarnated in the Republic, in order to counter the kind of ambition, thirst of power and self-aggrandizing exemplified by men such as Caesar and Mark Antony. The *De officiis* is divided in three parts, with the first book addressing the *honestum*, the second the *utile* (but viewed as directed by the *honestum*), and the third alleged potential conflicts between the *honestum* and the *utile*. It owes an explicit debt to the Stoic Panaetius, though Cicero claims to expand on the original threefold plan of Panaetius' presentation by also dealing with different degrees of the *honestum* and of the *utile* (1.9–10).

Wisdom and Community (*De officiis* Book 1)

The ending of book 1 of *De officiis* (from 1.153) represents a key notion in Cicero's thinking about sociability. This is how he defines "wisdom":

> The foremost of all the virtues is the wisdom (*sapientia*) that the Greeks call *sophia*. (Good sense (*prudentiam*), which they call *phronēsis*, we realize is something distinct, that is the knowledge of things that one should pursue and avoid.) But the wisdom (*sapientia*) that I declared to be the foremost is the knowledge of all things human and divine, and it includes the sociability and fellowship of gods and human beings with each other. If, as is certain, that wisdom is of the greatest importance, then necessarily the duty that is based upon sociability, is also of the greatest importance. (trans. Griffin and Atkins)

In this passage Cicero adopts a distinctly Stoic view of wisdom. That "wisdom is the knowledge of things human and divine" is a definition commonly attributed to the Stoics (which includes, in its fullest version, the knowledge of their causes).[5] More importantly, however, Cicero also includes in his definition (*in qua continetur*) sociability in the guise of the community of gods and human beings. In other words, sociability is intrinsic to this notion of wisdom. And as we know from other contexts, for the Stoics, being rational implies being social (but not the other way round, given that animals and prerational human beings display social behavior as well).[6]

In his next move Cicero deduces from the importance of wisdom *thus defined* the importance of "duty based upon sociability" (*quod a communitate ducatur officium*). The implications of this step in Cicero's reasoning have escaped a number of commentators because it is the specifically

---

[5] *SVF* 2.35–36, 1017; Cic. *Off.* 2.5; *Tusc.* 5.7; Sen. *QNat.* 1 Preface, and *Ep.* 89.5, 90.3.
[6] Reydams-Schils 2002.

Stoic – not Platonic, nor Peripatetic – view of wisdom that supports this move.[7] Thus we could rewrite the claims as follows:

> If as is certain, that wisdom *as manifested in the community of gods and men* is something of the greatest importance, then necessarily the duty that is based upon *sociability* is also of the greatest importance. (*Off.* 1.153; trans. Griffin and Atkins, my emphasis)

Because wisdom comes with this intrinsic social dimension and constitutes the most important virtue, Cicero can claim that social obligation makes up our most important duty. Therefore,

> learning about and reflecting upon nature is somewhat truncated and incomplete if it results in no action. Such action manifests itself most clearly in the protection of human interests, and therefore is concerned with the fellowship of the human race. For that reason this should be ranked above (mere) learning. (*Off.* 1.153; trans. Griffin and Atkins)[8]

The passage hinges on a distinction between "wisdom" (*sapientia*) and mere "learning" (*cognitio*, here coupled with *contemplatio*; see also 1.63). Unlike wisdom, we are meant to infer, mere learning is deficient to the extent that it does not lead to action. Wisdom, which encompasses the community of gods and men, on the other hand, appears to provide the foundation of not just any action but of action that serves the common good. Thus, in the space of a couple of lines Cicero has established a connection between wisdom, sociability, and action on behalf of the common good.

In this passage we catch an important glimpse of Cicero's overall attitude toward physics as the study of nature, one of the three main branches of philosophy, together with ethics and logic.[9] He has reservations about the value of this kind of inquiry when it is conducted for its own sake, but he acknowledges its value precisely insofar as it can provide a foundation of the social virtues and the common good – the kind of

---

[7] Miller 1913: 156–157; Atkins 1990: 258–259; Griffin and Atkins 1991: 60 n. 1. Dyck 1996: 340–344. Bellincioni 1974: 61–67 also overlooks the Stoic background.

[8] *Etenim cognitio contemplatioque naturae manca quodam modo atque inchoata sit si nulla actio rerum consequatur. Ea autem actio in hominum commodis tuendis maxime cernitur pertinet igitur ad societatem generis humani. Ergo haec cognitioni anteponenda est.* Atzert 1971 puts *naturae* in square brackets, following a suggestion by Unger to delete it; other editions, such as Testard 2002 and Winterbottom 1994 do not follow suit. The inclusion of *naturae* is justified by what follows, especially 3.154, which mentions "numbering the stars" and "measuring the size of the earth" as examples of the study of the *natura rerum*.

[9] Reydams-Schils 2015.

virtues, we may add, that were trampled underfoot by Caesar, who is foremost on Cicero's mind in the *De officiis* (1.26).

While the account of wisdom in *De officiis* borrows key elements from Stoicism, it is, taken in its entirety, specific to Cicero. As a comparison with the section on the history of philosophy in book 3 of the *De oratore* (esp. 56–57, 72) reveals, Cicero has construed wisdom in such as a way as to have it represent the virtue of his ideal Roman statesman, which includes the skill of oratory,[10] and this parallel indicates that this notion of wisdom was a leitmotif for Cicero throughout all his theoretical writings. As in *De officiis*, Cicero distinguishes here between the mere knowledge of natural philosophers, who not only neglect their own social obligations, but wrongly induce others to do so as well, and the wisdom of statesmen who put their philosophical and rhetorical training at the service of their communities. This type of wisdom constitutes what Cicero elsewhere calls "perfect philosophy" (*perfecta philosophia*, *Tusc.* 1.7).[11]

As Homeyer astutely points out,[12] Cicero's notion of *sapientia* is also at work in a letter to his brother (*QFr.* 1.1) about how to carry out one's political responsibilities in a province, even though Cicero in this context refers to Plato's philosopher-king (1.1.29). For Cicero, the relation between the active life and engaging in philosophy is not merely a matter of alternating phases in one's life. Rather, political responsibility and the study of philosophy are always meant to reinforce one another. In this respect, too, Cicero could have been inspired by the Stoics, and notably by their definition of the *bios logikos* as embracing both the active and the contemplative lives (Diog. Laert. 7.130).[13] Yet, again, the specific, and specifically Roman, coloring of the relation between action and study is Cicero's because of the centrality of the notion of the *res publica*.[14]

Duties and Sociability

The immediate context of the passage from *De officiis* underscores the importance of sociability for Cicero. Let us turn first to the manner in which he introduces his definition of wisdom:

[10] This issue is discussed in greater detail and in its fuller context in Remer (Chapter 13) in this volume.

[11] Nicgorski 2016: 73–76.   [12] Homeyer 1956: 308–310.

[13] On the implications of this position, see especially Bénatouïl 2007: 10–13 and 2009. So, *pace* McConnell 2014, ch. 3, I do not think that Cicero's position can be explained solely or primarily on the basis of what we know about the Peripatetic Dicaearchus' views (Cic. *Att.* 2.16.3 = 36 SB).

[14] Lévy 2012; Baraz 2012.

In my view those duties that have their roots in sociability conform more to nature than those drawn from learning. This can be confirmed by the following argument: suppose that a wise man were granted a life plentifully supplied with everything he needed so that he could, by himself and completely at leisure, reflect and meditate upon everything worth learning. But suppose also that he were so alone that he never saw another man: would he not then depart from life? (1.153; trans. Griffin and Atkins)

Here Cicero starts out with a dichotomy between (duties arising from) sociability (*communitas*) and (those that arise from) learning (*cognitio*), claiming that the former "conform more to nature." This claim already suggests that *nature* has a role in helping one determine what is right and wrong. Cicero engages in an interesting thought experiment. What would happen to a sage who had all his needs taken care of, could devote himself entirely to learning (*cognitio*), but was completely cut off from human society? Such a sage, Cicero avers, would "depart from life," possibly through suicide. What is at stake here, I submit, is not an existential consideration, that the sage could not handle such loneliness, but rather that a complete isolation from others would undermine the very exercise of wisdom. In that sense, a sage in isolation would be annihilated. The Stoics, as I have argued elsewhere, have a response to this challenge in their claim that a human being, in whichever circumstances she finds herself, is in fact never excluded from the community of gods and men, even if contemplation of the order of the heavenly bodies is the only option left.[15] Though Cicero does not mention this solution here, the definition of wisdom that he advances presupposes it: wisdom always comes with a social dimension. (And he alludes to it when he claims that Scipio Africanus the Elder used to say that he was never less alone than when he was alone: *Off.* 3.1; see also *Rep.* 1.27).

Once Cicero has proposed this definition of wisdom, he goes on, in the remainder of book 1 of *De officiis*, to expand on this fundamental insight in a series of amplifications. Who, he asks, would be so immersed in the *natura rerum* as not to drop everything when one's fatherland, parent, or friend was in danger (1.154)? But even people who have devoted their entire life to study have put that learning to the service of the common good, he argues, by teaching and making others better citizens, not only during their lifetime, but also in the written works they leave behind. In pursuing knowledge of laws, customs, and governance, these thinkers have dedicated their leisure (*otium*) to the active engagement (*negotium*) of

---

[15] Reydams-Schils 2005 and 2016.

others. Using the medium of words is to be preferred to mere solitary thought, no matter how profound, precisely because speech connects us to the community of human beings. Bees, he argues, do not gather to make the honeycomb, but rather make the honeycomb because they are by nature gregarious. Similarly, but to a much higher degree, human beings, who are by nature social, put to use their skill in thinking and acting. Thus it is not true, as "some have claimed," that human beings gather merely for the sake of taking care of necessities. As in the case of the sage with which Cicero set out, even if all of our needs were taken care of, we would seek the company of others, and pursue learning together. He holds that neither would the sage do anything scandalous for the sake of his country, nor would his country expect this of him. Finally, he lays out some principles for the gradation of duties in case of conflict between them (a topic he will continue to pursue in the remainder of *De officiis*): (a) priority should be given to those duties that pertain to the community and (b) among social duties, there is a natural hierarchy of duties – first, duties toward the gods; second, toward one's fatherland; third, toward one's parents; and so on. In this model the more private social duties are listed alongside the public ones.[16] Even though the notion of *officium* in Cicero's Latin is not entirely coextensive with its Greek Stoic counterpart *kathēkon*, like the latter it applies primarily to the sphere of social relations.[17] And thus the social aspect of virtue provides the dominant perspective throughout the *De officiis*. (It is worth recalling that for the ancients and many philosophical schools in Antiquity, virtue, as excellence, is not limited to what we might call social behavior but also refers to the proper order of one's soul). As in his *De legibus* and *De finibus* (see below), Cicero follows the Stoics in anchoring sociability squarely in nature, with the love for offspring being shared by animals and humans alike, but the sociability of humans being stronger because of speech and reason (*Off.* 1.11–12, 22, 50–57; 3.21–28, 69).

In his rendering of the four cardinal virtues, Cicero systematically foregrounds their social importance and implications. There appears to be a tension between his claim, when he first defines the four virtues as four headings of the honorable (*honestum*), that the pursuit of learning (i.e. the virtue of reason) most closely relates to human nature (*maxime naturam attingit humanam*, 1.18) and his statement toward the end, which we discussed already, that the "duties that have their roots in sociability conform more to nature than those drawn from learning" (1.153). It is

---

[16] See also *Off.* 1.50–57 and Atkins (Chapter 15, p. 246–249) in this volume.   [17] Gourinat 2014.

this tension, I have argued, that Cicero tries to resolve by positing a form of wisdom that includes sociability. It is striking that he devotes only two paragraphs (18–19) to the virtue associated with reason, and, as in his *De oratore* (see above), when he returns to the pursuit of learning in his discussion of the other virtues, he sounds a cautionary note against abandoning one's sociopolitical responsibilities for the sake of this pursuit (1.69–71, 92).

Instead of the traditional virtue of justice, Cicero presents a broader category (1.15): the fellowship of human beings or sociability as such (which includes justice and beneficence: 1.20). That broader heading is parsed immediately into "assigning to each his own" (*tribuendo suum cuique*) and "faithfulness to agreements one has made" (*rerum contractarum fide*). *Fides* (trust and faithfulness) is particularly on Cicero's mind, as exemplified by Regulus (first introduced at 1.39; 3.99–115) who, when released from captivity by the Carthaginians to negotiate an exchange of captives, not only made the case against such an exchange (because it would not be in the interest of Rome do so), but even returned to Carthage to face torture and death because he had given his word.

In his discussion of magnanimity, which replaces the traditional cardinal virtue of courage, Cicero explicitly expresses his concern about the damage that great personalities can do by distinguishing between a kind of magnanimity that is driven by selfish desire and one that serves the common good (1.68). He attempts to hedge in this dangerous trait by positing that true magnanimity entails overlooking one's own advantage and caring for the Republic in its entirety, and not just for one group (1.85).

The importance of sociability and of specifically Roman sensitivities leads Cicero to replace the traditional notion of "temperance" with the much broader category of *decorum* (1.93: *prepon* in Greek), which both relates to all virtues and is closely associated with *honestas*, while also referring to a more specific subcategory of virtue pertaining to "modesty" (*modestia*).[18]

The discussion of the notion of the befitting (*decorum*, πρέπον), which also plays a central role in Cicero's analyses of rhetoric,[19] is framed by the theory of four roles (*personae*) that can be assigned to any human being, allegedly derived from Panaetius. These roles are determined by (1) the faculty of reason which all human beings share; (2) one's individual disposition (1.107); (3) the circumstances in which one finds oneself; and (4) one's choice of occupation (1.115). The framework relies on and

---

[18] Schofield 2012.   [19] On this topic, see also Remer (Chapter 13, p. 207–208) in this volume.

expresses the relational aspect of a human being's existence, that is, how one sees oneself in relation to others in society and is in turn perceived by others.[20] "To neglect what others think about oneself is the mark not only of arrogance, but also of utter laxity," Cicero avers (1.99).

Of the first factor that determines our position in life, reason, Cicero emphasizes that it is the key feature that distinguishes human beings from animals and, more importantly, that it is shared by all human beings. Thus, again, Cicero highlights immediately that rationality creates a bond among all human beings. (We can easily imagine, by contrast, the image of a lonely and isolated seeker of knowledge, but we already know how Cicero addresses this scenario – see above.) The other factors determine individual differences, not of isolated individuals, but of people in relation to one another. The key purpose of paying attention to one's individual disposition, in body and what we may call temperament, the second factor, is to choose tasks and responsibilities to which one is suited (1.114) and to achieve a constancy in the manner in which one leads one's life.

The other two roles are determined by circumstances (chance) and by choice, specifically the choice of an occupation. But, given that our choices are often influenced by our ancestry, there is a strong connection, and not a radical opposition, between these two factors. Yet we can also expect the *homo novus* Cicero (that is, the first of his family to rise to senatorial rank and to be elected consul) to state that nature (both in the general and the specific sense) is more important than circumstance in determining one's choice of life (1.120).

Perhaps the most challenging emphasis on the common good in his *De officiis* occurs in the formula (*formula*), or the rule of procedure (3.19–20), that Cicero presents to adjudicate apparent tensions between the *honestum* and the *utile* in book 3: the key distinction is between actions done on behalf of the common good and those done for the sake of oneself. Actions that normally do not fall under the *honestum* can be justified if done not for personal advantage and glory, but to serve the common good. The example Cicero uses is one of a sage dying of hunger, and the conclusion he arrives at is that "the law of nature itself, which preserves and maintains that which is beneficial to men, will undoubtedly decree that the necessities of life should be transferred from an inactive and useless person to someone who is wise, good, and brave, who, if he were to die, would greatly detract from the common benefit" (3.31). Conversely, "each should attend to what benefits him himself, so far as may be done without

---

[20] Gill 1988. Cf. Lévy 2006.

injustice to another" (3.42). With these principles in mind, Cicero can make the case for a son legitimately killing his father (putting "the safety of his fatherland before that of his father") when the latter is a tyrant and all other means of changing the father's behavior and choices have failed (3.90). The allusion to Brutus' part in Caesar's murder could not be clearer (see also 3.32).

Cicero's Earlier Thinking about Sociability

Many aspects of Cicero's theoretical framework for his discussion of duties in the *De officiis* echo his earlier work.[21] Thus *De officiis* can also attest to the importance and continuity of these themes in Cicero's overall outlook. A first set of connections takes us back to Cicero's work of the mid-fifties BCE, his *De legibus* and *De republica*, and, in the case of the *De inventione*, even to his earliest work.

We find a more detailed exposition of the connection mentioned in *De officiis* between the community of gods and men on the one hand, and justice on the other, in book 1 of Cicero's *De legibus* (52 BCE, but it is possible that he kept working on this exposition up to his death). The laws and justice, he argues at great length in his own name, have their basis in Nature (a theme also addressed in *Off.* 3.23–27)[22] – more specifically, in right reason as "applied to command and prohibition" (1.33) – and they rely on the sociability of gods and men, which also implies the kinship between all human beings (1.23–24). Moreover, Cicero claims, in case we miss the point, that "out of all the material of the philosophers' discussions, surely there comes nothing more valuable" (1.28; trans. Keyes) than these insights. As in *De officiis*, there is a distinctly Stoic touch to his interpretation of wisdom (*sapientia*, 1.58), even if here it is presented as a broader consensus. This wisdom includes physics, as the study of the heavens and all existing things (*natura rerum omnium*). And the mind . . .

> . . . when it almost lays hold of the god who rules and governs the universe, and when it realizes that it is not shut in by walls of some fixed spot, but is a citizen of the whole universe, as it were of a single city – then in the midst of this universal grandeur, and with such a view and comprehension of nature, ye immortal gods, how well it will know itself, according to the precept of the Pythian Apollo! (*Leg.* 1.61; trans. Keyes, modified)

---

[21] Nicgorski 2016: ch. 3, esp. 101, 169–170.
[22] On this passage, see also Schofield 1995b: 199–200. Schofield aligns and compares Cicero, *Leg.* 1 with *Off.* 1.11–12, 3.27 and *Fin.* 3.62–63. But I argue here that more revealing parallels emerge from *Off.* 1.153 and *Fin.* 3.64–71: see below.

In this context, the study of nature comes with the realization that one's citizenship in the universe is the ground for any civic activity.

The most striking example in Cicero's writings of this positive use of a "cosmic viewpoint," to borrow a phrase from Gareth Williams,[23] occurs in his "Dream of Scipio" at the end of his *De republica* (completed perhaps in 51; see also 1.26). Like Seneca in his *Naturales quaestiones* (see especially the preface to book 3), Cicero here adopts the view from the universe as a whole.[24] But, unlike Seneca, Cicero uses this viewpoint to underscore the value of the active life and political duties, or, in Williams' words, "the Senecan emphasis remains on self-development, and not [as in Cicero's case] on public service as the highest form of moral action." The view from above can teach us how puny any desire for personal fame and glory would be. Virtue is its own reward, Cicero avers, but virtue for him is still first and foremost "justice and duty, which are indeed strictly due to parents and kinsmen, but most of all to the fatherland" (6.16 = 6.20 Powell) or "the defense of one's native land" (6.29 = 6.33 Powell; see also 6.13 = 6.17 Powell).

The theme of the natural underpinning of human sociability in the *De republica* is not limited to the "Dream of Scipio." It already occurs in the definition of a commonwealth with which Cicero's Scipio sets out (1.39; see also 1.1, 3).[25] A commonwealth, he claims, is not just any random collection of people, but an association based on an agreement about justice and the common good. As such, this type of community is not based on human flaws, but on a sociability that is part of human nature (*naturalis quaedam hominum quasi congregatio*). Even if (s)he could live in prosperity, a human being would not want to be isolated from other humans. The parallels between this definition and the account at the end of book one of *De officiis* are striking, and confirm that Cicero here has the Stoic rather than the Aristotelian foundation of human sociability in mind. Human beings do not congregate merely because of a certain weakness, or, we may add based on *De officiis* (1.157–158), merely in order to take care of necessities. Nature has engrained sociability in human beings. And, as in *De officiis* (1.153), Cicero mentions here the scenario of a human being provided with everything he or she needs, to register again, presumably, the point that sociability is essential to what it means to be human.

The prelude to this definition of a commonwealth involves a discussion of the value of the study of physics that is in line with what we have seen so

[23] See Williams 2012.   [24] Williams 2012: 28–29.
[25] On this definition, see Nicgorski (Chapter 14, p. 224–226) in this volume.

far. The pretext is the alleged appearance of two suns. In this discussion, and in anticipation of the "Dream of Scipio," Scipio Africanus the Younger is presented as defending the opinion that the "view from above" (i.e. the cosmic perspective) is indispensable for the proper governance of human affairs (1.26; see also 1.56) – even though he mentions with approval how Socrates allegedly called philosophy down from the heavens (1.15). Laelius comes across as the most doubtful of the value of this kind of inquiry (1.19, 30 ff.), whereas it is Philus who explicitly raises the question of whether an understanding of the *cosmos* as the community of gods and men would not be indispensable for understanding human communities (1.19). In the *De republica*, Cicero has given Scipio's perspective the final word. Moreover, even if no (Greek) philosophy can do away with the need for practical experience in Roman affairs (1.35), it is striking that the Stoic Panaetius is mentioned for *both* his interest in astronomy (and related questions), of which Scipio does not entirely approve (1.15), and his expertise in political philosophy (1.34).

In his earliest published treatise, the *De inventione* (84 BCE), Cicero appears not yet to have adopted the thesis of the natural sociability of human beings. In this work (1.2) he describes the original condition of humans as being bestial. Humans wandered aimlessly, hardly used their reasoning ability but relied mostly on bodily strength to satisfy their basic needs, and knew no reverence for the gods, social structure, or laws. He posits the existence, however, of (an) individual(s) who did rise above this condition, and through the combination of wisdom and eloquence (this is where rhetoric comes in) succeeded in persuading human beings, despite some reluctance on their part, to form communities and join in a more civilized way of life.

Once communities were established, how, without this same combination of wisdom and eloquence, could

> men possibly have been induced to learn to cultivate integrity and to maintain justice, and to be accustomed willingly to obey others, and to think it right not only to encounter toil for the sake of the general advantage, but even to run the risk of losing their lives? Undoubtedly no one, if it had not been that he was influenced by dignified and sweet eloquence, would ever have chosen to condescend to appeal to law without violence, when he was the most powerful party of the two as far as strength went; so as to allow himself now to be put on a level with those men among whom he might have been preeminent, and of his own free will to abandon a custom most pleasant to him, and one which by reason of its antiquity had almost the force of nature. (*Inv. rhet.* 2; trans. Yonge)

Something has to counter the right of the strongest, Cicero avers here. Yet even in this context we can already detect some features of his later position. Cicero hesitates to call the "right of the strongest" natural; it acquires something like a force of nature (*naturae vim*) merely because it represents the oldest phase of human existence. If we leave aside the question of how the exceptional individuals who turned things around could have emerged in such circumstances, it is still the case even in this narrative of origins that wisdom, through its combination with eloquence, is intrinsically social. The original human beings somehow fall short of what it means to be human precisely because their use of reason is very weak, and they do not have the art of rhetoric at their disposal. As in his later writings, Cicero is not interested here in just any use of reason and wisdom, but in reason and wisdom so construed that together with eloquence they can provide a foundation for human sociability, expressed in reverence for the gods, the fulfillment of one's duties in social relations (*humani officii ratio*), the care for the common good in the commonwealth (even to the point of sacrificing one's life), and the rule of law.

De officiis, De finibus, and the *Tusculanae disputationes*

Cicero's *De officiis* not only picks up themes from earlier phases in his writing career, it also has strong connections with other works from his final period in which his philosophical works were written (46–44 BCE). There are significant structural parallels between, on the one hand, the *De legibus* and *De officiis*, two accounts that Cicero presents in his own authorial voice, and, on the other, book 3 of the *De finibus*, in which the character Cato presents the Stoic position. The structural parallels are underscored by the fact that in his preface to book 1 of the *De officiis* (5–6; see also 3.11, 20) Cicero alludes to the topic of the *De finibus*, and that book 1 of the *De legibus* devotes a brief digression to the same topic (1.52–56). In the *De finibus* Cicero does not present Stoic views in his own name, and the Stoic position is submitted to sustained criticism. Yet these two features of the account do not imply that there is nothing in the character Cato's exposition that Cicero thought worth holding on to. The parallels with his other works can help one discern which features of Stoicism even in Cato's exposition could have been attractive to Cicero. The Stoic grounding of human sociability, I submit, is one such feature.[26]

---

[26] On this issue, see also the contribution by Woolf (Chapter 11) in this volume.

Cato turns to sociability toward the end of his overview of Stoicism (*Fin.* 3.62–71, 73), starting with the natural sociability present in animals. In human beings, however, sociability is actually much stronger:

> Yet the ties between human beings are far closer. Hence we are fitted by nature to form associations, assemblies, and states. The Stoics hold that the universe is ruled by divine will, and that it is virtually a single city and shared by humans and gods. Each one of us is a part of this universe. It follows naturally from this that we value the common good more than our own. (*Fin.* 3.63–64; trans. Woolf)

Once again the community of gods and humans beings provides the foundation for the social aspect of virtue, as it pertains to the common good. In this passage, as in that from the *De legibus* quoted above (1.61), Cicero also introduces a divine will that governs the universe, and hence the material presented here can help us better understand Cicero's sympathies for the Stoic notion of Providence in his *De natura deorum* (as opposed to his criticism of what he considers the rigid determinism of the Stoics in his *De fato* and *De divinatione*).[27] In what follows after this statement about the foundation of human sociability, as mentioned already, we can detect many parallels between this account in the *De finibus* and the *De legibus* and *De republica*, on the one hand, and the *De officiis* on the other:

(1) the importance of laws to encode this preference for the common good;

(2) the centrality of the specific example of dying on behalf of one's fatherland;

(3) the fact that "no one would choose to live in splendid isolation, however well supplied with pleasures" (*quodque nemo in summa solitudine vitam agere velit ne cum infinita quidem voluptatum abundantia*);[28]

(4) the emphasis on the social responsibility of teaching what one knows, and especially of the "principles of practical reason" (*rationibus prudentiae*);

(5) the compatibility of the notion of the cosmopolis with private property (see *Off.* 1.20–21).

---

[27] See also Auvray-Assayas and Begemann (chapters 8 and 9) in this volume.

[28] See also *De amicitia* 87, with Cicero's anchoring of friendship in human beings' natural sociability, passim.

Before concluding his speech, Cicero's Cato briefly returns to the other two branches of philosophy besides ethics, namely logic and physics.[29] In this context Cicero could not be more explicit about the importance of the foundation provided by nature not only for ethics in general, but also for social ethics specifically – and there is no indication in the remainder of the *De finibus* that Cicero would not be willing to adopt this perspective himself. Cato's succinct summary of physics shows clear echoes of views explicitly attributed to Chrysippus in other sources.[30] Once again, for Cicero, the main advantage of Stoic physics is the foundation it provides for the *social* aspect of virtues. Whereas the fragment from Chrysippus in Diogenes Laertius (7.87–88) mentions the connection between virtue and happiness defined as the "good flow of life" (εὔροια βίου) in general, Cicero focuses on justice, friendship, the other social relations, and piety toward the gods. With this move he clearly signals, as in other contexts, why and the extent to which Stoic physics matters to him.

It should come as no surprise, then, that in the final book of his *Tusculan Disputations* (5.69–72) Cicero provides his readers with the most detailed positive account of the study of nature, not only of the heavens and other natural phenomena, but also of a human being's privileged connection with the divine mind that governs the chain of causes in the natural realm. Here, too, the view from the universe in its entirety not only bestows calm (*tranquillitas*) but also provides the foundation for the knowledge of the virtues (*hinc illa cognitio virtutis exsistit*): "Discovery is made of what nature regards as the end in what is good and the last extremity in what is evil [the topic of *De finibus*], the object of our duties and the rule for the conduct of life that must be chosen [the topic of *De officiis*]" (5.71; trans. King). Finally, through this type of inquiry, Cicero avers, one can also establish that virtue is sufficient for the happy life.

How Cicero's consistent commitment to the Stoic notion of the community of gods and men sits with his Academic allegiance remains a puzzle. The least we can say, however, is that calling into question the importance of a philosophical foundation for *communitas et societas* was never an option for Cicero, in any of his theoretical writings.

---

[29] Inwood 2015 overlooks this passage, as well as the earlier discussion by Reydams-Schils 2002 and the other relevant secondary literature. See also Reydams-Schils 2015.
[30] See Plut. *De Stoicorum repugnantiis* 1035C–D = *SVF* 3.68 and *SVF* 3.4 = Diog. Laert. 7.87–88.

Further Reading

The introductions by Testard 2002, originally published in 1965, and by Griffin and Atkins 1991 lay out the key themes of the *De officiis*. Dyck 1996 is a scholarly commentary on the entire *De officiis*. Gill 1988 provides an analysis of the four *personae* theory. Schofield 1995b examines Cicero's philosophical approaches to justice. Lévy 2012, Baraz 2012, and Nicgorksi 2016 provide a framework for Cicero's commitment to political activity throughout his career, also in his philosophical writings. On Stoic cosmopolitanism, see especially Schofield 1999 and Vogt 2008. Reydams-Schils 2005 assesses Cicero in the context of what we know about Stoic sociability, and Reydams-Schils 2015 looks specifically at Cicero's assessments of the value of the study of nature for his normative ideal. Bénatouïl 2007 and 2009 discuss the relation between action and contemplation in Stoicism in the context of broader philosophical debates.

CHAPTER 13

Philosophy, Rhetoric, and Politics

Gary Remer

We live in a world today in which most people consider politics an immoral vocation and regard rhetoric, especially political rhetoric, as "language characterized by insincere expression" or as "inflated or empty verbiage."[1] Meanwhile, philosophy is viewed by the public as an academic field with little to no practical significance, unrelated to real-life politics. Cicero, however, would have rejected these characterizations. For Cicero, rhetoric, politics, and philosophy are so interconnected that they are, or at least should be, a unity under the rubric "eloquence." To be sufficiently capacious to include all three, eloquence means something different to Cicero than to us, with its current meaning of fluent or persuasive expression. Rather than simple (or even outstanding) facility in language, eloquence for Cicero is public speech, especially political speech, rooted in wisdom. As we shall see, Cicero, most especially in his rhetorical master-piece, *De oratore* (*On the Ideal Orator*), deems the *eloquens*, the man of (true) eloquence, to be the perfect orator who is, at the same time, the ideal statesman, unfolding "the thoughts and counsels of the mind in words, in such a way that it can drive the audience in whatever direction it has applied its weight" (3.55).[2] Because of the danger inherent in such forceful persuasion, the eloquent orator must apply his rhetorical skills only after "having acquired all-embracing knowledge" (3.55). Thus, Cicero's orator-cum-statesman is also a philosopher of a kind – a philosopher who is a man of action, who uses his wisdom to promote the common welfare, unlike those philosophers who shirk "politics and its responsibilities on deliberate principle," and who criticize and scorn the orator-statesman's practice of speaking (3.59-60).

---

[1] *Oxford English Dictionary*, s.v. rhetoric, 2c.

[2] Translations of Cicero generally follow those in the Loeb classical library. Exceptions to this rule include *De republica* (Zetzel 1999), *De officiis* (Griffin and E. M. Atkins 1991), and *De oratore* (J. M. May and Wisse 2001).

How Cicero conceives of the unity between philosophy, rhetoric, and politics is the subject of this chapter. In the next section, we shall examine how Cicero melds rhetoric and politics together – an approach that was obvious to Cicero, but which became less apparent after the end of the Republic, when the *populus* was largely excluded from political participation. Then, in the subsequent section, we shall discuss Cicero's argument that rhetoric and politics must be reconciled with philosophy, which is an argument consistent with Cicero's conviction that the moral cannot be separated from the beneficial.

Rhetoric and Politics

Although Cicero, in *De oratore*, considers political oratory to be of "paramount importance,"[3] politics does not, initially, appear to be the focal point of his rhetoric. Rather, of the three *genera* of oratory originally identified by Aristotle – deliberative (political), forensic (judicial), and epideictic (occasional) – many if not most current scholars consider the forensic *genus* to be of greatest importance to Cicero.[4] Because of the political nature of much judicial speech in Republican Rome, however, forensic oratory was often subsumed – if not formally, then in practice – under the deliberative genre: "All trials before *iudicia* [judicial assemblies] were by their nature 'political,' because ... they tended to involve persons engaged in political careers that were profoundly affected by a person's conduct in such cases and by the good or bad reputation gained; and because they were exposed to and much affected by crowd reactions."[5] Accordingly, despite the important role played by forensic oratory in Roman Republican speech and in Cicero's own rhetorical theory, the deliberative genre predominates in Ciceronian rhetoric, in importance if not also in frequency of use.

In the Roman Republic, rhetoric was most visibly joined to politics in the orators' speeches before two political bodies, the *contio* and the Senate. The *contio* was the informal, non-voting popular assembly, which often met several weeks before formal voting political assemblies (in which

---

[3] Fantham 2004: 209.

[4] Thus, in *De inventione*, Cicero devotes most attention to judicial oratory. And in *De oratore*, most of the discussion of both *inventio* and *dispositio* are dedicated to judicial, not deliberative (political), oratory. Cicero's position in *De inventione*, however, is not determinative, as he himself denies the authority of *De inventione* when he later dismisses it as "the sketchy and unsophisticated work" of his youth (*De or.* 1.5).

[5] Millar 1998: 87–88.

public debate was prohibited) were convened.[6] In the *contio*, orators sought to win public support for their positions before legislation was formally voted upon. Success at passing legislation by eliciting public enthusiasm through persuasive speech was one of the most significant means by which a politician advanced his career. At the same time, the *contio* was the primary venue in which the people could observe and publicly support (or reproach) a politician, thereby ensuring that political orators justify their proposed actions in words before the *populus Romanus*, as represented by the contional audience.[7] Especially during tumultuous times, politicians would collectively deliver more than one speech a day in *contiones*, leading Robert Morstein-Marx to refer to the *contio* as perhaps the most important of settings "for the purposes of self-advertisement, communication, and ritualized communal action" and as "quite simply, center stage for the performance and observation of public, political acts in the Roman Republic."[8] Aware of the political significance of the *contio*, Cicero himself is presumed to have addressed this body frequently.[9]

Deliberation within the more formal Senate differed from that of the *contio*. As opposed to *contiones*, where orators spoke to the common people, senators expressed their views before other senators, who were, invariably, members of the elite; the public was excluded from directly observing senatorial deliberations. Debate in the Senate began with the presiding magistrate speaking and then typically submitting the issue to be discussed to the Senate – with usually somewhere between two hundred to slightly over four hundred senators attending;[10] he would subsequently ask for their opinions on the matter. Senators were accorded the right to address the body according to rank, with those of consular rank dominating discussion. Eventually, the presiding magistrate called for a vote on a proposal or proposals that he put before them. Because the Senate was not a legislature, but, nominally, "a council summoned by magistrates to tender advice," its decrees took the form of recommendation (*senatus consultum*), not law.[11] Although the plebeian tribune could veto the Senate's recommendation – thus nullifying the force of the recommendation – the Senate's decrees carried great weight and were usually obeyed in practice.[12]

---

[6] Morstein-Marx 2004: 7–12. For more on the *contio* and more generally on oratory and politics in Republican Rome, see also the essays in Steel and van der Blom 2013.
[7] Morstein-Marx 2004: 8–9; Millar 1998: 45.   [8] Morstein-Marx 2004: 9.
[9] Only eight of Cicero's speeches before the *contio*, however, survive (out of fifty-eight extant speeches): Manuwald 2012: 153–154.
[10] Ramsey 2007: 124.   [11] Brunt 1988: 14.   [12] Brunt 1988: 14.

Cicero's key concept in explaining how orators persuade *in contione* and in the Senate (or, for that matter, in any audience) is *decorum*. In the *Orator*, Cicero confirms the centrality of *decorum* for rhetoric (70, 123): "For after all the foundation of eloquence, as of everything else, is wisdom," and "the form of wisdom that the orator must especially employ" is to "observe what is fitting (*quid deceat*) ... to adapt himself to occasions and persons." Although, for Cicero, *decorum* is the fundamental principle of rhetoric, nevertheless, "in an oration, as in life, nothing is harder than to determine what is appropriate (*quid deceat*), [i.e.,] ... *decorum*." *Decorum* requires that the orator not use "the same style and the same thoughts ... in portraying every condition in life, or every rank, position or age, [adapting oneself instead to what is proper to the object one talks about,] and in fact a similar distinction must be made in respect of place, time and audience [concerning what is proper to the particular audience]. The universal rule, in oratory as in life, is to consider propriety (*quid deceat*)" (71-72)).

Based on *decorum*, the orator should address each political body differently. Because the audience *in contione* was composed of the public, Cicero presents himself to the listeners there as a man of the people, a *homo popularis*, even referring to himself in *De lege agraria* 2 (10) – delivered *in contione* – as *consul popularis*, the People's consul.[13] In the same oration, Cicero identifies himself with Tiberius and Gaius Gracchus – tribunes and *populares* who supported the redistribution of land and were detested by Cicero's fellow optimates. Nevertheless, when orating before a popular crowd, Cicero describes the Gracchi as "two of the most illustrious citizens, the most able and devoted friends of the Roman people ... by whose advice, wisdom, and laws ... many departments of the administration were set in order" (*Leg. agr.* 2.10).

In speeches to the aristocratic Senate and in his writings for elite consumption, by contrast, Cicero adopts the elitist perspective of the optimates, which presented the senatorial elite as "superior to the common people in point of wisdom, experience, public service, and *auctoritas*."[14] For example, he refers to the common people as *animi imperitorum*, ignorant minds (*Cat.* 4.17; *Har. Resp.* 41). His self-presentation *in contione* is shaped, if not determined, by the need to adapt himself to the audience's perspective, not by his privately held views – at least not by those views he shares with members of the upper classes. Thus, in *De amicitia* (95), a philosophical treatise on friendship that would not have been read by the

---

[13] Morstein-Marx 2004: 194-95.   [14] Yakobson 2010: 286.

common people, Cicero belittles the *populus* even more forcefully than in
his senatorial speeches, describing the *contio* as "composed of very ignorant men (*quae ex imperitissimis constant*)." Similarly, in a letter to his
friend Atticus (1.16.11), in which Cicero was at liberty to speak frankly,
he refers to the common people as "the dregs of the city populace (*sordem
urbis et faecem*)"[15] and to those who attend *contiones* as "this wretched
starveling rabble." Moreover, in contrast to his speech in the *contio*, in
which he lauds the Gracchi, Cicero, addressing the Senate in *Catilinarian*
1 (29), declares that "our leading men and most distinguished citizens
have been honored rather than besmirched by the blood of ... the
Gracchi."

For Cicero, however, *decorum*,) is not only an aesthetic sensibility, but,
as he contends in *De officiis* (*On Duties*), a moral obligation as well (1.93-
94) – an innovative position among ancient rhetoricians.[16] How, then, can
we make sense of the moral character of Ciceronian *decorum*, when
decorum)appears to demand that the orator manipulate his audience and
act insincerely and hypocritically. Perhaps no single answer will prove
altogether satisfactory. Cicero, however, appears to anticipate Michael
Walzer's position that even moral politicians cannot avoid "dirty hands."[17]
The well-being of the whole, Cicero believes, sometimes permits politicians to act in ways that are conventionally deemed immoral. Further,
concerning manipulation, we should not forget that the attitudinal differences between the elites and common people were not as great as may
appear to many today. Morstein-Marx has effectively shown that the
public ideology of the Late Republic, which was embraced by Cicero,
should be termed "popular" in broad terms: both elites and masses agreed
on the authority of the Senate, while defending the majesty and *libertas* of
the Roman People. And though the Roman populace may not have been
aware of Cicero's most derogatory comments about them (which, being
directed to the elites, may or may not have reflected fully Cicero's own
sincerely held beliefs), they were not likely hoodwinked by Cicero into
mistaking him "for a *popularis* in some radical and subversive sense."[18]

As *decorum* requires that political viewpoints be accommodated to the
audience at hand, Cicero maintains that oratorical style too must be
adapted to the listeners. In the *contio*, most appeals are to the vehement
emotions. In *De oratore*, Cicero associates the passionate speech called for

---

[15] As Neal Wood notes, *faeces* means not only dregs, but also "sewage, garbage, and quite literally
'shit'" (Wood 1988: 96–97).
[16] Remer 2017: 54–55.   [17] Walzer 1973: 166–168.   [18] Yakobson 2010: 297–298.

in a *contio* with "some grander, some more brilliant mode of oratory," which is required by "the passionate emotions of the crowd" (2.337). The audience at a public meeting, which ranged as high as 15,000 to 20,000 listeners,[19] provided the orator with his "greatest stage" (*De or.* 2.338), a setting that naturally stirs orators "to employ a more distinguished mode of oratory." Different emotional appeals were considered appropriate, however, for speeches to the Senate. In theory, at least, senatorial oratory was more restrained. As Marcus Antonius, one of the two main interlocutors in *De oratore* (the other being Lucius Licinius Crassus) observes, a speaker's advice in the Senate was to be handled "with less display, for this is a wise council, and many others must be given the opportunity to speak" (2.333); speech in the Senate was to be free, or largely free, of *pathos* and affect.[20]

But the link between rhetoric and politics is more profound for Cicero than the advice he proffers about how to address *contiones* or the Senate with propriety; Cicero conceives of rhetoric as more than a set of procedures that are employed to best your political opponent. In *De oratore*, Cicero is more concerned with the rhetoric of the perfect orator, who, with an almost all-encompassing knowledge (including philosophy), protects and ennobles the community through his oratory. Cicero typically terms this broader sense of rhetoric "eloquence," which is possessed by the perfect orator. Cicero has the character Antonius depict the "truly eloquent (*eloquens*)" orator as someone who could deliver an oration "in a more marvelous and magnificent way, and whose intellect and memory encompassed all the sources of the subjects that had any bearing on oratory" (1.93-95). Crassus extends the capacities of this perfect orator further yet, by focusing on his ability to speak to the moral life of the political community. Thus, he portrays "the real power of eloquence" wielded by the ideal orator as "so enormous that its scope includes ... virtues, moral duties, and all the laws of nature that govern human conduct" and the state (3.76). The chief contribution of this polymath, as suggested here and in Cicero's other rhetorical writings, is not his possession of knowledge per se, but his application of this knowledge to better the commonwealth.

Cicero has both Crassus and Antonius emphasize the practical effects of the orator's eloquence on the *res publica*. For example, Cicero has Crassus assert that the perfect orator not only defends the well-being of "countless individuals," but provides the chief basis "for the safety of the State at large" (*De or.* 1.34). Later, in the same dialogue (3.63), Cicero has Crassus describe the ideal orator as "an author of public policy, a guide in

---

[19] Ramsey 2007: 124.   [20] Mack 1937: 17.

governing the community." Similarly, Antonius lauds the perfect orator in recounting his obligations to promote the moral life of the political community: "It is his task to unfold his opinion with dignity when giving advice on affairs of supreme importance. . . . Who can exhort people to virtue more passionately than the orator, and who can call them back from vice more vigorously" (2.35)?

Thus, Cicero conflates the roles of the ideal orator and the ideal statesman, which is further demonstrated by his consistent use of the same terms, in *De oratore* and *De republica* (*On the Commonwealth*), to describe a singular orator-statesman, instead of two distinct or even related *personae*. The two dialogues share four appellations when referring to the orator-statesman: *rector, princeps, procurator,* and *tutor. Rector* and *princeps* concern political leadership, which underscores the significance of the orator-statesman, not only in an obviously political work such as *De republica,* but also in *De oratore. Procurator* and *tutor* denote guardianship and agency.

In *De oratore*, Antonius says of the statesman (1.211): "he who understands as well as utilizes the means by which the state's interests are secured and advanced should be regarded as the helmsman of the state (*reipublicae rector*) and the author of public policy." Antonius later (1.215) describes the statesman as *in procuratione civitatis egregius,* i.e., "outstanding in the management of the city." Antonius (1.216) then speaks of Pericles, "the most eloquent man in Athens," as the *princeps* (leader) in that community. Until this point in the discussion (i.e., prior to the beginning of the second book), Antonius differentiates between ideal orator and statesman, a position he later abandons in favor of the unity of orator and statesman – thereby linking terms signifying statesmanship with the more ambitious ideal of the orator-statesman.[21] *Procurator* appears again in *De oratore* (3.131), when Q. Lutatius Catulus describes Crassus, whom Cicero appears to conceive as an approximation of the ideal orator-statesman, as being engrossed in "the administration of the entire world (*orbis terrae procuratione*), and the government of a vast empire, [having] embraced the study of an enormous range of things, and [having] united all of that with

---

[21] The main sources for the terms signifying the ideal orator-statesman in *De oratore* (*auctor, procurator, princeps,* and *rector*) are 1.211, 215, 216. These words derive from a speech by M. Antonius, the trial lawyer, in which Antonius rejects L. Licinus Crassus' position that the ideal orator must be a man of broad wisdom acting for the common good of society. Although Antonius' standpoint implies opposition to the ideal of the orator-statesman, he later admits in the dialogue (2.41) that he does not believe the case he is arguing and approves of Crassus' broader concept of the orator (Fantham 2004: 313).

the knowledge and practical experience of a man whose counsel and speech make him an influential figure in this same community."[22].

Cicero introduces the third book of *De oratore* (3.3) with a description of Crassus' final speech before his death. In this defense of the Senate against the consul L. Marcius Phillipus, Crassus is said to have "lamented the Senate's misfortune of being reduced to orphanhood" by a "consul, who ought to be like ... a faithful guardian (*tutor*)." Although Crassus does not equate a consul with an orator-statesman here, "a consul's duty," like an orator-statesman's, is "to consult the interests of his native land" (1.165). The best example of the consul as a synthesis of statesman and orator is found in Cicero's speech *Pro Murena* (24) There, Cicero does not explicitly portray the eloquent consul as the ideal of *De oratore* or *De republica*, but depicts him as capable of bringing men to the highest point.[23]

As already noted, in *De republica* (2.51), Cicero designates the orator-statesman with four of the same terms found in *De oratore*. He introduces *tutor, procurator,* and *rector* in a single section of the dialogue in which Scipio Aemilianus contrasts the tyrant with the ideal statesman: The tyrant Tarquinius Superbius "by the unjust use of power that he already had, entirely overturned monarchic government." Scipio sets over and against this tyrant another type of man, the orator-statesman "who is good and wise and knowledgeable about the interests and the reputation of the state, almost a *tutor* (guardian) and *procurator* (manager) of the commonwealth; that, in fact, is the name for whomever is the *rector* (guide) and *gubernator* (helmsman) of the state. Make sure you recognize this man; he is the one who can protect the state by his wisdom and efforts." The fourth term appears when Gaius Laelius (1.34) addresses Scipio (who, like Crassus in *De oratore*, is portrayed as a possible model for the orator-statesman) as a *princeps,* leader of the commonwealth." All four terms connote the orator-statesman's service to the common good. As we shall see in the next section, protecting the common interest calls for wisdom, which, as Cicero recounts, was a necessary component of the orator's armamentarium.

Rhetoric, Politics, and Philosophy

In *De oratore* (3.37-38), Cicero has Crassus designate "appropriateness," *aptum,* (literally, "that which is fitted") as one of the four necessary

[22] Fantham 2004: 313.   [23] See Fox 2007: 117; Millar 1998: 100.

qualities of style in oratory.[24] When discussing appropriateness, however, Crassus presents this quality – which he equates with *decorum* in the *Orator*[25] – as more than a matter of style. Thus, Crassus contrasts appropriateness with the "precepts of the rhetoricians," by which he means, in large part, the technical aspects of style found in rhetorical handbooks. The speaker who addresses his audience with appropriateness, as opposed to speakers who manipulate words without a broader understanding of "what role they are assuming or what claim they are making," is the only "true orator" (*De or.* 3.54). This consummate orator alone can be described as eloquent because he, and no other, has "examined and heard and read and discussed and thoroughly treated all aspects of human life" – acquiring "all-embracing knowledge, [unfolding] the thoughts and counsels of mind in words, in such a way that it can drive the audience in whatever direction it has applied its weight."

Because of oratory's power, Crassus explains, it is especially necessary "to join it to integrity and the highest measure of good sense." To avoid doing so, i.e., to "put the resources of speech at the disposal of those who lack virtues... [does] not make orators of [these immoral speakers], but [instead] put[s] weapons into the hands of madmen" (3.54-55). As Cicero has Crassus observe, however, the danger of corrupt speechmakers leading their listeners to immoral action was obviated by uniting morality and persuasiveness. Thus, in pre-Socratic Greece, the predominant form of learning "seems to have taught both right actions and good speech. Nor were the teachers separated from each other, but the same people gave instructions for living and for speaking" (3.57).

Alas, this union of knowledge and speech did not suit everyone, particularly those who sought to pursue pure knowledge to the exclusion of politics and rhetoric. Foremost among those who "split apart the knowledge of forming wise opinions and of speaking with distinction" was Socrates, "easily ranked above all others, wherever he directed his attention – not only because of his intelligence, acumen, charm and refinement, but also because of his eloquence." Ironically, the eloquent Socrates was most culpable in killing true eloquence; he instigated "the rupture, so to speak, between the tongue and the brain" – a split that is deemed "quite absurd, harmful, and reprehensible, and which has resulted in our having different teachers for thinking and for speaking." Until the rupture, "[t]he people who discussed, practiced, and taught the subjects

---

[24] The other three are correct Latin, clarity, and speaking with distinction.

[25] "'[P]ropriety' is what is fitting (*quasi aptum esse*) to an occasion or person" (*Orat.* 74).

and activities we are now examining bore one and the same name (because knowledge of the most important things as well as practical involvement in them was, as a whole, called 'philosophy')" (3.60-61). The breach, however, spawned two distinct (and rival) studies, rhetoric and philosophy, which – preserved by all of Socrates' followers (3.72) – has not yet healed.

But appropriateness or *decorum* demands of the orator knowledge of what Socrates and his intellectual heirs – from the Cynics and Stoics to the Academic skeptics – call philosophy; there can be no full eloquence without reintegrating philosophy into rhetoric or reunifying the two fields. But why must philosophy be an integral part of eloquence? First, as just seen, persuasive speech without integrity endangers society. Cicero makes much the same argument in his opening to *De inventione* (1.1; see also *De or.* 3.142-43) when he states that "wisdom without eloquence does too little for the good of states, but . . . *eloquence without wisdom is generally highly disadvantageous and is never helpful* (emphasis added)." Second, as Giuseppe Ballacci observes, "the general knowledge provided by philosophy is . . . a necessary support for the orator/politician to argue on the great variety of questions involved in public affairs."[26] Third, philosophy provides the orator with "an understanding of human character and the whole range of human nature, and of the causes by which the feelings are stirred and calmed"; without this insight into human nature and, specifically, *pathos*, the orator's "speech will not achieve its purpose," i.e., will not persuade (*De or.* 1.53-54). And last, knowledge of philosophy enables the orator to teach the audience "about the nature and category of the matter on a general level," rather than concentrating on "the particular, individual controversy" alone – which, in turn, results in better decision-making (3.120).

Can eloquence be regained after the breach? Cicero offers up the persona of the perfect orator as embodying the reintegration of oratory and philosophy.[27] But Cicero adopts a maximalist and a minimalist approach to how oratory and philosophy are brought together in the person of the consummate orator. When espousing the maximalist approach, he suggests that full-fledged eloquence can only be revived with an orator who acquires complete philosophical knowledge. But when

---

[26] Ballacci 2018: 57; see also *De or.* 1.58-68. Although the discussion in this section speaks, principally, of the unity of orator and philosopher, it would be more accurate to speak of the unity of orator-statesman or orator-politician *and* philosopher. By uniting rhetoric and politics, as well as rhetoric/politics and philosophy, the perfect orator is master of all three fields.

[27] "[A]ll [the philosophers'] knowledge is present in the perfect orator, while the knowledge of the philosophers does not automatically imply eloquence" (3.142-43).

defending the minimalist approach, he claims that because the perfect orator cannot abandon politics for philosophical arcana, the ideal orator is only required to become adept at practically oriented philosophy.

Before the rupture, wisdom was part of eloquence. After the split, when orators largely abandoned wisdom for persuasive speech, Cicero vests only the ideal orator, out of all orators, with the full complement of wisdom. The perfect orator alone can lay claim to true eloquence, which is "so vast and important that it can only be covered by all the books of the philosophers, which none of those rhetoricians [of earlier years] has ever so much as touched" (3.81). Crassus is so overwhelmed by the power of eloquence, that he establishes its scope as including "the origin, essence, and transformations of everything" (3.76), which can only be mastered by the consummate orator. Crassus expresses similar maximalist views in other parts of *De oratore*, for example, when he broadens eloquence to include "speaking about the nature of heavens or of the earth, or about divine and human nature" – not restricting eloquence to the main oratorical *genera* (especially, forensic and deliberative, where the orator speaks "in trials, in the Senate, or from the *rostra*"), even expanding it beyond moral and political philosophy (3.23).

Cicero often deems the resurrection of true eloquence, in its entirety, to be an undertaking so daunting as to make it impossible in practice. Therefore, the character Crassus, in *De oratore*, acknowledges that only the ideal orator, whose perfection is unattainable, possesses such knowledge (*De or.* 3.85). Nevertheless, Cicero generally focuses on the consummate orator's need to master philosophy as it relates to oratory's practical ends. Consequently, even when affirming his maximalist position, as Cicero does in his prologue to *De oratore* 2 (5-6), he couples this position with the practical effects of wide-ranging knowledge: "Anyone who claims to have this power [of eloquence] must be able to speak well about everything that can possibly fall within the scope of human discussion, or else he cannot maintain a claim to the title of eloquence. . . . I maintain that such eloquence . . . could not have developed without a knowledge of everything that could in any way contribute to . . . *great practical insight* (*tanta prudentia*; emphasis added)."

Cicero's belief that philosophy must be linked to practice, most especially political practice, prompts Cicero to offer a more restricted account of the philosophical knowledge requisite for eloquence. While asserting in *De oratore* that the perfect orator needs *comprehensive* knowledge of philosophy – even "all aspects of human life" (3.54) – he alternates between this maximalist position and a more modest demand on the orator, thereby bowing to reality. Thus, in the same work, he, in the voice of Crassus, maintains that the orator, presumably still the perfect orator, must not spend all his time lost in philosophical subtleties, lest he fail at his primary role of bettering the *res publica* through speech (3.86). He concedes that the orator can only learn the philosophy necessary for his oratory and no more. To plumb the depths of philosophy requires a lifetime of work, more time than any orator can spare. Speaking of philosophy, Crassus comments: We orators "must apply [philosophy] to our knowledge of community life, with which it is concerned and at which it aims .... We must not waste an entire lifetime in learning this" (3.122-25).

When adopting the minimalist standpoint, Cicero abandons his Platonic-style conviction that the unity between oratory and philosophy can only be realized in theory, but never fully realized in practice. Accordingly, instead of denying the existence of any eloquent speakers, Cicero, in his prologue to book 1 (19), notes that "there are so few [but still some] eloquent speakers." And despite Crassus' denial that he is himself the consummate orator (3.84), Catulus remains unconvinced, implying that Crassus embodies the qualities of the perfect orator, i.e., by uniting philosophy and rhetoric (3.130-31). And even Crassus suggests that Scipio Africanus the Elder may qualify as the perfect orator (3.87).

Cicero – whether he is adopting his maximalist or minimalist standpoints – vests the perfect orator with the philosophical knowledge necessary to achieve true eloquence. But what, according to Cicero, is the philosophical perspective the orator should embrace in his quest for eloquence? Cicero's Crassus singles out three philosophical schools – the Stoics, the Peripatetics, and the Academic skeptics – as possibilities, inquiring of them "not which philosophy is the truest, but which has the most affinity with the orator" (3.64). Crassus first dismisses the Stoics, not because he disapproves of them as philosophers, but because their views and speaking style conflict with the generally held views and tastes of their audience. "Whether these [Stoic views] are true or not is irrelevant for our present purpose, but if we follow their ideas, we should never be able to make anything understood through speech" (3.66). Therefore, Crassus moves on to consider the Peripatetics and Academic skeptics for their compatibility with oratory. His conclusion: "if you have come to love the splendid and outstanding appearance and the beauty of the perfect orator, then you must master the power of Carneades [the Academic skeptic] or that of Aristotle [founder of the Peripatetics]" (3.71-72).

What the two schools share, according to Cicero, is that both investigate matters by arguing *in utramque partem*, on either side of a question, and, in the case of the Academic skeptics, against every opinion forwarded. As Crassus observes:

> If ... there should ever appear someone who can, in the manner of Aristotle, speak on both sides of an issue about all subjects and, having learned his precepts, in every case unfold two opposing speeches, or who argues, in the manner of Arcesilaus [founder of the Academic skeptics] and Carneades, against every proposition that is put forward, and who adds to that method and that practice, our manner and experience, our practice of speaking—*then he shall be the true, the perfect, the one and only orator* (3.81; emphasis added).

He opts for this two-sided argumentation "because [he] found it gave the best practice in oratory," that is, it allowed the orator to see the strengths and weaknesses of not only his own position but also that of his opponent (*Tusc.* 2.9).

Although Cicero maintains that his choice of the Academics and Peripatetics – and his rejection of the Stoics – is determined by their consonance with rhetoric and not truth per se, he justifies the orator's need for philosophy because of its ability to impart morality to the orator. The truth that such argumentation provides, however, is uniquely suited to the orator. In contrast to the Stoics, who demanded that truth offer certainty, the Academic skeptics accepted as persuasive the closest approximation to the truth. As Cicero points up in *De oratore* (2.336), and as rhetoricians who preceded and followed him have similarly maintained, deliberation in political oratory is limited only to those matters that can happen and that are not necessary; it is impossible to predict the consequences of political choices. Therefore, "all deliberation is immediately cut short when people realize that something is impossible, or when necessity is adduced."

It should come as no surprise, then, that Cicero himself identified as an Academic skeptic (2.7-8; 3.20; *Nat. D.* 1.11-12).[28] And in line with his philosophical allegiance, Cicero turns to argument *in utramque partem* to determine probability. By arguing the strengths and weaknesses of each position, the orator, like the skeptic, could then compare the different opinions and decide which is most persuasive (*De or.* 2.8; *Acad.* 2.7-8).[29] As we have seen, Cicero prefers this practice because "it gave the best

---

[28] See Brittain and Osorio (Chapter 2) and Reinhardt (Chapter 7) in this volume.

[29] It is possible to view Cicero's inclusion of the maximalist and minimalist approaches to the philosophical knowledge required of the perfect orator as an example of argument *in utramque partem*, where the strengths and weaknesses of each are pointed up. The coexistence of both suggests the possibility that each might be considered the more persuasive depending on context.

practice in oratory." But he also justifies his preference by arguing that "in no other way did I think it possible for the [persuasive] truth to be discovered in each particular problem" (*Tusc.* 2.9). By employing multi-sided argumentation, Cicero believes that the perfect orator is able to determine which action is most moral in a particular context, which enables the orator to retrieve from the Peripatetics and Academic skeptics what was once theirs: "among the ancients [argument *in utramque partem*] belonged to those who furnished the entire method [i.e., speaking] and the whole fullness [i.e., thinking] necessary for speaking about matters arising in public life" (*De or.* 3.107).[30] Cicero vacillates between maximalist and minimalist positions on philosophical knowledge, but he is resolute in his commitment to the primacy of argument *in utramque partem* and the determination of persuasiveness as essential to the perfect orator's wisdom.

By joining oratory with Academic skepticism, Cicero viewed himself as going far in the direction of reintegrating philosophy into rhetoric – at least by the standards of his minimalist position. Nevertheless, philosophers and orators continued to perceive themselves as distinct from, if not always in opposition, to one other. With the collapse of the *res publica* and the rise of the Principate, however, Cicero's hopes for a revived eloquence were dashed. The rule of emperors was inimical to the *vita activa*; rhetoric was severed from politics, and philosophy turned ever more inward, disconnected from public life.[31] The breach that Cicero longed to heal was not to be resolved, at least not in the Rome of antiquity, the locus of his dreams.

Further Reading

In recent years, the relationship between Cicero's rhetoric and late-Republican politics (including Cicero's role in political activity and theory) has received greater attention. An excellent analysis of the relationship between Cicero's rhetoric and his political thought is Connolly 2007b. Other worthwhile discussions of Cicero's rhetoric and politics (thought and action) are Fantham 2004 (focusing on Cicero's *De oratore*), Garsten

---

On Cicero's adopting opposing positions depending on which he finds most persuasive in a particular context, see Remer 2017: 81.

[30] Cicero maintains (*De or.* 3.79) that use of argument *in utramque partem* is not limited to the consummate orator but may also be employed by the run-of-the-mill orator.

[31] Cicero anticipates the decline of oratory in his *Brutus*, where he presents the history of oratory in Rome to highlight the threat to the continued existence of political oratory under the dictatorship of Julius Caesar.

2006 (Chapter 5), Remer 2017, and significant sections of Connolly 2015. Chapter 5 of J. W. Atkins 2018a covers Roman accounts of rhetoric, deliberation, and political judgment, including that of Cicero. Although a study of the connection between the practice of oratory and politics in late-Republican Rome more generally, Morstein-Marx 2004 is also the best account of Cicero's politics as manifested in his public speeches.

Cicero's philosophy, including its relationship to his politics, has also not been slighted in the past several decades. Most books, however, say little about the connection between his philosophy and rhetoric. An exception is Ballacci 2018 (Chapter 3), which seeks to bridge the gulf between rhetoric and philosophy, as well as rhetoric and political thinking. Many of the chapters in Nicgorski 2012 offer useful accounts of how Cicero's practical philosophy and politics interact.

CHAPTER 14

Cicero's Republicanism

Walter Nicgorski

Before Cicero, the idea of a republican government or a tradition of republicanism did not exist, at least under such names. For that matter, Cicero's writings do not contain a single term or concept that must be translated as "republican"; nor do we find in those writings a distinct set of related concepts that he designated as "republicanism." Yet in the years after Cicero attained the acme of his political career, the consulship of the Roman Republic, he did write a dialogue after Plato's *Republic*. Here in *De republica* he provides some reflections on his participation in the political struggles of the late Republic as well as a probing exploration of the political nature of the human person and the various ways humans might work with that nature and reason toward security and a good life. The history and institutions of the Republic loom large in the dialogue's response to its central question, "What is the best constitution?" As instructive as are Roman political achievements, Cicero's best *res publica* is not entirely captured in Rome's past ways. Cicero's model *res publica* is a political community properly constituted. Examining his elaboration of this *res publica* in this and his other writings points us toward the ideal in Cicero's thought that constitutes his republicanism.

Whether such an elaboration has ever been done in a clear and convincing fashion, either by Cicero or others, is a question caught up in the long-standing perplexities and seeming confusion about what it is to be republican, and, in fact, about what a republic is. However, Cicero's noble but painful engagement in political action in the faltering years of the world's most famous republic, his defense and writing about that republic, and his envisioning of something even better provide the apparent basis for many over the years to hold up Cicero as a chief source for, if not the founder of, the republican tradition in the West.

For critical responses to drafts of this essay, I am grateful to the editors, to Michael Zuckert, to Michael Hawley, and to the anonymous reviewer.

One such time in the history of the republican tradition is the American moment, the second half of the eighteenth century highlighted by the Revolution, the transformation of most colonial charters into republican state constitutions, and the drafting and ratification of a constitution, considered both federal and republican. When the Constitutional Convention of 1787 had completed its work in September of that year, Benjamin Franklin was asked what kind of government he and his fellow delegates had designed. The senior statesman of America's founding era responded, "A republic, if you can keep it!," a response suggesting a common understanding of what a republic is and an allusion to the historic instability of governments of the people down through the ages.[1] These birthing years for the United States saw frequent and often intense discussions concerning the nature and requisites of republican government.

Earlier in that same year of 1787, a leading contemporary of Benjamin Franklin, John Adams, pointed to Cicero for clarification and understanding of republicanism. Just months before the Constitutional Convention would meet, he published *A Defence of the Constitutions of Government of the United States of America*. By means of this lumbering, extensive study, he sought to put at the disposal of all who would heed him an analytical and historical study of the West's experience with republican government. He hoped to shed light on what was the essence of republican government and why such fine democratic republics as those in the American states of the time were failing. All of this was thought to be potentially helpful in the design of the new central government.

For Adams, Cicero was clearly the most important authority on republican government. He uses extant portions of Cicero's *De republica* to lay the groundwork for his understanding of the nature of republican government. He specifically builds from Cicero's definition of *res publica* (*Rep.* 1.39) and what follows into a theoretical framework for what he regards as sound mixed government.[2] Adams rightly interprets Cicero to have given to his age and those that followed such regime-types as a monarchical republic and aristocratic republic as well as the democratic republic which Adams finds the best. Adams famously introduces Cicero in the preface to his multivolume work: "As all the ages of the world have not produced a

---

[1] An anecdote reported years later by James McHenry, one of Franklin's fellow delegates at the Convention (though not exemplary in attendance). See Farrand 1966: III, 85.

[2] For a summary history of the idea of mixed or blended government in Western political philosophy before Cicero and up to Polybius, the Greek historian of Rome who significantly shaped Cicero's thinking on this matter, see Lintott 1997: 70–73; Atkins 2013a: 81–83.

greater statesman and philosopher united in the same character, his authority should have great weight."[3] So for Adams, Cicero – a man of much direct experience in the late Roman Republic, a man rich in historical knowledge, and a man of thought who has learned from the Greek theorists and who finds it useful to project a model or ideal constitution (*Rep.* 1.33 ff.) – is critical to recovering the republican experience by which to prepare the American nation for a new experiment in republican government.

By his own admission, Adams, even with Cicero's critical help, failed to get beyond a "patchwork of uses" for republicanism and reach a settled definition.[4] Twenty years later, Adams would confess his own failure to grasp or express definitively the nature of a republic and republicanism. He wrote Mercy Warren that not only had he never understood what a republic was, but he also believed that "no other man ever did or ever will."[5]

In our contemporary discourse and for some time now, there have been calls to defend and strengthen republican institutions and the qualities of a republican citizenry. What specifically are we seeking? Surely to be a republican is to be a free person and one who acts to develop and secure institutions consistent with and protective of that freedom. Such freedom suggests an important role for equality in political communities as well as a strong commitment to these communities marked by a willingness to make significant sacrifices for them. Is a republican persuasion necessarily a democratic one? How far does it go down the road of egalitarianism? Which human rights are critical to republican institutions? Republicanism seems to entail law abidance and a culture of civility where thought and argument are the critical tools of persuasion. Perhaps it might be said that it also requires a constitution and even a strong national defense. Amid these characteristics, what is or should be central or essential? If republicanism today is a coherent set of political principles or beliefs, it calls out for a clarification of just what they are and how they are ordered or interrelated.

Cicero's Republican Experience and *De republica*

In the present troubled times, challenged specifically by various forms of populism, there is new reason to try again Adams's route of examining

---

[3] Adams 1797: xvii. For more on Adams on Cicero, see Kapust (Chapter 17) in this volume.
[4] The phrase "a patchwork of uses" is Nelson's (2004: 17–18); he emphasizes the difficulty for Adams (for most of us?) in the face of such uses to make a "totalizing claim" about the nature of republicanism.
[5] Connolly 2015: 3, citing the research on Adams of Gordon Wood.

Cicero to better understand the strengths and weaknesses of our democratic republics. It can only be helpful to the thinking which must be done to return to the classic source for republicanism, Cicero, embedded so loyally, thoughtfully, and critically in the failing Roman Republic. Our resources are greater than Adams had at hand: we have more of Cicero's texts at our disposal, including what is most important for this inquiry, a much more complete *De republica*. We stand two generations into a renaissance of Cicero studies that overall takes him seriously as a political philosopher. This same period has seen vigorous conversation and much scholarship focused on republicanism, its history, nature, and relevance to the problems of our political communities.[6]

Cicero experienced a republic before the idea of a republic was understood and formulated. He experienced the Roman Republic through the historical awareness his family encouraged and in the contentiousness of his own day over appropriate laws and practices that followed from the liberation from monarchy.[7] Cicero was born into an ongoing Roman struggle over the legacy of republicanism even if republicanism as such was not known at the time. What was known was the legacy of the Republic's founder, Lucius Junius Brutus, *libertas*, and the long-standing, ongoing class struggle to work out the implications of laws and practices for being a free people.[8] That struggle penetrated and enlivened and often drove a rich history of developments giving shape to the Republic's "unwritten constitution"[9] down to the struggles of Cicero's own lifetime. Over that history there were any number of heroes and models, exemplars around whose experiences various constitutional crises and developments

---

[6] For an introduction to this significant recent discussion, see Atkins 2018a, ch. 2 and conclusion, and Atkins 2018b. For engagement of the earlier discussion by Q. Skinner and P. Pettit, see Arena 2012, esp. chs. 1 and 2 and, Connolly 2015, esp. intro., chs. 1 and 3, and conclusion. In much of this discussion Cicero is an important, if not the most authoritative, person. In much more sophisticated language than that of John Adams, Connolly 2015: 4, 14, 32 points back to the texts of Cicero and especially his *De republica*. By no means above criticism, he is for her "the leading Roman theorist of republicanism." This essay primarily intends to explicate and to clarify that republicanism. Cicero as well as the Roman experience in general are major sources for a recent effort to gain a better understanding of the nature of a republic and republicanism, especially for a European audience (Moatti and Riot-Sarcey 2009; Moatti 2018).

[7] Zarecki 2014: 78 observed that Cicero owed his own career to the opportunities afforded by the republican system.

[8] Cicero remarks of Brutus that he was the first to demonstrate that when the cause of preserving liberty is at hand, no one remains a private citizen (*Rep.* 2.26). See Schofield 2015: 113–114 on the significance of Brutus' legacy to Roman republican culture. See also Schofield 2015: 121, 125–126 and Arena 2012 on the class struggle within the shared context of *libertas* as freedom from domination.

[9] I owe this apt expression to Dugan 2009: 181.

clustered. Among these were the historic Scipio clan and other leading historical figures that Cicero placed in either or both *De oratore* and *De republica*.

Just before the 50s, a decade fertile for his political writings, Cicero experienced both the peak and nadir of his political career in his election to the consulship. He attained this highest office in the Republic after rising as early as possible through the ranks of major offices, the *cursus honorum*. His controversial prosecution of Catiline in his consular year (63) and the inability of his allies to convict the infamous Clodius had a fallout that brought wide contempt for Cicero and led to his exile. And so he was reminded firsthand of what it meant to live in "the dregs of Romulus" (*Att.* 2.1.8), and he believed that the Republic was far gone. At great personal cost he was at the center of an intense and complex struggle within the failing Republic. Though this would be far from the end of Cicero's troubles in politics, all of this occurred before his writings on politics in the 50s.

De republica, the main text of that decade's political literary efforts, is situated in the context of his other dialogues and speeches of the period, above all *Pro Sestio*, *De oratore*, and *De legibus*.[10] Foundational to the dialogue's argument, as John Adams thought, is the much-commented passage (*Rep.* 1.39, considered closely in the next section of this essay) proposing a definition of a model political community or republic (*res publica*). The very title and direction of this work, which includes important prefaces in Cicero's own voice to three of the six books of the dialogue, and the place of the passage in the dialogue, indicate its centrality to any effort to understand Cicero's republicanism. It is an essential source for this endeavor, and while some of his other writings contribute to our understanding of his republican ideal, as will be evident in later pages, it is what follows the core definition in *De republica* that provides the most direct and a very rich elaboration of his ideal.

Cicero's text, spoken chiefly through the consul and general Scipio Africanus, unfolds in the following way. The political community (*res publica*), constituted to serve human needs and aspirations, requires a settled governing authority, and that entails a choice of one of the basic forms of government. Through an encounter among advocates of monarchy, aristocracy, and democracy, Cicero displays what can be said

---

[10] Atkins 2013a: 108–110 treats the role of *Pro Sestio* in the context of the contentious political setting for Cicero's writing the *De republica* and how that setting represents continuity with the earlier period that forms the dramatic setting for the dialogue.

for and against each of these constitutions. In this display and in his introduction of a mixed constitution as combining the strengths of the basic forms and alleviating their weaknesses, Cicero presents the mixed constitution as the most stable and the best. At this point he is revealing his great dependence on Polybius (*Histories* 6),[11] though going beyond Polybius, Cicero elevates monarchy as the best among the simple constitutions. He seems interested in singling out what is simply best while recognizing what would be the best for most communities in more or less ordinary circumstances. That qualified best or mixed constitution looks a lot like the Roman way, Rome's laws and customs making up its unwritten constitution. Cicero does not shirk from such an identification but rather intends it, as he illustrates his analysis and the forging of a mixed constitution in Roman history, once again largely following Polybius. Cicero presents both in his analysis in book 1 and in the account of Roman history in book 2, the dynamic pattern of how constitutions rise and fall and the role of leaders in such processes. In these respects his ability to free himself from Polybius' more strictly empirically based analysis and sense of historical inevitability allows him to make judgments of what is better and best and to entertain higher expectations of human intervention in political life.[12] Those judgments and the analyses leading to them reveal the influence of Aristotle and Plato on Cicero's political philosophy.

Like Plato's *Republic*, Cicero's dialogue explores but comes to reject a view of justice as the will of the stronger. Book 3 sees a defense of natural law as right reason grounded in nature, a position that seems to undergird the normativity necessary to claim that one constitution is better than another and that can provide the basis for a critique as well as a defense of Roman imperialism.[13] Book 3, however, like the following three books of the dialogue, is afflicted with large gaps of missing sections and pages. What we have indicates, again following Plato, that there was a treatment of social institutions and customs, above all education, at the very least that of the potential statesman but likely intended also for all citizens.

---

[11] Polybius was said to be in the circle of friends and associates around the historical Scipio and is explicitly mentioned twice in *De republica* (1.34, 2.27).

[12] As in the case of many of Cicero's philosophical writings, here in the *Republic* Cicero's identifiable sources, like Polybius, are shaped and doctored to suit his own understanding and purpose. Cicero's differences from Polybius have been noted and discussed by Zetzel 1995: 19, 22–25, and 2013: 186–187; Lintott 1997: 81–85; and extensively by Atkins 2013a: 93–119. Atkins treats Polybius' break with Plato and Aristotle as reflecting and anticipating the issues between the thinking of Polybius and Cicero, and he draws out the implications for moral and political theory of the different conceptions of human nature held by Polybius and Cicero.

[13] See Atkins (Chapter 15) in this volume.

The responsibilities to assume leadership and to lead justly are reinforced both by ancestral injunction and by the hope of a glorious afterlife in the Dream of Scipio, a portion of book 6 that is complete and has had a life of its own in Western history. It functions in the dialogue as Plato's myths often do, though in the case of the Dream there is a distinctly Roman veneer.

Recall that this dialogue, which closes with Scipio reporting his Dream, had begun in earnest in book 1 when he was assigned the lead role in a discussion seeking to understand the best constitution or political community. He began by offering a definition of *res publica* that seems to represent common ground among the participants in the dialogue. These latter include his legendary good friend Gaius Laelius, his major partner in the dialogue, and other leading political figures from the second century. These chosen *personae* are portrayed on a holiday from the tumultuous and sometimes violent politics of their time, not unlike the moment, less than a hundred years later, when Cicero wrote this work. Their conversation is portrayed as neither inconsequential nor as merely relaxing but rather as useful in best sense of the term, namely, relevant to the political situation in Rome and the tasks before them.

Though there is feigned opposition, for the purpose of argument, to Laelius' later defense of justice and natural law, and though we come to hear, as already noted, the arguments of proponents of different constitutions, no difference emerges among speakers on the definition of a republic which Scipio proposes. This interpreter is thus inclined to see the definition as an effort by Cicero, not to put this up for argument as a hypothesis to be explained or tested, but rather to cast it as a redaction of his understanding of the essence of republicanism. It is an abstract formulation of a founding act that states the core of Roman practices and expresses the best that Rome has been about and thus an implicit norm to which to aspire. The passage is a moment of drawing from the past and projecting into the future, at least a hoped-for future with republicanism restored, at least to some degree. Before examining these elements of republicanism and what mature forms of them might have been manifested in Roman experience, a critical and necessary component of this foundational moment must be acknowledged, namely, the Greek additive.

Nearly everyone recognizes that *De republica* is not just a summing up of the principles and practices of Roman political experience but has also been deeply impacted by Cicero's loving engagement with Greek philosophy. This is explicit in the dialogue and in Cicero's praise for Plato as a philosopher that runs throughout his writings.[14] Through his long legal and political career, he attended to his love of philosophy as circumstances permitted, ever recognizing its importance to human well-being.[15] This is especially so of moral and political philosophy. While immersed in Roman experience he also carried the torch for philosophy and first brought those two dimensions of his past together in the 50s and especially in *De republica*. The very title of the work and its form as a search for the best constitution speaks loudly of the Platonic influence. The philosophical Greeks are guiding Cicero as he draws from significant Roman experiences and as he formulates his model regime, the best possible among those instantiated in human experience. What Cicero regarded as politically good and desirable is what we must regard as his republicanism. The Greek and specifically Platonic impact on this good is significant. Ciceronian republicanism is not the offspring of Roman stock alone.

Definition and Implied Aspiration

In turning to the definition, it is useful to be reminded that even with the nineteenth-century recovery of the text now in use,[16] we have only a third to a quarter of the original *De republica* according to well-informed estimates. So any interpretation of this text has a high bar of "speculation" to overcome. The missing portion of the text does not, however, seem likely to have much impact on the thesis here: Cicero, informed by Greek learning and drawing from Roman experience, is casting his principles of good government in the form of an enhanced Roman Republic, and his first move is to condense this republican ideal in the very definition (how very Platonic!) of a republic; the norm is implied in the very definition. At 1.39, Cicero wrote:

> A republic (*res publica*) is then a possession of the people (*res populi*); however, not every human association assembled in any manner constitutes a people, but only such a union of many as is held together by a consensus based on justice (*iuris consensu*) and by the common good (*utilitatis communione*).[17]

---

[14] *Leg.* 2.14, 39; 3.1; *Tusc.* 1.22, 39–40; *Orat.* 10; *Scaur.* 4; *Rab. Post.* 23; *Att.* 4.16; *QFr.* 1.1.29. See Nicgorski 1992 and Schofield (Chapter 6) in this volume. Cicero's love of this Greek thing philosophy is reflected in his youthful rhetorical treatise, *De inventione*, and there is more evidence of it in what we know of the education his father encouraged in the home and beyond (*Brut.* 315–316; *Nat. D.* 1.6–7; *Inv. rhet.* 1.1 and passim.)

[15] See Lévy 2012 for Cicero's alternating attractions to the life of politics and that of philosophy.

[16] Powell 2006 published a new critical edition of *De republica* based on his revisiting of the original Mai manuscript in the Vatican.

[17] Arena is among those who have pointed out the long and rich tradition of scholarship on the definition (2012: 119 n. 195, 250–251). Especially notable in this company is Malcolm Schofield's

Whatever the public "thing" (*res publica*) is, property or institutions, or space – real and/or virtual, what is here generally translated as "republic" – it is a possession of the people.[18] Already there is an implication of equality because *populus* is left undifferentiated. A stronger and necessary implication is found in the republic being a possession of the people. Like most possessions, it might be thought that owners can dispose of it as they see fit. This is what we have come to know as popular sovereignty. Yet what follows in the definition seems to rule out popular sovereignty simply exercised as popular will or majority will or as a whim of this *populus* empowered by nature. This is so because such arbitrary or merely willful decisions are seen as emanating from a union of many (*coetus multitudinis*) that is *not* joined in agreement arising from right or justice (*iuris consensu*)[19] and thus by common advantage or good. Without such an agreement, a gathering of individuals would not constitute a genuine people who could legitimately claim to exercise sovereignty. Any moral claim for popular sovereignty is undercut by such arbitrariness.

It is a high bar to qualify as "a people" under this definition, as is made even clearer in an observation Cicero employs later in this dialogue: he would not bestow the title *res publica* or republic on a group consenting to any common ground, as in a popular or democratic positivism, a form of conventionalism, but in fact only in those cases where true justice and interest are what is embraced. Cicero through Scipio (*Rep.* 3.43–47 = 3.35–36 Powell) holds that only a justly constituted republic is truly a

---

1995 essay, "Cicero's Definition of *Res Publica*," which has been the basis of much subsequent discussion. What Schofield suggests here with respect to *iuris consensu* is further developed in his later essay on political discourse in the late Roman Republic (2015: 120). The key point is that both proper translation and attention to other passages in *De Republica* make it very unlikely that Cicero has in mind a conventionalist or contractual understanding of justice in this phrase. Schofield has extended his research and analysis of the phrase *iuris consensu* in a forthcoming paper, "*Iuris consensu* revisited." The findings here as well as the themes of the essays noted above are treated in his book (Schofield 2021). My translation and interpretation of the entire passage has been impacted by Schofield's scholarship. Note Zetzel's handling of the two uses of *iuris consensu* related to the definition (2013: 189, 193).

[18] One can understand the attraction, for Brunt 1986: 15 n. 8, and some others, of rendering *res publica* in English as "commonwealth." It makes particular sense if the preferred translation of the amorphous *res* is property. Later views of property, like those of Locke, bring forward notions of life and liberty as well as all that might be made with them. The common's wealth could be conceived in Aristotelian fashion as all that the political community can provide for human development. Then, too, "political community" itself seems an interesting way to cast *res publica*, capable of being seen as expressing the political space created by a true people coming together.

[19] Atkins understandably wishes to keep options open on the best translation of *ius*, and so renders it "law/justice/rights" (2013a: 130ff.). Fott 2014: 47, in his recent edition of *De republica*, translates it as "right." See also Zetzel's approach to popular sovereignty at this point in Cicero's text (2013: 189–190).

res publica. Others bearing the name are simply called republics in customary and imprecise usage. With true justice and interest elevated, the hand of Plato shows,[20] and Cicero opens to Augustine and to the entire tradition of republicanism that follows the question of what constitutes a republic that is not one in name alone.[21]

Consent in right or justice and in true interest can imply an explicit process marked by deliberation. It need not imply such a process, and in fact it almost always does not imply one in Cicero's world or before. Consent seems to require, as Wiszubski and Connolly have noted, some form of participation and the need for persuasion.[22] A person who consents takes a role, chosen or acquiesced in freely, and gives agreement thereby to what is proposed. Consent clearly implies a robust "negative liberty"; it is "negative" in the sense that freedom from constraint and interference in acting must be present; it is "robust" in not allowing domination in any way, even if there is not actual physical constraint.[23] Meaningful consent also implies sufficient self-mastery. The consent that Cicero introduces is not a formulaic and legalistic process that would require an actual vote in the form of a plebiscite.[24] Consent as a requisite of legitimate government might only manifest itself in informed yet tacit approval of how matters have been and are unfolding. It must be ever renewed, and such seems to be what Cicero sees emerging even in the period of kings (*Rep.* 2). He goes out of his way to note that Roman kings, especially the good and sensible ones, sought popular approval upon their coming to the throne. The role of persuasion clearly does enter here and has been highlighted by Cicero in his descriptions of societal and political beginnings. Reason and speech must be united to draw humans into the riches of political community.[25] The need for persuasion reflects and thus reinforces equality as a norm and standard as well as a necessary inequality, a seeming tension to be explained in what follows.

[20] Nelson 2004: 1–2; Fox 2007: 80–81, 94.

[21] Augustine (*De civ. D.* 2.21, 19.21) objects to this rigorous demanding definition and then employs it to argue that there can be no true republic that is not a Christian republic.

[22] Wirszubski 1950: 14; Connolly 2007a: 142.

[23] Berlin 1969 formulated the concept "negative liberty" along with its sometime rival or ally, "positive liberty," in his influential 1958 lecture, "Two Concepts of Liberty." The concept is invoked here to highlight the contemporary discussion of republicanism (see note 6 above) which has brought Cicero's version of republican liberty into the heart of debates about the nature and adequacy of Berlin's analysis.

[24] See a fuller discussion of this in Nicgorski 2016: 176–177.

[25] *Inv. rhet.* 1.2–3; *Rep.* 3.3 = 3.2 Powell; *Off.* 1.12, 34–35. Connolly 2007b: 166. See Remer (Chapter 13) in this volume.

When Cicero moves on from his definition of origins to the need for a directing and deciding person or body, in effect for the need for a government (*Rep.* 1.41–42), the stage is set for the necessity of persuasion on a regular basis. Under such authorities, the claims of liberty represented strongly by the people and the claims for efficiency and wisdom must be acknowledged and balanced whether within a formal legislative branch or just simply in terms of a reconciliation or harmonization of the basic orders of the society. Rome's historic class divisions are seen as resources for a mixed government marked by institutional arrangements that contribute to security, stability, and prudent movement toward justice. The statesman/leader has an explicit role (*Rep.* 2.69) in maintaining balance and thus harmony between the upper, lower, and middle classes. Striving for this balance would be best facilitated in a mixed government where the aristocratic element of the leading classes is located in the consuls/kings and the Senate. That element is to predominate over the greater numbers of the lower class, yet their liberty and participation in the regime is critical.[26] This is the framework for the Republic Cicero has known and now embraces anew as his model. It is a republic of speech where civil discourse is meant to persuade to the right and the common good while continually encountering differences and contestations from its origins through its occasional need to reconstitute the bonds of civil society and into conflicts entailed in day-to-day governance.[27]

Insofar as there is a need for leadership and thus for differentiated rhetorical ability and practical wisdom, the very idea of a republic implies inequality.[28] The republican requisite of consent to the right and the true good implies the need for leadership and wisdom as well as implying that deliberation is a sham if it is not well-informed and thoughtfully exercised. At their best, inequalities are to be seen as in the service of justice and the common good, and thus inequalities are to be in the service of appropriate equalities such as an equality of opportunity that would facilitate bringing the genuinely best into the ruling class.[29] The dynamism toward equality rooted in popular sovereignty works side-by-side (at times in apparent tension) with the differentiating principle of merit and the accordant

---

[26] *Rep.* 1.42–43, 45, 69; 2.39, 56–57, 69.
[27] The emphasis in Connolly's interpretation of Roman republicanism: Connolly 2007b and 2015.
[28] *Off.* 1.43, 46, 53; 3.13–14. Contrary to Zarecki's suggestion, inequality can be seen as not at odds with a republican commitment (2014: 116).
[29] Connolly 2009: 137 seems right in finding that Cicero is pushing away from bias based on gender or class.

responsibilities of the ruling class especially manifest in *De officiis*, Cicero's last philosophical work (also, *Att.* 4.25). This tells us much about the principles for republican government in the eyes of Cicero.

The expansive interpretation of *ius*, *utilitas*, and *consensus* means that the model republic is a regime built on real approval by the people and a common ground, the basis for which would be true justice independent of convention. Known republics simply never meet the bar. Properly understanding the definition is understanding that bar; in that way we know the direction in which to move our "republics." All are but approximations to a regime where both consent of the people and true justice, not opinion, characterize the political community and set the tone and limits for all that is done in laws and practices subsequent to the founding of such a political society.[30]

Republican Features

These seeds or principles of Cicero's republicanism can be seen in more mature form by looking to their unfolding in the republican tradition that later develops, and their character and limits can be discussed more richly by viewing them against the developed and authoritative American tradition of modern republicanism. First and foremost, to be a republican is *to be free* as a person and as a community. The rejection of absolute monarchy in an act of revolution and in the name of the public interest is a foundational experience shared by ancient Rome, Cicero's political theory, and eighteenth-century America. In the regicide that brought the beloved Roman Republic, the people's right to such a change is not as evident as in the other two cases, where the principle of popular sovereignty clearly has emerged as fundamental. In these cases and similar ones, "the people" are warranted by nature to free themselves from absolute control of another and to surrender their independence, reserving oversight, to a community or leader. In these instances the concept of "the people" in practice was not, of course, as inclusive as in contemporary applications of popular sovereignty. However, one can say that more inclusive current usages are pointed to in the universal appeals to nature explicitly employed in the Declaration of Independence and in the implicit

---

[30] One formulation of Cicero suggests to readers of *De republica* that the common interest or good (*utilitas*) and, in fact, consent itself might be collapsed into true *ius* (*Rep.* 6.13 = 6.17 Powell), "communities joined in right"; see discussion in Nicgorski 2016: 170–171. To be joined in right is to have consented to the genuine common good.

basis for the authority Cicero gives a people joining together in right (*ius*) in his very definition of *res publica*. However indebted he is to the achievements of the Roman Republic, Cicero cannot be said to have restricted the possibility of a republic to Romans alone. A republican tradition is born in Cicero and reaffirmed in America, that government is to be of the people and by the people.

Secondly, "by the people" entailed equality of participation in foundational acts and thus a basis and condition of authority that may be claimed by the majority of any people. A *dynamism toward equality* along with the wider inclusiveness in the concept of "the people" is the large story of Western political development from Cicero's elevation of consent and the individual "dignity" entailed in it. This dynamism had an ever-stronger impact on constitutions and political practices as Cicero's star rose anew in the post-Renaissance West, just as had already occurred in his acceptance of the tribune's powers and a very open franchise in certain assemblies to all who claimed or were granted citizenship.[31] Jefferson reminded all that the majority's authority had to be reasonable, and this is a statement that can be seen as rooted in Cicero's insistence that the people, to act with authority, must find their unity in true justice and a genuine common good. Equality was not enough.[32] The Roman Senate's historic role, purified and strengthened to what was intended for it, was for Cicero to be the critical element in elevating the popular decisions of the Roman Republic.[33] Government by the people had to be government that was truly for the people.

Third, in order to attain that end of being genuinely "for the people," republics must have leaders and citizens marked by *wisdom and virtue* (*Off.* 1.17).[34] Equal rights inclusive of real property rights for citizens along with expectations for the rule of law, extending even to constitutionalism, could be a sign and pointer, as it seems to be for Cicero (*Leg.* 1.29), to a yet wider equality rooted in the very nature of human beings. For Cicero, as for the likes of Adams and Jefferson in the American

---

[31] On the office of tribune: *Leg.* 3.15–17, 19–26; also *Rep.* 2, passim. On the franchise: Arena 2012, ch. 2; Millar 1998.

[32] Jefferson 1801. *Leg.* 1.29; *Off.* 1.124, 2.41–42. There is equality under the law, but equality is not sufficient: *Rep.* 2.29.

[33] *Sest.* 137, where the Senate's authority is seen to be established based on popular support and constituted of those marked by merit. See discussion of this passage in Schofield 1995a: 78; Wirszubski 1950: 43 and passim. See Connolly 2007b: 161 and 2015: 16 on the importance of elite self-mastery and the Senate as a necessary "senior partner" in the Republic. For Cicero, the Republic was seen to need the dignity and authority of the Senate for good government.

[34] With respect to leaders or statesmen, especially rich is Powell 2012.

tradition, rights of citizens or civil rights draw on natural rights grounded
in the laws of nature, natural law.[35] Nature is the ground for testing and
measuring, by a republic's leaders, whether a government is serving justice
and the common good, and the zenith of the virtue of such leaders is to
live, and be prepared to die, for their republic.[36] Republics need ordering
and reordering by leaders so attuned, and only essentially good citizens will
allow such leadership. Cicero was interested in reaching both citizens and
potential leaders by helping to implant and nourish the qualities necessary
to sustain republican government.[37] These were convictions widely shared
in the America of John Adams.

Fourth, the institutions and constitutional devices so often associated
with republican government are noted here last. These constitute *indirect
rather than direct rule of the people, namely representative government*, and
what has been *called a mixed constitution or mixed government, a government
whose chief functions are assigned to different classes.* These characteristics are
given last here because they are the primary means of securing freedom,
the attendant potential for equality and the wisdom and virtue requisite to
their functioning effectively to the true end of political society and government. They are the fruit of practical wisdom and historical experience.
While both Cicero and key American founders viewed the goal of such
devices the same way, there are differences in just what is meant for each
by indirect democracy and mixed government. The Roman constitution of
Cicero's time did not specifically preclude every form of direct participation of the people; there were assemblies where all citizens were welcome,
but in practice this never really occurred in the fully inclusive sense the law
allowed. In effect, Rome had the indirect rule that characterized most early
American constitutions, and Cicero's theory welcomed the filter and shield
respecting popular opinion that such rule gave, and specifically looked to
the Senate for the qualities of leadership and stability necessary for a
republic. Regarding mixed government, this was not to be the way of

---

[35] See Atkins (Chapter 15) in this volume for the defense of natural law by Laelius in *De republica*.
Also in this volume, see Schofield (Chapter 6) for Cicero on natural law in *De legibus*.

[36] Note the important discussion of Atkins 2013a: 139–141 about how the natural basis of rights is
implicit in the space for judgment of an existing regime. The ultimate sacrifice is suggested in
Cicero twice (*Off.* 1.22; *Fin.* 2.45–46), approvingly referring to Plato's call to good men to
understand themselves as born for others, including the political community.

[37] Nicgorski 2016: 216–218, passim. Here and in Zarecki 2014, the reader can further explore the
important role of the model statesman in Cicero's thought. That statesman (*rector*, encompassed by
the term "leader" in this essay) is the key to mixed government working for stability and justice, the
basis of harmony; he is one who is able protect the political community by his counsel and deeds
(*Rep.* 2.51, 69).

the United States. What was to be, as defended in *The Federalist*, was a pure republic or a democratic republic, giving no branch or status to hereditary classes.[38] However, the institutional framework for this pure republic emulated the qualities as well as the checking and elevating potential of a mixed government.[39] The separation of the major functions of government into separate hands, accountable to the people through different channels and each having some means of defending themselves, amounted to an effort to secure the benefits of mixed government. Cicero once argued (*Phil.* 7.4) that the true democrat (*popularis*) secures the people's role by defending an overall sound constitution.

Conclusion

What then is Cicero's republicanism? It is, as indicated earlier, his understanding of the principles of the best government humans might and should attain. It has been learned from leading thinkers of the past and from experience, especially Roman experience. It is in substance a set of convictions about fundamental rule by the people in which consent and all it implies has an important position; it assumes that liberty, in the sense of robust negative liberty, is the chief goal for government and that this implies a very high regard for meaningful equality. It entails the necessary wisdom and virtue to provide that the protected liberties are not turned to license and folly, but rather to perpetuating the excellences that lives of wisdom and virtue exemplify. It appears then that the conditions of liberty are not solely negative.

Perhaps it is going too far to claim that Cicero is reaching in the direction of American republicanism. He did, however, play a key role in the thinking of the republican tradition he largely spawned and quite specifically in the inquiries and minds of some, like Adams, of the founding generation. Cicero's thinking, studied anew in the light of what we now have of his writings, can contribute to defending this American republic and other modern republics, and to developing them in ways appropriate to our contexts. It seems right in our challenging times to

---

[38] See especially *The Federalist* #10, 14, 39 in Carey and McLellan 2001.

[39] In encouraging what are often called "the checks and balances" among branches of government and in seeming to welcome the mutual checking of factions, the American founders might reasonably be thought to be more heirs of Polybius' understanding of the operation of mixed government than of Cicero's. However, there is a strong call among the founders, especially John Adams, for leaders marked by wisdom and virtue and for the cultivation of those qualities in citizens if a republic is to be "kept." For the reception of Cicero's thought at the Constitutional Convention, see Cole 2019.

strive "to keep" our republics, glorious products of human development. We seem often to lack the knowledge of how to do so. More pointedly, how does one in this twenty-first century develop the citizen virtue and leadership capacities necessary for republican government.

Further Reading

Schofield 1995a has provided a classic recent examination of Cicero's definition of a republic at *Rep.* 1.39. He has revisited this in chapter 3 of his book on Cicero's political philosophy (Schofield 2021). Much of his prior scholarship on Cicero is integrated into this book. Kempshall 2001 offers an opportunity to appreciate the role of *Rep.* 1.39 in a significant portion of Western political theory. Wirszubski's (1950) treatment of *libertas* is foundational to considering Cicero's republicanism and the role of freedom in the entire experience of Roman history. Moatti 2018 draws on Cicero and the Roman experience to better understand what republicanism is and might be in the present. Connolly's two books (2007b, 2015) focus on features of Cicero's and Rome's republicanism through engagement with *De oratore* and *De republica*, respectively. Atkins 2018a highlights Roman republicanism in his analytical survey of Roman political thought. Here and in his earlier book (2013a), Cicero's republicanism is a central concern. Kapust 2011b considers Cicero as key in his discussion of republicanism in the major Roman historians. Fox 2007 and Zarecki 2014 offer stimulating and sometimes provocative angles on Cicero's thinking as a republican.

CHAPTER 15

Empire, Just Wars, and Cosmopolitanism

Jed W. Atkins

Cicero's writings on political philosophy stand at the head of two important but divergent traditions. The first is republicanism. As we saw in the last chapter, republicanism is concerned with the preconditions for a free commonwealth or *res publica*, which in turn should be the object of its citizens' highest allegiance. Patriotism is a key virtue, and citizens' lives are embedded in and regulated by a particular set of laws, institutions, and political culture. However, no less important is Cicero's contribution to the second tradition: natural law theory. Here his work influenced, for example, the later legal philosophy of the seventeenth-century Dutch legal theorist Hugo Grotius and the cosmopolitanism of Immanuel Kant. While republicanism privileges the development of affective attachments to and promotion of the interests of particular polities, natural-law cosmopolitanism in the "Ciceronian tradition" focuses on human rationality, which yields "natural laws" that regulate the universal human community.

Each of Cicero's major works of political philosophy – *De republica* and *De legibus* from the 50s BCE, and *De officiis* written late in 44 BCE – combine the fundamental elements of subsequent republican and natural-law cosmopolitan traditions. A major, if not *the* major, problem for scholars has been understanding how Cicero meant to integrate these different "political moralities" into a coherent whole. Nowhere has this integration seemed more fraught than in his handling of topics that modern students of politics would classify under "international relations." In this chapter, we will consider Cicero's treatment of three topics in this area to which he made especially important contributions: the justice of empire, the morality of war, and the integration of the *res publica* into cosmopolitan thought. In treating these themes, I have three goals: (1) to

I am grateful to Thomas Bénatouïl, Walter Nicgorski, and Gretchen Reydams-Schils for helpful feedback on this essay. The material on just war and cosmopolitanism condenses and adapts material in Atkins (forthcoming a and forthcoming b, respectively).

demonstrate the specific character of Cicero's contributions in these areas; (2) to indicate something of their importance for later political thought; and (3) to argue that Cicero's integration of the republican and natural-law-cosmopolitan traditions is far more coherent and successful than is often recognized.

Empire and Roman Imperialism

The question of empire is central to Roman republican thought.[1] Thus, it is unsurprising that it is a key issue in Cicero's *De republica*. In the dialogue's first two books, we encounter two views of empire. The first, reflecting traditional Republican ideology, presents a strong and long-lasting Roman empire as an important good to aspire to. In his account of the founding of Rome in book 2, Scipio provides as an example of Romulus' "outstanding foresight" the fact that he selected a location for founding the city "in the hope of a long duration and empire" (2.5). However, earlier in book 1, Scipio presents a contrasting picture which diminishes the glory and eternality of Rome through comparison to the Stoic cosmic city of gods and sages, an idea first introduced by his conversation partner, Philus:

> But what among human affairs should be considered glorious by he who has observed this kingdom of the gods, or long-lasting by he who has recognized what is eternal, or glorious by he who has seen how small the earth is – first its entirety, then that part of it which human beings inhabit? We [Romans] are attached to a tiny part of it [the earth] and are unknown to most nations: are we still to hope that our name will fly away and wander far and wide? (*Rep.* 1.26)[2]

We encounter a similar cosmic perspective in the Dream of Scipio that concludes *De republica* 6. In his dream, Scipio, viewing earth from a vantage point high in the heavens, sees the glory of Rome's empire as limited in both extent and duration (6.20–25 = 6.24–29 Powell). However, here the cosmic perspective also reveals that the virtue that is "its own reward" is political virtue.[3] Virtuous statesmen display justice

---

[1] See Atkins 2018a, ch. 7. For a discussion of the sense in which we may speak of "republicanism" in Roman political thought, see Atkins 2018a: 2–3 and Nicgorski (Chapter 14) in this volume. In the present chapter, "Republican" indicates the particular Roman constitutional form and historical period, whereas "republican" indicates the more general (and generalizable) ideology.

[2] For the Stoic provenance of Philus' reference to the cosmic city, see Schofield (Chapter 6) in this volume.

[3] Reydams-Schils 2015: 102.

(*iustitia*) and devotion (*pietas*) (6.16 = 6.20 Powell) by preserving, assisting, and *increasing* their fatherland (6.13 = 6.17 Powell). The Dream thus suggests that while imperial glory is neither a good per se nor enduring, the promotion of empire may be consistent with justice under at least some conditions.[4]

Cicero most extensively treats the relationship between justice and empire in the dialogue's third book, which introduces the second day of the three-day conversation narrated in *De republica*. Here readers are asked to consider the justice of Rome's empire in light of more general questions about the nature of justice in politics, especially in "international relations." Is justice beneficial for empires? Or perhaps the opposite is true: the acquisition and maintenance of empire necessarily requires injustice? Much of book 3 has been lost, but we can piece together the outlines of the discussion from what survives of the original palimpsest, supplemented by quotations preserved by writers from antiquity who had access to the entire debate. (The fourth- and fifth-century CE North African Christian writers Lactantius and Augustine are especially important sources.)

Philus makes the case for "injustice."[5] Wishing to be seen as a good, patriotic Roman, he argues against justice – and against the justice of Rome's empire – by borrowing the words of a Greek philosopher, Carneades, the Academic skeptic who as part of the "philosophers' embassy" to Rome in 155 BCE spoke first on behalf of and then against justice.[6] Philus' argument has several parts. (1) He disputes the idea that there exists any natural justice (*ius naturale*). Instead, he defends a type of relativism based on his observance of the diversity of civic customs among different cities and even within Rome's history (*Rep.* 3.12–18 = 3.8–11 Powell). (2) He contends that all justice is civil justice (*ius civile*), that is, justice is a product of convention; it arises from a pact (*pactum*) made between different groups in society when all realize that no one group can completely get its way and that a compromise is better than being in a state of perpetually giving and suffering injury (3.23 = 3.17 Powell). (3) He argues that the pursuit of self-interest is the essential natural drive at the heart of politics, especially in "international relations." Wisdom is the virtue that guides individuals in seeking their own personal advantages (3.24–28) and leaders in seeking the advantage of their nation. National advantage is construed as acquiring and increasing the goods of imperial

---

[4] For the relationship between the Dream and empire, see Atkins 2019b.
[5] For Philus' speech and Carneades, see Ferrary 1977; Glucker 2001; Powell 2013b; Zetzel 2017.
[6] For more on this event, see Moatti (Chapter 1) in this volume.

rule: money, land, and power (3.24 = 3.18 Powell). Wisdom conflicts with justice, an other-regarding virtue which, out of concern for others' interests, thwarts one's attempts to increase one's own advantage. Finally, (4) Philus contends that empire, especially as illustrated by Rome's empire, requires the practice of injustice, for Rome expanded by taking for itself what belonged to others (cf. Lactant. *Div. inst.* 6.9.2–4). Imperial rule necessarily enslaves others, and such enslavement is unjust; hence, empire is unjust (August. *De civ. D.* 19.21).[7]

Laelius, generally portrayed in *De republica* as deeply committed to Rome and to politics, undertakes the defense of Rome's empire.[8] At the heart of his argument lies a challenge to Philus' relativism, conventionalism, and efforts to separate wisdom and advantage from justice. He draws on Stoic (though he does not identify it as such) natural law theory to provide the theoretical basis of this response. One of the most elegant passages in Cicero's philosophical writings, his description of natural law is worth quoting at length:

> True law is right reason (*recta ratio*) in agreement with nature, spread throughout all nations: It is constant and eternal. It calls to duty with its commands; it deters from wrongdoing with its prohibitions . . . It is wrong for this law to be contravened, nor is it permissible to modify it in any part, and it cannot be repealed in its entirety. We cannot be released from this law by either the Senate or the people, and there is no need to look for an exegete or interpreter like [the famous Roman jurist] Sextus Aelius. There will not be one law at Rome, another at Athens, one law now, another in the future; but a single, eternal, immutable law will bind all peoples at all times. And there will be, as it were, one common teacher and ruler of all – god. He is the author, expounder, and proposer of this law. Whoever does not obey it will be fleeing from himself. As he has scorned his human nature, by this very fact he will pay the greatest penalty, even if he escapes all the other things that are commonly regarded as punishments. (*Rep.* 3.33=3.27 Powell; trans. adapted from Atkins 2013a)

Laelius' definition of "law" as "right reason" brings to mind that offered by Chrysippus, the extremely prolific third head of the Stoic school – though we should also be aware, as Cicero surely was, that a definition of law as "right reason" was also available in Plato's *Laws*; in fact, in his later discussion of natural law in *De legibus*, Cicero presents the Stoic position as

---

[7] For a reconstruction of point 4, see Schofield 2017a.
[8] For Laelius' argument, see Ferrary 1974; Dumont 1983; Zetzel 1996; Atkins 2013a: 36–42; Schofield 2017a.

an elaboration of Platonic doctrine.[9] Laelius' account follows Stoicism (and Plato) in holding "reason" to be substantive and prescriptive, commanding what is good for human beings inasmuch as they are rational, sociable, and political animals.[10] This normative account of human nature and natural law has implications for how advantage is to be construed: for the Stoics, nothing can be advantageous that conflicts with what is morally appropriate; far from benefitting its perpetrators, an act of injustice contradicts our nature as sociable beings and harms society.[11]

With this philosophical background, Laelius defends the justice of empire on a number of grounds. First, he disputes Philus' strong disjunction between advantage and justice. Rule (*imperium*) is just when it promotes the interests of the ruled. Empire in turn may be justly acquired when it enables strong republics to rule for the benefit (*utilitas*) of the weak. Empires may especially contribute to the advantage of the weak by protecting them from injury caused by the wicked (August. *De civ. D.* 19.21.34–35 = *Rep.* 3.36), an argument Cicero offers in his later work *De officiis*, where he justifies Roman empire inasmuch as it made possible the defense of Rome's provinces and allies as the "protectorate of the whole world" (2.27).

Laelius offers a paternalistic argument for empire: it is right and natural for the more mature and stronger to rule over the less mature and weaker. He employs a number of analogies: master and slave, soul and body, king and citizens, and father and children. Laelius seems to have distinguished the rule of master over slave from that of father over children (August. *De civ. D.* 14.23). As Malcolm Schofield has recently argued, this distinction enables Laelius to counter Philus' efforts to equate all rule (*imperium*) with the sort of domination typified in a master's rule over his slaves. This opens up space for Laelius to speak of an *imperium* that protects and promotes the advantage of Rome's allies rather than unjustly enslaving and exploiting them to Rome's benefit.[12]

---

[9] The Latin *recta ratio* is a translation of the Greek *orthos logos*. For Chrysippus' definition, see Diog. Laert. 7.88 = Long and Sedley 63C; for law as "right reason" in Plato's *Laws*, see 715b, 890d. Atkins 2015 reconstructs the role of Plato's *Laws* in the development of Stoic natural law theory. For Cicero's presentation of natural law in *De legibus* as an elaboration of Platonic doctrine, see Annas 2013 and 2017; Atkins 2013a, ch. 5.

[10] See Schofield 1999.

[11] For the identity of the honorable and advantageous, see *Off.* 2.10, 3.11, 3.20. For the connection between natural law, the honorable, and the advantageous, see *Leg.* 1.37, 40–52.

[12] Schofield 2017a. For a different reading of the master-slave analogy that sees it functioning as a justification for empire, see Garnsey 1996: 40–43 and Lavan 2013: 115–119.

Laelius also challenges Philus' assumption that injustice "pays" when it comes to maintaining and promoting an empire. Philus' argument ignores the fact that there are natural penalties that apply to nations no less than individuals when they violate natural justice. Unjust empires, Philus argues, are punished by a natural death and lose their empire (3.34 = 3.33 Powell). When empires turn from just rule and harm their subjects (3.41 = 3.34 Powell), they may discover that corrupt action by governors in the provinces finds its way back home, thereby leading to the sort of freedom-sapping civic corruption that destroys republican constitutions (*Off.* 2.27–29). Second, having the reputation of one who will abide by one's treaties and promises, and more generally act honorably toward other nations, itself constitutes an important advantage and source of influence, which leaders will forfeit by acquiring a reputation to the contrary through unjust actions.[13]

So much for Laelius' answers to Philus' claims that injustice rather than justice is essential for the maintenance of imperial rule. What about Philus' claim that Rome has acquired its empire through unjust conquest? While it is impossible to be entirely confident of its place within Laelius' argument, we do know that Cicero discussed the doctrine of a "just war" in *De republica* 3. Just as not all imperial rule is unjust slavery, so not every war is an unjust act of conquest. Cicero returns to this theme at length later in *De officiis*. Between them Cicero's works make an important contribution to what is now known as "just war theory."

Cicero on the Justice of War

Modern-day just war theory, in line with the earlier tradition, draws a fundamental distinction between *ius ad bellum*, the justice of going to war, and *ius in bello*, justice within the context of conducting war.[14] Cicero's writings cover both, and he recognizes that these categories constitute two distinct-but-related areas of conduct. Thus, in his ideal law code of *De legibus*, Cicero declares, "Let them wage just wars justly" (3.9). This law acknowledges that there exists such a thing as a justly declared or undertaken war (indicated by the adjective "just") and just ways of waging war (indicated by the adverb "justly"). Let's consider in greater detail Cicero's

---

[13] For these points and supporting texts, see Atkins 2018a: 173–174.

[14] For contemporary just war theory, see Walzer 1977; for the history of the tradition, Johnson 1981. My account of just war theory below comes from Johnson 1981 and Orend 2008.

treatment of each of the aspects of justice as it relates to war, noting where his discussion anticipates modern just war theory.

First, consider the justice of going to war (*ius ad bellum*). Modern just war theorists emphasize that wars must have a just cause and must be publicly declared. So too Cicero: "No war is considered just unless it has been declared, unless it has been announced, unless reparation has been demanded" (*Rep.* 3.35 = 3.25 Powell). As Cicero points out elsewhere (*Off.* 1.36), this formulation echoes the traditional Roman fetial law, an institution that Scipio in *De republica* traces back to the third king of Rome, Tullus Hostilius, who ruled sometime in the seventh century BCE (*Rep.* 2.31). The *fetiales* were priests whose sphere of competence roughly covered international relations. When the Roman Senate believed Rome had suffered a wrong at the hands of another city, the priests would visit the alleged perpetrator, state their grievance, and demand reparation (*repetitio*). The accused party would then have roughly a month (thirty or thirty-three days, depending on the source) to provide satisfaction. If the injury remained unaddressed at the end of this period, then the ambassador-priests would invoke the gods as witnesses that the Roman cause was just and present a notification (*denuntiatio*) to the magistrates of the offending city that it was likely that Rome would wage war. If the Roman Senate voted for war, then a formal declaration of war (*indictio*) was made on behalf of the Senate and People of Rome. The Senate would send the *fetiales* to communicate the news by hurling a bloody spear into the enemy's city. Some ancient sources suggest that all three steps of the process needed to be completed for a war to be just, but modern scholars disagree about whether this was actually the case.[15]

Between *De republica* and *De officiis*, Cicero provides four different articulations of the grounds for a just cause for war based on the fetial code, and some work is required to reconcile discrepancies.[16] Following Jonathan Barnes, we might summarize Cicero's general position as follows: "A war is just only if both (i) it is notified and (ii) it is declared and (iii) it concerns rights which have been reclaimed and (iv) its aim is the expulsion of enemy forces or compensation of wrongs suffered."[17] However, Cicero allows that an extreme emergency presented by an enemy attack may

---

[15] Compare Ando 2010; Santangelo 2008; Barnes 2015: 59.
[16] The passages are *Rep.* 2.31; *Rep.* 3.35 = 3.25 Powell (two fragments preserved by Isidore of Seville in the seventh century); *Off.* 1.36. For a careful attempt at reconciling the differences, see Barnes 2015.
[17] Barnes 2015: 66.

justify the use of force without going through all three stages stipulated by the fetial code.[18]

We will soon return to Barnes's formulation. For now, we should note that Cicero's presentation of the fetial code does not exhaust his enumerations of the conditions for a justly begun war. In a passage in *De officiis* book 1, Cicero extends a more general discussion of paying back harm (*iniuria*) to encompass the rules of war (*iura belli*), famously arguing – the passage would later be adapted by Machiavelli in his *Prince* – that since "speech" is more suitable to human nature than "force," human beings should resort to physical violence only after diplomacy ("speech") has failed (*Off.* 1.34–35). As in modern just war theory, force is to be a last resort, undertaken "in order to live in peace without harm" (*sine iniuria*; 1.35). Cicero also anticipates the later tradition by stating that war must be waged by proper authorities. At *De officiis* 3.107, he argues that pirates are not proper authorities for conducting war and hence they do not fall under the protection of the laws of war.[19]

Cicero's treatment of just wars also anticipates many of the principles of *ius in bello* held by contemporary theorists. For example, *De officiis* 1.36–37 conveys that war is to be limited to formally recognized soldiers, a principle that anticipates the later idea of "discrimination" between soldiers and civilians, with only official soldiers being proper participants in war. *De officiis* 1.40 and 3.86 forbids poisoning, a classic example of means that are *mala in se* – "evils in themselves" – and are on this ground forbidden by just war theorists. Finally, Cicero's suggestion that soldiers should show leniency in punishment anticipates the modern idea of proportionality: the force that is employed should not be excessively out of proportion to one's objectives.

Cicero's discussion in *De officiis* also adds the following constraints on conduct within war: truces, treatises, oaths, and promises should be honored (1.38–40); acts that dishonor one's country should be avoided (1.40, 1.159, 3.86); and, once the fighting has ended, the victor should spare those who were not "cruel or savage in warfare" and give refuge to those who seek it (1.35).

Cicero has derived much of the content for his provisions of "justice within war" from what we may call the warrior's honor code of the ancient Mediterranean world. Consider for example poisoning, which Cicero

---

[18] Atkins forthcoming a.

[19] Cicero presumably excludes pirates because they, like tyrants, destroy rather than contribute to the human society.

discusses in *De officiis* 1.40 and 3.86 in the context of the consul Fabricius' treatment of the Greek King Pyrrhus of Epirus, with whom Rome was fighting in the early third century BCE. When a deserter offered Fabricius the opportunity to poison Pyrrhus, the Roman general declined – a decision that was praised by the Roman Senate. Poisoning Pyrrhus would have ensured Rome's supremacy and saved numerous lives by ending the war, "but it would have been a great shame and disgrace (*magnum dedecus et flagitium*) for us to have overcome, not by manly virtue but by crime, a man with whom we were competing for praise (*certamen laudis*)" (3.86). Cicero concludes that neither glory nor other advantages can be achieved in imperial combat when conduct in war is accompanied by wicked actions that bring disrepute (3.87).

Cicero's discussion of glory and honor in war raises questions. Scholars have detected inconsistencies between his discussion of the justice of going to war, based on the fetial principle (linked in turn to the legal notion of injury from the Roman law of delict; see below), and his discussion of conduct within war, based on the competitive honor code of the ancient Mediterranean world.[20] Scholars have also doubted Cicero's attempt to link the latter morality with the account of justice he inherited from the Stoic Panaetius, whose work *Peri tou kathēkontos* (*On Proper Function*) he took as his model. Cicero's treatment of just war allegedly exposes the inconsistency haunting his attempt to bring the Roman honor code into conformity with the Stoic account of justice based on human beings' rational nature.[21] Both these charges of inconsistency are greatly exaggerated.

The most problematic passages are those where Cicero attempts to justify wars undertaken on behalf of imperial glory. Consider for instance the following passage:

> But when one contends for empire and glory is sought in war, it is nevertheless fitting that there be present the same grounds (*causas*) that I said earlier were the just grounds (*iustas causas*) for wars. But those wars by which the glory of empire is displayed must be waged less bitterly. For as we contend differently with a fellow citizen if he is an enemy than if he is a competitor (with the latter there is a contest for honor and standing [*certamen honoris et dignitatis*], with the former for life and reputation), so with the Celtiberians and Cimbrians war was waged as with enemies to determine which state would survive, not to determine which state would rule. (1.38)

---

[20] Brunt 1988: 307–308; Griffin and Atkins 1991: 98 n. 4; Barnes 2015: 71.
[21] Brunt 1988: 308 n. 63.

Cicero concludes by quoting some verses from the early Latin poet Ennius describing Pyrrhus' attitude toward prisoner exchange, which Cicero takes to express the morality of the Mediterranean honor code exhibited in wars for imperial glory:

> My demand is not for gold; nor shall you give me a price. Let us each determine our lives by iron, not by gold, not by selling, but by fighting war. Let us test by our virtue whether Mistress Fortune wishes you or me to reign, or what she may bring. Hear these words too: if the fortune of war spares the virtue of any, take it as certain that I shall spare them their liberty. Take them as a gift, and I give them with the will of the great gods. (1.38; trans. Atkins)

"The just grounds for wars" Cicero mentions at the beginning of the first extract above clearly refers to the fetial rites, and in particular their formulaic request for satisfaction of injury: *res repetere* (cf. *Off.* 1.36 and *Rep.* 3.35). In order to understand these passages, we must situate the fetial principle within its various legal, social, and religious contexts. In his reconstruction of Cicero's "just grounds for war" enumerated earlier, Jonathan Barnes offers a largely juridical account of the fetial principle, and by noting parallels to treatments of *iniuria* in the Roman law of delict (a comparison that Cicero's own treatment at *Off.* 1.33–36 invites), he shows clearly how it relates to justice. In particular, he identifies how, in line with developments in Roman law within the previous two centuries,[22] Cicero conceives of the *res*, the object for which Romans may request reparation, as broader than physical property; it encompasses all of the Romans' "various rights, moral and legal."[23] However, we should also note the connection between *iniuria* and honor in the Roman law of delict. As Jill Harries points out, "violations of honor were at the root of *iniuria*." Indeed, "the ideology of the offense is rooted in Roman beliefs in the importance of honor and reputation."[24]

It is also important to keep in mind the religious and political contexts of the fetial code. Through the declaration of war, the Senate and priests are making a claim about justice – the offending party was "unjust by right" (Plautus, *Amphitryon* 247).[25] At the same time, this act also testifies to *maiestas*, a word with both religious and political orientations. *Maiestas* evokes the majesty of the gods and indicates a political community's "sovereignty" and "dignity."[26] Romans can speak of the *dignitas* ("worthy standing"), *maiestas*, and *gloria* of the *res publica*. The *dignitas* of the *res*

---

[22] For these legal developments, see Thomas 1980.   [23] Barnes 2015: 69.   [24] Harries 2007: 49.
[25] See Harris 1979: 169.   [26] Drexler 1988.

publica, no less than that of an individual, can be diminished.[27] To speak of the glory, sovereignty, and worthy standing of the Roman *res publica* was to speak abstractly about the *res publica*: its status and glory was not reducible simply to the glory of any individual or of one of its constitutive parts. At the same time, there is an intimate connection between the honor, glory, and standing of the *res publica* and that of the individual magistrates elected to promote its interests. As Louise Hodgson notes, magistrates conceived of insults or injuries to the *res publica* as insults or injuries to themselves, and vice versa.[28]

Of course, in international relations, unlike in civil law, there is no one to arbitrate instances in which rights have been violated and one's standing has been offended. Hence, the aggrieved party calls on the gods to judge and vindicate his claims through a favorable outcome in battle. The gods ensure that the outcome of a war proves who is in the right (cf. Livy 21.10.9 and Dante, *De monarchia* book 2).

These interconnected legal, religious, and social contexts explain why Cicero can easily draw a connection at *De officiis* 1.38 between requesting reparations for injury and glory in combat between imperial powers. Cicero here makes what would to Roman ears be an obvious point, that if you are engaged with another imperial power over a grievance, which the Romans would naturally take to involve a point of honor and standing (*certamen honoris et dignitatis*), you should compete honorably, as one worthy of that standing (1.38). In such a context, the desire to receive recognition from one's fellow competitors – a deep-seated desire in status-seeking honor cultures – leads to "less bitterly" waged wars, especially when one also recognizes the worthiness of one's competitors.

The logic of mutual recognition between honorable combatants is also evident in Pyrrhus' words quoted in Ennius. In addressing the case of Pyrrhus in both *De officiis* books 1 and 3, Cicero mentions that the Greek general is waging war unprovoked (*ultro*), and so, according to Cicero's analysis of just causes of war, Rome is justified in resisting. Perhaps Pyrrhus would dispute Rome's claims of wrongdoing. Hence the duel before the gods, eloquently described by Ennius, to determine whose claims will be vindicated.

In short, to separate claims of injury and justice from notions of honor and "fair play" befitting a "gentleman" is to make a distinction unknown to Cicero and the Romans.[29] Neither did some of Cicero's later readers

---

[27] For texts, see Drexler 1958: 24–30.   [28] Hodgson 2017: 29.

[29] For this basic distinction, see Ignatieff 1998: 120; von Heyking 2007; Barnes 2015: 69 (to which the above quotations refer).

draw such sharp distinctions: Glory and honor continued to be important themes in the reflections on just war by seventeenth-century legal thinker Hugo Grotius;[30] a century or so later, the Swiss jurist Emmerich de Vattel, in his *On the Law of Nations* – a work featuring as an epigraph a passage from Cicero's Dream of Scipio – expressly defended the logic whereby a nation's honor and status might become matters of a just war:

> It is of great advantage to a nation and is one of its most important duties to itself to make itself renowned. True renown consists in the good opinion which wise and enlightened men have of us ... Since a nation's renown is a real advantage, it has the right to defend that renown as it would any other possession ... We cannot, therefore, condemn the measures sometimes taken by sovereigns to uphold or avenge the honor of their crown. They are both just and necessary ... (1.191)

Vattel's logic is a useful starting point for seeing why Cicero's treatment of glory within the context of war need not suffer from the gross inconsistencies with his Stoic-inspired theory of justice alleged by his critics. Following the Stoics, Cicero conceives of glory and good reputation, like health and wealth, as "preferred indifferents." Though it holds no value apart from its virtuous handling, the desire for glory and recognition from others is both natural and advantageous. One may pursue glory just as one may pursue wealth, property, or any other preferred indifferent, provided only that one pursues it justly.[31] And justice for the Stoics requires giving to each his due. Given the preceding, the argument for wars involving questions of national honor would run as follows: When a nation has suffered an injury that has diminished its honorable standing – an advantage no less than the material goods of property or wealth – those representing its sovereign authority – whether a monarch in Vattel's example or the people and Senate in a republican context – may as a matter of justice undertake steps to recover the honor properly due to the nation. A war for honor, glory, and worthy standing may be waged as a consequence of justice on the Stoic's own theory of justice.

---

[30] For Grotius's debt to Cicero, see Straumann 2015.

[31] Greek Stoics distinguished between "fame" (*doxa*) and "glory" (*timē*), with the former a "preferred indifferent" and the latter a "good" possessed by the virtuous. Cicero maintains the distinction between the type of glory, praise, or good reputation as a preferred indifferent and the sort bestowed on the virtuous by the virtuous (*Tusc.* 1.109–111; *Leg.* 1.32). For glory as that which almost all men desire and which attends the virtuous, cf. *Off.* 1.65; *Tusc.* 1.109; *Leg.* 1.32. For the glory bestowed on leaders by the people as a preferred indifferent, see *Tusc.* 1.110 and *Off.* 2.31. At *Off.* 1.38, *gloria* and *honor* are both preferred indifferents. For further discussion and overview of Cicero's vocabulary, see Graver 2002: 77; Graver 2016; and Graver forthcoming.

The stance I am imputing to Cicero is consistent with how he generally handles glory throughout *De officiis*. Glory is an advantage that accompanies justice. For Cicero, following the Stoics, virtue pays and vice harms. Thus, in book 2, when he turns his attention to what is advantageous, he focuses on justice as the surest way to acquire glory. On the other hand, the loss of glory can be a penalty for unjust behavior and, as we saw in Cicero's discussion of empire, this penalty applies to nations no less than to individuals. A nation's honorable status can be lost if it behaves unjustly: Rome's unjust actions, Cicero warns, are causing it to lose both its republican form of government and its imperial glory (2.27–29). There is the occasional passage, especially in book 2, where Cicero speaks as if glory were a per se good.[32] Still, Cicero's overall strategy of handling glory in *De officiis* is to align glory and justice, much as I have argued he does in his account of just war.[33]

Many modern readers may find it troubling that Cicero includes honor among the advantages over which one may wage war. This raises, for example, a question regarding proportionality: what kind of injury to honor would be sufficient grounds for waging war? Surely rude words spoken to an ambassador on a diplomatic mission would not constitute grounds for war! However, Cicero's position becomes more comprehensible when we remember that to the Roman mind other grounds for a just war – *iniuriae* caused by harm done (or, on one of Cicero's formulations of the fetial principle, about to be done) to Roman territory, property, and lives – would also be seen as affronts to Roman honor. Due to this link between injury and dishonor, the question of proportion – whether an affront is grave enough to warrant the use of force – must be answered in any circumstance in which one seeks to wage a just war.

While Cicero's linking of just war theory and honor may feel very strange to readers in liberal democracies that no longer orient individual conduct around canons of nobility, it is ironically the presence of honor that may make Cicero's account most relevant to modern international relations theory. Scholars increasingly stress the important role that honor

---

[32] On these passages and Cicero's overall handling of glory in *De officiis*, see Long 1995b.

[33] *De officiis* 2.85 is sometimes seen as another passage that conflicts with Cicero's account of just war theory by providing "an economic rationale for Roman imperialism" (Griffin and Atkins 1991: 98 n. 4). However, Cicero is making a claim about the result of war rather than the purpose of going to war, and his argument here is consistent with his view that rule, glory, and resources can be acquired through a just war. For further discussion, see Keller 2012: 100–101 and Atkins forthcoming a, where I explore reasons for the remaining tensions in Cicero's treatment of just war within *De officiis*.

plays in international relations and thus point out the deficiencies of theories that ignore the important immaterial desire for standing and recognition.[34]

Cicero's Patriotic Cosmopolitanism

In his *De legibus*, Cicero returns to the theory of natural law articulated by Laelius in *De republica* book 3. By virtue of reason's prescriptive characteristics, "right reason" is law. This means that all who share reason are bound together by law and justice. Since human beings and gods share in reason, they also share in law and justice. We generally conceive of those whose lives are regulated by common codes of justice and law as fellow citizens. Hence, we can conceive of human beings and gods as members of a single city (*Leg.* 1.23). Cicero's argument displays the logic by which Stoics argued for "cosmopolitanism," the notion that by virtue of his or her rationality a human being may properly be designated a "citizen of the world" (in Greek: *kosmopolitēs*).

In Cynicism, where the term originated, and for the Greek Stoics who appropriated it, "cosmopolitan" was primarily a negative and critical term. To be a "citizen of the world" meant that one's natural, and thus proper, allegiances were *not* to conventional cities, which were unworthy of the name. Such a perspective is not absent in Cicero's philosophical writings; for instance, in the *Tusculan Disputations* the character M. quotes Socrates as regarding himself as "a native and citizen (*civis*) of the whole world," for "what value indeed can be attached to the sort of community (*civitas*) from which the wise and good are driven away?" (5.108–109). But Cicero's treatment of the cosmic city in *De legibus* places one's allegiance to conventional cities in a very different light. At the beginning of book 2, following his discussion of the Stoic cosmic city at the conclusion of book 1, Cicero speaks of the great patriotic devotion Roman citizens owe to Rome. Rome is the city for which "we ought to die and to which we ought to devote ourselves entirely and in which we ought to place and (so to speak) consecrate everything." "It is necessary," he explains, "for Rome to stand foremost in our affections" (*Sed necesse est caritate eam praestare*; 2.5).

This sentiment reflects traditional Roman patriotism.[35] But is Cicero's prioritizing of Rome merely an instance of his patriotism getting the best

---

[34] Lebow 2008; Dafoe, Renshon, and Huth 2014; May 2007 (honor applied to contemporary just war theorizing).

[35] Compare Lucilius 1207–1208 (Warmington, Loeb); Cic. *Off.* 1.57; Cic. *Fam.* 12.14.7; Plutarch, *Fabius Maximus* 24.2.

of him?[36] Does he have philosophical reasons for emphasizing his strong allegiance to the *res publica*? How precisely does Cicero envision the relationship between the cosmic city and Rome? Cicero addresses these questions, from different perspectives, in both *De legibus* and *De officiis*.

The greatest philosophy-related interpretive problem for readers of *De legibus* is how to reconcile the natural law enumerated in book 1 with the laws of his ideal law code in book 2. Malcolm Schofield discusses this problem and offers a solution in Chapter 6, above.[37] What interests us here is the related problem that arises from the universality of natural law that undergirds Cicero's argument for the cosmic city. If natural law prescribes what is good for all human beings, and if Cicero's law code, based on the Roman Republican constitution, reflects natural law, then perhaps Cicero's project in *De legibus* is to use the Stoic idea of the cosmic city to ratify the idea of Rome as a world-state? Such a transposition of Stoic cosmopolitanism onto empire is not unknown in the Roman world – Plutarch, for example, famously presented Alexander the Great's empire in this light in his *Life of Alexander*. Nor are aspirations for global political institutions, what is sometimes called "political" or "legal cosmopolitanism,"[38] absent from strains of modern cosmopolitan thought. However, Cicero's project is different due to his sensitivity to historical, political, and cultural particularity.

Cicero presents the mixed constitution as the best practicable or humanly attainable constitution suited to free peoples (*Leg.* 3.4) and, as we know from *De republica*, he sees the Roman constitution as the best example of this form of constitution. But he also stresses that the Roman constitution developed organically over generations as statesmen responded to numerous contingencies; hence, the exact provisions of the Roman constitution could not be replicated (unless by some miracle another city had experienced Rome's precise historical, cultural, and political developments). In the *Laws*, Cicero draws attention to the importance of accommodating political necessity (3.26, 37), and he acknowledges culturally diverse means of promoting the virtues enjoined by natural law, such as *pietas* (2.26).[39]

Cicero's *De legibus* thus combines a political particularism based on sensitivity to place, history, and culture with an ethical universalism

---

[36] See for instance Atkins 1990: 274, 281.
[37] For alternative solutions, see Girardet 1983; Asmis 2008; Annas 2013, 2017; Atkins 2013a, 2017; Sauer 2015; Straumann 2016.
[38] Pogge 1992; Held 2010.
[39] For a detailed defense of this argument, see Atkins 2017 and 2018a: 161–164.

derived from Stoic cosmopolitanism. His account anticipates later efforts by the modern liberal tradition to balance universalism (now usually formulated in the language of human rights) with attention to cultural, political, and historical constraints. In fact, the French political thinker Montesquieu, whose thought contributed so much to the later liberal project in the United States, drew on Cicero, especially the *De officiis*, in his own sensitive handling of a version of this problem.[40]

Cicero returns to the question of the relationship between Stoic cosmopolitanism and patriotic allegiance to the Roman Republic in *De officiis*. Human rationality unites human beings into a natural "fellowship (*societas*) of the entire human race" (1.50–51). As a consequence, we have cosmopolitan duties to all human beings simply by virtue of the fact that they are human beings and regardless of citizenship or fatherland (3.27–28).[41] Nevertheless, Cicero argues that a "rational outlook" (*ratione animoque*) will confirm that no fellowship (*societas*) is "weightier" or "dearer" (*carior*) than that which exists between us and the republic (*res publica*; 1.57).

Cicero argues that a "rational outlook" confirms the priority of the *res publica* because he believes that the *res publica* promotes, in an especially unique and valuable way, human sociability, the natural end of all forms of human fellowship (*Off.* 1.50–51). He grounds this argument in a close engagement with Stoic teachings on sociability, especially the emphasis they place on responding properly to natural human loves and needs.

The Stoics recognize that nature engenders a special love for one's self and one's children (*Off.* 1.12). From these loves, human sociability develops through a process known as *oikeiōsis*, "making something one's own" (see *Off.* 1.50–51, where the idea is translated by the Latin verb *concilio*).[42] As human beings mature (and develop rationally) they gradually come to identify their own interests with others, starting with their immediate family and continuing until they identify with all rational beings (i.e. all mature human beings). However, Cicero recognizes two potential pitfalls in this process. First, the love of one's own is prone to a nearsightedness that keeps us from seeing the interests of others and our duties to them due to undue self-love (1.30). On the other hand, an other-regarding love that encompasses all humanity is liable to lack

---

[40] See Callanan 2018, ch. 1.

[41] For the cosmopolitan nature of this passage, see Nussbaum 2000: 185 and in this volume (Chapter 18).

[42] For a discussion of *oikeiōsis* with special attention given to Cicero, see Reydams-Schils 2005, ch. 2 and Chapter 12 (in this volume).

enough intensity to enable us to feel the weightiness of other's interests. Cicero notes:

> It is difficult to be concerned about another's affairs. Although [the Roman comic poet] Terence's Chremes "thinks that nothing human is foreign to him," nevertheless we in fact do tend to notice and feel good things and bad things that happen to us more than those things that happen to others, which we see as if a great distance intervenes; accordingly, we judge others differently than ourselves. (*Off.* 1.30)

The *res publica* promotes human sociability precisely by broadening the love of our own and lending shape and intensity to our love for other human beings. The *res publica* "embraces all the affections (*caritates*) of all her inhabitants" (*Off.* 1.57). By this, Cicero means that it makes possible "the Roman's deepest loves" – all the activities and people that make life meaningful.[43] Moreover, the city places a new identity – "citizen" – on top of and beyond the identities and affections generated by the natural bonds of blood. Through the conventional devices of the city – laws, monuments, tombs, and temples – the *res publica* broadens and expands familiar blood relations (1.53–54).[44] At the same time, the boundaries of the *res publica* limit human love and furnish it with intensity. The patriotic citizen will even sacrifice his life for the city because he aligns his own interests with those of the city, thus reconciling the love of self with devotion to others (1.57).[45]

Of the various grades of fellowships (*societates*) surveyed by Cicero in book 1, the association of citizens within the republic best balances the breadth and intensity of love and best reconciles self-love and other-regarding love. The familiar bonds of blood – from immediate family to one's nation or ethnic group – are not open to those with whom one does not share these ties; thus, these societies not only lack the breadth of the *res publica*, but they also do not encompass an other-regarding love in the same way as friendship or patriotic allegiance. The ties of friendship, because they come to embrace someone who is not naturally your own by birth, do effectively reconcile the love of one's own with love for others,[46] but friendship is possible only among a few. At the other end

---

[43] Atkins 1990: 275.
[44] For the full text of this passage and a different but complementary interpretation, see Nussbaum (Chapter 18, p. 291) in this volume.
[45] Cf. Cic. *Fin.* 3.64, in which Cato, the Stoic spokesman, explicitly connects the patriotic sacrifice with the self-overcoming love of country.
[46] At *De officiis* 1.56 Cicero grounds friendship in the mutual love of virtue by men of good character, in which "each one is as equally delighted with the other as with himself." Cf. *Off.* 1.56 and *De amicitia* 56–57, 65–66, 79, 83.

of the spectrum, membership in the universal fellowship of human beings, while available to all, is too distant and abstract a concept to generate in individual human beings any strong sense of attachment. Therefore, inasmuch as human society requires some degree of reconciliation of self-love and other-regarding love, and inasmuch as the *res publica* best accomplishes this reconciliation, then Cicero's account implies that the *res publica* is the political form best equipped to foster human society.

In addition to natural loves, for the Stoics sociability also consists of meeting and virtuously responding to our natural needs, the necessities of life (*Off.* 1.11). The *res publica* and its leaders meet human need by ensuring "that there is an abundance of things that constitute the necessities for sustaining life" (2.74). Cities enable human beings to meet their mutual needs for life's necessities (2.15). But, Cicero argues, human beings must respond to these needs properly, that is, as rational and social beings; in particular, they must display the social virtues of justice and liberality. When human beings display these virtues when handling the necessities of life, they consequently strengthen and preserve "the fellowship (*societas*) and union of human beings" (1.17).[47] As Cicero makes clear, his account of the formation of society is not instrumental, such as those proposed by Protagoras or the Epicureans. When he speaks of society promoting human advantage, he is construing advantage in terms of the "common advantage of human beings" (1.51; cf. 1.52).

By supplying the necessities and advantages of life, the *res publica* thus contributes to the building up of human society. It does so not only by protecting life's necessities whose just handling allows human beings to build up society, but also by transforming human beings through the laws, customs, and habits constituting a "fixed way of life," so that their natures possess the "gentleness of spirit" and "sense of shame" that enhances sociability (2.15).

As in the case of love, so for the socially productive meeting of needs, the size and type of political society matters. Cicero's decision to pick out the *res publica* as the best society to achieve this was not arbitrary (see *Off.* 2.74). On one hand, the *res publica* – the form of society that requires "a union of a great number" (*Rep.* 1.39) – is large enough to have sufficient resources to meet its citizens' needs. On the other hand, it is small enough of a society to provide the knowledge of specific circumstances that Cicero believes is essential for exercising liberality in distributing material resources to the needy. As Cicero argues at *De officiis* 1.59, "In assigning

---

[47] For justice as the virtue that builds up society, see Atkins 1990.

all of these duties, we will have to see what each person needs the most and what each person could or could not obtain even without our help." Knowledge of particular circumstances (*gradus temporum*) as well as experience and practice (*usus, exercitatio*) is needed if we are to become "good calculators of our duties" (1.59–60; quotation at 1.59). Cicero's recognition of the difficulty of extending sufficient knowledge beyond the *res publica* to the community of all human beings is perhaps an important (though unarticulated) assumption guiding his recommendation to limit benefactions to non-citizens to resources that cost little or nothing (see *Off.* 1.51–52).[48] Once again, if the meeting of human need fosters human society, and if the *res publica* is the particular political society that best allows human needs to be meet, then the *res publica* is the political form best equipped to promote human society.

In the end, Cicero argues for the promotion of general human sociability through the limited, partial, and attached perspective of the citizen rather than from the detached perspective of cosmic justice. In this sense, Cicero's project may be said to anticipate what some have called "rooted" or "patriotic" cosmopolitanism.[49]

Patriotic attachments may lead citizens at times to harm other members of the larger human *societas* in the defense of their own *res publica*, a fact that may seem to be incompatible with Cicero's cosmopolitan commitments.[50] To this objection, there are two Ciceronian responses. The first is to stress that Cicero justifies war by grounding it in the same virtue that he believes is the foundation of human sociability – justice. For Cicero, to refrain from acting when you are in a position to prevent an injustice to those around you is itself an injustice (*Off.* 1.23, 28), and regrettably (so the just-war argument goes) this commitment to justice sometimes requires force.

The second response focuses on advantage. Cicero acknowledges that war takes a horrific toll on the human race: he cites the Peripatetic philosopher Dicaearchus' calculation that more human beings have perished from warfare and human violence than from all natural causes of death combined (*Off.* 2.16). Yet human beings also provide the greatest advantage for one another if their social instinct is fostered (2.17). Since the *res publica* is the form of society best able to foster human sociability, citizens who are devoted to their own *res publicae* are crucial for benefitting the universal human *societas*.

---

[48] For this suggestion, see Nussbaum 2000: 205–206.   [49] See Appiah 2006.
[50] For this objection, see Atkins 1990: 277.

To see the logic, let's adapt one of Cicero's own examples, taken in turn from the Stoic Hecato. Just as the *res publica* is generally benefitted by children who revere their parents, even if at times their loyalty to their parents is not in the short-term interest of the *res publica*, so human fellowship is ultimately best fostered by patriotic citizens who strive above all to see the flourishing of their own various *res publicae*, even if at times this commitment may lead to results that do not appear to be in the best short-term interest of the human race (i.e. the use of violent force to take human life).[51] In the long run, the destructive forces of human violence and natural disasters alike are most reduced through flourishing political societies.[52] Thus, according to Cicero, one best benefits the universal human society indirectly by making one's first and thickest allegiance to one's own republic. As Cicero declared in a remark at *De officiis* 1.50 that launched his entire discussion of the degrees of fellowship in the first place: "Human society and its union will be best preserved if your acts of kindness are conferred upon each person in proportion to the closeness of their relationship to you."

Conclusion

Cicero bequeathed to later political thought influential accounts of natural-law cosmopolitanism, empire, and just war theory. I have argued that Cicero's discussion of these themes evinces a nuanced and sensitive treatment of the universalism characteristic of the cosmopolitan tradition and the particularism of the republican tradition. Not only does Cicero's theorizing show a greater coherence than modern scholars often assume, but it offers a rich response to a question of immediate importance in contemporary politics given the recent rise of nationalist movements: how may our allegiances to our particular political communities square with our aspirations for global justice? For readers interested in "international relations," Cicero remains good to think with.

Further Reading

For the English translations of the texts discussed in this chapter, the reader should consult Zetzel 1999 (2nd ed. 2017) on *De republica* and *De*

---

[51] At *Off.* 3.90 Hecato urges that it is in a country's interest for a son to defend his treasury-robbing father out of a sense of *pietas* because having loyal citizens benefits the country in the long run.

[52] Compare *Off.* 2.15 and 2.17 in light of the above argument. Appiah 2006: 163, 167–168, citing research suggesting democracies suffer fewer natural disasters, argues that modern cosmopolitans should recognize the importance of healthy regimes for human flourishing.

legibus, and Griffin and Atkins 1991 on *De officiis*. Atkins 2018a, ch. 7 situates Cicero's treatments of these themes within the larger context of Roman republicanism. For the debate on empire in *De republica*, see especially Ferrary 1974 and 1977; Zetzel 1996; Schofield 2017a. For Cicero on just wars, see Keller 2012; Barnes 2015; Atkins forthcoming a. For Cicero on natural law, see Girardet 1983; Asmis 2008; Atkins 2013a; Annas 2013. For Cicero's cosmopolitanism, see Nussbaum 2000; Schofield 2013a; Atkins forthcoming b. Schofield 2021 includes discussion of Cicero's treatments of natural law, cosmopolitanism, and imperialism.

CHAPTER 16

Cicero and Augustine

Anne-Isabelle Bouton-Touboulic
Translated by Lucy Sheaf

No other author from Late Antiquity was more influenced by Cicero than Augustine. This influence can be measured quantitatively (through citations and allusions), but also manifests itself in the style of Augustine's writing. Furthermore, Cicero's philosophy had a profound effect on Augustine's thought. Various explanations can be given. Most obviously, we can appeal to the fact that Cicero's influence reached its peak between the end of the fourth century and the beginning of the fifth,[1] as can be seen in the work of other Christian authors such as Lactantius[2] and Ambrose (whose *De officiis ministrorum* of 386 was inspired by Cicero's *De officiis*),[3] as well as in Macrobius' commentary on the Dream of Scipio. We must also recall that the Eastern and Western parts of the Roman empire were divided by language during this period. This is particularly significant, as Augustine had little direct access to Greek (at least in his youth).[4]

The last century of research on Augustine was primarily focused on the question of the influence of Neoplatonism and the identification of the *Libri platonicorum* which Augustine credits with having an important influence on his thought (*Conf.* 7.9, 20; 8.2).[5] However, important studies have highlighted Augustine's debt to Cicero, while others have focused on particular themes, works, or passages, giving due attention to the circumstances in which Augustine read Cicero,[6] and shown how Augustine often strikingly rearranges and transforms Cicero's texts for his own purposes.

Augustine – the "doctor of grace" who converted to Christianity in 386 and was appointed bishop in 395 – was the most prominent representative of the Church at the end of Antiquity. Given Augustine's Christian

---

[1] Atkins 2002.   [2] Kendeffy 2015: 66–77.   [3] Atkins 2011b.
[4] Neuschäfer 2010: 1005–1006.
[5] See Alfaric 1918; Hadot 1960; Madec 1992; Bouton-Touboulic 2004b.
[6] Testard 1958; Hagendahl 1967; O'Donnell 1980.

identity, it was of course impossible for him to be "faithful" to Cicero's philosophical outlook. Indeed, his treatment of Cicero has even been termed a "parricide."[7] More recently, however, some scholars have described Augustine as *Cicero redivivus*[8] – a topos which is in fact already used by some of Augustine's contemporaries (e.g. Nect. *Ep.* 103.1). For these scholars, Augustine can be considered a true heir to Cicero the philosopher (and perhaps the only one in this period) precisely because he seeks to determine the scope of Cicero's philosophical project and takes that project seriously.

This reassessment of Augustine's debt to Cicero has been made possible by the fact that Cicero is no longer seen merely as an eclectic compiler[9] but rather as a philosopher in his own right.[10] We must therefore consider not only the extent to which Augustine was influenced by Cicero's philosophical works – and in some cases it is only thanks to Augustine that we have fragments of these works – but also the question of how he understands Cicero the philosopher.[11] Addressing these questions will allow us to shed light on Cicero's philosophy as well. In some ways, the rediscovery in 1819 of fragments of Cicero's *De republica* in a palimpsest of a work by Augustine serves as a symbol for this enterprise; in this palimpsest Cicero's text is transmitted by Augustine's text, but only after it has been erased in order to make way for Augustine's work.

My initial focus in this chapter will be on Cicero's *Hortensius*: First, I will explore the role played by this work in Augustine's intellectual and philosophical development; I will then turn my attention to the philosophical position that Augustine attributed to Cicero in his *Hortensius*. After that, two major philosophical contributions by Augustine will be studied: the Cassiciacum Dialogues and the *City of God*. Finally, I will consider the question of what can be said about Augustine's overall assessment of Cicero the philosopher.

The *Hortensius*

The *Hortensius* was written during the winter of 46–45 BCE. In Cicero's own assessment, this text marks the start of the philosophical project of his final years.[12] It is part of a trilogy with *Catulus* and *Lucullus*, which

---

[7] D'Onofrio 2002.   [8] "Cicero revived" or "reincarnated." See O'Donnell 2015.
[9] On this topic, see Glucker 1988.
[10] See Lévy 1992a; Woolf 2015: 2–3; Nicgorski 2016: 3–4 and the Introduction to this volume.
[11] Brittain 2011.   [12] *Tusc.* 2.4; *Div.* 2 (preface); *Fin.* 1.2.

together constitute the *Academica priora*.[13] Responding to Hortensius' objections to philosophy, Cicero praises it in a follow-up speech: he argues that every human being aims at happiness and that this cannot be grounded in false goods such as pleasure, wealth, or glory. The happy life does not consist simply in living as one desires, but rather in desiring appropriately, without any "depravity of the will" (cf. fr. 59 B Grilli).[14] He condemns the desire for riches – a desire which is represented by the character of Orata.[15] He also claims that philosophy is necessary for happiness, and that it prepares us for death and for the afterlife; questions relative to the post-mortem destiny of the soul are addressed at the end of Cicero's speech.

Augustine read the *Hortensius* when he was nineteen and studying rhetoric in Carthage.[16] In his account, in which he attributes the text to "a certain Cicero" (*quidam Cicero*)[17] and describes it as an "exhortation to philosophy," he does not praise the language of the *Hortensius*, as the scholarly conventions of his time might lead us to expect, but praises the author's "heart" (*pectus*), describing his work as "learned, of literary elegance and truthful." He focuses particularly on its philosophical dimension. Reading it was a transformative experience for Augustine:[18] it elicited new desires (*affectus*), which were directed toward God, and made him "long for the immortality that wisdom seems to promise" (*Conf.* 3.4.7).[19] In the Scriptures, wisdom is identified with Christ, whose name of course does not appear in the *Hortensius*, much to Augustine's disappointment. Furthermore, there can be no comparison between the Bible and Ciceronian *dignitas*. On the other hand, Augustine writes that Cicero "unmasks" a number of so-called philosophers, and that he exhorts the reader to seek "wisdom itself," and not "this or that sect." In his youth, Augustine's quest for wisdom had been handicapped by "childish superstition"[20] – a form of fideism which was hostile to intellectual inquiry. He was then led astray by the Manichaeans, who promised him reason.[21] Indeed, some Manichaeans knew of the importance of the *Hortensius* for Augustine.[22]

[13] Gigon 1962 and Reinhardt (Chapter 7) in this volume.
[14] Cf. August., *Beat. vit.* 2.10; *Ep.* 130.10; *Trin.* 13.5.8.
[15] *Beat. vit.* 2.10; *Sol.* 1.10.17. Cf. Doignon 1982.   [16] See Vössing 1997: 379.
[17] On the connotations of this phrase, see Testard 1958: 1, 19; Feldmann 1975: 394 and Solignac 1992: 667.
[18] Jeanmart 2006: 183.   [19] Trans. Boulding 1997: 41.   [20] Schlapbach 2006.
[21] BeDuhn 2010: 25.
[22] Strikingly, Secundinus compares Augustine to Hortensius in a letter to him (*Epistula Secundini ad Augustinum* 3).

In fact, the influence of *Hortensius* on Augustine's intellectual and personal development is emphasized by Augustine himself in five places (*Beat. vit.* 1.4; *Sol.* 1.10.17; *Conf.* 3.7–8, 6.11.18, 8.7.17). Of these, *Confessions* 8.7.17 includes a remarkable passage before the account of his final conversion in a garden in Milan. Reproaching himself for deferring the search for wisdom, he writes: "Yet even to seek it, let alone find it, would have been more rewarding than discovery of treasure."[23] This shows that even after reading the *Libri platonicorum*, Augustine regards his conversion to Christianity as completing a process set in motion by the *Hortensius*.

Augustine's use of the *Hortensius*[24] should also be seen in the context of a general development in his thinking which can be divided into three stages. These stages can be marked respectively by the Cassiciacum Dialogues written in 386, the *Confessions*, and finally three late works (i.e. written after 413) – the *De Trinitate* and the two treatises *Contra Iulianum* and *Contra Iulianum opus imperfectum*.

Book 1 of *Contra academicos* presents the ideal of a life dedicated to the search for wisdom – and one whose value does not depend on wisdom being finally discovered.[25] We have here a kind of *exercitatio* for two young pupils[26] who have just read the *Hortensius*, and are in a situation broadly similar to that in which Augustine found himself after his own reading of Cicero's dialogue. The *Contra academicos* certainly has a "protreptic scheme"[27] and includes certain elements of this genre, notably in the prologues. The *Beata vita* undoubtedly also includes citations and more oblique allusions to the *Hortensius* – as evidenced by its discussion on happiness.[28]

Much later, in books 12 and 13 of *De Trinitate*, while discussing the notions of *scientia* and *sapientia*, Augustine uses Cicero's definition of wisdom as "knowledge of things divine and human" and acknowledges its source as the *Hortensius*. But he breaks this definition down, and remodels it from a Christian point of view;[29] referring to St. Paul's words in 1 Cor. 12:8, he understands wisdom as "knowledge of divine things" and science as "knowledge of human things" (*Trin.* 14.1.2–3). So science fulfills the practical function of philosophy, whereas wisdom involves the contemplation of eternal goods (*Trin.* 12.14.21).[30]

---

[23] Trans. Boulding 1997: 159.
[24] Augustine is one of our principal sources for citations of the *Hortensius*. See the editions of this work by Müller 1879; Ruch 1958b; Grilli 1962; Straume-Zimmermann 1976; Bochet and Madec 2012.
[25] Cf. *Conf.* 8.7.17.   [26] See Hagendahl 1967: II, 192.   [27] Van der Meeren 2007.
[28] Cf. Altman 2016a: 68.   [29] Hagendahl 1967: II, 516.   [30] See Madec 1969: 169–170.

The fragment of the *Hortensius* on the universal desire for happiness (fr. 59 G) is in fact the one which is most often cited by Augustine, not only in his main works, from *De beata vita* to *De Trinitate*, but also in his sermons. In *De Trinitate* 13.8.11 f., he completes this sentence by saying that immortality of the soul is necessary for real happiness. Goods that make man happy can be acquired through the four virtues; those four virtues are "necessary only in this life, which we observe to be full of trials and errors" (14.9.12).[31] In *De Trinitate* 14.9.12 and *Contra Iulianum* (written 421) Augustine also uses fragments from the *Hortensius* which relate to eschatology and the post-mortem destiny of the soul. (In the "Islands of the Blessed," which are promised to those who have dedicated their lives to philosophy, the cardinal virtues are no longer necessary.)

As *Contra Iulianum* is a polemical work, it is perhaps not surprising that Augustine says that he prefers Cicero to Julian because the former, "prompted by the evidence," recalls that ancient philosophers emphasized the extent of human misery – an emphasis which Augustine shared. These philosophers appropriated Aristotle's analogy between souls which are condemned to remain in a body and prisoners yoked to a corpse by Etruscan bandits.[32]

Let us now turn to a controversial question for contemporary scholars: which philosophical position – if any – should be attributed to Cicero, both the author of the *Hortensius* and the character in that dialogue?[33] Augustine's writings point us toward an answer. A key text here is *Contra academicos* 1.3.7, of which this excerpt is worth considering: "Cicero emphatically declares that man cannot perceive anything and that the only thing left for the wise man to do is to search for the truth carefully. If the wise man assented to uncertain matters then, even if they perhaps were to be true, he couldn't be free from error."[34] Grilli takes these words emphasizing *akatalepsia* and the universal suspension of assent to be from the *Hortensius*,[35] whereas Ruch argues that in this case Augustine has "contaminated" the *Hortensius* with the *Academica*.[36]

---

[31] Trans. Hill 1991: 381.
[32] *C. Iul.* 4.78 (= *Hort.* fr. 112 G.); see Aristotle, *Protr.* 59–61, ed. Rose: 1886.
[33] Hirzel 1883: 297 n. 2 vs. Grilli 1962: 148; Hagendahl 1967: ii, 492; Schlapbach 2006: 427. Straume-Zimmermann 1976: 198.
[34] Trans. King 1995: 9.
[35] Fr. 107 Grilli 1962: 149. See Ohlmann 1897: 37 (cf. Straume-Zimmermann 1976: 198; Schlapbach 2003: 95f.) vs. Hirzel 1883: 297 n. 2. See Reinhardt (Chapter 7, n. 14) in this volume.
[36] See Ruch 1958b: 168; Altman 2016a: 74.

Can we go further and argue that, even in the *Hortensius*, Cicero endorses some (if not all) of the teachings of the Academics, even if he does so only briefly? Cicero's intention could be to present these teachings as a possible solution to the problem of how to attain happiness.[37] His purpose could also be to suggest that to be a philosopher is to be a skeptic. After all, Cicero takes philosophy to be *amor sapientiae* (fr. 93 Grilli) or the search for truth,[38] so to dedicate oneself to philosophy is to dedicate oneself to skeptical philosophy.[39]

The Cassiciacum Dialogues

Somewhat surprisingly, immediately after his "complete" conversion to Christianity, in Cassiciacum Augustine engaged fairly systematically with Cicero's philosophical works. He wrote three dialogues featuring himself and other historical characters – his students or members of his family – which are supposed to recount their discussions in the villa of Cassiciacum in the fall of 386. Augustine takes philosophy to be divided into three parts – logic, ethics, and natural science. These distinct realms are the concern of the *Contra academicos*, the *De beata vita*, and the *De ordine*, respectively. In the *Contra academicos* he challenges the epistemology of the Academic skeptics; *De beata vita* is concerned with the question of the good life, and in *De ordine*, he addresses the question of the origin of evil in a world governed by God. He draws on the *Academica* in his *Contra academicos*, on the *De finibus* and *Tusculan Disputations* in his *De beata vita* (3.16–18).[40] In his *De ordine*, the central concept is order (*ordo*), which is relevant not only to the question of God's creation, but also to divine providence and foreknowledge. In answering these two questions, Augustine draws on Cicero's *De natura deorum* 2, *De divinatione*, and *De fato*.[41]

The structure, literary form, and the themes of the Cassiciacum Dialogues (to which we can add the *Soliloquies*)[42] make it clear that they

---

[37] This interpretation is supported by the similarity between *C. acad.* 1.3.7 and fr. 115 Grilli (= *Trin.* 14.19.26). Licentius' words at *C. acad.* 1.3.9 and 1.18.23 are an interesting parallel here. See Grilli 1962: 151.

[38] See Cic. *Acad.* 2.7.   [39] Schlapbach 2003: 19 and 91; Schlapbach 2006: 427.

[40] Cf. Foley 1999: 68.

[41] Augustine will again refer to book 2 of *De natura deorum* to celebrate the marvels of the created world: see *De civ. D.* 22.24 (Testard 1954) and the recently rediscovered *Sermo de providentia Dei* (= *Sermo* Dolbeau 29).

[42] There is also an affinity between Augustine's *Soliloquies* (a neologism) and the *Tusculan Disputations*. See Cataudella 1966; cf. Lévy 2002a: 31.

are an "imitation" of Cicero.[43] As Foley emphasizes, just as Cicero used eloquence to introduce philosophy to Rome, so too Augustine uses eloquence to introduce Christianity to the empire.[44] These dialogues are also the fruit of philosophical leisure enjoyed in some *villa*, and can be seen both as a continuation of the teaching in rhetoric (*schola*) he had given in Milan[45] and also as a break with this teaching. This tension is consistent with the complex relationship which Cicero establishes between *otium* and *negotium* during the writing of his philosophical books, although he also seeks to reconcile rhetoric and philosophy.[46]

His reworking of Cicero should not blind us to the fact that Augustine is often profoundly original. For example, while Cicero gives pride of place to men of letters and those involved in politics,[47] the characters who feature in Augustine's work can be of low social status (including women such as his mother Monica).[48] And even if these dialogues contain few biblical citations, they are clearly Christian works and, as such, hardly inspired only by Cicero.

The influence of Cicero affects both the logic and the development of the *Contra academicos*. In book 3, Augustine refutes the claims of Neo-Academic gnoseology (using arguments which are clearly taken from the *Academica*), though he is also appropriating Cicero's text for his own ends. For example, Cicero's account of the cataleptic impression allows Augustine to emphasize the subjectivity of the truths regarding which we have a certainty.[49] Furthermore, Augustine couples *ratio* with *auctoritas* (*C. acad.* 3.20.43). This pairing – which is undoubtedly influenced by Cicero's treatment of the topic in *Academica*[50] – is central to Augustine's epistemology: it is thanks to this double emphasis – where *auctoritas* precedes *ratio* – that we are "impelled" to learn. For Augustine, *auctoritas* is a precondition for reasoning, and he accuses Academic skeptics of paying greater head to *auctoritas* than to *ratio*, contrary to what they claim.

---

[43] O'Donnell 2015: 104.   [44] Foley 1999: 76.   [45] Steppat 1980.
[46] Boyancé 1970: 89–113; Luciani 2010: 68–95.
[47] Conybeare discusses Augustine's motivation for using this literary genre, which is synonymous with *otium liberale*. See Conybeare 2006: 20.
[48] Conybeare 2006: 63f.; Ribreau 2012.
[49] See Reinhardt 2016. Augustine will also use the notion of "assent" for his own conception of faith: Fuhrer 1992; Catapano 2016.
[50] See Cic. *Acad.* 2.60. See also Lütcke 1968: 35f.; Fuhrer 1997: 475.

The *City of God*

Obviously, Augustine's idea of the heavenly city comes from the Bible,[51] but its development also involves a deep engagement with Cicero, as shown by the letters to Nectarius from 408/9, just before Augustine began work on the *City of God*. Through these letters we can see again that in Late Antiquity cultured men all spoke the language of Cicero fluently, but they did not all understand his words in the same way. Nectarius, a high-ranking official from Calama, pleads the cause of his fellow citizens who are guilty of violence against Christians. This violence had erupted after they ignored Honorius' imperial edict of 408, which forbade pagans from engaging in public religious celebrations. Nectarius appeals to the notion of "care for the country" (*caritas patriae*) and cites an unpublished fragment from the *De republica* in which Cicero suggests that this *caritas* should be without "limit" (*Ep.* 91.1).[52] Augustine responds by setting up a contrast between a "fatherland of your birth in the flesh"[53] and a "certain heavenly fatherland"[54] into which we are "born by faith" (*Ep.* 91.6). He invites his correspondent to allow his fellow citizens to enter this homeland by abandoning traditional religion. He argues that the moral ideal (of continence) extolled by the protagonists of the *De republica* was incompatible with civic religion, and that it is now "taught and learned" in the churches (*Ep.* 91.1, 3).[55] Nectarius then identifies this "heavenly fatherland" with the "dwelling" (*domicilium*; Nect. ad August., *Ep.* 103.2)[56] promised to great men in the Dream of Scipio. But, in the third letter, a third place is mentioned: the "terrestrial [city] common to everyone" (*mundana ... communis omnibus* [*civitas*]; *Ep.* 103.2).[57] Here Nectarius is drawing on Stoic cosmopolitanism, which cannot be accommodated in Augustine's binary scheme. However, in the remaining correspondence Augustine makes no mention of his definitive account of the two cities which are "mingled" in this world – which he started elaborating around 400 and completed in *City of God*.[58]

The intended audience of the *City of God* is learned pagans in the aftermath of the sack of Rome by Alaric in 410. When he started to write this text in 412, Augustine was prompted to reread Cicero[59] – this was, after all, a text which was aimed at learned pagans. From this point on, he

---

[51] Van Oort 1997: 163–164. [52] Cf. *Rep.* 1, fr. 1 Powell. See O'Daly 1999: 25.
[53] Trans. Teske 2001: 368. [54] Trans. Teske 2001: 363. [55] Trans. Teske 2001: 368.
[56] Trans. Teske 2003: 40; cf. Cic. *Rep.* 6.29 = 6.33 Powell.
[57] Cf. *Rep.* 1.19 [The character Philus is speaking]. See Bermon 2011: 531–532.
[58] See Van Oort 1997. [59] Hagendahl 1967: II, 572.

considers Cicero's works in their own context and not in the fragmented or decontextualized way which sometimes characterized his earlier readings of Cicero's texts.

Populus

Cicero's *De republica* had a systematic influence on the *City of God*. Both these works are concerned with politics in a context where the question of Romanness and the very survival of Rome are at stake. We can appreciate why Augustine chose to draw on *De republica* if we recall that the *City of God* is an apologetic work, in which he seeks to show that even before the birth of Christ (*De civ. D.* 2.21) – and during the period of the Republic – misfortunes befell Rome and that its political system was far from perfect. Indeed, this system could even be described as tainted. In making this point, Augustine rejects Cicero's suggestion that the institutions of the Roman Republic embodied a political ideal.[60] At a time of crisis for the Roman empire – an empire which was an autocratic power – he tries to show the futility of Cicero's non-Platonist hope that the ideal and the real could coincide.[61] In contrast, Augustine suggests that it is only in the next life, in the heavenly city, that we will experience the harmonious concord which is enjoyed once justice is established.[62] The extent of Augustine's engagement with Cicero can be seen in the way he follows the development of Cicero's argument in books 2 to 5. The fact that he often cites those books at length surely suggests that he either had Cicero's text in front of him or had reread it very recently.[63]

Cicero defines *res publica* as *res populi* and a people (*populus*) as "not every association, but an association brought together by a common sense of what is right (*ius*) and by shared utility (*utilitas*)" (*Rep.* 1.39).[64] Augustine's rejection of Cicero's definition of a republic raises the question of how justice is to be established in an earthly city. It also prompts him to offer an alternative definition of a republic – a definition in which the idea of love is central. Book 19 of the *City of God* completes what Augustine set out to do in book 2: he shows that even if we use Scipio's definition of a republic, Rome was never a true republic because it lacked the true justice which exists only in the *res publica* of which Christ is the "founder and ruler" (*De civ. D.* 2.21). Cicero had already suggested the paradoxical view

[60] Girardet 1995. [61] Cf. August. *De civ. D.* 2.21 and Cic. *Rep.* 2.21–22; see Atkins 2011a: 464.
[62] Cf. August. *De civ. D.* 2.21 and Cic. *Rep.* 2.69. [63] Hagendahl 1967: II, 572; O'Donnell 1980.
[64] Trans. O'Daly 1999. See Schofield 1995a and Nicgorski (Chapter 14) in this volume.

that the Republic no longer existed.[65] It might continue to exist in name, but it did not exist in reality, like a "picture" which had lost its colors (*Rep.* 5.2 = 5.1 Powell). Augustine pushes this paradox further. In doing so, he applies Scipio's account of degenerate forms of government to the case of Rome (*Rep.* 3.43 = 3.35 Powell):[66] "Augustine does not disagree with Cicero's definition. The philosophers are right in pointing to justice as the healthy condition of cities, but they are unable to secure its performance."[67]

Augustine therefore says that he will offer definitions of the republic which are "more convincing" (*probabiliores*) – an academic term worth emphasizing. These definitions, Augustine suggests, will enable us to see that the *respublica Romana* was "better administrated by the early Romans than by their descendents" (2.21).[68] The new definition which Augustine offers is this: a republic is "an assembled multitude, not of animals but of rational creatures, and is joined together by common agreement on the objects of its love" (*De civ. D.* 19.24).[69] The fact that this definition does not appear until book 19 can no doubt be explained by the fact that until this point Augustine has argued that the Roman Republic did not worship the true God, whereas *vera iustitia* depends on *vera religio*. His *retorsio* (*De civ. D.* 19.21)[70] against Cicero is based on the analysis of the two elements of the definition of *populus* given by Scipio: he suggests that there is no possible *ius*, and thus no possible *consensus iuris*, without true justice.[71] But even the idea of *utilitatis communio* is untenable: for what benefit could there be in living in impiety, or worshiping demons?

City of God *Book 5: The* De fato *Reexamined*

Augustine acknowledges the greatness of the Roman empire in book 5 of the *City of God*. He attributes that greatness not to the divinities of the city but rather to a cause which is "neither chance nor fate" (*De civ. D.* 5.1). Augustine appeals to Cicero's *De fato* to refute the view that our lives are determined by the stars. Then he assumes a Stoic conception of *fatum* that

---

[65] Cicero goes beyond Sallust, who describes the Roman Republic simply as *flagitiosissima* (*Cat.* 5.9, in *De civ. D.* 2.18).
[66] Cf. Hagendahl 1967: II, 548.   [67] Fortin 1997: 48.   [68] Trans. Babcock 2012: 59.
[69] Trans. Babcock 2013: 385. This passage shows that Augustine subscribes to the Roman ideal of *concordia* (see also *Ep.* 138.10, written in 412). Cf. Cicero's image in *Rep.* 2.70.
[70] See Bouton-Touboulic 2004a: 609.
[71] Cf. the anecdote about the *regna* reduced to *magna latrocinia* (*De civ. D.* 4.4) when Augustine recalls the pirate's words to Alexander = *Rep.* 3, fr. 1 Powell.

he defines as the "order and chain of causes" (Cic. *Div.* 1.125), and to this
extent he takes "destiny" to refer to "the divine order"; finally, he suggests
that *fatum* should in fact be called "providence." After this, Augustine's
attitude to Cicero changes significantly, and he challenges Cicero's critical
approach to Stoic doctrines. Cicero suggests that those who accept
divination[72] – and therefore attribute foreknowledge to the gods[73] – are
committed to a view of destiny which is incompatible with human
freedom (Cic. *Fat.* 20). However, in Augustine's eyes, Cicero ends up
denying all divine foreknowledge.[74] Such a denial, Augustine suggests, is
worse than any adherence to astral fatalism, since it comes down to a denial
of God.

Augustine acknowledges that the "insane" idea that God does not exist
is not one which Cicero directly "sounded out" (*temptavit*) himself (*De civ.
D.* 5.9). Instead, it is defended at *De natura deorum* 3.95 by the Academic
Cotta,[75] before Cicero adopts the views of the Stoic Balbus.[76] Augustine
does not take any account of the fact that Cotta repeatedly makes it clear
that he is not denying the existence of gods, but is simply rejecting the
arguments used by his opponents to establish their existence.[77] This
suggests that Augustine is relying on an interesting distinction between
the different *personae*[78] in this dialogue in order to discern Cicero's own
views – a task with which scholars are still engaged today. For Augustine,
Cicero is a "masked" presence as he attacks the existence of the gods using
Cotta as an intermediary. Cicero then abandons the idea of divine pre-
science in the *De divinatione*. This allows him to reject the notion of
destiny and to emphasize human freedom in the *De fato*. Indeed, the
character "Cicero" can be found in both these works.[79] When he considers
the development of Cicero's thought here, Augustine sees a "crazy" dis-
proportionality between Cicero's intended aim of preserving human
freedom and the means which he uses: "In his desire to make men free
he made them irreligious" (*De civ. D.* 5.9). In Augustine's eyes, human
free will is not incompatible with divine foreknowledge. In fact, the latter
serves to guarantee the former. In this way, Augustine claims, he is able to
avoid the traps that stymied Cicero's Carneades' efforts to refute
Chrysippus.[80]

---

[72] See *Div.* 1.128.   [73] According to the definition of divination given by Quintus, Cic. *Div.* 1.1.
[74] See Cic. *Div.* 2.18; cf. *Fat.* 32.
[75] For a discussion of the view that Cicero is "insincere," see Lévy 1992a: 558 n. 5.
[76] Cf. August. *De civ. D.* 5.9. See Lévy 1992a: 580–581.   [77] Testard 1958: II, 47.
[78] Cf. Brittain 2011: 108–109.   [79] See Pic 1997: 214–217.
[80] See further Bouton-Touboulic 2004a: 381–387.

The Passions

Cicero's influence on the *City of God* is marked by another major theme, the question of the passions in books 9 and 14. There are in fact two questions which Augustine addresses in these books; first, how to define the passions and second, whether they have a place in Christian life. Augustine makes some use of Seneca and Aulus Gellius here, but the definition of the passions as *perturbationes*[81] in book 4 of the *Tusculan Disputations* is particularly important to him. He places even greater emphasis on Cicero's use of the Stoic notion of "good emotions" (*eupatheiai* or *constantiae*; *De civ. D.* 14.8), characteristic of the wise man,[82] though he claims to go beyond the strict distinction between *perturbationes* and *constantiae*. Furthermore, he proposes a new norm by which we can measure all these affects: *voluntas* (whether good or bad). In this way, he draws on Cicero's critique of the Stoic Cleanthes' method of consolation – a consolation which consists only in arguments and would not be neither effective nor appropriated in the case of Alcibiades, as his sadness is justified because he grieves for his own foolishness (*Tusc.* 3.77).[83] In the latter case, Augustine even speaks of a "sadness useful and desirable" (*utilis optandaque tristitia*; *De Civ. D.* 14.8) and "a sadness according to God" (2 Cor. 7:10).[84] While Cicero is noncommittal toward Stoicism, Augustine does not hesitate to turn Cicero's comment on Cleanthes into a systematic critique and to erase the Stoic distinction between good emotions and passions,[85] since in his judgment the *apatheia* of the sage is not attainable in this life.

Augustine's Point of View: A *Cicero Academicus*?

At least one crucial question remains. What is Augustine's judgment of Cicero? Does he use Cicero only when it suits him or does he engage with Cicero's views deeply enough to form an assessment of him as a philosopher? Does he identify Cicero with a particular philosophical school? It is certainly worth noting that, while Augustine often describes Cicero as an eloquent orator, he describes him as a philosopher only on rare occasions. Sometimes his judgment of this pagan author is harsh, but he also emphasizes the fact that certain elements of Christian faith are found in

---

[81] Testard 1958: I, 210 n. 5 (cf. *Tusc.* 4.14). [82] E.g. *cautio, gaudium*, and *voluntas*.
[83] Cf. Pl. *Symp.* 215e–216c. See Luciani 2010: 344. [84] See Bouton-Touboulic 2016: 492–493.
[85] Brachtendorf 1995.

his works (*C. Iul.* 4.14.72). For present purposes, the most significant question is this: to what extent does Augustine take Cicero to be an *academicus* (i.e. affiliated with the New Academy)? And does Augustine see a tension between Cicero's skepticism and the more "dogmatic" positions he takes in some of his writings?[86] These tensions – which are central to recent studies on Cicero[87] – did not escape Augustine. We cannot be sure of Augustine's reasons for proposing the view that the Neo-Academics were characterized by an "esoteric dogmatism"[88] – their skepticism was merely a façade,[89] which allowed them to safeguard Plato's dogmatic claims by protecting them from the objections put forward by Stoics or Epicureans. In any case, this hypothesis, which Augustine presents at the end of the *Contra academicos*, refers the reader to Cicero's own words: "Furthermore, if anyone thinks that the Academicians also held this view, let him hear Cicero himself" (3.20.43).[90]

It is an open question whether Augustine has a particular text by Cicero in mind here – a text which he could have interpreted in his own way, of course.[91] Whatever the case, it is clear that Augustine believes that he is able to reveal Cicero's true intention. This intention could also be revealed in Cicero's own use of the adjective *verisimile*.[92] However, when Augustine summarizes the history of the Academy – by turns evincing both indifference[93] and interest[94] in this history – he represents Cicero as playing a key role in this project of safeguarding and communicating Plato's legacy. Cicero uses oratory that is "full of hot air" (i.e. excessive and vain) to attack Antiochus (a "Platonic straw man"). In a dialectical way, this oratory allows him to staunchly defend Plato's innermost sanctuary (*C. acad.* 3.18.41).[95] Indeed, *Tullius noster* is presented as the defender of the Academic tradition maintained by the New Academy and by Philo of Larissa. Augustine continued to suggest that the New Academy was

---

[86] Quite apart from the question of whether Cicero's intellectual life can be divided into different periods ("skeptical" or otherwise). See Glucker 1988: 66.

[87] Glucker 1988; Lévy 1992a; Woolf 2015; Nicgorski 2016.

[88] It is clear that Augustine began to hold this view when he was in Milan. Cf. *Conf.* 5.14.25.

[89] Before Augustine, other thinkers had proposed this theory: see Lévy 1978.

[90] Trans. King 1995: 92.

[91] Cf. *Acad.* 2.60 and the term *mysteria* or a passage from the *Acad. post.* that is now lost (Glucker 1978: 303). See Bouton-Touboulic 2009: 112–113.

[92] *C. acad.* 2.11.26, which cites a passages from the *Academica* (= fr. 19 Müller = Plasberg 1996: 22, 3–8) that is now lost. See Lévy 1992a: 289 for a discussion of the "Platonic register," which this term calls to mind, as well as Bouton-Touboulic 2009: 106; Fuhrer 1993.

[93] Glucker 1978: 326. See also Bouton-Touboulic 2018.

[94] Brittain 2001: 68–70; Lévy 2005: 71.   [95] Trans. King 1995: 90.

characterized by an esoteric dogmatism until at least 410: in his Letter 118, Augustine describes Cicero as an author who explicitly suggests that on the Platonist scheme "the highest good and the cause of things and the trustworthiness of reason" (August. *Ep.* 118.20)[96] – i.e. the three parts of philosophy[97] – should be seen in the context of divine wisdom. Augustine distinguishes this Cicero from "Cicero the *academicus*" who seeks only to refute the arguments of others.

In two late texts (*De Trinitate* 13.4.7, written after 415, and *Contra Iulianum opus imperfectum* 6.26, written after 428) where Cicero is presented as *patronus* of the Academics, Augustine notes the irony that even when he "doubts everything," Cicero's starting point is the certainty that there is a universal desire for happiness. In the *De Trinitate*, Augustine renews his critique of the *Nova Academia*. He also cites the *Hortensius* (fr. 115 G) as evidence that Cicero's position on the immortality of the soul is ambiguous. While Augustine attributes Cicero's confusion on this point to the fact that he had been excessively influenced by the *Nova Academica*, and therefore insufficiently faithful to the Platonic tradition, he nonetheless celebrates his judgement: "He certainly did not have to learn this from the philosophers whose praises he sings so enthusiastically; this opinion smacks of that New Academy in which he was persuaded to doubt even the most evident things" (*Trin.* 14.19.26).[98] Still, the hesitation Augustine sees in Cicero here is consistent with his attitude in the *Tusculan Disputations* book 1.[99]

The theory that Cicero is characterized by an esoteric dogmatism does not feature in the *City of God*.[100] In that work Cicero is often called *academicus* and his apparent skepticism is criticized[101] because Augustine takes doubt to be incompatible with Christian doctrine (*De civ. D.* 19.18).[102] Nonetheless, in the *City of God*, Augustine appreciates Cicero's attachment to the philosophy of Plato.[103] In book 22, for example, he notes with approval that Cicero's views on the imperishability of the world are consistent with the position of the *Platonici*.

[96] Trans. Teske 2003: 116.   [97] See *De civ. D.* 8.4.   [98] Trans. Hill 1991: 393.

[99] Lévy 2002b: 83–84.

[100] Cf. Bouton-Touboulic 2009: 110; Brittain 2011: 89 suggests that this change in Augustine's assessment of Cicero comes about after 415, and that it should be seen in the context of his rereading of Cicero as he starts working on the *City of God*.

[101] See *De civ. D.* 4.30 and 6.2, written c. 415.

[102] Cf. the *cogito* in *Trin.* 15 and *De civ. D.* 11.26.

[103] At *De civ. D.* 22.6, as is noted in Brittain 2011: 110.

Conclusion

Augustine is often said to offer creative "syntheses"[104] between elements of pagan philosophy and Christian dogma. But it seems more appropriate to speak of Augustine's "appropriation" of Cicero. Indeed, for Augustine, Cicero is by no means only a renowned orator. Augustine sees him first and foremost as the author who encouraged him to engage with philosophy and who provided him with the definition of philosophy as "love of wisdom." On many issues, Augustine is faithful to the vision outlined in the *Hortensius*. These points of agreement include eudaimonism,[105] the fate of the soul after death, a rejection of the goods associated with the sensible realm, the misery of earthly life, and the emphasis on the search for truth. Especially in his early works, he sees Cicero as the spokesperson for the truths conveyed by Platonism (an assessment which surely exaggerates Cicero's interest in spiritual questions),[106] even if Augustine is certainly well aware of Cicero's attachment to the New Academy. This attachment is first sidelined and then ridiculed by Augustine, who realizes that Cicero represents a challenge to Christian faith because he is a philosopher who embraces doubt.

For Augustine, Cicero is also a witness to the great controversies that were discussed by Hellenistic philosophers and covered various questions: the *summum bonum*, divine providence and divination, the passions, and the different kinds of knowledge that are available to human beings. Augustine picks up some of the arguments Cicero uses against the Epicureans and the Stoics, he also appeals to Cicero in his efforts to combat Pelagianism (though in this case he relies on rather distorted interpretations of Cicero's arguments). Furthermore, some of the key motifs in Augustine's thought derive from his reading of Cicero: among them, the pairing of *ratio* and *auctoritas*; *adsensio*; the republic. Although these concepts can be traced to Cicero, they are of course reinterpreted by Augustine from a Christian point of view. To this extent, Augustine played a crucial role in preserving Cicero's conception of Romanness: many of Cicero's ideas about this would have been lost had they not been transmitted by Augustine. In the end, Cicero is seen by Augustine as the main authority on the question of Roman thought – and as an authority who had been shaped by Plato's legacy.

---

[104] See Uhle 2012: 4; Madec 1994: 318 rejects this notion.   [105] On this topic, see Holte 1962.
[106] Testard 1986: 927.

Further Reading

Modern English translations for almost all of Augustine's works can be found in New City Press's series, The Works of Saint Augustine: A Translation for the 21st Century. Besides this, the additional main English translations of works covered in this chapter include the following editions: O'Meara 1951 (*Contra academicos*); King 1995 (*Contra academicos* and *De magistro*); Foley 2019a and Foley 2019b (*Contra academicos* and *De beata vita*). Dodaro and Atkins 2001 includes translations of political themes in a selection of Augustine's sermons and letters. Dyson 1998 is a translation of the *City of God*. Commentaries include O'Donnell 1992 (*Confessions*); Fuhrer 1997 and Schapbach 2003 (*Contra academicos*); Trelenberg 2009 (*De ordine*); O'Daly 1999 is a reader's guide to the *City of God*.

The *Augustinus Lexikon* (ed. Mayer et al. 1986–) is an essential tool that offers a wide range of articles dealing with Cicero and Ciceronian themes. For Ciceronian *testimonia* and general influence on Augustine's works, see first and foremost Testard 1958 and Hagendahl 1967 (Testard's focus is on the history of sources; Hagendahl's on the history of ideas). Madec 1969; Catapano 2001; and Bochet and Madec 2012 deal with the philosophical reception of *Hortensius* by Augustine. For scholarly debate about the value and the meaning of *Contra academicos* for the history of Academic Skepticism, see Glucker 1988; Lévy 1992a and 2005; Brittain 2001; Nicgorski 2015. On the value of Augustine for interpreting Cicero's philosophy more broadly, see Glucker 1988 and Altman 2016a. Brittain 2011; O'Donnell 2015; and Bouton-Touboulic 2018 provide overviews of Augustine's judgment of Cicero's philosophical affiliation. For Cicero's influence on Augustine's epistemology, see Fuhrer 1993; Bermon 2001; Catapano 2016; Reinhardt 2016. For Augustine's debts to Stoicism through Cicero's writings in matters of anthropology, ethics, politics, and theology, see Colish 1985; Girardet 1995; Bouton-Touboulic 2004a and 2017; Byers 2013. For Augustine's debts to Cicero on political thought, see Fortin 1997; O'Daly 1999; Dodaro and Atkins 2001; Atkins 2002; Bouton-Touboulic 2004a; and Moatti 2018.

CHAPTER 17

Cicero and Eighteenth-Century Political Thought

Daniel J. Kapust

"The fame of Cicero flourishes at present; but that of Aristotle is utterly decayed": thus wrote Hume in his *Enquiry Concerning Human Understanding*.[1] In the English-speaking world of the eighteenth century, Cicero was often simply "Tully"; Middleton's *Life of Cicero*, published in 1741, sold well. Voltaire penned a play, *Rome Saved, or Catiline*, aimed to "make young people who go to the theatre acquainted with Cicero."[2] Diderot called Cicero "first of the Roman philosophers," American universities often "mandated a basic knowledge of Cicero,"[3] and Hamilton signed as "Tully" his papers condemning the Whiskey Rebellion. If in the seventeenth century Cicero's skepticism attracted figures such as John Locke, Cicero the republican orator-statesman assumed a central role in the eighteenth century.

There are many reasons beyond his role in the eighteenth-century educational curriculum to explain why he had such a prominent place. Not the least of these, and one which is directly related to much of my discussion, is Cicero's centrality to the republican tradition in political thought, a tradition that was of paramount importance on both sides of the Atlantic in the eighteenth century.[4] But we might also point to the centrality of Cicero, especially *De finibus*, to one of the key debates in eighteenth-century political and ethical thought: the debate over sociability. In these debates, as Hont has shown, Epicureanism and Stoicism served "as proxy categories" to denote two fundamental positions: "Epicureanism stood for a position in which a foundational sociability of man was missing . . . whereas Stoicism stood as a proxy theory of sociability."[5] Indeed, no less a pair of luminaries in eighteenth-century debates on

---

[1] Hume 1902: 7. Material in this paragraph was adapted from Kapust and Remer 2021: 7–8.
[2] Gay 1966: 106.   [3] Richard 2015: 125, 129.
[4] See Pettit 1999; Skinner 1998 and Nicgorski (Chapter 14) in this volume.
[5] Hont 2015: 14–15.

sociability than Smith and Kant drew from Cicero's *De finibus* in their lectures on moral philosophy.

Less clear is what *sort* of role. On the one hand, some are cautious regarding Cicero's influence, Matthew Fox's essay in the *Cambridge Companion to Cicero* being a key example. Fox remarks, "Cicero's thought does not have any coherent philosophical system, a lack that comes to be seen as a failing on his part only as the Enlightenment nears its end."[6] As a result, as Fox puts it, "although it can be argued that [Cicero] did influence a few figures strongly, unless an assumption is made about what Cicero's thought consists of, it is difficult to find a close correspondence between particular theories developed in the Enlightenment and views that can be attributed to Cicero."[7] There are, however, good reasons to think that Cicero is a coherent thinker, as recent work by both Walter Nicgorski and Raphael Woolf attests. Even if one does not think Cicero was systematic, a range of eighteenth-century sources testify to Cicero's influence on their thought.

On the other hand, some overplay Cicero's influence, a tactic in Paul MacKendrick's *Philosophical Books of Cicero*, which often locates a claim in Cicero and suggests influence given a source's familiarity with Cicero. Thus MacKendrick suggests Adam Smith's "conviction that the pursuit of enlightened self-interest contributes to the public welfare can also be found in Cicero *On Duty* 1.93–145," though Smith had a range of ancient and modern sources.[8] More strikingly, after remarking that Montesquieu's *On the Spirit of the Laws* "has been hailed ... as anticipating nineteenth-century sociology," MacKendrick suggests that "all Montesquieu's alleged innovations are already to be found in Cicero."[9] It would be an overstatement to suggest that Cicero was *the* source for doctrines found in later thinkers who knew him, as MacKendrick at times tends to do; after all, eighteenth-century thinkers were well-read in both the classics and modern – not to mention medieval – thought.

I position myself between Fox and MacKendrick, arguing that Cicero inspired and influenced a range of eighteenth-century thinkers – whether in the adoption of Ciceronian arguments or the use of Cicero as theoretical foil. My tactic is to put Cicero into conversation with eighteenth-century figures on key themes: ethics, eloquence, civil religion, law, and the active

---

[6] Fox 2013: 319.
[7] Fox 2013: 319. For a pointed critique of Fox, see Sharpe 2015. For readings of Cicero as coherent, see Nicgorski 2016 and Woolf 2015.
[8] MacKendrick 1989: 281.   [9] MacKendrick 1989: 277.

life. I select these themes, which I approach in what follows, not because they are exhaustive, but because they allow us to gauge Cicero's place in a range of key eighteenth-century political thought. My aim is less a representative sample, let alone a full survey, but rather a discussion broad enough to see different approaches to Cicero in the period. Prior to turning to eighteenth-century thought, though, I deal briefly with Locke, whose engagement with Cicero will serve as a precursor to and model for approaching later eighteenth-century engagements.

Cicero and Locke

Cicero played a pivotal role in Locke's education, especially when it came to rhetoric;[10] among the volumes Locke owned were many editions of Cicero's writing on rhetoric.[11] Wood argues for Locke's Ciceronianism most forcefully: he notes, as evidence of Locke's "genuine admiration for the ancient," his citation of *De natura deorum* on the title page of *An Essay Concerning Human Understanding*, suggesting that "some of Cicero's axiomatic social values must have found a receptive audience in Locke: the emphasis upon private property . . . the distinction between gentlemen and non-gentlemen; the stress on moderation, proportionate equality, and decorum in gentlemanly conduct; and the belief in fundamental moral equality joined with an acceptance of widespread social and political inequalities."[12]

Yet also Locke exemplifies the complexity of Cicero's reception. If we focus on where and when Locke *mentions* Cicero by name, Locke does so neither in the *First* nor *Second Treatise on Government*. Both Wood and MacKendrick suggest that Cicero is the key source for Locke's theory of property; I am skeptical. To be sure, both Cicero and Locke point to preserving property as a key state function, but *why* they do so fundamentally differs: Locke provides in *The Second Treatise of Government* a prepolitical account of property acquisition based on mixing labor and rights, writing, "Whatsoever . . . he removes out of the State that Nature hath provided . . . he hath mixed his *Labour* with, and joined to it something that is his own, and thereby makes it his *Property*."[13] Cicero agrees that "no property is private by nature," but he holds that it becomes so "by long

---

[10] Dawson 2007: 65.   [11] See Harrison and Laslett 1963: 108–109.
[12] Wood 1983: 29. For a recent interpretation of Locke's relationship to Cicero that departs from Wood, see Nacol 2021.
[13] Locke 1988: 287–288.

occupation ... or by victory ... or by law, by settlement, by agreement, or by lot" (*Off.* 1.21; trans. Griffin and Atkins). And he seems more concerned with what redistribution *does* to political association given the harm it does to the security of property that led pre-political humans to seek "protection in cities" (*Off.* 2.73; trans. Griffin and Atkins). Less controversial, given direct textual evidence, is the role Cicero plays in Locke's *Essay Concerning Human Understanding.* Locke cites Cicero to support the claim that "virtue is every-where that which is thought praiseworthy; and nothing else but that which has the allowance of public esteem is called virtue. Virtue and praise are so united, that they are called often by the same name."[14] He points specifically to *Tusculan Disputations* 2.46, where Cicero writes, "far the best for man is that which is desirable in itself and for itself, has its source in virtue or rather is based on virtue, is of itself praiseworthy, and in fact I should prefer to describe it as the only rather than the highest good" (*Tusc.* 2.46; trans. King). Later, Locke refers to *De legibus* 2.16 to support his argument for the existence of God as rooted in our consideration "of ourselves and what we infallibly find in our own constitutions," leading to the truth "that *there is an eternal, most powerful, and most knowing being,* which whether anyone will please to call "*God,*" it matters not."[15]

Though Locke cites Cicero approvingly, and appeals to his authority, he displays an uneasy relationship to him, in part because he embraces the seventeenth-century worry about rhetorical *elocutio,* which could, through metaphor and other figures, breach what Dawson describes as "the semantic contract"[16] – that is, the idea that common usage provides meaning to words. Thus Locke argues, in *Essay Concerning Human Understanding* 3.10.34, that "all the artificial and figurative application of words eloquence hath invented, are for nothing else but to insinuate wrong ideas, move the passions, and thereby mislead the judgment, and so indeed are perfect cheats," thus making such eloquence "wholly to be avoided" in any speech seeking "to inform or instruct."[17] In *De oratore,* by contrast, Cicero has Crassus suggest that a speech "be sprinkled, as it were, with flowers of language and thought ... to hold the attention of our audience" (*De or.* 3.96–97; trans. May and Wisse), pleasing them without pleasing them too much. Locke knew and drew on Cicero, but at least when it comes to the nature of figures of speech, he also uses Cicero as a foil.

---

[14] Locke 1824: I, 373.   [15] Locke 1824: II, 190; emphasis added.   [16] Dawson 2007: 78.
[17] Locke 1824: II, 41.

Cicero and Eighteenth-Century Ethics

Let us move from Locke to the eighteenth century by stating the obvious: not all eighteenth-century ethical theories are Ciceronian. Indeed, the greatest eighteenth-century ethical thinker – Immanuel Kant – is arguably anti-Ciceronian. It's worth being more cautious than MacKendrick, who suggests, for example, that Kant's Categorical Imperative in the *Groundwork for the Metaphysics of Morals* was "inspired" by Garve's 1783 translation and commentary of *De officiis*.[18] Kant knew Cicero well, and he knew Garve. Yet Kant's ethical system is decidedly non-Ciceronian, insofar as a Ciceronian ethical theory owes its account of the formation of moral character and its operation to a framework shaped by affections and a sense of shame, along with a deep awareness of the importance of human embeddedness.[19] To be sure, Cicero says in *De officiis*, "Reason therefore commands, and impulse obeys. All action should be free from rashness and carelessness; nor should anyone do anything for which he cannot give a persuasive justification (*cuius non possit causam probabilem reddere*): that is practically a definition of duty" (*Off.* 1.101; trans. Griffin and Atkins). Kant's categorical imperative has a faint echo: "I am never to act otherwise than so *that I could also will that my maxim should become a universal law.*"[20] But Cicero's view is not what Kant intended by the *a priori* foundations of morality, since Cicero uses a skeptical term (*probabile*) to articulate his reasoning. Cicero is far from Kant's ethical vision, prioritizing as he did what Kant terms "the *principle of volition* by which the action has taken place, without regard to any object of desire."[21] Notwithstanding the point that Cicero was certainly an influence on Kant, as Nussbaum has shown, especially when it comes to Kant's cosmopolitanism, I find Woolf's claim compelling that Cicero's view in *On Duties* shows him to be sympathetic to ethical particularism. That is to say, "A Ciceronian agent who strives to serve the common good will not ... be able to do so by following rules."[22]

Much more sympathetic to Ciceronian ethics is sentimentalism. Standing at the head of this tradition is a figure, Anthony Ashley Cooper, third Earl of Shaftesbury, whose life spanned the late seventeenth and early eighteenth century. Shaftesbury's relationship to Cicero helps

---

[18] MacKendrick 1989: 284.
[19] On these points, Woolf 2015 is especially helpful, particularly chs. 5 and 6.
[20] Kant 1949: 19; emphasis original.   [21] Kant 1949: 17; emphasis original.
[22] Woolf 2007: 344. See Nussbaum 1997.

explain his rejection of Thomas Hobbes's (apparent) egoism and his corollary emphasis on human sociability. Sympathy forms an important part of Shaftesbury's moral theory, and especially his criticisms of Hobbes, as Peart and Levy show;[23] we might point to this passage from "An Inquiry Concerning Virtue or Merit":

> It will be consider'd how many the Pleasures are, of *sharing Contentment and Delight with others*; of receiving it in Fellowship and Company; and gathering it, in a manner, from the pleas'd and happy States of those around us, from accounts and relations of such Happinesses, from the very Countenances, Gestures, Voices and Sounds, even of Creatures foreign to our Kind, whose Signs of Joy and Contentment we can anyway discern. So insinuating are these Pleasures of Sympathy, and so widely diffus'd thro' our whole Lives, that there is hardly such a thing as Satisfaction or Contentment, of which they make not an essential part.[24]

Later in the *Characteristicks*, in "The Moralists; A Philosophical Rhapsody," Shaftesbury draws upon Cicero to support his claim for the interdependence of the universe and living creatures by quoting the Latin text of *De oratore*, which translates as:

> those great men of the past, having grasped in their minds something of a higher order, have thereby seen much more than our mind's eye today is able to contemplate: they said that all the universe above and below is a unity and is bound together by a single, natural force and harmony (*unum esse et una vi atque [una] consensione naturae constricta esse dixerunt*).[25]

For Shaftesbury, then, an account of human psychology prioritizing interdependence and sympathy owes its inspiration to Cicero.

When we turn from Shaftesbury to Adam Smith, the greatest of the sentimentalists, we see him define sympathy in *The Theory of Moral Sentiments* as "our fellow-feeling with any passion whatever."[26] The term *sympatheia* was central to Stoic doctrine, though Smith's contemporary, John Gillies, thought Smith may have borrowed the term from Polybius.[27] Notwithstanding the possible link to Polybius, in *De divinatione* – a text Smith surely knew – Cicero translates the Greek term thus: "What natural tie, or what 'symphony,' so to speak, or association (*coniunctione naturae et quasi concentu atque consensus*), or what 'sympathy', as the Greeks term it, can there be between a cleft in a liver and a petty addition to my purse?" (*Div.* 2.34; trans. Falconer). To be sure, his use of the term in this context

---

[23] Peart and Levy 2008.   [24] Shaftesbury 2001: II, 62.   [25] Shaftesbury 2001: II, 161.
[26] Smith 1982: 10.   [27] Vivenza 2001: 44–46.

is cosmological, denoting the relationship "between objects apparently unrelated" (*Div.* 2.34; trans. Falconer). And while Cicero doesn't always use the Greek *sympatheia*, he emphasizes the need, in *De officiis*, to consider "what others think about oneself," holding that "the part of justice is not to harm a man, that of a sense of shame (*verecundiae*) not to outrage him" (*Off.* 1.99; trans. Griffin and Atkins). Given the bonds of human fellowship, we ought to look to what others think of us to gauge moral action; in this regard, Cicero suggests we look to poetry as a model for harmony between character and action.[28]

Cicero's account of consideration and the role of shame occurs in the context of him describing *decorum*, a Latin term that may be rendered in English as propriety or appropriateness. Smith, early in his account of sympathy's role in moral judgment, introduces propriety with the following remark: "When the original passions of the person principally concerned are in perfect concord with the sympathetic emotions of the spectator, they necessarily appear to this last just and proper, and suitable to their objects."[29] Sympathy is the capacity allowing for such judgments. While Smith's use of the term sympathy may, indeed, owe to his Stoic sources – or Polybius, or even Cicero's *De divinatione* – his account of the desire to seek harmony when it comes to human interactions strikes me as less obviously Stoic. If for Smith it is true that "in the suitableness or unsuitableness, in the proportion or disproportion which the affection seems to bear to the cause or object which excites it, consists the propriety or impropriety, the decency or ungracefulness of the consequent action,"[30] one can certainly make the case that his approach to propriety is Ciceronian, like that of Shaftesbury.

Cicero and Eighteenth-Century Eloquence

Hume was deeply influenced by Cicero, a point he makes in a 1739 letter to Frances Hutcheson, remarking "I desire to take my Catalogue of Virtues from Cicero's *Offices*, not from the *Whole Duty of Man*. I had, indeed, the former Book in my Eye in all my Reasonings."[31] His attitude, though, differs when it comes to Cicero's rhetoric. As Adam Potkay argues, Hume's account of eloquence is a "*dialogue* between the assumptions of modern politeness and the claims of ancient eloquence, or, more precisely, a debate in which politeness is increasingly, though never conclusively,

---

[28] On echoes of this metaphor in Smith, see Griswold 1999: 183.   [29] Smith 1982: 16.
[30] Smith 1982: 18.   [31] Quoted in Gay 1966: 66.

given the upper hand."[32] Potkay's distinction between eighteenth-century understandings of eloquence and politeness is helpful: the prior "serves as the metonymy for an imagined *scene* of ancient oratory in which the speaker moves the just passions of a civic assembly and implants a sense of community with his words." Stylistically and substantively, the country writers of the early eighteenth century were devotees of eloquence; republicans *par excellence*, they "equate eloquence with 'virtue,' steadfastly maintaining that only the good citizen could be a good speaker." Politeness, "an ethos of concealment," by contrast, sought "to place or stabilize rather than, as with eloquence, to make things happen."[33] We can thus appreciate why Hume saw Cicero as *impolite*. He writes in *Of Eloquence* that Cicero was "the most eloquent speaker, that had ever appeared in Rome," understanding eloquence to be "speaking in public." And yet he suggests, after discussing the "blaze of eloquence" from a passage in Cicero's *Verrines*, "Should this sentiment even appear to us excessive, as perhaps it justly may, it will at least serve to give an idea of the stile of ancient eloquence, where such swelling expressions were not rejected as wholly monstrous and gigantic."[34]

Cicero, though an influence, was also Hume's foil. Thus, at times, Hume finds Cicero "too florid and rhetorical: His figures are too striking and palpable: The divisions of his discourse are drawn chiefly from the rules of the schools: And his wit disdains not always the artifice even of a pun, rhyme, or jingle of words."[35] Hume seems to prefer Demosthenes, who was "more chaste and austere." And yet, Hume has a profoundly Ciceronian view of eloquence:

> The principles of every passion, and of every sentiment, is [*sic*] in every man; and when touched properly, they rise to life, and warm the heart, and convey that satisfaction, by which a work of genius is distinguished from the adulterate beauties of a capricious wit and fancy. And if this observation be true . . . it must be peculiarly so, with regard to eloquence; which, being merely calculated for the public, and for men of the world, cannot, with any pretence of reason, appeal from the people to more refined judges; but must submit to the public verdict, without reserve or limitation.[36]

Cicero says something very similar about the efficacy and judgment of oratory in his work *Orator*.[37]

---

[32] Potkay 1994: 5.   [33] Potkay 1994: 2, 3, 5.   [34] Hume 1985b: 101.
[35] Hume 1985b: 105.   [36] Hume 1985b: 107.
[37] On this point, and the criterion of *decorum* more broadly, see Kapust 2011a.

The eloquence of orators has always been controlled by the good sense of the audience, since all who desire to win approval have regard to the goodwill of their auditors, and shape and adapt themselves completely according to this and to their opinion and approval. (24; trans. Hubbell)

Cicero and Hume would seem close when it comes to the *evaluation* of and *constraints* on oratory. And yet Hume makes a striking comment:

ancient eloquence, that is the sublime and passionate, is of a much juster taste than the modern or the argumentative and rational; and, if properly executed, will always have more command and authority over mankind ... For, if I mistake not, our modern eloquence is of the same stile or species with that which ancient critics denominated ATTIC eloquence, that is, calm, elegant, and subtile, which instructed the reason more than affected the passions, and never raised its tone above argument or common discourse.[38]

Hume is being tendentious: Cicero favored the style he dubbed Asiatic in opposition to Atticism, the latter looking to Athenian models of "purity and simplicity," and the former extolling emotional engagement and decorative speech.[39] Cicero did not, however, think that one should *only* deploy the emotional and decorative Asiatic style: such an orator "seems to be a raving madman among the sane, like a drunken reveler in the midst of sober men" (*Orat.* 99; trans. Hubbell). But if one cannot speak in the Asiatic style when appropriate, one is not an ideal orator, since the orator must be able "to sway or persuade," a task suited to the Asiatic style. Hume thinks something like the Asiatic mode is necessary, or at least has been necessary, in certain political moments; thus Potkay suggests Hume certainly had "Cicero's story of the origins of civil society" in *De oratore* in mind as he argued against contract models,[40] emphasizing, as Hume did in *Of the Original Contract*, that early rulers "ruled more by persuasion than command."[41]

Smith, too, seemingly rejects Cicero – and Quintilian – when it comes to style, where "they tell us all the beauties of language, all that is noble, grand and sublime, all that is passionate, tender and moving is to be found." He disagrees:

When the sentiment of the speaker is expressed in a neat, clear, plain and clever manner, and the passion or affection he is poss<ess>ed of and intends, *by sympathy*, to communicate to his hearer, is plainly and cleverly hit off, then and then only the expression has all the force and beauty that

---

[38] Hume 1985b: 108.   [39] May and Wisse 2001: 27 n. 33.   [40] Potkay 1994: 58.
[41] Hume 1985a: 468.

language can give it. It matters not the least whether the figures of speech are introduced or not . . . They neither add to nor take from the beauty of the expression . . . They have no intrinsick worth of their own.[42]

This is not to say that Smith is unappreciative of Cicero's style; in the passage above, Smith emphasizes sympathetic communication, and does not reject Cicero, per se. Indeed, Smith later remarks that Cicero's style suited his times: "The Nobleman of Rome would . . . find himself greatly superior to the far greater part of mankind . . . His discourse would be pompous and <o>rnate and such as appeard to be the language of a superior sort of man." By contrast, "At Athens . . . the Citizens were all on equall footing . . . In the one country the People at least the Nobles would converse and harangue with Dignity, Pomp and the air of those who speak with authority. The language of the others would be that of freedom, ease and familiarity." Thus, "Cicero abounds with all those figures of spee<ch> which are thought to give dignity to language," while Demosthenes "abounds with all the Common phrases and Idioms, and Proverbs."[43]

Smith, like Hume, holds that there is something about Ciceronian oratory improper to the eighteenth-century age of commerce.[44] But he understands speech to be most beautiful *and* most forceful when it works by sympathy to produce its desired effects. Even though Cicero seems to be Smith's foil, Cicero refers to something like sympathy in his rhetoric: we might note, for instance, that he warns against excessive use of rhythm in forensic oratory: "If you use it constantly, it not only wearies the audience, but even the layman recognizes the nature of the trick: further- more, it takes the feeling out of the delivery, it robs the audience of their natural sympathy, and utterly destroys the impression of sincerity" (*Orat.* 209; trans. Hubbell).[45]

Cicero and Civil Religion

Jean-Jacques Rousseau, one of the greatest eighteenth-century French political thinkers, poses a puzzle when it comes to Cicero. As Cranston shows, Rousseau requested Cicero's works from Jacques Barillot, which, in

---

[42] Smith 1985: 25–26.   [43] Smith 1985: 158–159.
[44] On this point, see Kapust and Schwarze 2016.
[45] The term that Hubbell 1939 translates here as "sympathy" is *humanum sensum*; Kaster translates it more literally, as "fellow feeling" (2020: 236). Such a rhetorical performance makes it impossible for the orator's audience to experience the emotions he wishes to arouse in them.

conjunction with a number of acquisitions, would serve him: "I have now embarked on a programme of studies which I am pursuing as systematically as my health permits."[46] And in a poem Rousseau wrote in 1738, *The Orchard of Madam de Warens*, Rousseau names Cicero, with a number of other figures, as one of "his companions"; Cranston remarks that "it would seem that Rousseau read more philosophy than literature at this time."[47]

He does not, however, mention Cicero or his works by name frequently in his major political writings; when he does, it is typically not favorable. He rejects, for instance, Cicero's criticism of Roman electoral practice in his chapter on the Roman *comitia* in the *Social Contract*. More damning is his accusation of Cicero in the context of discussing the Catilinarian crisis: "he himself, though a Roman, loved his glory more than his fatherland, he sought not so much the most legitimate and certain way to save the State as the way to get all the honor in this affair."[48] The only work of Cicero that Rousseau mentions by name in his major works, so far as I can tell, is *De officiis* (though he alludes to the *Tusculans* in *Emile*), and he does so to dismiss its importance: "One does not need to know Cicero's *Offices* to be a good man."[49] Cicero, it would seem, is very much Rousseau's foil.

Yet he mentions Cicero in the context of discussing civil religion in the *Social Contract*, specifically in a footnote to support his claim that "a purely civil profession of faith" serves to promote "sentiments of sociability, without which it is impossible to be either a good Citizen or a loyal subject," which he explains thus: "Caesar pleading for Catiline tried to establish the dogma of the mortality of the soul; to refute it Cato and Cicero did not waste time philosophizing: they contented themselves with showing that Caesar was speaking like a bad Citizen and advancing a doctrine pernicious to the State."[50]

Rousseau's sole source here cannot be Sallust's *Bellum Catilinae* (*War with Catiline*); for though Sallust gives long versions of the speeches of Cato and Caesar in the Senate, he gives few details about the speeches Cicero gave there. Nor do we find such an account in Plutarch's *Life of Cicero*. Rousseau is likely referring to Cicero's *Fourth Catilinarian*, where he responds to Caesar's claim that "death has been ordained by the immortal gods not as a means of punishment but as a necessity of nature or a relief from all our toil and woe" (*Cat.* 4.7; trans. MacDonald). As he argues, "to confront evil-doers with some fear in this life, those men of old would have had us believe that punishments of this kind were ordained for

---

[46] Cranston 1983: 117.   [47] Cranston 1983: 136.   [48] Rousseau 1997: 140.
[49] Rousseau 1979: 408.   [50] Rousseau 1997: 150.

malefactors in the next world because, obviously, they realized that without this prospect, death by itself was nothing very frightening" (*Cat.* 4.8; trans. MacDonald).

In criticizing Caesar, Cicero shows that certain theological doctrines are tied to the social order; this is a common theme in Cicero, perhaps most famously at the beginning of *De natura deorum*. There he remarks that,

> if the gods have neither the power nor the desire to help us, if they have no interest whatever and they pay no attention to our activities ... what reasons have we for addressing any acts of worship or honours or prayers to the immortal gods? ... Once these disappear, our lives become fraught with disturbance and great chaos. It is conceivable that, if reverence for the gods is removed, trust and the social bond between men and the uniquely preeminent virtue of justice will disappear. (*Nat. D.* 1.3; trans. Walsh)

If we assume that Rousseau read the Cicero he purchased, Cicero's discussions of the political importance of religion are noteworthy given Rousseau's argument in *Social Contract* book IV, chapter 8. There, just after he notes Cicero's response to Caesar, Rousseau describes the "dogmas of the civil Religion," which "ought to be simple, few in number, stated with precision, without explanations or commentary. The existence of the powerful, intelligent, beneficent, prescient, and provident Divinity, the life to come, the happiness of the just, the punishment of the wicked, the sanctity of the social Contract and the Laws."[51] Cicero would likely agree, given his rejection of Caesar's arguments, and it seems plausible that Rousseau had in mind Cicero's own arguments about religion and civil order when he wrote book IV, chapter 8.[52]

Cicero and Law

To explore Cicero's influence on legal thought, I turn to James Wilson. One of the first justices of the Supreme Court, Wilson gave a series of *Lectures on Law* to the College of Philadelphia, beginning in December 1790. The published *Lectures* are massive – nearly 700 pages – and cover a range of topics: "philosophy of law ... the relationship of politics to law ... the role of God in the development of law."[53] These lectures reveal a wide range of sources and influences – Scottish thinkers, English thinkers, and, not least, Cicero, whom he cites often, both as an authority

---

[51] Rousseau 1997: 150–151.
[52] On the connection between Cicero and Rousseau, see Atkins 2017 and Atkins 2018a, ch. 6.
[53] Wilson 2007: xxi.

and as someone whose thinking informed his own. Cicero, for Wilson, is a key source for understanding the law of nature, which Wilson describes as "immutable; not by the effect of an arbitrary disposition, but because it has its foundation in the nature, constitution, and mutual relations of men and things." The natural law is commensurate with "the supreme power of an all-perfect Being," who "is the author of our constitution; he cannot but command or forbid things as are necessarily agreeable or disagreeable to this very constitution." A "universal" law, he continues, it "has an essential fitness for all mankind, and binds them without distinction."[54]

To drive his point home, he turns to Cicero: "This law, or right reason, as Cicero calls it, is thus beautifully described by that eloquent philosopher. 'It is, indeed,' says he, 'a 'true law, conformable to nature, diffused among all men, unchangeable, eternal.'" Given his clear debt to Cicero, it is no wonder that Cicero illustrates the relationship between law and human nature – "*Natura juris a natura hominis repetenda est* [the nature of law is to be sought in the nature of man] is the judgment of Cicero. It is a judgment, not more respectable on account of the high authority, which pronounces it, than on account of its intrinsick solidity and importance."[55] Cicero, too, illustrates and informs his view of the importance of sympathy and mutual assistance, which he describes thus: "Take away society, and you destroy the basis, on which the preservation and happiness of human life are laid." A long citation of *De officiis* 1.22 follows; I quote only the beginning: "There is nothing more certain . . . than the excellent maxim of Plato – that we are not intended solely for ourselves; but that our friends and our country claim a portion of our birth."[56] Cicero's account of natural law and sociability would seem to go hand in hand with Wilson's own understanding of the common law, the benefits of which he illustrates by reference to Cicero: "To those, who enjoy the advantages of such a law as has been described, I may well address myself in the words of Cicero [*Caecin.* 26], "Believe me, a more inestimable inheritance descends to you from the law, than from those who have left, or may leave you fortunes."

Cicero as Model

I wish now to turn to Cicero as something more than source or foil: a model. We may approach this by recalling that Cicero was not indifferent to glory; as he writes in *De officiis*, "A true and wise greatness of spirit

---

[54] Wilson 2007: 523.   [55] Wilson 2007: 583–584.   [56] Wilson 2007: 631.

judges that deeds and not glory are the basis of the honourableness that nature most seeks. It prefers not to seem pre-eminent but to be so: he who is carried by the foolishness of the ignorant mob should not be counted a great man" (*Off.* 1.65; trans. Griffin and Atkins). And, in a rather (in) famous letter to Lucius Lucceius, he desires that his "name should gain luster and celebrity" through the history he wanted Lucceius to write (*Fam.* 5.12; trans. Shackleton Bailey). Cicero's concern with his own glory did not win him universal praise in antiquity: Plutarch suggests that "Cicero's immeasurable boasting of himself in his orations argues him guilty of an uncontrollable appetite for distinction" (*Cic.* 24; trans. Clough). Cicero himself thought the desire for glory could be dangerous, hence his reference to Caesar's domination as rooted in a desire for "complete pre-eminence" (*Off.* 1.64; trans. Griffin and Atkins).

A Ciceronian concern with glory, on the one hand, and the awareness that such a concern could be dangerous on the other were common themes in eighteenth-century thought. No less an eighteenth-century icon than Montesquieu homed in on Cicero's love of glory as a positive feature of his thought in his early *Discourse on Cicero*, written around 1717, and a negative feature of his personality in the later *Considerations on the Causes of the Greatness of the Romans and Their Decline* (1734). In the former, Montesquieu praises Cicero's love of glory: "Cicero is, of all the ancients, the one who had the most personal merit, and whom I would prefer to resemble; there is not one of them who had possessed finer and greater qualities, who had loved glory more, who had acquired for himself a more solid glory, and who had arrived at it by less beaten paths."[57] In the latter work, Cicero seems a dupe, "flattered" by Octavian and manipulated by "all the artifices of which vanity is never distrustful"; compared to Cato, Cicero's "genius was superb, but his soul was often common. With Cicero, virtue was the accessory, with Cato, glory."[58]

John Adams – whom Farrell terms "the American Cicero"[59] – knew Cicero well. Adams was moved, from an early age, by a desire for glory, admonishing himself thus:

> Which, dear youth, will you prefer, a life of effeminacy, indolence, and obscurity, or a life of industry, temperance, and honor? Take my advice; rise and mount your horse by the morning's dawn, and shake away, amidst the great and beautiful scenes of nature that appear at that time of the day, all the crudities that are left in your stomach, and all the obstructions that are left in your brains.

[57] Montesquieu 2002: 733.   [58] Montesquieu 1999: 115–116.   [59] Farrell 1989: 520.

He includes, in a plan for his development, this commandment: "Study Seneca, Cicero, and all other good moral writers."[60] It was not just Adams who looked to Cicero in order to understand his own life; his friend, Jonathan Sewell, wrote him in a 1760 letter:

> But if, in the estimation of the world, a man's worth riseth in proportion to the greatness of his country, who knows but in future ages, when New England shall have risen to its intended grandeur, it shall be as carefully recorded among the registers of the *literati*, that Adams flourished in the second century after the exodus of its first settlers from Great Britain, as it is now that Cicero was born in the six hundred and forty-seventh year after the building of Rome?[61]

Adams's reply is striking:

> And reason will despise equally a blind, undistinguishing adoration of what the world calls fame. She is neither a goddess to be loved, nor a demon to be feared, but an unsubstantial phantom, existing only in imagination. But with all this contempt, give me leave to reserve (for I am sure that reason will warrant) a strong affection for the honest approbation of the wise and good both in the present and in all future generations.[62]

Adams did not simply look to Cicero as inspiration; he modeled his own actions, and understood them, in Ciceronian terms, a point evident in a March 1809 letter to Benjamin Rush, where he compares himself to Cicero:

> I am weary, My Friend of that unceasing Insolence of which I have been the object for twenty years. I have opposed Nothing to it, but Stoical Patience, unlimited Submission, passive Obedience, and Non Resistance. Mausauleums [*sic*], Statues, Monuments will never be erected to me. I wish them not. Panegyrical Romances will never be written, nor flattering orations Spoken to transmit me to Posterity in brilliant Colours, No Nor in true Colours. All but the last I loath. Yet I will not die wholly unlamented. – Cicero was libelled, Slandered, insulted by all Parties.[63]

Adams looked to Cicero's life as a mirror for his own: "Cicero was not sacrificed to the vengeance of Antony ... more egregiously than John Adams was to the unbridled and unbounded ambition of Alexander Hamilton."[64] It is perhaps no wonder that toward the end of his life, he cited Cicero's Dream of Scipio, *De amicitia* (*On Friendship*), and *De senectute* (*On Old Age*) – ostensibly in support of his religious views, but

---

[60] Adams 1856: 45–46.   [61] Adams 1856: 50–51.   [62] Adams 1856: 52.   [63] Adams 2017.
[64] Letter by J. Adams to J. Lloyd (Feb. 11, 1815) quoted in Farrell 1989: 507.

one imagines, too, as a consolation. Thus he writes to Samuel Miller, in a letter dated July 7, 1820, "That you and I shall meet in a better World, I have no more doubt than I have, that we now exist on the same Globe – If my natural reason did not convince me of this Cicero's dream of Scipio, and his Essays on Friendship, and Old Age would have been sufficient for the purpose."[65] Adams, who looked to Cicero's example eleven years earlier as consolation for his defeats, may have had in mind this passage from book 6 of *De republica*: "do not give yourself to the words of the mob, and do not place your hopes in human rewards: virtue itself by its own allurements should draw you towards true honor. Let others worry about what they say about you – and they will say things in any case" (*Rep.* 6.25; trans. Zetzel).

Adams's concern for reputation, Ciceronian to the core – and filtered through the lens of Cicero – is, in a sense, a mere reflection of Adair's thesis concerning the love of fame in late eighteenth-century America, but it is also something more:[66] Adams was confronted, like Cicero, with the fact that virtue is not always met with its earthly due. In his experience of misrecognition, Cicero served as consolation.

Further Reading

Gay 1966 is a classic account of Cicero's place in the eighteenth century, while MacKendrick's 1989 overview of Cicero's reception in *The Philosophical Books of Cicero* is excellent, if at times overstated. Fox's chapter (2013) on Cicero's eighteenth-century reception in Steel's *Cambridge Companion to Cicero* is informative, as are Sharpe's and Richard's chapters (2015) in Altman's *Brill's Companion to the Reception of Cicero*. In addition to his chapter in Altman's volume, Richard 1995 provides an excellent overview of Cicero's place in eighteenth-century America, along with Roman thought more broadly, while Corwin 1955 discusses Cicero's place in American constitutionalism. Garsten's 2006 discussion of Cicero and Kant in *Saving Persuasion* provides a good overview of their relationship. In addition to Atkins's work (2017, 2018a) on Rousseau cited above, also worth attention is his essay "A Revolutionary Doctrine? Cicero's Natural Right Teaching in Mably and Burke" (2014). For further study of Cicero's influence on Burke, Mill, and the *Federalist* papers, Remer 2017 is an important work.

[65] Adams 2016: 659.   [66] Adair 1998.

CHAPTER 18

Cicero and Twenty-First-Century Political Philosophy

Martha C. Nussbaum

For too long, contemporary philosophers treated Cicero with disdain, thinking him at best a source for the ideas and arguments of the Greek Hellenistic thinkers, not as a thinker worthy of close attention in his own right. In part, this judgment was influenced by a baneful stereotype about Romans in general: they were good at action, not so good at thinking. In part, too, it was influenced by many philosophers' disdain for the topics at which Cicero excels: applied political thought, thought about the emotions, and the topics of aging and friendship. All these topics[1] have been denigrated throughout much of the tradition of Anglo-American philosophy. And finally, the negative judgment comes from a dislike of Cicero the man, who seems to some too egotistical, to others too conservative, to others too long-winded – and after all, many think, he did not even choose philosophy as his way of life, but did it only when circumstances made political action temporarily impossible.

As this chapter will show, I think every single one of these criticisms profoundly mistaken. Cicero uses Greek sources, but he makes original contributions as well. The Ciceronian topics I have mentioned are topics of high importance, and Cicero's contributions are all the more significant because so many centuries of philosophers have neglected them. And Cicero, with whatever personal failings (and what philosopher would look blameless were his deeds similarly open to view?), was both heroic and appealingly human, and this heroic commitment to the Roman Republic, far from undercutting his claim to philosophize about it, actually infuses his writings with a special depth and urgency.

My choice of topics is idiosyncratic and incomplete. In order to make my case, I have chosen to focus on three topics where Cicero speaks to contemporary philosophical problems with special urgency and relevance:

---

[1] See also the Introduction to this volume. This chapter draws at several points on material published in a different form in Nussbaum and Levmore 2017 and Nussbaum 2019.

cosmopolitanism, aging, and friendship. It speaks to the range of Cicero's thought that I could just as easily have chosen to support my case by examining his contributions to republican thought, ethics, or the emotions.[2] Cicero's short works on aging and on friendship may seem to be ethical rather than political – but I do not agree, and nor does Cicero. They are both ethical and political, and a decently reflective society ignores them at its peril.

Cosmopolitan Political Thought: *De officiis* (*On Duties*)

De officiis is Cicero's last work, written in 43 BCE, shortly before his assassination by the minions of Mark Antony, while he was heading for the coast to join Brutus and Cassius in Asia. Perhaps the most influential work in the Western tradition of political philosophy, its ideas were further developed in the Middle Ages by thinkers such as Aquinas, Suarez, and Gentili; they were the basis for Grotius's account of just and unjust war, which inaugurated the entire modern tradition of thought on that topic; they strongly influenced many aspects of the work of Wolff, Pufendorf, and Kant.[3] *De officiis* was so popular that non-philosophers in public life – all over the world – read it and justified their conduct with reference to it. African philosopher Kwame Anthony Appiah mentions that his father, Joe Appiah, one of the founders of the modern nation of Ghana, had two books on his bedside table: the Bible and *De officiis*.[4] The work is rightly understood as a key source for contemporary "cosmopolitanism." ("Cosmopolitanism" standardly means the view that we owe our primary ethical duties to human beings everywhere, although it can also refer to the weaker view that we owe *some* demanding duties to human beings everywhere. Cicero holds the weaker view, giving reasons why we may prefer our own republic in some instances.) Moreover, although it is clear from his letters that Cicero used Stoic texts to compose the work, there are undeniable signs of his own personal contribution, particularly in the section on "passive injustice" and the section on love of one's own republic.

According to Cicero's account, duties of justice (*iustitia*) are strict and impose burdens wherever a person is. They require, first, doing no harm to anyone, unless provoked by a wrongful act. Second, they require "using

---

[2] For these topics, see in this volume McConnell (Chapter 10, on emotions), Woolf and Reydams-Schils (chapters 11 and 12, on ethics), and Nicgorski (Chapter 14, on republicanism).

[3] For Cicero's reception in early modern philosophy, see Kapust (Chapter 17) in this volume.

[4] Appiah 1992. For *De officiis* as a work of social ethics, see Reydams-Schils (Chapter 12) in this volume.

common things as common, private possessions as one's own." (The strong defense of property rights in this section of the work, not very convincingly developed, may be inspired by Cicero's opposition to Julius Caesar's program of land redistribution.) Cicero makes it clear that justice requires us to treat our adversaries with respect and honesty. Trickery of any sort must be avoided. (Later he employs this view to oppose the use of spies in wartime.) Even wrongdoers must be treated morally; there is a strict limit to vengeance and punishment, and the main goal of punishment should be reform and deterrence.

So far, we might think that the duties of justice are purely negative: we can fulfill them completely without acting at all. But in one of the most important contributions of the work, Cicero argues that the failure to prevent injustice, when one can do so without great cost (a boundary never clarified), is itself injustice. Not to help someone who is being attacked – anywhere, apparently – is like deserting your friends or family. He plainly relies on a moral tradition in which the failure to defend friends and family is a paradigmatic moral failing. What he does is to extend that account to areas in which people do not usually think such thoughts.

Especially fascinating is Cicero's attack on his own philosophical colleagues (1.28–29). They love what they are doing, and they don't like the idea of getting messed up in politics. So, as Plato imagines, they will have to be forced to take part in the affairs of state. Cicero replies that they do wrong if they do not take part of their own choice. Like misanthropes and obsessive moneymakers, they do harm to humanity by failing to aid it. This theme is of urgent significance to Cicero, who is about to be murdered for having made a different choice, and he returns to it later, saying that such a life of retirement has been chosen by "the noblest and most distinguished philosophers, and also certain strict and serious men who could not bear the conduct of the people or their leaders" (1.69). What they were after is clearly appealing: "They wanted the same thing kings do: to need nothing, to obey nobody, to enjoy their liberty, which is defined as doing as you like." Cicero is even prepared to concede that sometimes that choice may perhaps be blameless – if people have retired because of ill health or "some other very serious reason," and, he now adds, if they have extremely fine minds and are devoting themselves to learning. (Here he seems to go back on what he said about Platonic philosophers, albeit in an uncertain and half-hearted way.) But anyone else is surely in the wrong to pursue a life that does not involve service to others through political action.

This section of the *De officiis* is analytically very important for its rejection of the active-passive distinction and for its passionate defense of the life of committed political service, even on the part of philosophers. It needs to be pondered by all, in our current era of segmentation between the academy and the public sphere.

Cicero now turns from these general observations to the conduct of warfare.[5] About the waging of war, he insists, first, that negotiated settlement is always preferable to war, since the former involves behaving humanly (and treating the other party as human), whereas the latter belongs to beasts (1.34). War should be a last resort when all negotiation has failed. Cicero offers as a good example the ancient Roman fetial law, which insists that all warfare be preceded by a formal demand for restitution (1.37). And of course war is justified, in his view, only when one has been grievously wronged by the other party first. In general, war should always be limited to what will make it possible to live in peace without wrongful acts (1.35). After conflict has ended, the vanquished should be given fair treatment, and even received into citizenship in one's own nation where that is possible (1.35).

During conflict, the foe is to be treated mercifully: for example, Cicero would permit an army to surrender unharmed even after the battering ram has touched their walls (1.35); in this he is more lenient than traditional Roman practice. Promises made to the enemy must be faithfully kept: Cicero cites with honor the example of Regulus, who returned to a terrible punishment because he had promised the Carthaginians that he would (1.39). Even a powerful and egregiously unjust enemy leader should not be murdered by stealth (1.40). Cicero ends this section by reminding his readers that the duties of justice are to be observed even to slaves (1.41).

In general, Ciceronian duties of justice involve an idea of respect for humanity, of treating a human being like an end rather than a means. (That is the reason Kant was so deeply influenced by this account.) In book 3 Cicero returns to the duties of justice, elaborating on his claim that they are the basis for a truly transnational law of humanity. Since the useful frequently conflicts with the honorable, he writes, we need a rule (*formula*) to follow. The rule is that of never using violence or theft against any other human being for our own advantage. This passage, more rhetorical than book 1's account, is the text that most deeply influenced Grotius, Smith, and Kant:

---

[5] For a fuller account of Cicero's "just war theory," see Atkins (Chapter 15) in this volume.

> Then for someone to take anything away from another and for a human being to augment his own advantage at the cost of a human being's disadvantage, is more contrary to nature than death, than poverty, than pain, than all the other things that can happen to his body or his external possessions. For to begin with, it removes human fellowship and social life. For if we are so disposed to one another that anyone will plunder or assault another for the sake of his own profit, it is necessary that the fellowship of the human kind, which is most of all in accordance with nature, will be torn apart. Just as, if each limb had the idea that it could be strong if it took the strength of the adjacent limb for itself, the whole body would necessarily weaken and perish, so too, if each one of us should take the advantages of others and should snatch away whatever he could for the sake of his own profit, the fellowship and common life of human beings must necessarily be overturned. (3.21–22)

The point is, presumably, that the universal law condemns any violation which, should it be general, would undermine human fellowship. Klaus Reich has found in this passage the origins of Kant's formula of universal law.[6] Whether this is right or wrong, we certainly should see a strong similarity between Cicero's argument and Kant's idea.

Cicero now calls this principle a part of "nature, that is the law of peoples," and also "nature's reason, which is divine and human law." He notes that it is also widely recognized in the laws of individual states. We should all devote ourselves to the upholding of this principle – as Hercules did, protecting the weak from assault, a humanitarian act for which he was made into a god. In general:

> If nature prescribes that a human being should consider the interests of a human being, no matter who he is, just because he is human, it is necessary that according to nature what is useful for all is something in common. And if this is so, then we are all embraced by one and the same law of nature, and if that is so, then it is clear that the law of nature forbids us to do violence to (*violare*) anyone else. But the first claim is true, so the last is also true. (3.27)

Cicero remarks that it is absurd for us to hold to this principle when our family or friends are concerned, but to deny that it applies to all relations among citizens. But then, it is equally absurd to hold to it for citizens and deny it to foreigners. People who make such a distinction "tear apart the common fellowship of the human kind" (3.28). (Hercules, his salient example of nature's law, was a cosmopolitan in his aid to the weak.)

---

[6] Reich 1939.

This section makes it very clear that Cicero's duties of justice are fully global. National boundaries are morally irrelevant, and Cicero sternly reproves those who think otherwise. At the core of Cicero's argument is an idea of not doing violence to human dignity – and, when we add in the distinction from book 1 (and the Hercules example), of not allowing people to be violated when you can help them. *Violare* includes physical assault, sexual assault, cruel punishment, torture, and also the taking of property. Cicero now links to that idea of humanity as an end the idea of a universal law of nature: conduct is to be tested by asking whether it could be made into such a law. Cicero clearly wants the world citizen to be Hercules-like in his determination to create a world where such violations of humanity do not occur, a world that accords with nature's moral law. The law of nature is not actual positive law, but it is morally binding on our actions, even when we are outside the realm of positive law.

This is the material in Cicero that became the foundation for much of modern international law, including both the law of war and human rights law. Grotius's *De lege belli atque pacis* is, we might say, a commentary on these passages. Kant's *Perpetual Peace* also follows them very closely. Particularly influential was Cicero's moral rigor, his insistence that all promises be preserved: in the form of the Grotian maxim *pacta sunt servanda*, this is the basis for modern conceptions of treaty obligation – although of modern thinkers only Kant follows Cicero all the way to his praise of Regulus.

So far so good: these aspects of Cicero's argument have vital relevance to current debates without much in the way of reformulation. This is not so with the part of book 1 that discusses our duties of material aid. Here Cicero announces that these duties, unlike those of justice, are very elastic, and may be completely satisfied without giving to people outside our own immediate context. This section of the work, alas, has had enormous influence as well, explaining in good measure why our doctrines of human rights and global duties include little or nothing about duties of material aid (although Grotius began to correct this asymmetry).

What is wrong with the bifurcation of duties? First of all, the absence of material aid (food, housing, medical care) is at least as serious, as a source of human suffering, as violence and war. So it seems inconsistent to address human suffering with urgency and compassion in the one instance, but with indifference in the other. But things are worse still: for fulfilling the duties of justice, as Cicero formulates them, costs a lot of money. To defend allies from assault will probably prove more expensive than to feed the hungry.[7] So there is an internal inconsistency in the doctrine. Third, if Cicero had held that we must simply avoid active wrongdoing, then he might get away with the bifurcation. But he actually holds that doing nothing at all is not morally blameless, when human life is at risk. And if he should try to say that duties of justice involve an active wrongdoer, while material poverty does not, he would simply be wrong: hunger isn't just a matter of natural catastrophe, but a matter of defective political arrangements.[8] Cicero, then, has evaded a set of questions that are actually crucial for contemporary debates. And his evasion has generated centuries of evasion, extending all the way to the modern human rights movement, which has well-worked-out doctrines in the areas covered by the duties of justice, but none in the area of material aid.

Despite this problem, the material aid section of the work does contain an extremely important insight. Later thinkers who recognize global duties often have a hard time giving any role at all to one's own nation-state. Thus, in contemporary philosophy we basically have forms of resolute globalism with no clear role for the nation-state, and, on the other side, views that begin from the nation-state, and regard international duties as posterior, to be approached only after the structure of the nation and its internal distribution of wealth and income has already been settled. Views of the latter sort, such as those of Immanuel Kant and John Rawls, give international duties a very thin role. Nor, since they begin from the nation, do they even offer an account of why the nation has such great importance.

A beginning of a richer view was made by Grotius, who argues that the nation has moral importance because it is the largest unit that represents the voices of its citizens, thus satisfying their interest in autonomy, that is, literally, in self-given law. And it is also the largest unit that is decently accountable to its citizens. So Grotius recognizes strong global duties, but he also holds that our own republic may legitimately occupy a special place in our moral concern. This insight actually originates with Cicero. In the material aid section of the work is a paragraph that actually has importance for all of our duties, so it is misplaced. (The work was written in great haste, as Cicero changed dwellings frequently.) First, Cicero says that the shared associational activities provided by one's own republic – "a forum, temples, porticoes, roads, laws, rights, courts, elections" – are a unique source of "goodwill and love" (1.54–55), and these associational structures deserve a high measure of our concern. He then concludes:

---

[7] See Shue 1996.   [8] See Sen 1993.

But when you look at everything with your reason and mind, of all the forms of fellowship none is weightier, none more dear, than that which each of us has with the republic. Parents are dear, children, relatives, acquaintances are dear; but the republic embraces all these loves of all of us together, and what good person would hesitate to die for her if it would help her? How much more detestable, then, is the monstrosity of those men who have cut up their country with every type of crime, and have been, and are still, engaged in her utter destruction! (1.57)

Cicero here appears to distinguish our affiliation with the institutions of our republic even from the shared association he previously mentioned, that of fellow citizens who share a forum, temples, and so forth. The affiliation praised here is with the republican institutions themselves, which are justifiably objects of very great love and concern, and which demand our service, even unto death.

This moving passage is obviously Cicero's reflection on his own love for the Roman Republic and the sacrifice that love will shortly exact. It makes the Grotian argument in both institutional and psychological terms, and is still quite possibly the most nuanced account of how a contemporary world citizen should think and feel, in a world where the needs of distant strangers and the institutions of our own nation both demand our concern.[9]

The *De officiis* was written in haste, with death, in the form of Mark Antony's minions, waiting in the wings. It is therefore not a perfect or finished work of political philosophy. But it has rightly influenced some of the best in contemporary thought about global duties – not least in its loving praise of Rome.

De senectute (On Aging)

Aging is an enormously important part of ethical and political philosophy. For Cicero, the time spent as a *senex* extends at least from his own age – sixty-two at the time he wrote the work in 45 BCE (since he describes himself as a *senex* in its preface) – at least up through the age of his chosen interlocutor, Cato the Elder, who at the dialogue's dramatic date (150 BCE) was eighty-three, one year before his death. That large chunk of the human life cycle, which is getting longer in our own time, poses many questions for the thoughtful: how to enjoy and wisely use those years; what special duties or possibilities that time might offer; how to make wise

---

[9] For further analysis of this passage, see Atkins (Chapter 15, p. 247) in this volume.

choices about pleasure, friendship, physical and mental activity, the disposal of one's property; how to prepare for death. Indeed, Cicero announces that he is writing precisely because, for both himself and Atticus (then sixty-five), aging can seem a burden, whether it is "already pressing" or "at least approaching," and one role for philosophy is to examine topics that seem troubling, and to show that they can be made enjoyable. Indeed, he offers the dialogue to Atticus as a pleasant distraction from the political upheavals that are weighing on both of them.

The topic poses issues for political as well as ethical philosophy. Since the aging are stigmatized in a variety of ways, as Cicero shows, society might be thought to have the obligation to protect them from discrimination by law, and to educate its younger members so that they will not imbibe prejudice and will become capable of respect. Cicero's society did not force aging men, at least, to retire from public life; in fact, as he points out, in the context of the Roman Senate the word *senex* is honorific, and the Senate was indeed full of aging men. But the social stigma was widespread, he insists, and needed confronting. Cicero indeed dramatizes this issue by introducing as his other interlocutors in the dialogue two younger men then in their thirties, Scipio and Laelius. They have come to visit Cato in order to learn about aging, since, as they announce, they will get there eventually unless they should die first; and since Cato seems to be doing quite well they want to scout the territory ahead. Cato uses his opportunity to tell the two visitors about the common prejudices and why they are wrong. The challenge of aging, then, is a challenge for all, not just for the aging themselves.

How rarely, however, philosophers have taken up this challenge. Cicero's treatise is one of only two well-known works on this topic in the Western tradition of political philosophy, the other being Simone de Beauvoir's *La vieillesse* (1970), an inferior work that appears but a repository of familiar clichés, in which those clichés masquerade as necessary truths. By contrast, Cicero's work is clear, cogent, and crisply argued. It is also one of his most polished and entertaining uses of the dialogue form. Cato is a real character, unlike many of Cicero's interlocutors. He has not only arguments but also a personal life story: he enjoys learning Greek, for example, and, above all, he is devoted to farming. Cicero, who seems totally lacking in any passion for that standard Roman hobby, which approximates the British mania for gardening – and who probably had been bored like so many of the real-life Cato's readers by his long-winded treatise on that topic, *De agri cultura* – represents his Cato as discoursing at tiresome length about the wonderful properties of manure, without taking note of the lack of uptake by the young men. In this way Cicero engages in mild and quite funny satire of aging people, who all too often talk too much and listen too little. What's more, he represents Cato himself as aware of his own failing: "Old age is by nature rather long-winded, just so you don't think that I am trying to defend it against every single charge" (55).

The core of the dialogue, however, is Cato's forceful defense of old age against stigma and prejudices. He organizes his argument around four common charges (which are still made ubiquitously in the twenty-first century):

1. Aging people are inactive and don't contribute much.
2. Aging people have lost their physical strength.
3. Aging people can no longer enjoy bodily pleasures (especially eating, drinking, and sex).
4. Aging people are closing in on death, which is horrible.

On charge number 4, Cato's reply is unconvincing, since he deploys a Platonic account of the immortality of the soul, which was not generally accepted then and is not so now. Given that the work is dedicated to Atticus, who, as an Epicurean, believed that life ended at death, he could have come up with something better. On the other three charges, however, he does very well. On the first, part of his reply is to say that the stereotype is simply untrue. Cato gives many examples of outstanding contributions made by aging people, and the people he mentions are on average at least twenty years older than Cicero and Atticus. Particularly effective is the story of the poet Sophocles, whose heirs took him to court to have him declared incompetent so that they could get their hands on his fortune (still a problem for aging people today!). Sophocles recited to the jury some speeches from his *Oedipus at Colonus*, which he had just been composing (at the age of around ninety). He then asked the jury whether they thought this the work of a mentally incompetent person. He won (23). More generally, Cato grants that some activities that require a lot of physical strength are harder for aging people, but leadership and deliberation do not diminish: the captain of a ship would not be called incompetent because he could not ply the oars (17). It is here that Cato dwells on the Senate, a name signifying the belief that a *senex* possesses wisdom, experience, and deliberative capacity. If a senator were to live to a hundred, would he be useless? No, says Cato, because the job does not require "running and leaping, or long-distance spear-throwing, or hand-to-hand sword play," but, rather "reflection, reason, and judgment" (19). Cato does admit that memory and other mental faculties can decline with age, but he insists that exercise and practice can ward off this problem (21).

To some extent, Cato's insights correspond to what we now know, to some extent they don't. For he makes no mention of Alzheimer's disease, the great fear of us all as we age. But now evidence is mounting that Alzheimer's is caused by environmental factors unknown to the ancients, air pollution especially. So probably Cato simply didn't know of it. Romans also had a healthy diet and did not use tobacco, and of necessity they did regular walking and other physical exercise. So they were following what are now the instructions doctors would give for improving our odds. To this Cato adds memory exercises and learning new languages, which again are just what we are currently rediscovering. He later gives a detailed account of his daily pursuits. Cato exercised his mind by writing history, studying law, and learning Greek; he trained his memory by reviewing the details of each day; and he kept active by providing counsel for friends and attending Senate meetings (47).

As for physical strength, the second charge: certainly there is decline, says Cato, but to a great extent it can be warded off by regular physical activity. He cites many examples of people who continue vigorous walks, horseback riding, and other exercises into their nineties (34). (Here we should remember that Romans, in addition to constant walking, were expected to serve in the military, and Cicero himself, as proconsul in Cilicia, stormed a mountain fortress at the head of his troops at the age of fifty-seven.) As for himself, says Cato, he can't do what he once did on the battlefield, but he still loves his farming, and nobody can complain that he is slacking in his political tasks or in entertaining his guests or helping his friends (32). Moreover, one important part of one's physical equipment is the voice, and oratorical skill declines less rapidly than other physical abilities, and to the extent that there is decline one can shift to a quieter, less bombastic style. (This is probably Cicero praising himself, for his voice was not terribly strong, and he was praised for his subtle and non-bombastic delivery.) Finally, if you can't do something you can still teach it! All of this is now being rediscovered by aging dancers, athletes, and opera singers (since ancient oratory, unmiked, was more like opera than like today's oratory in its physical requirements.) Furthermore, abrupt decline can be caused by illness at any time of life (35). Cato now summarizes this part of his argument:

> My young friends, we should resist old age; we should compensate for its defects by watchful care; we should fight against it as we would fight against a disease; we should adopt a regimen of health; we should do regular

moderate exercise; and we should eat and drink just enough to replenish our strength, not so much as to crush it. Nor, indeed, should we give our attention only to the body. Much greater care should be given to the intellect and the mental faculties. For they, too, like lamps, grow dim with time, unless we keep them supplied with oil. (35–36)

One more observation concludes the response to the first and second charges. The aging, Cato says, often have more social influence (*auctoritas*) than younger people. But that is so only on condition that the aging person confidently claims respect from others, refusing to be ground down by stigma. "Old age is honored only on condition that it defends itself, maintains its rights, is subservient to no one, and to the last breath rules over its own domain." Aging people who want respect should also avoid whining and complaining, and this flaw can be curbed by self-discipline (65).

We now reach the third argument, concerning bodily pleasures. Cato's approach to this topic is similar to his treatment of physical strength: the aging have what they need, they don't miss what they don't have, and they spare themselves a lot of trouble. If you don't overeat or overdrink, you are healthier. If you feel somewhat less sexual desire, you are less likely to break up families or to get in trouble with the law. And many hobbies that give sensory pleasure can be pursued with undiminished zeal – here is the place of that tiresome digression on farming, which certainly shows his undiminished zeal!

Cato's, and thus Cicero's, arguments are excellent, arguments that modern culture forgot more or less until now, and we can still learn a lot from this engaging work. Cicero himself never got to apply his own advice, since he died by assassination only two years later. But Atticus may well have used its arguments, since he lived to be seventy-seven, dying of what seems to have been stomach or intestinal cancer. He was certainly reputed to have lived well until shortly before that time, although (or perhaps because) he always steered clear of politics, the passionate pursuit of both Cicero and his Cato. The Roman Republic did not have a tranquil old age, nor did those who loved it.

De amicitia (*On Friendship*)

The topic of friendship is not as completely neglected by philosophers as the topic of aging, but Cicero has one advantage over his distinguished predecessor Aristotle: he writes as an immersed political man, thinking about friendship in a thick social and political context. Aristotle's analysis of friendship is very schematic, with no particular examples, no real people. (No doubt Aristotle's dialogues were different, but we don't have them.) Cicero, here again, uses the dialogue form with grace and aptness, and as they talk the characters illustrate their reflections with many historical and recent examples. It is no surprise that *De amicitia* has been one of Cicero's most beloved works over the ages.

The dialogue seems to have been written after *De senectute*, since in the dedication to Atticus, Cicero alludes to it in the past tense: "As in that other book, an aging man myself, I wrote to another aging man about aging, so in this book, with the greatest friendliness I have written to a friend about friendship." In *De senectute*, set in 150 BCE, Scipio and Laelius, famously close friends, appear as young men in their thirties. *De amicitia*, set in around 129 BCE, shows this same Laelius, the second dialogue's main character, mourning the recent death of his dear friend Scipio. Provoked by two younger relatives, he describes the benefits of friendship. Cicero (born in 106) immediately points out that one of these younger characters, when he became an aging man much later, taught Cicero law and became a much-admired mentor. So the dramatic choices link the two works to one another and to Cicero's own life; they give further emphasis to the themes of aging and friendship. As does the dedication to Atticus. The two essays are "a gift that both of us can enjoy together."

De amicitia is a justly admired analysis and encomium of long-lived friendship. Some of its good ideas are: the importance of good will for enduring friendship (19); the value of intimacy, and the relief of discovering that one can talk about things that one usually conceals from others (22); the way friends make life better by sharing both joy and adversity (22); the way that friendship nourishes hope (23). Even though these are familiar ideas, Cicero presents them with moving realism and restrained eloquence.

Even better, because more surprising, is Cicero's critique of the Stoic account of friendship, an account that was plainly very popular at this time of trouble. The Stoics "who, I am informed, are considered sages in Greece" say something that Cicero's Laelius finds quite "astonishing": namely, that we should avoid too much intimacy in friendships, so that one doesn't become bogged down by the anxieties of others (45). Each person has enough on his own plate, and it is troublesome to be too much involved in other people's business. In short, "it is best to hold the reins of friendship as loosely as possible, so that we may either draw them up or slacken them at will; for, they say, an essential condition of a happy life is freedom from care, and this the soul cannot enjoy if one man is, as it were, in labor for many."

Laelius replies that this model of friendship is too self-insulating to be really good: for virtue is generous, and does not shrink from caring for another's pain on account of the difficulty it may bring. And he then goes one step further, to say that taking this risk-incurring generosity out of friendship would take away what is finest and most delightful in it, which is love. The Stoics make friendship something self-centered, but that removes "the most delightful link in the chain of friendship" (51): for love, which is generous and uncalculating, is much more rewarding than utility.

An equally impressive contribution is the dialogue's critique of another common picture of friendship. A popular view says that we should measure our good will to our friends by their good will toward us. Friendship is an accounting game, and you should never give, or feel, more than you have received or can expect to receive (56–57). Laelius utterly rejects this way of thinking:

> It surely is calling friendship to a very close and petty accounting to require it to keep an exact balance of credits and debits. I think true friendship is richer and more abundant than that and does not narrowly scan the reckoning lest it pay out more than it has received; and there need be no fear that some bit of kindness will be lost, that it will overflow the measure and spill upon the ground, or that more than is due will be poured into friendship. (58)

This error is closely linked to that of the Stoics, since the behavior described here is frequently a sign of excessive self-protectiveness.

In all of this, Cicero goes well beyond Aristotle, who apparently had no opponents with such self-insulating views. And he also explores persuasively the complicated tensions that friends who are immersed in politics may face, when a friend puts pressure on them to do something that their morality opposes.

In fact, it is where Cicero most resembles Aristotle that he is least convincing. For Laelius claims that a good friendship is characterized by harmony of beliefs and tastes, and by agreement. "For friendship is nothing else than an accord (*consensio*) in all things, human and divine, conjoined with mutual good will and affection" (20). Later he goes even further: "there should be between them complete harmony of opinions and inclinations in everything without exception" (60).

This sounds high-minded, but is it true? Laelius does not go into the topic very deeply. He does not distinguish differences of taste from differences of opinion, nor both of these from differences of temperament. Large-scale differences of taste and pursuit probably threaten friendship more than differences of opinion, since one can respect and even discuss differences of opinion – as Cicero knew perfectly well. In one of his earliest letters to Atticus, written on December 5, 61, he reassures Atticus that he did not need to insist that he is above petty concern with money, since Cicero knew that already. (Atticus was essentially a banker, so he probably felt defensive on that score; Cicero's letter is not only about friendship, it is an act of friendship.) Cicero then adds a more general reflection of a very surprising nature:

> I have never felt any difference between us – apart from our overall choices of a total mode of life (*praeter voluntatem institutae vitae*). What one might call desire for glory has led me to seek political office. But a different, and unexceptionable, course of reasoning (*minime reprehendenda ratio*) has led you to seek a virtuous detachment (*honestum otium*). (*Att.* 1.17)

What could be a greater difference of opinion than one about "a total mode of life"? And that was indeed the disagreement they had. Atticus, an Epicurean, believed that one should avoid the tumult of politics. Cicero believed that the republic is worthy of a person's most intense love and even sacrifice. He makes light of this view here, calling it "desire for glory," which he surely had as well, in spades. But it's well to remember that *De amicitia* omits and even negates salient features of the great real-life friendship that linked its author and its dedicatee.

Furthermore, the two men also differed greatly in temperament, and this seems not to have been an obstacle to friendship but a valuable ingredient. Atticus was urbane, witty, a great host, and also calm and caring. Cicero was prey to intense emotions, and what one could certainly call tantrums. It is perfectly clear that this difference in temperament was a valuable ingredient in the friendship. At his daughter Tullia's death (just before the two dialogues were written), Cicero turns to Atticus for support in his overwhelming grief. He writes to him every day when they are apart.[10] Atticus' calm temperament helps him process emotions that are almost too great to bear. At other times, too, the presence of this calm and

---

[10] See the letters from March to August 45 BCE (*Letters to Atticus* books 12–13).

witty friend helps Cicero convert fear into play. One of the most famous letters in the whole correspondence is Cicero's account of Julius Caesar's ominous arrival at his country estate, where he proceeds to billet two thousand soldiers (*Att.* 13.52; December 21, 45 BCE). Since Cicero was very hostile to Caesar (he later sympathized with Brutus and the other conspirators), and Caesar no doubt knew this, the occasion was fraught with peril. Cicero narrates it as high comedy, as the story of an odd and unwelcome guest. And we might see Cicero even teasing himself for the fear he no doubt feels, by writing in this mode to his calmer friend. In short, the correspondence shows an intimate play of difference and similarity, which becomes finally a delighted complementarity and interdependence. And it shows something more, which is omitted from *De amicitia*: the role in any good friendship of small talk, jokes, silliness. As Cicero puts it in a letter written in May 45 BCE, around the time he was composing *De senectute*: "Even if I have nothing to write to you about, I'm writing anyway, because it makes me feel as if I'm talking to you" (*Att.* 12.53; May 22, 45 BCE).

De amicitia is one of the Western tradition's most valuable philosophical works about friendship, and especially for its exploration of friendship as an element of a political life. But philosophy is not always very good at jokes, or the intimate texture of dailiness, or the collisions of emotions that mark the ups and downs of real friendship in a turbulent time. So the reader of *De amicitia* would be well advised to pore through the *Letters to Atticus*, which complicate and deepen Cicero's analysis.

I believe that Cicero is the political philosopher of the Greco-Roman world whom our era needs to study seriously, even more than Plato and Aristotle. He dealt with many topics, so my treatment is woefully incomplete. But I hope to have shown that he deals with three urgent and very contemporary problems extremely well, and with a flawed and passionate humanity that shows us what it is to take arguments seriously.

Further Reading

Readable modern English translations of *De senectute* and *De amicitia* can be found respectively in Freeman 2016 and Freeman 2018. Konstan 1996 provides an accessible account of attitudes toward friendship in the classical world, including Cicero's. Nussbaum and Levmore 2017 offers contemporary reflections on a range of matters related to aging and includes a chapter on Cicero. Nussbaum 2019 traces the development of the cosmopolitan tradition in the ancient and early modern worlds and examines thorny contemporary problems related to cosmopolitanism. Atkins 2019a, drawing on *De officiis* and *De amicitia*, offers a Ciceronian intervention in debates over conscientious refusal in contemporary medical ethics.

Bibliography

Achard, G. (1994) *Cicéron:* De l'invention. Paris.

Ackrill, J. (1973) *"Anamnēsis* in the *Phaedo,"* in *Exegesis and Argument: Studies in Greek Philosophy Presented to Gregory Vlastos,* ed. E. Lee and A. Mourelatos. Assen: 177–195.

Adair, D. (1998) *Fame and the Founding Fathers.* Indianapolis.

Adamietz, J. (1989) *Marcus Tullius Cicero* Pro Murena *mit einem Kommentar.* Darmstadt.

Adams, C. F. (1856) *The Works of John Adams, Second President of the United States: With a Life of the Author, Notes and Illustrations,* Vol. 1. Boston.

Adams, J. (1797) *A Defence of the Constitutions of Government of the United States of America.* Philadelphia.

(2016) "Letter to Samuel Miller, July 7, 1820," in *John Adams: Writings from the New Nation 1784–1826,* ed. G. Wood. The Library of America. New York: 658–659.

(2017) "From John Adams to Benjamin Rush, 23 March 1809," *Founders Online.* National Archives, http://founders.archives.gov/documents/Adams/ 99-02-02-5324.

Adams, J. N. (2003) *Bilingualism and the Latin Language.* Cambridge.

Albrecht, J., Degelman, C., Gasparini, V., et al. (2018) "Religion in the making: The lived ancient religion approach," *Religion* 48: 568–593.

Alexander, M. (2002) *The Case for the Prosecution in the Ciceronian Era.* Ann Arbor.

Alfaric, P. (1918) *L'Évolution intellectuelle de Saint Augustin.* Paris.

Algra, K., Barnes, J., Mansfeld, J., and Schofield, M. (2003) (eds.) *The Cambridge History of Hellenistic Philosophy.* Cambridge.

Allen, J. (2014) "Why there are ends of both goods and evils in ancient ethical theory," in *Strategies of Argument: Essays in Ancient Ethics, Epistemology, and Logic,* ed. M.-K. Lee. Oxford: 231–254.

Altman, W. H. F. (2008) "How to interpret Cicero's dialogue on divination," *Interpretation* 35: 105–121.

(2009) "Womanly humanism in Cicero's *Tusculan Disputations,"* *Transactions of the American Philological Association* 139: 411–45.

(2015) (ed.) *Brill's Companion to the Reception of Cicero.* Leiden.

(2016a) *The Revival of Platonism in Cicero's Late Philosophy:* Platonis aemulus *and the Invention of Cicero.* Lanham, MD.

(2016b) "Interpreting Plato's dream in *De divinatione*," in *The Revival of Platonism in Cicero's Late Philosophy:* Platonis aemulus *and the Invention of Cicero,* W. H. F. Altman. Lanham, MD: 179–195.

Ando, C. (2010) "Empire and the laws of war: An archaeology," in *The Roman Foundations of the Law of Nations: Alberico Gentili and the Justice of Empire,* ed. B. Kingsbury and B. Straumann. Oxford: 30–52.

Annas, J. (2013) "Plato's *Laws* and Cicero's *De legibus*," in M. Schofield (2013c): 206–224.

(2017) *Virtue and Law in Plato and Beyond.* Oxford.

Annas, J. and Betegh, G. (2016) (eds.) Cicero's *De finibus:* Philosophical Approaches. Cambridge.

Annas, J. (ed.) and Woolf, R. (trans.) (2001) *Cicero:* On Moral Ends. Cambridge.

Apolloni, D. (1996) "Plato's affinity argument for the immortality of the soul," *Journal of the History of Philosophy* 34: 5–32.

Appiah, A. (1992) *In My Father's House: Africa in the Philosophy of Culture.* Oxford.

(2006) *Cosmopolitanism: Ethics in a World of Strangers.* New York.

Arena, V. (2012) Libertas *and the Practice of Politics in the Late Roman Republic.* Cambridge.

Arena, V. and Mac Góráin, F. (2017) (eds.) *Varronian Moments.* London. [= *BICS* 60.2, Dec. 2017.]

Arena, V. and Piras, G. (2016) (eds.) "Reconstructing the Republic: Varro and Imperial Authors (Rome, 22nd & 23rd September 2016)," special issue of *Res publica litterarum* 39.

Arnim, J. von (1903–1905) (ed.) *Stoicorum veterum fragmenta.* 3 vols. Leipzig.

Asmis, E. (1984) *Epicurus' Scientific Method.* Ithaca, NY and London.

(1990) "Philodemus' Epicureanism," *Aufstieg und Niedergang der römischen Welt* 2.36.4: 2369–2406.

(2008) "Cicero on natural law and the laws of the state," *Classical Antiquity* 27.1: 1–33.

Atkins, E. M. (1990) "'*Domina et regina virtutum*': justice and *societas* in *De officiis*," *Phronesis* 35: 258–289.

(2002) "Old philosophy and new power: Cicero in fifth-century North Africa," in G. Clark and T. Rajak (2002): 251–269.

Atkins, J. W. (2011a) "L'argument du *De republica* et le Songe de Scipion," *Les Études philosophiques* 99: 455–469.

(2011b) "The *officia* of St. Ambrose's *De officiis*," *Journal of Early Christian Studies* 19.1: 49–77.

(2013a) *Cicero on Politics and the Limits of Reason:* The Republic *and* Laws. Cambridge.

(2013b) "Cicero on the relationship between Plato's *Republic* and *Laws*," in A. Sheppard (2013): 15–24.

(2014) "A revolutionary doctrine? Cicero's natural right teaching in Mably and Burke," *Classical Receptions Journal* 6.2: 177–197.

(2015) "Zeno's *Republic*, Plato's *Laws*, and the early development of Stoic natural law theory," *Polis* 32.1: 166–190.

(2017) "Natural law and civil religion: *De legibus* book II," in *Ciceros Staatsphilosophie: Ein Kooperativer Kommentar zu* De re publica *und* De legibus, ed. O. Höffe. Klassiker Auslegen 64. Berlin: 167–186.

(2018a) *Roman Political Thought*. Cambridge.

(2018b) "Non-domination and the *Libera res publica* in Cicero's republicanism," *History of European Ideas* 44.6 (2018): 756–773. [Repr. as ch. 6 in *Liberty: Ancient Ideas and Modern Perspectives*, ed. V. Arena. London, 2021.]

(2019a) "Integrity and conscience in medical ethics: A Ciceronian perspective," *Perspectives in Biology and Medicine* 62.3: 470–488.

(2019b) "Espoir et empire dans le songe de Scipion" (trans. C. Murgier), *Les Cahiers Philosophiques* 159.4: 27–41.

(forthcoming a) "Cicero on the justice of war," in N. Gilbert, M. Graver, and S. McConnell (forthcoming).

(forthcoming b) "Patriotism and cosmopolitanism in Cicero's *De officiis*," in *The Cambridge Critical Guide to* De officiis, ed. R. Woolf. Cambridge.

Atzert, C. (1971) (ed.) *Cicero*: De officiis-De virtutibus. Leipzig.

Aubert, S. (2011) "La φιλοστοργία chez Fronton, une vertu sans équivalent latin?," *Aitia. Regards sur la culture hellénistique au XXIe siècle* 1, https://journals.openedition.org/aitia/.

Aubert-Baillot, S. (2008) "Cicéron et la parole stoïcienne: polémique autour de la dialectique," *Revue de Métaphysique et de Morale* 57: 61–91.

(2014) "L'influence de la *disputatio in utramque partem* sur la correspondance de Cicéron," *Vita Latina* 189–190: 21–39.

(2015) "Un cas particulier de παρρησία: la parole sans détour (εὐθυρρημοσύνη) des Stoïciens," *Rhetorica* 33: 71–96.

(2018) "Terminology and practice of dialectic in Cicero's letters," in T. Bénatouïl and K. Ierodiakonou (2018): 254–282.

(2021) *Le grec et la philosophie dans la correspondance de Cicéron*. Turnhout.

Auvray-Assayas, C. (2006) *Cicéron*. Paris.

(2016) "Which protohistory of the text can be grasped from Carolingian manuscripts?," in *From the Protohistory to the History of the Text*, ed. X. Velaza. Frankfurt am Main: 45–53.

(2019) (ed., trans., introd.) La nature des dieux. *Cicéron*. Caen, www.unicaen.fr/puc/sources/ciceron/accueil/.

Babcock, W. (ed.) (2012) The City of God, *Books 1–10, The Works of Saint Augustine: A Translation for the 21st Century, 1/6*, introduction and translation by W. Babcock, notes and edited by B. Ramsey. New York.

Babcock, W. (2013) The City of God, *Books 11–22, The Works of Saint Augustine: A Translation for the 21st Century, 2/6*, introduction and translation by W. Babcock, notes and edited by B. Ramsey. New York.

Ballacci, G. (2018) *Political Theory between Philosophy and Rhetoric: Politics as Transcendence and Contingency*. London.

Baltussen, H. (2013) "Cicero's *Consolatio ad se*: Character, purpose and impact of a curious treatise," in *Greek and Roman Consolations*, ed. H. Baltussen. Swansea: 67–92.

Baraz, Y. (2012) *A Written Republic: Cicero's Philosophical Politics*. Princeton.

Barnes, J. (1997) "Antiochus of Ascalon," in *Philosophia Togata*, Vol. 1: *Essays on Philosophy and Roman Society*, ed. M. Griffin and J. Barnes. Oxford: 51–96.

(2015) "Cicero and the just war," in *Mantissa: Essays in Ancient Philosophy*, Vol. 4, ed. J. Barnes. Oxford: 56–79.

Beard, M. (1986) "Cicero and divination: The formation of a Latin discourse," *Journal of Roman Studies* 76: 33–46.

(2015) *S.P.Q.R.: A History of Ancient Rome*. New York.

Beard, M., North, J., and Price, S. (1998) *Religions of Rome*. 2 vols. Cambridge.

BeDuhn, J. D. (2010) *Augustine's Manichaean Dilemma*, Vol. 1: *Conversion and Apostasy, 373–388 C. E.* Philadelphia.

Begemann, E. (2012) *Schicksal als Argument. Ciceros Rede vom fatum in der späten Republik*. Stuttgart.

(2015) "Damaged go(o)ds: Cicero's theological triad in the wake of German historicism," in W. H. F. Altman (2015a): 247–280.

(forthcoming) "Was haben die Götter mit Gerechtigkeit zu tun? Ciceros Theologie zwischen ratio und Resonanz," in *Zwischen Skepsis und Staatskult. Neue Perspektiven auf Ciceros De natura deorum*, ed. C. Diez and C. Schubert. Bern.

Belayche, N., Bendlin, A., Rosenberger, V., and Rüpke, J. (2005) "Divination romaine," *Thesaurus Cultus et Rituum Antiquorum* 3: 79–104.

Bellincioni, M. (1974) *Cicerone politico nell'ultimo anno di vita*. Brescia.

Bénatouïl, T. (2007) "Le débat entre platonisme et stoïcisme sur la vie scolastique: Chrysippe, la Nouvelle Académie et Antiochus," in *Platonic Stoicism – Stoic Platonism*, ed. M. Bonazzi and C. Helming. Leuven: 1–21.

(2009) "*Theôria* et vie contemplative du stoïcisme au platonisme: Chrysippe, Panétius, Antiochus et Alcinoos," in M. Bonazzi and J. Opsomer (2009): 3–31.

(2016) "Structure, standards and Stoic moral progress in *De finibus* 4," in J. Annas and G. Betegh (2016): 198–220.

Bénatouïl, T. and Ierodiakonou, K. (2018) (eds.) *Dialectic after Plato and Aristotle*. Cambridge.

Benferhat, Y. (2005) *Ciues Epicurei. Les épicuriens et l'idée de monarchie à Rome et en Italie de Sylla à Octave*. Brussels.

(2014) "*Noua uerba*: réflexions sur la place des néologismes lucretiens dans la création d'un vocabulaire philosophique latin," *Latomus* 73: 596–614.

Berlin, I. (1969) "Two concepts of liberty," in *Four Essays on Liberty*, Vol. 1. Oxford : 118–172.

Bermon, É. (2001) *Le Cogito dans la pensée de saint Augustin*. Paris.

(2011) "Le *Songe de Scipion* dans la correspondance entre saint Augustin et Nectarius de Calama," *Les Études philosophiques* 99.4: 521–542.

Berry, D. H. (2000) (ed.) *Cicero: Defence Speeches*. Oxford.

Besnier, B. (1993) "La nouvelle Académie selon le point de vue de Philon de Larissa," in *Scepticisme et exégèse: Hommages à Camille Pernot*, ed. B. Besnier. Fontenay and Saint-Cloud: 85–140.

Bishop, C. (2019) *Cicero, Greek Learning, and the Making of a Roman Classic*. Oxford.

Bobcock, W. (2012) (trans.) The City of God *(1–10)*. New York.

(2013) (trans.) The City of God *(11–22)*. New York.

Bobzien, S. (1998) *Determinism and Freedom in Stoic Philosophy*. Oxford.

Bochet, I. and Madec, G. (2012) "Augustin et l'*Hortensius* de Cicéron," in *Augustin philosophe et prédicateur: hommages à Goulven Madec*, ed. I. Bochet. Paris: 195–294.

Boes, J. (1990) *La philosophie et l'action dans la correspondance de Cicéron*. Nancy.

Bonazzi, M. (2009) "Antiochus' ethics and the subordination of stoicism," in M. Bonazzi and J. Opsomer (2009): 33–54.

Bonazzi, M. and Opsomer, J. (2009) (eds.) *The Origins of the Platonic System: Platonisms of the Early Empire and Their Philosophical Contexts*. Leuven.

Boulding, M. (1997) *St. Augustine:* The Confessions. New York.

Bourbon, M. (2019) *Penser l'individu: genèse stoïcienne de la subjectivité*. Turnhout.

Bouton-Touboulic, A.-I. (2004a) *L'ordre caché: la notion d'ordre chez saint Augustin*. Paris.

(2004b) "L'approche philosophique de l'œuvre d'Augustin au miroir de la Revue des Études Augustiniennes," *Revue des études augustiniennes* 50.2: 325–347.

(2009) "Augustin lecteur de Cicéron dans le *Contra academicos*," *Revue d'Études Anciennes* 111.1: 95–114.

(2016) "*Affectus sunt, amores sunt*: saint Augustin ou les passions revisitées," in *L'hommes et ses passions. Actes du Congrès Budé, organisé à Lyon, août 2013*, ed. J.-L. Ferrary and S. Franchet d'Espèrey. Paris: 483–498.

(2017) "Justice et châtiment. Augustine et la notion de *poena*," in *L'amour de la justice: de la Septante à Thomas d'Aquin*, ed. A.-I. Bouton-Touboulic. Pessac: 183–200.

(2018) "'Os illud Platonis': scepticisme, platonisme et néoplatonisme dans le *Contra academicos* d'Augustin," in *Plato Latinus: Aspects de la transmission de Platon en latin dans l'Antiquité*, ed. J.-B. Guillaumin and C. Lévy. Turnhout: 233–256.

Boyancé, P. (1967) "Cicéron et la vie contemplative," *Latomus* 26: 3–26. [Repr. in *Études sur l'humanisme cicéronien*, Collection Latomus 121 (1970): 89–113.]

(1969) "Trois citations de Platon chez Cicéron," in *Hommages à Marcel Renard*, ed. J. Bibauw. Brussels: 126–132.

(1970) *Études sur l'humanisme Cicéronien*. Brussels.

Brachtendorf, J. (1997) "Cicero and Augustine on the passions," *Revue des études augustiniennes* 43: 289–308.

Brennan, T. (2009) "Stoic souls in Stoic corpses," in *Body and Soul in Ancient Philosophy*, ed. D. M. Frede and B. Reis. Berlin: 389–407.

Brittain, C. (2001) *Philo of Larissa: The Last of the Academic Sceptics*. Oxford.
  (2006) (trans. and intro.) *Cicero:* On Academic Scepticism. Indianapolis.
  (2008) "Philo of Larissa," The Stanford Encyclopedia of Philosophy (Fall 2008 Edition), Edward N. Zalta (ed.), http://plato.stanford.edu/archives/fall2008/entries/philo-larissa/.
  (2011) "Augustine as a reader of Cicero," in *Tolle Lege: Essays on Augustine and on Medieval Philosophy in Honor of Roland J. Teske*, ed. R. C. Taylor, D. Twetten, and M. Wreen. Milwaukee, WI: 81–114.
  (2012) "Self-knowledge in Cicero and Augustine (*De trinitate*, x, 5, 7–10, 16)," *Medioevo* 37: 107–135.
  (2016) "Cicero's sceptical methods: The example of the *De finibus*," in J. Annas and G. Betegh (2016): 12–40.
Brouwer, R. (2014) *The Stoic Sage: The Early Stoics on Wisdom, Sagehood and Socrates*. Cambridge.
Brunschwig, J. and Sedley, D. N. (2003) "Hellenistic philosophy," in *The Cambridge Companion to Greek and Roman Philosophy*, ed. D. N. Sedley. Cambridge: 151–183.
Brunt, P. A. (1986) "Cicero's *officium* in the civil war," *Journal of Roman Studies* 76: 12–32.
  (1988) *The Fall of the Roman Republic and Related Essays*. Oxford.
Büchner, K. (1984) (ed.) *M. Tullius Cicero:* De re publica. Heidelberg.
Burkert, W. (1965) "Cicero als Platoniker und Skeptiker," *Gymnasium* 62: 299–318.
Burnyeat, M. (1982) "Gods and heaps," in *Language and Logos*, ed. M. Nussbaum and M. Schofield. Cambridge: 315–338.
  (unpublished) "Carneades was no probabilist," https://fr.scribd.com/document/341395731/Carneades-Was-No-Probabilist.
Bury, R. G. (1936) (trans. and intro.) *Sextus Empiricus:* Against the Physicists. Cambridge, MA and London.
Byers, S. (2013) *Perception, Sensibility, and the Moral Motivation in Augustine: A Stoic-Platonic Synthesis*. Cambridge.
Bywater, I. (1869) "On a lost dialogue of Aristotle," *Journal of Philology* 2: 55–69.
Callanan, K. (2018) *Montesquieu's Liberalism and the Problem of Universal Politics*. Cambridge.
Cambiano, G. (2002) "Cicerone e la necessità della filosofia," in *Interpretare Cicerone. Percorsi della critica contemporanea*, ed. E. Narducci. Florence: 66–83.
Cappello, O. (2019) *The School of Doubt: Skepticism, History and Politics in Cicero's* Academica. Leiden.
Cardauns, B. (2001) *Marcus Terentius Varro: Einführung in sein Werk*. Heidelberg.
Carey, G. W. and McLellan, J. (2001) (eds.) *The Federalist: The Gideon Edition*. Indianapolis.
Caston, V. (2001) "Dicaearchus' philosophy of mind," in W. W. Fortenbaugh and E. Schütrumpf (2001): 175–193.

Catapano, G. Catapano, G. (2001) *Il concetto di filosofia nei primi scritti di Agostino. Analisi dei passi metafilosofici dal "Contra academicos" al "De uera religione."* Rome.

(2005) (ed.) *Agostino:* Contro gli Accademici. Milan.

(2016) "Errore, assenso e fede. La critica dello scetticismo accademico nell'*Enchiridion* di Agostino," in *Scepticisme et religion. Constantes et évolutions, de la philosophie hellénistique à la philosophie médiévale*, ed. A.-I. Bouton-Touboulic and C. Lévy. Turnhout: 219–233.

Cataudella, Q. (1966) "I 'Soliloqui' di Agostino e i libro I delle *Tusculane*," *Aevum* 40: 550–552.

Cavallo, G. (1983) *Libri, scritture, scribi a Ercolano: introduzione allo studio dei materiali Greci*. Naples.

Charpin, F. (1991) (ed. and trans.) *Lucilius.* Satires. Paris.

Clark, G. and Rajak, T. (2002) (eds.) *Philosophy and Power in the Graeco-Roman World: Essays in Honour of Miriam Griffin*. Oxford.

Clark, M. and Ruebel, J. (1985) "Philosophy and rhetoric in Cicero's *Pro Milone*," *Rheinisches Museum für Philologie* 128.1: 57–72.

Clavel, V. H. (1868) *De M. T. Cicerone graecorum interprete*. Paris.

Clough, A. H. (1992) (trans.) *Plutarch:* Life of Cicero, *in* The Lives of the Noble Grecians and Romans, Vol. 2. New York.

Cole, T. B. (2019) "Ciceronian thought at the constitutional convention," *Global Intellectual History*, doi:10.1080/23801883.2019.1637271.

Colish, M. L. (1985) *The Stoic Tradition from Antiquity to the Early Middle Ages*, Vol. 2: *Stoicism in Christian Latin Thought through the Sixth Century*. Leiden.

Connolly, J. (2007a) "The new world order: Greek rhetoric in Rome," in *A Companion to Greek Rhetoric*, ed. I. Worthington. Oxford: 139–165.

(2007b) *The State of Speech: Rhetoric and Political Thought in Ancient Rome*. Princeton.

(2009) "The politics of rhetorical education," in *The Cambridge Companion to Ancient Rhetoric*, ed. E. Gunderson. Cambridge: 126–141.

(2015) *The Life of Roman Republicanism*. Princeton.

Conybeare, C. (2006) *The Irrational Augustine*. Oxford.

Corbeill, A. (1996) *Controlling Laughter: Political Humor in the Late Roman Republic*. Princeton.

(2013) "Cicero and the intellectual milieu of the Late Republic," in C. Steel (2013a): 9–24.

Corwin, E. S. (1955) *The "Higher Law" Background of American Constitutional Law*. Ithaca, NY.

Couissin, P. (1983) "The stoicism of the New Academy," in *The Skeptical Tradition*, ed. M. Burnyeat. Berkeley: 31–63.

Craig, C. (1986) "Cato's stoicism and the understanding of Cicero's speech *Pro Murena*," *Transactions of the American Philological Association* 116: 229–239.

Cranston, M. (1982) *Jean-Jacques Rousseau: The Early Life and Work of Jean-Jacques Rousseau 1712–1754*. Chicago.

Dafoe, A., Renshon, J., and Huth, P. (2014) "Reputation and status as motives for war," *Annual Review of Political Science* 17: 371–393.

Dawson, H. (2007) *Locke, Language and Early-Modern Philosophy*. Cambridge.

de Beauvoir, S. (1970) *La Vieillesse*. Paris.

DeFilippo, J. (2000) "Cicero vs. Cotta in *De natura deorum*," *Ancient Philosophy* 20: 169–187.

Des Places, É. (1973) (ed.) *Numénius: Fragments*. Paris.

Diels, K. and Kranz, W. (1951–1952) (eds.) *Die Fragmente de Vorsokratiker*. Berlin.

Dodaro, R. and Atkins, E. M. (2001) (eds.) *Augustine: Political Writings*. Cambridge.

Dolbeau, F. (1996) *Vingt-six sermons au peuple d'Afrique*. Paris.

D'Onofrio, G. (2002) "Il parricidio di Cicerone. Le metamorfosi della verità tra gli *Academica* ciceroniani e il 'Contra Academicos' di Agostino (*lettura di testi*)," in *Enosis kai Philia. Unione e Amicizia: Omaggio a Francesco Romano*, ed. M. Barbanti, G. R. Giardina, and P. Manganaro. Catania: 207–236.

Doignon, J. (1982) "L'enseignement de l'*Hortensius* de Cicéron sur les richesses devant la conscience d'Augustin jusqu'aux *Confessions*," *L'Antiquité classique* 51: 193–206.

Dominik, W. and Hall, J. (2007) (eds.) *A Companion to Roman Rhetoric*. Oxford.

Douglas, A. E. (1965) "Cicero the philosopher," in *Cicero*, ed. T. A. Dorey. London: 135–170.

(1995) "Form and content in the *Tusculan Disputations*," in J. G. F. Powell (1995a): 197–218.

Drexler, H. (1958) "*Res publica* (II parte)," *Maia* 10: 3–37.

(1988) *Politische Grundbegriffe der Römer*. Darmstadt.

Drogula F. K. (2019) *Cato the Younger: Life and Death at the End of the Roman Republic*. New York.

Dubuisson, M. (1992) "Le grec à Rome à l'époque de Cicéron, extension et qualité du bilinguisme," *Annales* 47: 187–206.

(2005) "Le grec de la correspondance de Cicéron: questions préliminaires sur un cas de bilinguisme," *Ling* 41: 69–86.

Ducos, M. (2005) "Nigidius Figulus," in *Dictionnaire des Philosophes antiques*, Vol. 4, ed. R. Goulet. Paris: 703–712.

Dugan, J. (2005) *Making a New Man: Ciceronian Self-Fashioning in the Rhetorical Works*. Oxford.

(2009) "Rhetoric and the Roman Republic," in *The Rhetoric*, ed. E. Gunderson. Cambridge: 178–193.

(2013) "Cicero's rhetorical theory," in C. Steel (2013a): 25–40.

Dumont, J. C. (1983) "Conquête et esclavage chez Cicéron: *De republica*, III, 36–37," *Ktema* 8: 113–128.

Düring, I. (1961) *Aristotle's Protrepticus: An Attempt at Reconstruction*. Gothenburg.

Dyck, A. R. (1996) *A Commentary on Cicero*, De officiis. Ann Arbor.

(2003) *Cicero*: De natura deorum. Cambridge

(2004) *A Commentary on Cicero's* De legibus. Ann Arbor.

Dyson, R. W. (1998) (ed.) *Augustine:* The City of God against the Pagans. Cambridge.

Eckerman, C. (2013) "Lucretius' self-positioning in the history of Roman epicureanism," *Classical Quarterly* 63: 785–800.

Elder, O. and Mullen, A. (2019) *The Language of Roman Letters: Bilingual Epistolography from Cicero to Fronto.* Cambridge.

Erler, M. and Schofield, M. (1999) "Epicurean ethics," in K. Algra, J. Barnes, J. Mansfeld, and M. Schofield (2003): 642–674.

Erskine, A. (1990) *The Hellenistic Stoa: Political Thought and Action.* Ithaca, NY.

Ewbank, W. W. (1933) *The Poems of Cicero.* London.

Falconer, W. A. (tr. and intro.) (1923) *Cicero:* De senectute, De amicitia, De divinatione. Cambridge, MA and London.

Fantham, E. (2004) *The Roman World of Cicero's* De Oratore. Oxford.

(2013) *Cicero's* Pro L. Murena Oratio. New York.

Farrand, M. (1966) (ed.) *The Records of the Federal Convention of 1787.* 3 vols. New Haven.

Farrell, J. M. (1989) "John Adams's *Autobiography*: The Ciceronian paradigm and the quest for fame," *The New England Quarterly* 62.4: 505–528.

Feeney, D. (2010) "Fathers and sons: The Manlii Torquatii and family continuity in Catullus and Horace," in *Ancient Historiography and Its Contexts: Studies in Honour of A. J. Woodman,* eds C. S. Kraus, J. Marincola, and C. Pelling. Oxford: 205–223.

Feldmann, E. (1975) *Der Einfluss des Hortensius und des Manichäismus auf das Denken des jungen Augustinus von 373.* Münster.

Ferrary, J.-L. (1974) "Le discours de Laelius dans le troisième livre du *De re publica* de Cicéron," *Mélanges de l'École française de Rome* 86.2: 745–771.

(1977) "Le discours de Philus (Cicéron, *De re publica* III, 8–31) et la philosophie de Carnéade," *Revue des études latines* 55: 128–156.

(1988) *Philhellénisme et impérialisme. Aspects idéologiques de la conquête romaine du monde hellénistique, de la seconde guerre de Macédoine à la guerre contre Mithridate.* Rome.

Fletcher, R. (2016) "Philosophy in the expanded field: Ciceronian dialogue in Pollio's letters from Spain (*Fam.* 10.31–33)," *Arethusa* 49: 549–573.

Fögen, T. (2000) *Patrii sermonis egestas:* Einstellungen lateinischer Autoren zu ihrer Muttersprache: ein Beitrag zum Sprachbewusstsein in der römischen Antike. Heidelberg.

Foley, M. P. (1999) "Cicero, Augustine and the philosophical roots of the Cassiciacum Dialogues," *Revue des études augustiniennes* 45: 51–77.

(2019a) (trans. and commentary) Against the Academics: *Saint Augustine's Cassiciacum Dialogues,* Vol. 1. New Haven and London.

(2019b) (trans. and commentary) On the Happy Life: *Saint Augustine's Cassiciacum Dialogues,* Vol. 2. New Haven and London.

Font, A. (1894) *De Cicerone graeca vocabula usurpante.* Paris.

Fortenbaugh, W. W. (2013) "Cicero's *Letter to Atticus* 2.16: 'A Great Controversy'," *Classical World* 106: 515–519.

Fortenbaugh, W. W. and Schütrumpf, E. (2001) *Dicaearchus of Messana: Text, Translation, and Discussion.* New Brunswick.

Fortenbaugh, W. W. and Steinmetz, P. (1989) (eds.) *Cicero's Knowledge of the Peripatos.* New Brunswick.

Fortin, E. L. (1997) "Justice as the foundation of the political community: Augustine and his pagan models," in *Augustinus* De civitate Dei, ed. Christoph Horn. Berlin: 41–62.

Fotheringham, L. (2013) *Persuasive Language in Cicero's* Pro Milone*: A Close Reading and Commentary.* London.

Fott, D. (2012) "The politico-philosophical character of Cicero's verdict in *De natura deorum*," in W. Nicgorski (2012): 152–179.

(2014) (ed. and trans.) *Cicero,* On the Republic *&* On the Laws. Ithaca, NY.

Fox, M. (2007) *Cicero's Philosophy of History.* Oxford.

(2013) "Cicero during the Enlightenment," in C. Steel (2013a): 318–336.

Frede, D. (1978) "The final proof of the immortality of the soul in Plato's *Phaedo* 102a–107a," *Phronesis* 23: 27–41.

Frede, M. (1986) "The Stoic doctrine of the affections of the soul," in *The Norms of Nature: Studies in Hellenistic Ethics,* ed. M. Schofield and G. Striker. Cambridge: 93–110.

(1987) "The skeptic's two kinds of assent and the question of the possibility of knowledge," in *Essays in Ancient Philosophy,* ed. M. M. Frede. Oxford: 201–222.

(1992) "Plato's arguments and the dialogue form," in *Methods of Interpreting Plato,* ed. J. Klagge and N. Smith. Oxford: 201–220.

(1996) "The literary form of the *Sophist*," in *Form and Argument in Late Plato,* ed. C. Gill and M. M. McCabe. Oxford: 135–151.

(1999) "Stoic epistemology," in K. Algra, J. Barnes, J. Mansfeld, and M. Schofield (2003): 295–322.

(2011) *A Free Will: Origins of the Notion in Ancient Thought,* ed. by A. A. Long with a Foreword by D. N. Sedley. Berkeley.

Freeman, P. (2016) How to Grow Old*: Ancient Wisdom for the Second Half of Life.* Princeton.

(2018) How to Be a Friend*: An Ancient Guide to True Friendship.* Princeton.

Fuhrer, Th. (1992) "Das Kriterium der Wahrheit in Augustins *Contra Academicos*," *Vigiliae Christianae* 46: 257–276.

(1993) "Der Begriff *ueri simile* bei Cicero und Augustin," *Museum Helveticum* 50: 107–125.

(1997) *Augustin,* Contra Academicos (uel De Academicis) *Bücher 2 und 3. Einleitung und Kommentar.* Berlin and New York.

Furley, D. (1989) "Aristotelian material in Cicero's *De natura deorum*," in W. W. Fortenbaugh and P. Steinmetz (1989): 201–219.

Gallagher, R. L. (2001) "Metaphor in Cicero's *De re publica*," *Classical Quarterly* 51.2: 509–519.

Garbarino G. (1973) *Roma e la filosofia greca dalle origine alla fine del II secólo A.C.* 2 vols. Turin.

Garcea, A. (2012) *Caesar's* De analogia: *Edition, Translation, and Commentary.* Oxford.

Garnsey, P. D. A. (1996) *Ideas of Slavery from Aristotle to Augustine.* Cambridge.

Garsten, B. (2006) *Saving Persuasion: A Defense of Rhetoric and Judgment.* Cambridge, MA.

Gasparini, V., Patzelt, M., Raja, R., Rieger, A.-K., Rüpke, J., and Urciuoli, E. (2020) (eds.) *Lived Religion in the Ancient Mediterranean World: Approaching Religious Transformations from Archaeology, History and Classics.* Berlin.

Gawlick, G. and Görler, W. (1994) "Cicero," in *Die Philosophie der Antike,* Vol. 4: *Die Hellenistische Philosophie,* ed. H. Flashar. Basel: 991–1168.

Gay, P. (1966) *The Enlightenment: The Rise of Modern Paganism.* New York.

Gee, E. (2001) "Cicero's astronomy," *Classical Quarterly* 51: 520–536.

Gigante, M. (2001) "Philodème dans l'histoire de la littérature grecque," in *Cicéron et Philodème,* ed. C. Auvray-Assayas and D. Delattre. Paris: 23–50.

Gigon, O. (1962) "Die Szenerie des ciceronischen *Hortensius,*" *Philologus* 106: 223–245.

Gilbert, C. D. (1973) "Marius and Fortuna," *Classical Quarterly* 23: 104–107.

Gilbert, N. (2015) Among Friends: Cicero and the Epicureans. Unpublished PhD dissertation, Toronto.

Gilbert, N., Graver, M., and McConnell, S. (forthcoming) (eds.) *Power and Persuasion in Cicero's Philosophy.* Cambridge.

Gildenhard, I. (2006) "Reckoning with tyranny: Greek thoughts on Caesar in Cicero's *Letters to Atticus* in early 49," in *Ancient Tyranny,* ed. S. Lewis. Edinburgh: 197–209.

(2007) *Paideia Romana: Cicero's* Tusculan Disputations. Cambridge.

(2011) *Creative Eloquence: The Construction of Reality in Cicero's Speeches.* Oxford.

(2013a) "Of Cicero's Plato: Fictions, forms, foundations," in M. Schofield (2013c): 225–275.

(2013b) "Cicero's dialogues: Historiography manqué and the evidence of fiction," in *Der Dialog in der Antike,* ed. S. Föllinger and G. M. Müller. Berlin: 235–274.

Gill, C. (1988) "Personhood and personality: The four-personae theory in Cicero *De officiis* 1," *Oxford Studies in Ancient Philosophy* 6: 169–199.

Girardet, K. (1983) *Die Ordnung der Welt: Ein Beitrag zur philosophischen und politischen Interpretation von Ciceros Schrift* De legibus. Wiesbaden.

(1995) "Naturrecht und Naturgesetz: eine gerade Linie von Cicero zu Augustin?," *Rheinisches Museum für Philologie* 138: 286–298.

Glucker, J. (1978) *Antiochus and the Late Academy.* Göttingen.

(1988) "Cicero's philosophical affiliations," in *The Question of Eclecticism,* ed. J. M. Dillon and A. A. Long. Berkeley: 34–69.

(1992) "Cicero's philosophical affiliations again," *Liverpool Classical Monthly* 17: 134–138.

(1995) "*Probabile, veri simile* and related terms," in J. G. F. Powell (1995a): 115–144.

(2001) "Carneades in Rome: Some unsolved problems," in J. G. F. Powell and J. North (2001): 57–82.

Gorman, R. (2005) *The Socratic Method in the Dialogues of Cicero*. Stuttgart.

Görler, W. (1974) *Untersuchungen zu Ciceros Philosophie*. Heidelberg.

(1987) "Hauptursachen bei Chrysipp und Cicero: Philologische Marginalien zu einem vieldiskutierten Gleichnis (*De fato* 41–44)," *Rheinisches Museum für Philologie* 130: 254–274.

(1994) "Cicero: Philosophie," in *Grundriss der Geschichte der Philosophie, Die Philosophie der Antike*, Vol. 4: *Die Hellenistische Philosophie, Zweiter Halbband*, ed. H. Flashar. Basel: 1084–1118.

(1995) "Silencing the troublemaker: *De legibus* 1.39 and the continuity of Cicero's scepticism," in J. G. F. Powell (1995a): 85–113.

(1996) "Zum literarischen Charakter and zur Struktur der *Tusculanae*," in ΛΗΝΑΙΚΑ: *Festschrift für Carl Werner Müller*, ed. C. Mueller-Goldingen and K. Sier. Stuttgart: 189–216.

(1997) "Cicero's philosophical stance in the *Lucullus*," in *Assent and Argument: Studies in Cicero's Academic Books*, ed. B. Inwood and J. Mansfeld. Leiden: 36–57.

(2011) "Cicero, *De finibus bonorum et malorum*, Buch 5. Beobachtungen zur Quelle und zum Aufbau," *Elenchos* 32: 329–354.

Gottschalk, H. D. (1971) "Soul as *harmonia*," *Phronesis* 16: 179–198.

Gourinat, J.-B. (2014) "Comment se détermine le *kathekon*? Remarques sur la conformité à la nature et le raisonnable," *Philosophie Antique* 14: 13–39.

Graver, M. (2002) (trans. and comm.) *Cicero on the Emotions:* Tusculan Disputations *3 and 4*. Chicago.

(2009) "Cicero's philosophy of religion," in *History of the Western Philosophy of Religion*, Vol. 1, ed. G. Oppy and N. Trakakis. Durham: 119–132.

(2016) "Honor and the honorable: Cato's discourse in *De finibus* 3," in J. Annas and G. Betegh (2016): 118–146.

(forthcoming) "The psychology of honor in Cicero's *De republica*," in N. Gilbert, M. Graver, and S. McConnell (forthcoming).

Green, W. M. (1970) *Sancti Aurelii Augustini* Contra academicos, De beata vita, De ordine, De magistro, De libero arbitrio. Turnhout.

Griffin, M. T. (1995) "Philosophical badinage in Cicero's letters," in J. G. F. Powell (1995a): 325–346.

(1997a) "From Aristotle to Atticus: Cicero and Matius on friendship," in *Philosophia Togata*, Vol. 2: *Plato and Aristotle at Rome*, ed. J. Barnes and M. T. Griffin. Oxford: 86–109.

(1997b) "The composition of the *Academica*: Motives and versions," in *Assent and Argument: Studies in Cicero's Academic Books*, ed. B. Inwood and J. Mansfeld. Leiden: 1–35.

(2001) "Piso, Cicero and their audience," in *Cicéron et Philodème, La polémique en philosophie*, ed. C. Auvray-Assayas and D. Delattre. Paris: 85–99.

Griffin, M. T. and Atkins, E. M. (1991) (eds.) *Cicero:* On Duties. Cambridge.

Grilli, A. (1962) *M. Tulli Ciceronis:* Hortensius. Milan.

(1971) *I proemi del* De republica *di Cicerone*. Brescia.

Griswold, C. L. (1999) *Adam Smith and the Virtues of Enlightenment*. Cambridge.

Gruen, E. (1965) "The Lex Varia," *Journal of Roman Studies* 55: 59–73.

Guillaumont, F. (2008) "Cicéron et les *Lettres* de Platon," in Epistulae Antiquae *5:* Actes du Ve colloque international "L'épistolaire antique et ses prolongements européens" (Université François-Rabelais, Tours, 6–7–8 septembre 2006), ed. P. Laurence and F. Guillaumont. Leuven-Paris: 127–137.

Hadot, P. (1960) "Citations de Porphyre chez saint Augustin (à propos d'un ouvrage récent)," *Revue des études augustiniennes* 6: 205–244.

Hagendahl, H. (1967) *Augustine and the Latin Classics*. 2 vols. Gothenburg.

Hall, J. (2007) "Oratorical delivery and the emotions: Theory and practice," in W. Dominik and J. Hall (2007): 218–234.

(2013) "Saviour of the Republic and father of the fatherland: Cicero and political crisis," in C. Steel (2013a): 215–229.

Harries, J. (2006) *Cicero and the Jurists: From Citizens' Law to the Lawful State*. London.

(2007) *Law and Crime in the Roman World*. Cambridge.

Harris, W. V. (1979) *War and Imperialism in Republican Rome, 327–70 BC*. Oxford.

(2003) "Roman opinions about the truthfulness of dreams," *Journal of Roman Studies* 93: 18–34.

Harrison, J. and Laslett, P. (1963) (eds.) *The Library of John Locke*. Oxford.

Hatzimichali, M. (2013) "The texts of Plato and Aristotle in the first century bc," in M. Schofield (2013c): 1–27.

Held, D. (2010) *Cosmopolitanism: Ideals and Realities*. Cambridge.

Henry, M. Y. (1927) "Cicero's treatment of the free will problem," *Transactions of the American Philological Association* 58: 32–42.

Hill, E. (1991) (ed.) The Trinity. New York.

Hine, H. (2015) "Philosophy and *philosophi*: From Cicero to Apuleius," in G. Williams and K. Volk (2015): 13–29.

Hirzel, R. (1877) *Untersuchungen zu Cicero's philosophischen Schriften, 1. Theil:* De Natura Deorum, Leipzig.

(1882) *Untersuchungen zu Cicero's philosophischen Schriften, 11. Theil:* De finibus. De officiis. Leipzig.

(1883) *Untersuchungen zu Cicero's philosophischen Schriften, 111. Theil:* Academica Priora, Tusculanae Disputationes. Leipzig.

(1895) *Der Dialog. Ein literarhistorischer Versuch.* 2 vols. Leipzig.

Hodgson, L. (2017) Res Publica *and the Roman Republic: "Without Body or Form."* Oxford.

Hoenig, C. (2018) *Plato's* Timaeus *and the Latin Tradition*. Cambridge.

Hollis, A. S. (2007) *Fragments of Roman Poetry (60 BC–20 CE)*. Oxford.

Holte, R. (1962) *Béatitude et Sagesse, Saint Augustin et le problème de la fin de l'homme dans la philosophie ancienne*. Paris.

Homeyer, H. (1956) "Zu Bedeutungsgeschichte von '*Sapientia*'," *L'Antiquité Classique* 25.2: 301–318.

Hont, I. (2015) *Politics in Commercial Society: Jean-Jacques Rousseau and Adam Smith*. Cambridge, MA.

Horsfall, N. (1979) "*Doctus sermones utriusque linguae?*," *Échos du monde classique* 23: 85–95.

Hösle, V. (2013) *The Philosophical Dialogue: A Poetics and a Hermeneutics*. Notre Dame.

Houston, G. W. (2013) "The non-Philodemus book collection in the villa of the Papyri," in J. König, K. Oikonomopoulou, and G. Woolf (2013): 183–208.

Hubbell H. M. (1939) (trans.) Orator. Cambridge, MA.

Hume, D. (1902) *Enquiries Concerning the Human Understanding and Concerning the Principles of Morals by David Hume*, ed. L. A. Selby-Bigge. Oxford.

(1985a) "Of the original contract," in *Essays Moral, Political, and Literary*, ed. E. Miller. Indianapolis.

(1985b) "Of eloquence," in *Essays Moral, Political, and Literary*, ed. E. Miller. Indianapolis.

Hunt, H. (1954) *The Humanism of Cicero*. Melbourne.

Hutchinson, G. (1998) *Cicero's Correspondence: A Literary Study*. Oxford.

Ignatieff, M. (1998) *The Warrior's Honor: Ethnic War and the Modern Conscience*. New York.

Inwood, B. (1990) "*Rhetorica Disputatio*: The strategy of *de Finibus II*," *Apeiron* 23: 143–164.

(2015) "The voice of nature," in J. Annas and G. Bétegh (2015): 147–166.

Inwood, B. and Mansfeld, J. (1997) (eds.) *Assent and Argument: Studies in Cicero's Academic Books*. Leiden.

Ioppolo, A. M. (1986) *Opinione e scienzia: il dibattito tra Stoici e Accademici nel III e nel II secolo A. C.* Naples.

Jacotot, M. (2013) *Question d'honneur. Les notions d'*honos*, honestum et honestas dans la République romaine antique*. Rome.

Jaeger, W. W. (1923) *Aristoteles: Grundlegung einer Geschichte seiner Entwicklung*. Berlin.

Jeanmart, G. (2006) *Herméneutique et subjectivité dans les* Confessions *d'Augustin*. Turnhout.

Jefferson, T. (1801) First inaugural address, bartleby.com/124/pres16.html.

Jocelyn, H. D. (1982) "Varro's *Antiquitates rerum divinarum* and religious affairs in the late Roman Republic," *Bulletin of the John Rylands University Library of Manchester* 65: 148–205.

Johnson, J. T. (1981) *Just War Tradition and the Restraint of War: A Moral and Historical Inquiry*. Princeton.

Kant, I. (1949) *Fundamental Principles of the Metaphysics of Morals*, trans. T. K. Abbott. London.

(1952) *The Critique of Judgement*, trans. J. C. Meredith. Oxford.

Kapust, D. (2011a) "Cicero on decorum and the morality of rhetoric," *European Journal of Political Theory* 10.1: 92–112.

(2011b) *Republicanism, Rhetoric and Roman Political Thought*. Cambridge.

Kapust, D. J. and Schwarze, M. A. (2016) "The rhetoric of sincerity: Cicero and Smith on propriety and political context," *American Political Science Review* 110.1: 100–111.

Kapust, D. J. and Remer, M. G. (2021) *The Ciceronian Tradition in Political Theory*. Madison.

Kaster, R. A. (2006) *Cicero:* Speech on Behalf of Publius Sestius. Oxford.
(2020) *Cicero:* Brutus *and* Orator. Oxford.
Keller, A. (2012) *Cicero und der gerechte Krieg: Eine ethisch-staatsphilosophische Untersuchung*. Stuttgart.
Kempshall, M. (2001) "*De re publica* 1.39 in medieval and Renaissance political thought," in J. Powell and J. North (2001): 91–135.
Kendeffy, G. (2015) "Lactantius as Christian Cicero, Cicero as shadow-like instructor," in W. H. F. Altman (2015a): 57–78.
Kerferd, G. (1971) "Epicurus' doctrine of the soul," *Phronesis* 16: 80–96.
Kerschensteiner, J. (1986) "Cicero und Hirtius," in *Studien zur Alten Geschichte. S. Lauffer zum 70. Geburtstag am 4. August 1981 dargebracht von Freunden, Kollegen und Schülern. Band 11*, ed. H. Kalcyk and S. Lauffer. Rome: 559–575.
Kidd, D. (1997) (ed.) *Aratus:* Phaenomena. Cambridge.
King, J. E. (1971) (trans.) *Cicero:* Tusculan Disputations. Cambridge, MA.
King, P. (1995) (trans., introd. and notes) *Augustine:* Against the Academicians *and* The Teacher. Indianapolis and Cambridge.
Koch, B. (2006) *Philosophie als Medizin: Untersuchungen zu Ciceros* Tusculanae Disputationes. Palingenesia 90. Stuttgart.
König, J., Oikonomopoulou, K., and Woolf, G. (2013) (eds.) *Ancient Libraries*. Cambridge.
Konstan, D. (1996) *Friendship in the Classical World*. Cambridge.
(2008) *A Life Worthy of the Gods: The Materialist Psychology of Epicurus*. Las Vegas.
Koyré A. (1948) "Du monde de l'à-peu-près à l'univers de la précision," *Critique* 4: 806–823. [Repr. in *Etudes d'histoire de la pensée philosophique*. Paris, 1971: 311–329.]
Kragelund, P. (2001) "Dreams, religion and politics in Republican Rome," *Historia* 50: 53–95.
Kreter, F. (2006) *Kann Fabius bei einer Seeschlacht sterben? Die Geschichte der Logik des Kontingenzproblems von Aristoteles,* De interpretatione *9 bis Cicero,* De fato. Trier.
Krostenko, B. (2000) "Beyond (dis)belief: Rhetorical form and religious symbols in Cicero's *de Divinatione*," *Transactions of the American Philological Association* 130: 353–391.
Laks, A. (2000) "The *Laws*," in *The Cambridge History of Greek and Roman Political Thought*, ed. C. Rowe and M. Schofield. Cambridge: 258–292.
Laks, A. and Schofield, M. (1995) (eds.) *Justice and Generosity: Studies in Hellenistic Social and Political Philosophy*. Cambridge.
Lambardi, N. (1982) *Il "Timaeus" ciceroniano: arte e tecnica del vertere*. Florence.
Lavan, M. (2013) *Slaves to Rome: Paradigms of Empire in Roman Culture*. Cambridge.
Lebow, R. N. (2008) *A Cultural Theory of International Relations*. Cambridge.
Lehmann, Y. (1997) *Varron théologien et philosophe romain*. Latomus 237. Brussels.

Leeman, A. (1982) "The technique of persuasion in Cicero's *Pro Murena*," in *Eloquence et rhétorique chez Cicéron*, ed. W. Ludwig. Geneva: 193–228.

Leeman, A., Pinkster, H., and Nelson, H. (1985) (eds.) *M. Tullius Cicero:* De oratore libri *III*. Vol. 2. Heidelberg.

Lefèvre, E. (2008) *Philosophie unter der Tyrannis*. Heidelberg.

Leonardis, I. (2019) *Varrone, unus scilicet antiquorum hominum. Senso del passato e pratica antiquaria*. Bari.

Leonhardt, J. (1999) *Ciceros Kritik der Philosophenschulen*. Munich.

Levine, P. (1957) "The original design and publication of the *De natura deorum*," *Harvard Studies in Classical Philology* 62: 7–36.

(1958) "Cicero and the literary dialogue," *Classical Journal* 53: 146–151.

Lévy, C. (1978) "Scepticisme et dogmatisme dans l'Académie: 'l'ésotérisme' d'Arcésilas," *Revue des études latines* 56: 335–348.

(1984) "La dialectique de Cicéron dans les livres II et IV du *De finibus*," *Revue des études latines* 62: 111–127.

(1992a) *Cicero Academicus: recherches sur les Académiques et sur la philosophie Cicéronienne*. Collection de l'Ecole Française de Rome 162. Rome.

(1992b) "Cicéron créateur du vocabulaire latin de la connaissance," in *La langue latine langue de la philosophie*, ed. P. Grimal. Rome: 91–106.

(1995) "Le mythe de la naissance de la civilisation chez Cicéron," in *Mathesis e Philia. Studi in onore di Marcello Gigante*, ed. S. Cerasuolo. Naples: 155–168.

(1996) "Doxographie et philosophie chez Cicéron," in *Le concept de nature à Rome. La physique. Actes du séminaire de philosophie romaine de Paris XII-Val de Marne (1992–1993)*, ed. C. Lévy. Paris: 109–123.

(2001) "Cicéron et l'épicurisme: la problématique de l'éloge paradoxal," in *Cicéron et Philodème. La polémique en philosophie*, ed. C. Auvray-Assayas and D. Delattre. Paris: 61–75.

(2002a) "Les *Tusculanes* et le dialogue cicéronien: exemple ou exception?," *Vita Latina* 166: 23–31.

(2002b) "L'Âme et le moi dans les *Tusculanes*," *Revue des études latines* 80: 78–94.

(2003) "Cicero and the *Timaeus*," in *The* Timaeus *as Cultural Icon*, ed. G. Reydams-Schils. Notre Dame: 95–110.

(2005) "Les petits Académiciens: Lacyde, Charmadas, Métrodore de Stratonice," *L'eredità Platonica. Studi sul platonismo da Arcesila a Proclo*, ed. M. Bonazzi and V. Celluprica. "Elenchos" 45. Naples: 51–77.

(2006) "Y a-t-il quelqu'un derrière le masque? À propos de la théorie des *personae* chez Cicéron," in *Vivre pour soi, vivre pour la cité, de l'Antiquité à la Renaissance*, ed. P. Galand-Hallyn and C. Lévy. Paris: 45–58.

(2008) "Cicéron, le moyen platonisme et la philosophie romaine: à propos de la naissance du concept latin de *qualitas*," *Revue de métaphysique et de morale* 57: 5–20.

(2012) "Philosophical life versus political life," in W. Nicgorski (2012): 58–78.

Lévy, C. and Guillaumin, J.-B. (2018) "Présentation," in *Plato Latinus: aspects de la transmission de Platon en Latin dans l'Antiquité*, ed. J.-B. Guillemain and C. Lévy. Turnhout: 7–29.

Lintott, A. (1997) "The theory of the mixed constitution at Rome," in *Philosophia Togata*, Vol. 2: *Plato and Aristotle in Rome*, ed. J. Barnes and M. T. Griffin. Oxford: 70–85.

Locke, J. (1824) *An Enquiry Concerning Human Understanding*, in *The Works of John Locke in Nine Volumes*, Vol. 2. London.

    (1988) *Second Treatise of Government*, in *Two Treatises of Government*, ed. P. Laslett. Cambridge.

Long, A. A. (1995a) "Cicero's Plato and Aristotle," in J. G. F. Powell (1995a): 37–61.

    (1995b) "Cicero's politics in De officiis," in A. Laks and M. Schofield (1995): 213–240.

Long, A. A. and Sedley, D. N. (1987) *The Hellenistic Philosophers*. 2 vols. Cambridge.

Long, A. G. (2015) "Academic eloquence and the end of Cicero's *De finibus*," *Ancient Philosophy* 35: 183–198.

Luciani, S. (2010) *Temps et éternité dans l'œuvre philosophique de Cicéron*. Paris.

Lütcke, K. H. (1968) *"Auctoritas" bei Augustin. Mit einer Einleitung zur römischen Vorgeschichte des Begriffs*. Stuttgart, Berlin, Cologne, and Mainz.

MacBain, B. (1982) *Prodigy and Expiation: A Study in Religion and Politics in Republican Rome*. Brussels.

MacCormack, S. (2013) "Cicero in late antiquity," in C. Steel (2013a): 251–305.

Mack, D. (1937) *Senatsreden und Volksreden bei Cicero*. Würzburg.

MacKendrick, P. (1989) *The Philosophical Books of Cicero*. London.

Madec, G. (1969) "L'*Hortensius* de Cicéron dans les livres XIII–XIV du *De trinitate*," *Revue des études augustiniennes* 15: 167–173.

    (1992) "Augustin et Porphyre. Ébauche d'un bilan des recherches et des conjonctures," in ΣΟΦΙΗΣ ΜΑΙΗΤΟΡΕΣ. *"Chercheurs de sagesse": Hommages à Jean Pépin*, ed. M.-O. Goulet-Cazé, G. Madec, and D. O'Brien. Paris: 367–382.

    (1994) "Les embarras de la citation," *Petites Études augustiniennes*. Paris: 307–318.

Madvig, N. (1839) De finibus bonorum et malorum libri quinque. Hanse.

Magnaldi, G. (1991) *L'οἰκείωσις peripatetica in Ario Didimo e nel "De finibus" di Cicerone*. Turin.

Mankin, D. (2011) (ed.) *Cicero: De oratore, Book III*. Cambridge.

Mansfeld, J. (1990) "Doxography and dialectic: The Sitz im Leben of the 'Placita,'" *Aufstieg und Niedergang der römischen Welt* 36.4: 3056–3229.

    (1995) "Sources," in *The Cambridge Companion to Early Greek Philosophy*, ed. A. A. Long. Cambridge: 22–44.

Manuwald, G. (2012) "The speeches to the people in Cicero's oratorical corpora," *Rhetorica* 30:153–175.

Maso, S. (2008) *Capire e dissentire. Cicerone e la filosofia di Epicuro*. Naples.

    (2015) *Grasp and Dissent: Cicero and Epicurean Philosophy*. Turnhout.

May, J. M. and Wisse, J. (2001) (trans. and intro.) Cicero: *On the Ideal Orator*. Oxford.

May, L. (2007) *War Crimes and Just War*. Cambridge.

Mayer, P. Feldmann, E., Geerlings, W. et al. (1986–) *Augustinus Lexikon*. Basle and Stuttgart.

Mayor, J. B. (1880–1885) M. T. Ciceronis De natura deorum. Cambridge.

McConnell, S. (2014) *Philosophical Life in Cicero's Letters*. Cambridge.

Merguet, H. (1905) *Handlexikon zu Cicero*. Leipzig.

Michel, A. (1960) *Les rapports de la rhétorique et de la philosophie dans l'œuvre de Cicéron. Recherches sur les fondements philosophiques de l'art de persuader.* Paris.

   (1973) "Rhétorique et philosophie dans les traités de Cicéron," *Aufstieg und Niedergang der römischen Welt* 1.3: 139–208.

Millar, F. (1998) *The Crowd in Rome in the Late Republic*. Ann Arbor.

Miller, W. (1913) *Cicero: De officiis, with an English Translation*. Cambridge, MA.

Mirhady, D. (2001) "Dicaearchus of Messana: The sources, text and translation," in W. W. Fortenbaugh and E. Schütrumpf (2001): 1–142.

Moatti, C. (2015) *The Birth of Critical Thinking in Republican Rome*. Cambridge. [Originally published as *La Raison de Rome: naissance de l'esprit critique à la fin de la République*. Paris, 1997.]

   (2018) Res publica. *Histoire romaine de la chose publique*. Paris.

Moatti, C. and Riot-Sarcey, M. (2009) (eds.) *La République dans tous ses états*. Paris.

Momigliano, A. (1984) "The theological efforts of the Roman upper class in the first century BC," *Classical Philology* 79: 199–211.

Montesquieu, C. (1999) *Considerations on the Causes of the Greatness of the Romans and their Decline*. Indianapolis.

   (2002) "Discourse on Cicero" (trans. David Fott), *Political Theory* 30.5: 733–737.

Morel, P.-M. (2016) "Cicero and Epicurean virtues (*De finibus* 1–2)," in J. Annas and G. Betegh (2016): 77–95.

Moreschini, C. (1979) "Osservazioni zu lessico filosofico di Cicerone," *Annali della Scuola Normale Superiore di Pisa* 3.9: 99–178.

Morrell, K. (2017) *Pompey, Cato and the Governance of the Roman Empire*. Oxford.

Morstein-Marx, R. (2004) *Mass Oratory and Political Power in the Late Roman Republic*. Cambridge.

Müller, C. F. W. (1879) *M. Tulli Ciceronis Opera* IV.3. Leipzig.

Musial, D. (2001) "*Sodalicium Nigidiani*: les Pythagoriciens à Rome à la fin de la République," *Revue de l'Histoire des Religions* 218: 339–367.

Nacol, E. C. (2021) "Locke and Cicero on property, labor, property, and value," in *The Ciceronian Tradition in Political Theory*, ed. D. J. Kapust and G. Remer. Madison, WI: 140–159.

Nails, D. (1995) *Agora, Academy, and the Conduct of Philosophy*. Dordrecht.

Nederman, C. J. (2020) *The Bonds of Humanity: Cicero's Legacies in European Social and Political Thought, ca. 1100–ca. 1550*. University Park, PA.

Nelson, E. (2004) *The Greek Tradition of Republican Thought*. Cambridge.

Neuschäfer, B. (2010) "Lingua graeca," in *Augustinus Lexikon,* Vol. 3.7–8, ed. C. Mayer et al. Basel: 1005–1011.

Nicgorski, W. (1992) "Cicero's Socrates: Assessment of 'the Socratic turn,'" in *Law and Philosophy: The Practice of Theory,* Vol. 1, ed. J. Murley, R. Stone, and W. Braithwaite. Athens, OH: 213–233.

(2012) (ed.) *Cicero's Practical Philosophy.* Notre Dame.

(2016) *Cicero's Skepticism and His Recovery of Political Philosophy.* New York.

Nicolas, C. (1996) Utraque lingua: *le calque sémantique: domaine gréco-latin.* Louvain.

Nisbet, R. G. M. (1961) *Cicero:* in L. Calpurnium Pisonem Oratio. Oxford.

Nussbaum, M. (1994) *The Therapy of Desire: Theory and Practice in Hellenistic Ethics.* Princeton.

(1997) "Kant and Stoic cosmopolitanism," *The Journal of Political Philosophy* 5.1: 1–25.

(2000) "Duties of justice, duties of material aid: Cicero's problematic legacy," *The Journal of Political Philosophy* 8.2: 176–206.

(2001) *Upheavals of Thought: The Intelligence of Emotions.* Cambridge, MA.

(2019) *The Cosmopolitan Tradition: A Noble but Flawed Ideal.* Cambridge, MA.

Nussbaum, M. and Levmore, S. (2017) *Aging Thoughtfully: Conversations about Retirement, Romance, Wrinkles, and Regret.* Oxford.

Nussbaum, M. and Rorty, A. (eds.) (1992) *Essays on Aristotle's* De anima. Oxford.

Obbink, D. (1996) *Philodemus* On Piety *Part 1: Critical Text with Commentary.* Oxford.

(2002) "'All gods are true' in Epicurus," in *Traditions of Theology,* ed. D. M. Frede and A. Laks. Leiden: 183–221.

O'Daly, G. (1999) *Augustine's* City of God*: A Reader's Guide.* Oxford.

O'Donnell, J. J. (1980) "Augustine's classical readings," *Recherches Augustiniennes* 15: 144–175.

(1992) *Augustine's* Confessions. 3 vols. Introduction, Text, and Commentary. Oxford.

(2015) "Augustine – Cicero 'Redivivus'," *Kampf oder Dialog? Conflict/Dialog? Augustine's Engagement with Cultures in* De ciuitate dei, *International Symposium, 25–29 September 2012,* ed. C. Müller in cooperation with R. Dodaro and A. D. Fitzgerald. Würzburg: 103–113.

Ohlmann, A. D. (1897) De S. Augustini Dialogis in Cassiciaco scriptis, Inaugural Dissertation. Argentorati.

O'Meara, J. J. (1951) (ed. and trans.) *Augustine:* Against the Academics. New York.

Opsomer, J. (1998) *In Search of the Truth: Academic Tendencies in Middle Platonism.* Brussels.

Orend, B. (2008) "War," in *The Stanford Encyclopedia of Philosophy,* ed. E. N. Zalta (Fall 2008 edition), http://plato.stanford.edu/archives/fall2008/entries/war/.

Paulson, Lex (forthcoming) Voluntas populi: *Free Will and the Fall of Cicero's* Republic. Cambridge.

Patzig, G. (1979) "Cicero als Philosoph, am Beispiel der Schrift *De finibus*," *Gymnasium* 86: 304–322.

Peart, S. J. and Levy, D. M. (2008) "Adam Smith and his sources: The evil of independence," *The Adam Smith Review* 4: 57–87.

Pease, A. (1955–1958) (ed.) *M. Tulli Ciceronis* De Natura Deorum. 2 vols. Cambridge, MA.

Pettit, P. (1999) *Republicanism: A Theory of Freedom and Government*. Oxford.

Pic, A. (1997) "Saint Augustin et l'impiété de Cicéron: Étude du *De Ciuitate Dei* v, 9," *Studia Patristica* 33: 213–220.

Pizzolato, L. (1974) "L'amicizia in sant'Agostino e il 'Laelius' di Cicerone," *Vigiliae Christianae* 28: 203–215.

Plasberg, O. (1996) *M. T. Cicero*: Academica. Leipzig.

Pogge, T. (1992) "Cosmopolitanism and sovereignty," *Ethics* 103.1: 48–75.

Poncelet, R. (1957) *Cicéron traducteur de Platon: l'expression de la pensée complexe en latin classique*. Paris.

Potkay, A. (1994) *The Fate of Eloquence in the Age of Hume*. Ithaca, NY.

Powell, J. G. F. (1988) (ed.) *Cicero*: Cato Maior de Senectute. Cambridge.

(1995a) (ed.) *Cicero the Philosopher: Twelve Papers*. Oxford.

(1995b) "Cicero's works and their background," in J. G. F. Powell (1995a): 1–35.

(2001) "Were Cicero's *Laws* the laws of Cicero's *Republic?*," in J. G. F. Powell and J. North (2001): 7–39.

(2006) (ed.) *M. Tulli Ciceronis*: De re publica, De legibus, Cato major, De senectute, Laelius, De amicitia. Oxford.

(2012) "Cicero's *De re publica* and the virtues of the statesman," in W. Nicgorski (2012): 14–42.

(2013a) "Cicero's reading of Plato's *Republic*," in Sheppard (2013): 35–57.

(2013b) "The embassy of the three philosophers to Rome in 155 B.C.," in *Hellenistic Oratory: Continuity and Change*, ed. C. Kremmydas and K. Tempest. Oxford: 219–247.

Powell, J. G. F. and North, J. (2001) (eds.) *Cicero's* Republic. London.

Powell, J. G. F. and Paterson, J. (2004) (eds.) *Cicero the Advocate*. Oxford.

Press, G. (2000) (ed.) *Who Speaks for Plato? Studies in Platonic Anonymity*. Lanham.

Prost, P. (2006) "*Humanitas*: originalité d'un concept cicéronien," *Philosophies de l'humanisme, L'art du comprendre* 15: 31–46.

Purinton, J. (1999) "Epicurus on free volition and the atomic swerve," *Phronesis* 44: 253–299.

Ramsey, J. (2007) "Roman senatorial oratory," in W. Dominik and J. Hall (2007): 122–135.

Rasmussen, S. W. (2003) *Public Portents in Republican Rome*. Rome.

Rawson, E. (1975) *Cicero: A Portrait*. London.

(1985) *Intellectual Life in the Roman Republic*. London.

Reich, K. (1939) "Kant and Greek ethics," *Mind* 48: 338–354, 446–463.

Reinhardt, T. (2004) (ed.) *Cicero's* Topica. Oxford.

(2016) "Cicero and Augustine on grasping the truth," in *Philosophie in Rom, römische Philosophie, Kultur-, literatur- und philosophiegeschichtliche Perspektiven*, ed. G. M. Müller and F. Mariani Zini. Berlin: 305–323.

(2018) "*Pithana* and *probabilia* in Sextus and Cicero," in T. Bénatouïl and K. Ierodiakonou (2018): 218–253.

Remer, G. (2017) *Ethics and the Orator: The Ciceronian Tradition of Political Morality*. Chicago.

Reydams-Schils, G. (1999) *Demiurge and Providence: Stoic and Platonist Readings of Plato's* Timaeus. Turnhout.

(2002) "Human bonding and *oikeiôsis* in Roman stoicism," *Oxford Studies in Ancient Philosophy* 22: 221–251.

(2005) *The Roman Stoics: Self, Responsibility, and Affection*. Chicago.

(2015) "Teaching Pericles: Cicero on the study of nature," in K. Volk and G. Williams (2015): 91–107.

(2016) "Dio of Prusa and the Roman Stoics on how to speak the truth to oneself and to power," in *Philosophy and Political Power in Antiquity*, ed. C. Arruzza and D. Nikulin. Leiden: 134–147.

Ribreau, M. (2012) "Quand une chrétienne prend la parole: Monique dans le *De ordine* et le *De beata uita* d'Augustin," *Cahiers "Mondes anciens"* 3, http://mondesanciens.revues.org/index773.html.

Richard, C. J. (1995) *The Founders and the Classics*. Cambridge, MA.

(2015) "Cicero and the American founders," in W. H. F. Altman (2015a): 124–143.

Riggsby, A. (1999) *Crime and Community in Ciceronian Rome*. Austin.

Robertson, D. (2010) *The Philosophy of Cognitive Behavioural Therapy: Stoic Philosophy as Rational and Cognitive Psychotherapy*. London.

Rose, V. (1886) Aristotelis qui ferebantur librorum fragmenta, 3rd ed. Leipzig.

Rose, H. J. (1921) "The Greek of Cicero," *The Journal of Hellenic Studies* 41: 91–116.

Rosenberger, V. (1998) *Gezähmte Götter: Das Prodigienwesen der römischen Republik*. Stuttgart.

Ross, W. D. (1958) *Aristotelis Fragmenta selecta*. Oxford.

Rousseau, J.-J. (1979) *Emile, or On Education*, trans. A. Bloom. New York.

(1997) *Of the Social Contract*, ed. and trans. V. Gourevitch. Cambridge.

Rowe, C. (2003) "The status of the 'myth' in Plato's *Timaeus*," in *Plato Physicus. Cosmologia e antropologia nel Timeo*, ed. C. Natali and S. Maso. Amsterdam: 21–31.

Ruch, M. (1958a) *Le préambule dans les œuvres philosophiques de Cicéron. Essai sur la genèse et l'art du dialogue*. Paris.

(1958b) *L'Hortensius de Cicéron. Histoire et reconstitution*. Paris.

Rüpke, J. (2006) "Communicating with the gods," in *A Companion to the Roman Republic*, ed. R. Morstein-Marx and N. Rosenstein. Oxford: 215–235.

(2012) *Religion in Republican Rome: Rationalization and Ritual Change*. Philadelphia.

(2013) "New perspectives on ancient divination," in *Divination in the Ancient World: Religious Options and the Individual*, ed. V. Rosenberger. Stuttgart: 9–20.

Santangelo, F. (2008) "The fetials and their *ius*," *Bulletin of the Institute of Classical Studies* 51: 63–93.

(2015) *Divination, Prediction and the End of the Roman Republic*. Cambridge.

Sauer, J. (2015) "Dichotomy in the conception of natural law in Cicero's *De legibus?*" (trans. A. Lewis), "Gesetz-Rhetorik-Gewalt," special issue of *Ancilla Iuris*, ed. T. Vesting: 125–153.

Schallenberg, M. (2008) *Freiheit und Determinismus: Ein philosophischer Kommentar zu Ciceros Schrift* De fato. Berlin.

Schlapbach, K. (2003) *Augustin* Contra Academicos *(uel* De Academicis*): Buch 1*. Berlin.

(2006) "Hortensius," in *Augustinus Lexikon*, Vol. 3.3–4, ed. C. Mayer et al. Basel: 425–436.

Schmitt, C. B. (1972) *Cicero Scepticus: A Study of the Influence of the* Academica *in the Renaissance*. The Hague.

Schofield, M. (1980) "Preconception, argument and God," in *Doubt and Dogmatism*, ed. M. Schofield, M. Burnyeat, and J. Barnes. Oxford: 283–308.

(1986) "Cicero for and against divination," *Journal of Roman Studies* 76: 47–65.

(1995a) "Cicero's definition of *Res publica*," in Powell (1995a): 63–84.

(1995b) "Two Stoic approaches to justice," in A. Laks and M. Schofield (1995): 191–212.

(1999) *The Stoic Idea of the City*, expanded ed. Chicago.

(2002) "Academic therapy: Philo of Larissa and Cicero's project in the *Tusculans*," in G. Clark and T. Rajak (2002): 91–107.

(2003) "Stoic ethics," in *The Cambridge Companion to the Stoics*, ed. B. Inwood. Cambridge: 233–256.

(2008) "Ciceronian dialogue," in *The End of Dialogue in Antiquity*, ed. S. Goldhill. Cambridge: 63–84.

(2012) "The fourth virtue," in W. Nicgorski (2012): 43–57.

(2013a) "Cosmopolitanism, imperialism, and justice in Cicero's *Republic* and *Laws*," *Intellectual History and Political Thought* 2.1: 5–34.

(2013b) "Writing philosophy," in C. Steel (2013a): 73–87.

(2013c) (ed.) *Aristotle, Plato and Pythagoreanism in the First Century* BC. Cambridge.

(2015) "Liberty, equality and authority: A political discourse in the later Roman Republic," in *A Companion to Greek Democracy and the Roman Republic*, ed. D. Hammer. London: 113–127.

(2017a) "Cicero on imperialism and the soul," in *Selfhood and the Soul: Essays on Ancient Thought and Literature in Honour of Christopher Gill*, ed. R. Seaford, J. Wilkins, and M. Wright. Oxford.

(2017b) "Cicero's Plato," in *From Stoicism to Platonism*, ed. T. Engberg-Pedersen. Cambridge: 47–66.

(2021) *Cicero: Political Philosophy*. Oxford.

(forthcoming) "*Juris consensus* revisited," in N. Gilbert, M. Graver, and S. McConnell (forthcoming).

Schubert, C. (2017) "Remarks on the philosophical reflections of fate in the writings of Seneca," *Mythos: Rivista di Storia delle religioni* 10: 125–154.

Schultz, C. E. (2014) *A Commentary on Cicero,* De divinatione 1. Ann Arbor.

Schwameis, C. (2014) *Die Praefatio von Ciceros* De inventione. Munich.

Sedley, D. N. (1998) *Lucretius and the Transformation of Greek Wisdom.* Cambridge.

   (2009) "Epicureanism in the Roman Republic," in *The Cambridge Companion to Epicureanism,* ed. J. Warren. Cambridge.

   (2011) "Epicurus' theological innatism," in *Epicurus and the Epicurean Tradition,* ed. J. Fish and R. K. Sanders. Cambridge: 29–51.

   (2012) (ed.) *The Philosophy of Antiochus.* Cambridge.

   (2013) "Cicero and the *Timaeus,*" in Schofield (2013c): 187–205.

Sen, A. (1993) *Poverty and Famine: An Essay on Entitlement and Deprivation.* Oxford.

Setaioli, A. (2013) "Cicero and Seneca on the fate of the soul: Private feelings and philosophical doctrines," in *The Individual in the Religions of the Ancient Mediterranean,* ed. J. Rüpke. Oxford: 455–488.

Shackleton Bailey, D. R. (1965–1970) (ed.) *Cicero's* Letters to Atticus. 7 vols. Cambridge.

   (1977) (ed.) *Cicero:* Epistulae ad Familiares. 2 Vols. Cambridge.

   (1980) (ed.) *Cicero:* Epistulae ad Quintum fratrem et M. Brutum. Cambridge.

Shaftesbury, A. A. C. (2001) *Characteristicks of Men, Manners, Opinions, Times.* 3 vols. ed. D. Den Uyl. Indianapolis.

Sharpe, M. (2015) "Cicero, Voltaire, and the *philosophes* in the French Enlightenment," in W. H. F. Altman (2015a): 329–356.

Sharples, R. W. (1991) *Cicero:* On Fate & *Boethius:* The Consolation of Philosophy. Warminster.

Sharples, R. W. and Sorabji, R. (2007) (eds) *Greek and Roman Philosophy: 100 BC–200 AD.* London.

Sheppard, A. (2013) (ed.) *Ancient Approaches to Plato's* Republic. *Bulletin of the Institute of Classical Studies supplement* 117. London.

Shue, H. (1996) *Basic Rights: Subsistence, Affluence, and U.S. Foreign Policy,* 2nd ed. Princeton.

Skinner, Q. (1998) *Liberty before Liberalism.* Cambridge.

Smith, A. (1982) *The Theory of Moral Sentiments,* ed. D. D. Raphael and A. L. Macfie. Indianapolis.

   (1985) *Lectures on Rhetoric and Belles Lettres,* ed. J. C. Bryce. Indianapolis.

Smith, C. (2019) "Varro and the contours of Roman antiquarianism," *Latomus* 77: 1090–1118.

Smith, P. (1995) "'A self-indulgent misuse of leisure and writing'? how not to write philosophy: Did Cicero get it right?," in Powell (1995a): 301–323.

Solignac, A. (1992) (ed.) Les Confessions. Paris.

Sorabji, R. and Sharples, R. W. (2007) *Greek and Roman Philosophy, 100 BC–200 AD.* 2 vols. *Bulletin of the Institute of Classical Studies* 94. London.

Steel, C. (2013a) (ed.) *The Cambridge Companion to Cicero.* Cambridge.

   (2013b) "Structure, meaning and authority in Cicero's dialogues," in *Der Dialog in der Antike,* ed. S. Föllinger and G. M. Müller. Berlin: 221–234.

Bibliography

Steel, C. and van der Blom, H. (eds.) (2013). *Community and Communication: Oratory and Politics in Republican Rome.* Oxford.

Steele, R. B. (1900) "The Greek in Cicero's epistles," *The American Journal of Philology* 21: 387–410.

Steinmetz, P. (1989) "Beobachtungen zu Ciceros philosophischem Standpunkt," in W. W. Fortenbaugh and P. Steinmetz (1989): 1–22.

Stem, R. (2006) "Cicero as orator and philosopher: The value of the *Pro Murena* for Ciceronian political thought," *Review of Politics* 68.2: 206–231.

Steppat, M. P. (1980) *Die Schola von Cassiciacum: Augustins "De ordine."* Frankfurt.

Stone, A. (1980) "*Pro Milone*: Cicero's second thoughts," *Antichthon* 14: 88–111.

Straumann, B. (2015) *Roman Law in the State of Nature: The Classical Foundations of Hugo Grotius' Natural Law Theory.* Cambridge.

(2016) *Crisis and Constitutionalism: Roman Political Thought from the Fall of the Republic to the Age of Revolution.* Oxford.

Straume-Zimmermann, L. (1976) *Ciceros Hortensius.* Bern and Frankfurt.

Straume-Zimmermann, L., Broemser, F., and Gigon, O. (eds.) (1990) *Marcus Tullius Cicero: Hortensius, Lucullus, Academici Libri.* Munich and Zürich.

Stroh, W. (1975) *Taxis und Taktik: die advokatische Dispositionskunst in Ciceros Gerichtsreden.* Stuttgart.

Stull, W. (2012) "Reading the *Phaedo* in *Tusculan Disputations* 1," *Classical Philology* 107: 38–52.

Striker, G. (1995) "Cicero and Greek philosophy," *Harvard Studies in Classical Philology* 97: 53–61.

Swain, S. (2002) "Bilingualism in Cicero? The evidence of code switching," in *Bilingualism in Ancient Society*, ed. J. N. Adams, M. Jansse, and S. Swain. Oxford: 128–167.

Taran, L. (1987) "Cicero's attitude towards stoicism and skepticism in *De natura deorum*," in *Florilegium Columbianum: Essays in Honor of Paul Oskar Kristeller*, ed. K.-L. Selig and R. Somerville. New York: 1–22.

Tarrant, H. (1985) *Scepticism or Platonism? The Philosophy of the Fourth Academy.* Cambridge.

ten Berge, B. (2013) "Dreams in Cicero's *De divinatione*: Philosophical tradition and education," *Archiv für Religionsgeschichte* 15: 53–66.

Teske, R. J. (2001) (ed.) *Augustine:* Letters. New York.

(2003) (ed.) *Augustine:* Letters *100–155.* New York.

Testard, M. (1954) "Note sur *De ciuitate Dei* XXII, 24: exemple de réminiscences cicéroniennes de saint Augustin," in *Augustinus Magister: congrès international augustinien*, Vol. 1. Paris: 193–200.

(1958) *Saint Augustin et Cicéron.* 2 vols. Paris.

(1986) "Cicero," in *Augustinus Lexikon*, Vol. 1, ed. C. Mayer. Basel: 913–930.

(2002) (ed. and trans.) *Cicéron: Les devoirs.* 2 vols, 3rd ed. Paris.

Thomas, Y.-P. (1980) "*Res*, chose et patrimoine (Note sur le rapport sujet-objet en droit romain)," *Archives de philosophie du droit* 25: 413–426.

Thorsrud, H. (2009) *Ancient Scepticism.* Stocksfield.

(2010) "Arcesilaus and Carneades," in *The Cambridge Companion to Ancient Scepticism*, ed. R. Bett. Cambridge: 58–80.

(2012) "Radical and mitigated skepticism in Cicero's *Academica*," in W. Nicgorski (2012): 133–151.

Trelenberg, J. (2009) (ed.) *Augustins Schrift "De ordine."* Tübingen.

Tutrone, F. (2013) "Libraries and intellectual debate in the late Republic: The case of the Aristotelian corpus," in J. König, K. Oikonomopoulou, and G. Woolf (2013): 152–166.

Uhle, T. (2012) *Augustin und die Dialektik*. Tübingen.

Van der Meeren, S. (2007) "La sagesse 'droit chemin de la vie': lecture d'une métaphore du *Contra Academicos* à la lumière de la tradition du protreptique philosophique," *Revue des études augustiniennes et patristiques* 53: 81–111.

(2011) *Exhortation à la philosophie. Le dossier grec: Aristote*. Paris.

Van Oort, J. (1997) "*Civitas dei-terrena civitas*: The concept of the two antithetical cities and its sources (book 11–14)," in *Augustinus De civitate Dei*, ed. C. Horn. Berlin: 157–169.

Vesperini, P. (2012) *La* philosophia *et ses pratiques d'Ennius à Cicéron*. Rome.

Vitelli, C. (1979) (ed.) *M. Tullii Ciceronis* Consolationis *fragmenta*. Florence.

Vivenza, G. (2001) *Adam Smith and the Classics*. Oxford.

Vogt, K. M. (2008) *Law, Reason, and the Cosmic City: Political Philosophy in the Early Stoa*. New York.

Volk, K. (2017) "Signs, seers and senators: Divinatory expertise in Cicero and Nigidius Figulus," in *Authority and Expertise in Ancient Scientific Culture*, ed. J. König and G. Woolf. Cambridge: 329–347.

Volk, K. and Williams, G. (2015) (eds.) *Roman Reflections: Studies in Latin Philosophy*. Oxford.

Von Heyking, J. (2007) "Taming warriors in classical and early medieval political theory," in *Ethics, Nationalism, and Just War: Medieval and Contemporary Perspectives*, ed. H. Syse and G. M. Reichberg. Washington, DC: 11–35.

Vössing, K. (1997) *Schule und Bildung im Nordafrika der römischen Kaiserzeit*. Brussels.

Wachsmuth, C. (1894) *Ioannis Stobaei* Anthologii *libri duo priores*. Berlin.

Walsh, P. G. (1997) (trans. and intro.) *Cicero:* The Nature of the Gods. Oxford.

Walzer, M. (1973) "Political action: The problem of dirty hands," *Philosophy and Public Affairs* 2: 160–180.

(1977) *Just and Unjust Wars: A Moral Argument with Historical Illustrations*. New York.

Wardle, D. (2006) *Cicero* On Divination*: De divinatione* Book 1, trans. with intro. and comm. Oxford.

Warren, J. (2001) "Epicurus and the pleasures of the future," *Oxford Studies in Ancient Philosophy* 21: 135–179.

(2006) "Epicureans and the present past," *Phronesis* 51: 362–387.

(2013) "The harm of death in Cicero's *First Tusculan*," in *The Metaphysics and Ethics of Death: New Essays*, ed. J. Taylor. Oxford: 44–70.

(2016) "Epicurean pleasure in Cicero's *De finibus*," in J. Annas and G. Betegh (2016): 41–76.

Watts, N. H. (1931) (ed.) *Cicero:* Pro Milone, In Pisonem, Pro Scauro, Pro Fonteio, Pro Rabirio Postumo, Pro Marcello, Pro Ligario, Pro Rege Deiotaro. Loeb Classical Library 252. Cambridge, MA.

White, G. F. (2015) Copia verborum: *Cicero's Philosophical Translations.* Unpublished PhD dissertation, Princeton.

White, S. (1995) "Cicero and the therapists," in Powell (1995a): 219–246.

Williams, B. (1973) "A critique of utilitarianism," in *Utilitarianism for and Against*, ed. J. Smart and B. Williams. New York: 77–150.

   (1985) *Ethics and the Limits of Philosophy.* London.

Williams, G. D. (2012*) The Cosmic Viewpoint: A Study of Seneca's* Natural Questions. New York.

Wilson, J. (2007) *Collected Works of James Wilson*, Vol. 1, ed. K. L. Hall and M. D. Hall. Indianapolis.

Winterbottom M. (1994) (ed.) *M. Tulli Ciceronis:* De officiis. Oxford.

Wirszubski, C. (1950) Libertas *as a Political Idea at Rome during the Late Republic and Early Principate.* Cambridge.

Wisse, J. (1989) Ethos *and* Pathos*: From Aristotle to Cicero.* Amsterdam.

Wissowa, G. (1912) *Religion und Kultus der Römer.* Handbuch der klassischen Altertumswissenschaft 4. Munich.

Wood, N. (1983) *The Politics of Locke's Philosophy: A Social Study of "An Essay Concerning Human Understanding."* Berkeley.

   (1988) *Cicero's Social and Political Thought.* Berkeley.

Woolf, R. (2007) "Particularism, promises, and persons in Cicero's De officiis," *Oxford Studies in Ancient Philosophy* 33: 317–346.

   (2015) *Cicero: The Philosophy of a Roman Sceptic.* London.

Wynne, J. P. F. (2014) "Learned and wise: Cotta the sceptic in Cicero's On the Nature of the Gods," *Oxford Studies in Ancient Philosophy* 47: 245–273.

   (2019) *Cicero on the Philosophy of Religion:* On the Nature of the Gods *and* On Divination. Cambridge.

Yakobson, A. (2010) "Traditional political culture and the people's role in the Roman Republic," *Historia* 59: 282–302.

Zarecki, J. (2014) *Cicero's Ideal Statesman in Theory and Practice.* London.

Zetzel, J. E. G. (1995) (ed.) *Cicero:* De republica, *Selections.* Cambridge.

   (1996) "Natural law and poetic justice: A Carneadean debate in Cicero and Vergil," *Classical Philology* 91.4: 297–319.

   (1999) (ed. and trans.) *Cicero:* On the Commonwealth *and* On the Laws. Cambridge.

   (2003) "Plato with pillows: Cicero on the uses of Greek Culture," in *Myth, History and Culture in Republican Rome: Studies in Honour of T. P. Wiseman*, ed. D. Braund and C. Gill. Exeter: 119–138.

   (2013) "Political philosophy," in C. Steel (2013a): 181–195.

   (2017) "The attack on justice: Cicero, Lactantius, and Carneades," *Rheinisches Museum für Philologie* 160: 299–319.

Zoll, G. (1962) Cicero Platonis Aemulus*: Untersuchungen über die Form von Ciceros Dialogen, besonders von* De oratore. Zürich.

Index of Cicero's Texts

General Index

OTHER VOLUMES IN THE SERIES OF CAMBRIDGE
COMPANIONS *(continued from page ii)*